HATE SPEECH AND
DEMOCRATIC CITIZENSHIP

Hate Speech and Democratic Citizenship

ERIC HEINZE

Professor of Law and Humanities, Queen Mary, University of London

OXFORD
UNIVERSITY PRESS

Great Clarendon Street, Oxford, OX2 6DP,
United Kingdom

Oxford University Press is a department of the University of Oxford.
It furthers the University's objective of excellence in research, scholarship,
and education by publishing worldwide. Oxford is a registered trade mark of
Oxford University Press in the UK and in certain other countries

First published 2016
First published in paperback 2017

Published in the United States of America by Oxford University Press
198 Madison Avenue, New York, NY 10016, United States of America

British Library Cataloguing in Publication Data

Data available

Library of Congress Cataloging in Publication Data

Data available

ISBN 978–0–19–875902–7 (Hbk.)
ISBN 978–0–19–881641–6 (Pbk.)

This book is dedicated, with admiration and affection, to the Media Diversity Institute (MDI) and to its founder and Executive Director Milica Pešić.

Acknowledgements

For their valuable comments on various earlier drafts or portions of this book, I would like to thank Timothy Garton Ash, Uladzislau Belavusau, Erik Bleich, Thomas Brudholm, Ian Cram, Antony Duff, Stanley Fish, Katharine Gelber, Kay Goodall, Kent Greenawalt, Alan Haworth, A.R. Heinze, Steven Heyman, Morten Kinander, Rae Langton, Mary Kate McGowan, Sandra Marshall, Jacob Mchangama, Jo Murkens, Aernout Nieuwenhuis, Gavin Phillipson, Wayne Sumner, Joseph Tanega, Alexander Tsesis, Eugene Volokh, James Weinstein, Susan Williams, and the anonymous reviewers, as well as all participants in the Academic.edu online discussion group on Chapter 1 of this book, along with Nicole Lieberman for research assistance, and István Zöld for the cover design. Many thanks also to Alex Flach, Natasha Flemming, and Elinor Shields of Oxford University Press's editorial staff, to Gayathri Viswanathan of Newgen, and to this book's copy editor, Elissa Connor.

I have been grateful for the invitation by Oxford University's Foundation for Law, Justice and Society (FLJS) to deliver the 2015 Max Watson Memorial Lecture at Wolfson College, 29 October 2015, along with opportunities to present the views set forth in this book at other conferences and seminars, including 'Liberté d'expression et "discours de haine"', Université de Lyon III—Jean Moulin, 27 March 2015, organized by Erik Bleich and Charles Girard; 'Debate on Free Speech', North London Literary Festival, 24 March 2015, organized by Sarah Wardle, Lorna Gibb, and James Martin Charlton; 'Denialism and Human Rights', Maastricht University, 22–23 January 2015, organized by Roland Moerland, Hans Nelen, Jan Willems, Fons Coomans, and Jasper Krommendijk; 'War of Words: International Conference on Media, Armed Conflict, and Hate Speech', International Federation of Journalists, Residence Palace, Brussels, 25 April 2014; 'Conference on Online Hate Speech' of the European Law Students Association, Oslo, Norway, 3–8 December 2013; a staff seminar at the School of Law, University of Surrey, Wednesday 13 November 2013; Media-4-Change Conference, 'Hate Speech and the Role of the Media', Cagliari, Sardinia, 24–26 October 2013, organized by Neringa Jurčiukonytė; UK Law Commission conference, 'Hate Crime: The Case for Extending the Existing Offences', Queen Mary, University of London, 17 September 2013, on the invitation of Professor David Ormerod; a staff seminar of the Department of Cross-Cultural and Regional Studies, University of Copenhagen, 31 June 2013, organized by Birgitte Schepelern Johansen and Thomas Brudholm; a seminar of the Norwegian Civitas Academy, at Oxford University, 15 September 2012, organized by Morten Kinander and Torkel Brekke; the International Political Science Association World Congress, Madrid, Spain, 8–12 July 2012, session organized by Katharine Gelber; the public debate 'Hate Speech Bans: For and Against' (with Henning Koch), Department of Cross-Cultural and Regional Studies, University of Copenhagen, 6 April 2011, organized by Thomas Brudholm; 'Multiculturalism—Dilemmas, Paradoxes,

Traps', Villa Decius, Krakow, Poland, 15 October 2009; 'Seminar on Media and Diversity', Prague, 5–7 February 2009, organized on behalf of the European Commission by the International Federation of Journalists, Internews Europe, and the Media Diversity Institute; the conference 'Sexuality, Hatred and Law', Durham University Law School, 6 May 2008, organized by Helen Fenwick and Neil Cobb; at the conference 'Extreme Speech and Democracy: A Comparative View', Cambridge University Law School, 23 April 2007, organized by Ivan Hare and James Weinstein; at the conference 'Religious Pluralism and Human Rights in Europe: Where to Draw the Line?', Utrecht University, 9–10 May 2006, organized by Titia Loenen and Jenny Goldschmidt; 'Hate Speech: Conference and Consultation', Central European University, Budapest, 30 March–1 April 2006; 'Mainstreaming Diversity', organized by the Luxemburg Ministry for Foreign Affairs, Mondorf-les-Bains, Luxemburg, 27–28 June 2005; and at various seminars and class sessions within the Law Department at Queen Mary, University of London, organized by colleagues or visiting staff, including Gavin Sutter and Marloes van Noorloos, as well as student members of Queen Mary's European Law Students Association.

The discussion of defamation in Section 2.8 is adapted from the opinion piece, 'British MP Exploits Vague Defamation Law to Sue Guardian Journalist', published online in *The Conversation*, 11 February 2015. This book's concluding chapter is adapted from 'Nineteen Arguments for Hate Speech Bans—and Against Them', first published online in *Free Speech Debate*, 31 March 2014, and later reprinted online as 'The Case Against Hate Speech Bans' in *Eurozine*, 31 March 2014.

Translations from modern languages are mine, unless otherwise indicated.

Contents

List of Abbreviations

CEE	Central and Eastern Europe
CoE	Council of Europe
ECHR	European Convention on Human Rights
ECRI	European Commission against Racism and Intolerance
EU	European Union
ICCPR	International Covenant on Civil and Political Rights
ICERD	International Convention on the Elimination of All Forms of Racial Discrimination
IERA	Islamic Education and Research Academy
LSPD	longstanding, stable, and prosperous democracy
NGO	non-governmental organization
NPD	German National Democratic Party
RWB	Reporters Without Borders
UCL	University College London
UDHR	Universal Declaration of Human Rights

Die eigentliche *Radikalkur der Zensur wäre ihre Abschaffung*.

—*Karl Marx**

---

* 'The truly *radical cure for censorship would be its abolition*.' Marx, [1843] 1976, p. 25 (original emphasis).

1

Introduction

In late September 2005, an ordinary newspaper sparked an extraordinary war. The Danish *Jyllands-Posten* dropped not a single bomb—except one sketched into the Prophet's turban. As the New Year arrived, disputes around its twelve Muhammad cartoons were still mostly confined to Denmark. But within the month, reprints began to emerge in Norway, France, Italy, Germany, Belgium, and the Netherlands. Reports soon rushed in about 'anger flashing through the Muslim world'.[1] Syrians sacked and burned the Danish and Norwegian embassies. Protests in Afghanistan and Somalia claimed several lives.[2]

It was a war about free expression. The Iranian-American scholar Reza Aslan blasted the cartoons as 'fodder for the clash-of-civilizations mentality that pits East against West'.[3] Yet the British columnist Bruce Anderson railed at 'soggy liberals' in the West to 'stop cringing' and 'stand up for our own values'.[4] The French writer Pierre Jourde saw some irony. 'In the West, the most sacred God, the one we dare not touch, is Allah. We laugh at Jesus and his father as much as we like.'[5] Jourde's compatriot Régis Debray fired back: 'The lack of historical sensitivity among the hard-and-fast libertarians betrays a thoroughly imperial attitude. We may have removed our imperial hats, but our bearing remains colonial: the world must do as we do, lest it be declared primitive or savage.'[6]

Predictably pungent were the views of Ayaan Hirsi Ali. Born in 1969 in Mogadishu, Ali had risen, by the age of 33, to the rank of elected representative to the Dutch parliament. She received death threats after writing a screenplay for Theo van Gogh's *Submission*. The film depicts controversial Koranic verses being projected onto the body of a naked woman.[7] Ali condemned intellectuals who 'live off of free speech, but then accept censorship'.[8] She chided Western cowardice:

In 1980 the British network ITV showed a documentary about the stoning of a Saudi Arabian princess who had reportedly committed adultery. When the Riyadh government complained, British authorities apologised. We saw the same appeasement in 1987 for a sketch about Ayatollah Khomeini. Then, in 2000, the play *Aisha*, about the Prophet's

---

[1] Fisk, 2006. Cf. Bleich, 2011, pp. 3–4.   [2] BBC News, 2006.   [3] Aslan, 2006.
[4] Anderson, 2006.   [5] Jourde, 2006.   [6] Quoted in Fredet, 2006.
[7] Van Gogh was murdered in Amsterdam in November 2004 by the 26-year-old son of Moroccan immigrants. See Burke, 2004.
[8] Quoted in van Walsum, 2006.

youngest wife, was cancelled even before its premiere in Rotterdam....Since van Gogh's murder, writers, journalists and artists shut their mouths. Everyone is afraid to criticize Islam. *Submission* is still not shown in cinemas.[9]

Meanwhile there are those who would censor insults to their own views, but relish the freedom to offend others. Sir Iqbal Sacranie, then Secretary General of the Muslim Council of Britain, protested that 'Muslims respect and love the Prophet as being dearer to them than their own families.'[10] Scarcely a month later, he publicly declared that gays are 'harmful', 'immoral', and 'spread disease'.[11]

The Italian politician Roberto Calderoli unbuttoned his suit during a televised interview to flaunt a T-shirt picturing a cartoon image of the Prophet.[12] A week later Pope Benedict XVI warned, 'To promote peace and understanding among peoples and individuals, it is necessary and urgent that religions and religious symbols be respected.'[13] Within a few months, the Pontiff would nevertheless proclaim: 'Show me just what Muhammed brought that was new, and there you will find things only evil and inhuman.' Not his own words, but those of a fourteenth-century Byzantine emperor. Benedict later apologized, but not before damage had been done. 'The Pope's aggressive, insolent statement', proclaimed a Turkish official, 'appears to reflect both the hatred within him towards Islam and a Crusader mentality. He has destroyed peace.'[14]

1.1 Hatred and Value Pluralism

Many have challenged the 'sticks and stones' adage that 'words can never hurt me'. Words, they argue, can hurt as much as physical attacks.[15] Racist, sexist, homophobic, and similar epithets become, in the words of Charles Lawrence, Mari Matsuda, and other American critical race theorists, 'weapons to ambush, terrorize, wound, humiliate, and degrade'.[16] Lawrence reminds us that '[t]he experience of being called "nigger," "spic," "Jap," or "kike" is like receiving a slap in the face. The injury is instantaneous.'[17]

Two other leading American proponents of hate speech bans, Richard Delgado and Jean Stefancic, recall that, as far back as the Bible, we find 'the first known discussions of hate speech' in the Western canon. Judeo-Christian Scripture condemns 'cursing the deaf, rebuking neighbours, or scorning others'.[18] Aristotle reproaches people who 'speak evil' (κακηγορεῖν).[19] The French philosopher Jean-Luc Nancy sees the hate

---

[9] Quoted in Traufetter, 2006.
[10] Quoted in 'Danish Cartoons Depicting the Prophet Muhammad Abuse Our Freedoms', 2005.
[11] 'Muslim head says gays "harmful"', 2006.   [12] Cavalli, 2006.
[13] Accattoli, 2006.   [14] Owen & Erdem, 2006.
[15] See generally, e.g., Delgado & Stefancic, 1999, pp. 3–26; Delgado & Stefancic, 2004; Langton, 1993; Matsuda et al., 1993.
[16] Lawrence et al., 1993, p. 1.
[17] Lawrence, 1993, pp. 67–8. Cf. Nancy, 2013, pp. 7–8.
[18] Delgado & Stefancic, 2004, p. 1 (citing Leviticus 19:14, 19:17; Proverbs 29:8)
[19] *Nicomachean Ethics* 5.2.1129^{b}23, *in* Aristotle, [4th century BCE] 1984, vol. 2, p. 1782 (also translated as 'reviling', 'verbally abusing', or 'slandering'). Cf. text accompanying Section 4.12, note 175.

speaker as acting on an 'impulse' that 'can go so far as to seek the destruction of the other'.[20] The German scholar Claudia Hoppe recalls the simultaneously deterrent and symbolic role of hate speech bans as a necessary response to European history. 'Millions of Jews', she recalls, 'were exterminated on grounds of the so-called "race theory".' Hate speech in the Weimar Republic fed fascism, which then overthrew German democracy utterly, leading to history's worst atrocities: 'subsequent generations maintain the responsibility—even if they are not directly guilty—to ensure that such things *never happen again.*'[21]

Today, almost all nations—the United States being a notorious, oft-criticized exception[22]—impose penalties for some form of expression because of its hateful content. Most Western democracies assume what can be called *value pluralism*. They expect their legislatures and courts to limit the democratic freedoms of some citizens in order to safeguard the interests of other citizens.[23]

Limiting democracy in order to strengthen it is nothing new. Consider our familiar doctrines of separations of powers[24] and of constitutional checks and balances. They are designed in part, as hate speech bans are designed, with the goal of protecting the vulnerable. No modern democracy, for example, could legitimately hold an election on whether an individual criminal suspect ought to be found guilty. We fear that an innocent suspect could perish under the 'tyranny of the majority'.[25] Of course, courts are as vulnerable to prejudice as are electoral majorities. Still, we want courts, not voters, to render such judgments. We de-democratize that element of democracy in order to protect the very citizens who constitute the democracy.

Modern democracies' regimes of higher-order rights[26] equally serve as limits on democracy aimed at protecting democracy. An individual right of free expression protects unpopular speakers—political dissidents, social critics—from popular hostilities. In most democracies today,[27] however, the right is curbed against citizens who spread hatred. That limit, too, aims to keep society fair for all citizens. '[A]s a matter of principle', observes the European Court of Human Rights, 'it

---

[20] Nancy, 2013, pp. 7–8.

[21] Hoppe, 2008, pp. 2–3 (emphasis added). Cf. Günther, 2000; Grimm, 2009b, p. 561; Kailitz, 2004, pp. 11–12; Pech, 2003, p. 160; Suk, 2012; Tsesis, 2002, pp. 11–27; Zwagerman, 2009, pp. 8–9. Cf. text accompanying Section 5.7, notes 196–7.

[22] See, e.g., Boyle, 2001; Matsuda, 1993, pp. 26–31; Molnar, 2015; Richards, 1999, pp. 2–6, 30–3, 161–80; Stefancic & Delgado, 1992–93; Waldron, 2012a, pp. 1–6.

[23] On non-citizens, see Section 4.11, text accompanying note 169.

[24] Cf., e.g., Kelsen, 1920, p. 20.

[25] *De la démocratie en Amérique*, I:7, *in* de Tocqueville, [1835] 1999, pp. 348–51; *On Liberty*, ch. 1, *in* Mill, [1869] 1991a, p. 8.

[26] Higher-order rights can claim both *de jure* and *de facto* existence. Some weaker democracies formally adopt higher-order rights, e.g., in their constitutions, or by statute or treaty, but then largely disregard them. Others, such as Britain, may maintain strong doctrines of parliamentary sovereignty, unbound by higher law, yet can be said to observe higher-order rights *de facto* on par with other democracies.

[27] See generally, e.g., Bleich, 2011; Cohen-Almagor, 2005; Josende, 2010; Nieuwenhuis, 2011; Noorloos, 2012; Parekh, 2012; Pech, 2003; Robitaille-Froidure, 2011; Stefancic & Delgado, 1992–93; Thiel, 2003a.

may be considered necessary in certain democratic societies to sanction or even prevent all forms of expression which spread, incite, promote or justify hatred based on intolerance.' For the Court, 'tolerance and respect for the equal dignity of all human beings constitute the foundations of a democratic, pluralistic society'.[28] Sometimes, then, less democracy is 'really' more democracy. According to the British House of Lords member Bhikhu Parekh:

> Although free speech is an important value, it is not the only one. Human dignity, equality, freedom to live without harassment and intimidation, social harmony, mutual respect, and protection of one's good name and honour are also central to the good life and deserve to be safeguarded. Because these values conflict, either inherently or in particular contexts, they need to be *balanced*.[29]

1.2 Rights, Security, and Citizenship

We face a complicated dialectic. With each step, our reasoning strays ever further from democratic foundations. At one remove from democratic processes, the right of free expression protects unpopular speakers by limiting the ability of legislatures or judges to silence them. The right carves out an exception to the rule of democratic processes in order to safeguard democracy itself. At a second remove, however, hate speech bans place limits *upon* those limits. That second step equally aims to protect vulnerable citizens, and so to preserve democracy. But then at a third remove, those hate speech bans must face limits of their own. Legislatures and courts must determine how far they extend. They must therefore place *limits on the limits on the limits* imposed upon democracy.

I shall challenge the view that public discourse can legitimately be regulated under our prevailing rights regimes, which place public discourse at three removes away from the very democracy which it constitutes. My objection arises not from the complexity of rights regimes as such. Human expression is intrinsically complex, and the law must reflect that complexity.[30] The wisest legal system could never adequately regulate free expression through a few simple formulas. Moreover, even three degrees of removal from some core principle—exceptions to exceptions to exceptions—are in themselves nothing unusual in law. We witness such intricacy in any number of tax or commercial codes. Nor is my intention to banish rights regimes entirely. They do have a role to play in preserving free expression.[31]

Democratic public discourse, however, demands a stronger protection. It must be safeguarded not only as an *individual right*, but as an essential *attribute of democratic citizenship*. It is a perennial mistake to equate the demands imposed upon the state through a regime of rights with the demands imposed upon it as a regime

---

[28] *Gündüz v. Turkey*, ECHR, no. 35071/97, judgment of 4 December 2003, para. 40; cf. *Erbakan v. Turkey*, ECHR, no. 59405/00, judgment of 6 July 2006, para. 56.
[29] Parekh, 2012, p. 43 (emphasis added).   [30] See Sections 2.5 and 5.3.
[31] See Section 4.4.

of democracy. Limits must certainly be placed upon democracy in order to maintain it for all citizens. Those limits must themselves be limited, however, when that function encroaches upon the elements that *make* the state a democracy.

Those two strands of law, the strand of individual rights and the strand of democratic citizenship, certainly overlap. But they are not identical. Much of our talk about democratic citizenship becomes clouded by our talk about individual rights, as if the latter subsume the former. Nor is that the only confusion. We further tend to conflate those two strands with a third, namely, the strand of state *security.* Hate speech bans may indeed under some circumstances promote the state's security. Protection of vulnerable persons or groups is a standard security concern.[32] But bans *never promote the state's democracy.* This book therefore rejects the positions of Delgado and Stefancic, Lawrence, Matsuda, Nancy, and Parekh. In fact, it rejects the views of almost all legislatures, courts, and international organizations today.

I am by no means the first to challenge hate speech bans. But most writers wage their opposition by claiming the kinds of individual rights or freedoms appearing on our familiar charters of 'constitutional', 'civil', or 'human' rights and freedoms, including our numerous bills and treaties of rights. That view tempts us to view problems surrounding expression as self-contained. Self-expression becomes just one of an assortment of rights and freedoms on the 'human rights checklist'.

Free expression is, of course, no more important to individual or collective welfare than a number of other interests, such as fair trials, protection from torture, or access to food and water. It is, however, the only distinctly democratic interest. A state could easily release its political prisoners or stop torturing without becoming a democracy. It might well provide food and water without becoming a democracy. It might even offer a considerable margin of free expression without becoming a democracy. It cannot be a democracy, however, without guaranteeing what I shall call *the citizen's prerogative of expression within public discourse.* Even the right to vote, the more conventional hallmark of democracy, is nothing but an occasional, formalized procedure for exercising that more basic prerogative of expression within public discourse. Voting is a derivative of speaking.[33]

We must distinguish carefully among those three strands of law: the strand of national security, the strand of individual rights, and the strand of democratic citizenship.[34] They interweave, but one strand can never wholly blend into another without destroying democracy entirely. We fail to regulate expression legitimately until we identify the extent to which expression is not just an important right within democracy, but is materially constitutive *of* democracy.

---

[32] Violence against members of a social group most clearly illustrates the state's concern with hatred as a security interest. The modern state is defined, in part, with reference to its monopoly on defining lawful violence either by state agents (e.g., the military or police) or private agents (e.g., defence of oneself or of an innocent third party). Cases in criminal law, e.g., are commonly denominated as 'the state *versus*' the defendant.

[33] See Section 3.4, text accompanying notes 35–6.

[34] See Section 4.7, text accompanying note 88.

No democracy can be seen as constituted solely through one or a series of legal enactments, not even through a comprehensive written 'constitution'. All democratic constitutions confirm the possibility of their own abolition or amendment. On their own terms, that can only mean through public discourse.[35] Through such abrogation options, democratic constitutions present themselves as constituted through nothing *but* an ongoing process of public discourse. That process had established the democracy in the first place, and can at any time re-constitute it. Within a democracy, public discourse is the constitution *of* the constitution. It is the *Urverfassung*. That primordial status of viewpoints expressed, however repulsively, within public discourse cannot legitimately lend itself to outright regulation within those democratic legal processes which it constitutes.[36] Viewpoint-selective penalties imposed upon expression within public discourse can never offer 'less democracy for the sake of more democracy'. They serve only to de-democratize the state, even if they do in some circumstances, like certain other de-democratizing measures, serve a security interest.

Contrary to widespread opinion, challenges to speech bans in no way assume a value-neutral state. Such an entity is a conceptual impossibility. Even the most libertarian state would by definition promote libertarian values merely through its actions and omissions. Through word and deed, the modern democracy proclaims all sorts of values, even conflicting ones, every day.[37]

Serious opponents of bans do not seek a state callous to inequality. They in no way expect the state to preach that vulnerable groups 'should learn to live with'[38] hostilities and prejudices. To preserve itself as a democracy, a state must certainly take effective steps to protect the vulnerable and to promote social and civic pluralism. Such measures are indeed legitimately coercive. They include well-established anti-discrimination laws extending to commerce, education, and employment. But it is never 'less democracy for the sake of more democracy' to penalize citizens for expressing within public discourse attitudes even grotesquely hostile to those pluralist values.

My challenge to bans on democratic grounds aims to avoid some common misunderstandings. One would be the assumption that opposition to bans necessarily entails 'marketplace', 'libertarian', 'Americanized', 'neo-liberal', or indeed 'neo-conservative' values. Particular points of US free speech law will certainly prove invaluable, in view of the degree of detail with which it has been articulated and refined over many years. That does not mean that those doctrines must be incorporated wholesale along with broader political assumptions underlying US legal or political culture. US law provides helpful insights into democracy, not exhaustive ones.

A related misunderstanding concerns the post-Second World War model of the European social-welfare state. That model, it has been assumed, justifies bans as

---

[35] See Chapter 4, text accompanying notes 1–5.
[36] See Section 4.3, text accompanying note 43.   [37] See Section 4.11.
[38] Waldron, 2012a, p. 3; Waldron, 2012b, p. 331.

means of balancing the supposedly conflicting values of liberty and equality, often portrayed as a standoff between 'American' and 'European' approaches. The democratic model I shall propose will serve to overcome that assumption. It envisages a state that promotes pluralist, anti-hate worldviews, without having to punish citizens who, within public discourse, crudely spurn that ideal. That model will serve to challenge the widespread view that abolition of bans is, through a kind of historical determinism, suited only to US law and culture.[39] Northern European social-welfarist democracies will prove to be the *best* situated to abolish bans.

Pondering democracy's legitimating conditions may smack of an eighteenth-century quaintness. It may seem scarcely suited to the mammoth machines of our post-industrial regulatory, administrative, and surveillance states, often managed by anonymous bureaucracies, corrupted by commercial influence, and tempted to exaggerate state security needs, all the while governing disaffected constituencies.[40] What delusions can we, in the twenty-first century, be chasing by seeking yet another holy grail of democratic legitimacy? How much democracy is there left to theorize? Does a focus on democracy presuppose, moreover, an outmoded, Enlightenment-era assumption of perfectly rational, autonomous legal subjects? Advocates of bans unsurprisingly depict them as remedies for the decline of equal citizenship, a decline characteristic of atomized and technocratically managed mass societies, which have long drifted from any hope of collective endeavour in the ways Rousseau had once imagined.

Democratic theory must certainly take account of our de-democratized spheres.[41] We must distinguish, however, between the descriptive 'is' of observing defects of modern democracies, and the normative 'ought' of deciding which legal rules and social attitudes most legitimately and most effectively redress them. Our post-industrial, regulatory, and administrative societies present dozens of social and technical problems for which democratic theory as such has little to offer. But the citizen's relationship to public discourse is not one of them. After centuries of political theory, basic relationships among democracy, freedom, rights, and citizenship remain poorly clarified. One of the chances still available to us for tempering the dominion of technocratic and managerial spheres is to seize back into our hands our societies' vestiges of citizen-driven democracy.[42] Crucial to that aim is insight into democracy's roots in public discourse.

1.3 Overview

But what about the immediate dangers of hate speech? One problem for many writers has been to treat them in political abstraction. That reproach may, in two opposed senses, seem odd. From one standpoint, such a reproach seems to

---

[39] See Section 6.1.
[40] See, e.g., Crouch, 2004; Nancy, 1990; Nancy, 2013, pp. 4–8; Rancière, 2004; Rancière, 2005, p. 29 (discussing Baudrillard), pp. 58–60, 80–1; Rorty, 2004. Cf. Post, 1996–97 (discussing Fiss).
[41] See Section 4.7, text accompanying note 88.
[42] See Section 4.1, text accompanying note 20.

underestimate both the problem of hate speech and the passionate reactions to it. Hateful expression, after all, inherently entails political meanings. Protagonists on all sides often take vibrant political stands. From that perspective, it seems strange to suggest that the debate has neglected politics.

From an opposite point of view, my reproach seems to overestimate the character of hate speech—to attribute to it more politics than it deserves. Jeremy Waldron, for example, insists on the materiality of hateful expression. He repeatedly uses metaphors drawn from our responses to the physical world. He speaks in naturalist terms about its 'slow-acting poison', which 'become a disfiguring part of the social environment'.[43]

That metaphor's aim is clear. Problems posed by the physical environment, like quicksand or bee stings, take on the veneer of objectivity. They retain their harmful qualities irrespective of the political contexts in which they arise. The harm of a bee sting, and by extension the harm of hate speech, becomes the same in Sweden and in Saudi Arabia. That is why Delgado and Stefancic can, in an essentialist vein, trace the problem of hate speech, which they see in their own world, back to what they view as a sufficiently similar problem within Biblical communities that lived thousands of years ago. From that standpoint, removal of the problem from political contingencies, by bestowing a fixed, material objectivity upon it, seems justified. Advocates often emphasize hate speech bans' quasi-universality. They point to bans embraced across the globe, irrespective of differences among political systems.[44]

I shall agree with the bans' supporters that hateful expression is experienced in painful ways. I disagree, however, that such a harm remains constant in its nature, irrespective of the social and political context in which it arises. Unlike the bee sting, hateful expression is by no means the same thing in Weimar Germany or 1994 Rwanda that it is in early twenty-first-century Western Europe. Certain solutions may be appropriate for some societies, but not for others. That hypothesis will guide this book's journey. I shall certainly examine the harms attributed to hateful expression, but only towards the end, in Chapter 5. I shall considerably postpone, then, what many writers ordinarily assume to be the foremost question: Is hate speech harmful? Unlike the bee sting, we cannot examine the harms attributed to hateful expression 'as such'. We must first examine the political and social contexts in which such expression arises. That is the task of Chapters 2–4.

Given what I am claiming to be the constitutive role of public discourse, basic legal and political concepts will enter from the outset. Chapter 2 begins with a review of some familiar, liberal perspectives on free expression. It also briefly surveys the alternative perspectives of republican, communitarian, and critical legal scholars. The discussion then pinpoints certain problems arising around such core

[43] Waldron, 2012a, pp. 4, 30, 31, 33, 37, 39, 45, 59, 65–9, 72, 96–7, 116–17; Waldron, 2012b, p. 331. Cf., critically, Heinze, 2013b, p. 614.
[44] See Section 1.1, text accompanying note 22, and Section 3.1. But see also Section 6.1, text accompanying notes 40–6.

concepts as 'freedom', 'liberty', 'liberal', 'speech', 'expression', 'content', 'viewpoint', 'hatred', 'legitimacy', and 'public discourse', as well as differences between consequentialist and deontological approaches.

Chapter 3 examines certain failures of our dominant, rights-based systems to recognize the requirements of democracy. Leading liberals like John Rawls or Ronald Dworkin had hailed liberal rights regimes as shields against outright legislative and judicial balancing of conflicting social interests. Rights regimes have, however, themselves become entrenched within those balancing processes. Regimes of individual or human rights may well offer benchmarks for assessing *state* legitimacy, but in no way provide, nor were they historically conceived to provide, criteria of specifically *democratic* legitimacy. We must distinguish between the state's legitimacy *as a state* and its legitimacy *as a democracy*. Whatever anchor free expression may find in rights, we must also recognize its distinct grounding in democratic public discourse. We must distinguish between a liberal or human *right* of expression and a democratic citizen *prerogative* of expression.

Supporters of bans often deny that democracies can guarantee any particular safety from the harmful effects of speech. They note that atrocities traceable to hate speech arose in democracies like Germany's Weimar Republic, Rwanda, or the former Yugoslavia. In Chapter 4 it is argued that an historically recent form of democracy has emerged since the 1960s. It can be called the 'longstanding, stable, and prosperous democracy' (LSPD). That model displays internal social and political dynamics that equip LSPDs better than non-LSPDs (non-democracies or weaker democracies) to counter the risks of hate speech. LSPDs offer more politically legitimate and more practically effective ways of preventing the harms of hate speech without having to censor speakers.

The bans' defenders rightly note the historical dangers of hate speech. In Chapter 5, however, it is argued that their empirical claims, made over decades, have never been substantiated for LSPDs. The bans' advocates alternatively postulate notions of indirect or 'symbolic' causation, that 'slow-acting poison', whereby hate speech, even if not reliably traceable to harmful material effects, nevertheless acts in subtler yet still deleterious ways. But such views of indirect causation fail to circumscribe a sphere of harmful speech within the public discourse of LSPDs. In view of those difficulties surrounding both direct and indirect causation of harm within LSPDs, defenders of bans have also taken 'dignitarian' positions. They present hate speech as a *malum in se*, harmful not through further effects, but rather inherently harmful, through its aim to diminish the equal respect and equal citizenship due to all members of society. That claim rests, however, on a category error. A metaphorical denial of citizenship becomes implausibly equated with a material denial of citizenship.

Chapter 6 locates the LSPD model against the broader backdrop of hate speech controversies since the late twentieth century. From the beginnings of global and comparative conversations, a 'US *versus* the rest of the world' model has emerged. That dualism styles the anti-ban position as aberrantly American, indeed in ways linked to other aberrations of US politics and society. It is a misleading dichotomy, however, both in historical and political terms. It breeds an historical determinism that oversimplifies the broader approaches, and the character of public discourse, not only among democracies, but also between democracies and non-democracies. The LSPD model offers a more credible lens for distinguishing between those democracies which may, and those which may not legitimately maintain bans. The analysis concludes, in Chapter 7, with a point-by-point review of common arguments favouring bans, and the replies that the LSPD model can offer.

2

Concepts and Contexts

Concern about hatred has surged not only within the public and the media, but across academic disciplines. Vocabularies arising out of that cross-disciplinary field are not always mutually understood. This chapter begins by recalling how perspectives both within and outside our dominant, rights-based tradition have shaped the debates. The aim of distinguishing a democratic foundation for expression from the liberal, rights-based approaches requires, moreover, some definition of 'liberal'. That term has a history of divergent, mutually contradictory meanings. We must also distinguish between 'freedom' and 'liberty', 'speech' and 'expression', 'content' and 'viewpoint', 'hate speech' and 'hateful expression'.

2.1 Liberal and Democratic Models

This book's conception[1] of democracy will stand between two extremes. At one extreme, Ronald Dworkin enters the debate to declare his rejection of hate speech bans.[2] Dworkin ordinarily counts as a stalwart of rights-based liberalism. Yet that approach tacitly recedes in his analysis of free speech, in favour of a distinctly democratic rationale. The importance of that shift from rights-based to democratic principles has gone unnoticed, including by him, not least through his and our tendency to conflate democratic principles with liberal rights principles, as if they each make broadly the same assumptions or entail the same results.

Dworkin's view is extreme, as he assumes a timeless, universal model of democracy. He recognizes 'deep controversy' about 'what democracy really is',[3] but maintains a fixed 'conception' of 'government subject to conditions ... of equal status for all citizens'.[4] Free expression, on that view, 'is not just instrumental to democracy but constitutive of [it].'[5] Dworkin ignores differences between the Anglo-American culture central to his analysis and the democracies of, for example, the pre-Nazi Weimar Republic, post-colonial democracies, or post-Soviet Central and Eastern Europe. In his only, stunningly anecdotal concession to

---

[1] Cf., e.g., Rawls, 1999, p. 5 (distinguishing between a general, normative 'concept', such as 'justice', and specific, often divergent 'conceptions' of it, e.g., Aristotelian, Kantian, Marxist, etc.).
[2] See, e.g., Dworkin, 1992; Dworkin, 2009; Dworkin, 2012.
[3] Dworkin, 1996, p. 15.   [4] Dworkin, 1996, p. 17.
[5] Dworkin, 1996, pp. 200–1; Dworkin, 2009, p. v.

non-US approaches, Dworkin recalls Europeans describing their history as 'darker than that of the United States',[6] as if Europe's hate speech bans betray a cultural pathology, while US history shines bright.

Dworkin rightly doubts the claims that causally link hateful expression within modern democracies to acts of violence or discrimination.[7] That scepticism is scarcely plausible, however, unless we can account for the times in—often very recent—history when hate speech surely led to atrocities. Dworkin veers off, then, onto a sweepingly *generalist* path. He extrapolates from US constitutional principles to absolute principles of democracy by neglecting every other democracy. That naïve universalism recapitulates errors made by his rivals, advocates of speech bans, who equally fail to distinguish among various types of democracy.[8] So Dworkin leaves a basic question unanswered. Even if we were to assume opposition to bans within some democracies to be justified, would that view necessarily presuppose a justified opposition to bans in all democracies?

Yale Law Dean Robert Post, arguably the subtlest opponent of bans by the later twentieth century,[9] joins Dworkin's challenge. Post, however, swings to the opposite extreme. He, too, focuses on US law, but with attention to its historical and political contexts. That focus leads him in a *particularist* direction. He shuns pushing American norms on other democracies.[10] Post arrives at that conclusion, opposite to Dworkin's, yet through a curiously similar pathologizing of non-US democracies. Momentarily overlooking dissident views within the US, and sidestepping the fact that Australia, Canada, or New Zealand also have bans, Post dually essentializes what 'American eyes' would see as 'European habits of deference to political authority'. In Europe, 'democracy is a comparative newcomer to millennia-old forms of highly deferential structures of political governance.' Consequently, 'elite norms retain a hegemonic status that they have lost in America'.[11] In a similar vein, Richard Posner smirks at 'the *less democratic cast* of European politics, as a result of which elite opinion is more likely to override public opinion than it is in the United States'.[12]

Many a European might bristle at such condescension.[13] The problem is not that these writers' observations are wholly wrong. Being formulated in such open-ended terms, who could really tell? Did fourteenth- or fifteenth-century Europe display 'millennia-old' deference in the way the seventeenth century did? Is democracy in Alabama or Mississippi something other than a 'newcomer'? Do

---

[6] Dworkin, 2012, p. 343.   [7] Dworkin, 2009, p. vi. Cf. Sections 5.1–5.3.
[8] See Section 5.2.
[9] See generally, e.g., Post, 1994–95; Post, 1995; Post, 1996–97; Post, 2006; Post, 2009; Post, 2011a; Post, 2011b.
[10] Molnar & Post, 2012, p. 25. See, critically, Heinze, 2013b, pp. 593–4.
[11] Post, 2009, pp 137–8. Cf. Section 6.1, text accompanying notes 17–19. In fairness, it would be wrong to overstate Post's particularism, which he presents as conjecture.
[12] Posner, 2005, p. 86 (emphasis added).
[13] See, e.g., Heinze, 2009a. To be sure, we find that same reductionism towards other countries among leading American advocates of bans. See Heinze, 2008a. Conversely, non-US writers have also at times overly simplified US approaches. See Section 5.5, note 103; Section 5.6, note 172; and, generally, Section 6.1.

the histories of Denmark or the Netherlands reveal a 'less democratic cast' than the histories of Texas or Georgia, or indeed of Connecticut or Illinois?

The problem, rather, is that the trophy ends up being awarded to a land steeped in corporate dominance, military adventurism, botched death sentences, abusive incarceration, and police brutality.[14] For Dworkin, that side-lining of non-US democracies means that his universal model reflects the law of only one democracy—his own. All others turn into aberrations. On the other hand, it draws Post back into an American exceptionalism, leaving him agnostic about any shared conception of democracy. Post turns on its head the question Dworkin had left us with. We must now ask: even if we accept the legitimacy of opposing hate speech bans for one democracy, does that position presuppose nothing about the legitimacy of opposing bans for other democracies?

Opposition to speech bans needs a model pitched between those two extremes. That model will hopefully teach us not just about speech, but, more importantly, about democracy. I shall navigate between, on the one hand, Dworkin's ahistorical focus on the universalist demands of democracy per se and, on the other hand, Post's concern about the historical and cultural limits of any single model. I shall certainly follow Dworkin in asking what democracy as such requires. But I will also ask about the historical conditions under which particular democracies can or cannot be expected to conform to such an ideal.

James Weinstein joins Dworkin and Post as an authority on US law. Weinstein hints at that aim to synthesize democracies' structurally essential elements with their historically contingent elements. Weinstein agrees with Post in taking 'historical and cultural differences'[15] into account. But he also echoes Dworkin: 'there remains a core free speech principle that must be respected in any democracy worthy of that name.'[16] What it means to be 'worthy' of the name of democracy now demands closer study. I therefore hope to reconcile conceptually universalist with historically relativist notions of democracy. Once its elements have been examined, I shall, in Chapter 6, call that model a *democratic-historicist* theory of political legitimacy. It will present democracy's 'core free speech principle' not irrespective of historical and social conditions, but as the fruit of them.

Dworkin, Post, Weinstein, and other US experts write within the rights-based framework of the First Amendment to the US constitution. Meanwhile, many non-US scholars work within rights-based frameworks of their respective national, regional, or international instruments. Within those frameworks, democracy is certainly treated as crucial, but still as only one factor to consider for purposes of

[14] Cf., e.g., Gilens & Page, 2014 (examining systemic flaws in US democratic processes). One leading study places more than ten European states, in addition to Australia, Canada, and New Zealand, ahead of the US on a synthesis of democratic indicators. See Section 4.1, text accompanying notes 8–9. See also Section 5.4, text accompanying note 96. On the criteria I shall set forth in this book, whole swathes of the US, notably in the South, certainly maintained a white, mob-rule majoritarianism (cf. Section 3.3, text accompanying notes 31–2; Section 6.1, text accompanying notes 28–36), which is largely the antithesis of democracy, but could scarcely have been called mature democracies much before the late twentieth century.
[15] Weinstein, 2009a, p. 23.   [16] Weinstein, 2009a, pp. 23–4.

interpreting a *right* of free expression. Under article 10(1) of the European Convention on Human Rights[17] (ECHR), for example, '[e]veryone has the right to freedom of expression.' However, under article 10(2), '[t]he exercise of these freedoms … may be subject to such formalities, conditions, restrictions or penalties as … are *necessary* in a democratic society' to any protect any number of overriding interests.[18]

The case law seals that subordination of democracy. Democracy ends up tossed into a blend of principles, all of which are then to be weighed and balanced. Recall the Court's aforementioned view that 'it may be considered necessary in certain democratic societies to sanction or even prevent' hateful expression.[19] Rights regimes serve indeed to ensure that democratic excesses will not endanger vulnerable citizens. But the sheer recitation of that motive, with no requirement on a government to show any material evidence of such danger,[20] becomes an exercise in deploying rights as a means of limiting democracy, with no demand that demonstrated compensatory protections for vulnerable citizens be shown. I shall examine that problem more closely in Chapter 3, in order to develop one of this book's core theses. Democratic citizen prerogatives certainly form a necessary element of higher-law *rights* of free speech. They do so, however, because, as I shall argue, they form a necessary element of democratic legitimacy *irrespective of rights*. Democratic citizen prerogatives are compatible with, and applicable to, but remain conceptually independent of the status of higher-law rights within any given constitutional order.

2.2 Alternative Contexts

The shift among otherwise liberal writers like Dworkin or Post to democratic principles hints at the inadequacy of classically liberal or rights-based assumptions. Some writers go further, challenging liberal or rights-based frameworks categorically. Many *communitarian* writers challenge what they see as modernity's exaggerated focus on individual legal entitlements.[21] Opponents of speech bans, on that view, exhibit their obsession with individual freedom at the expense of interpersonal respect and social cohesion.

Some *civic republican* theorists seek to limit the capacity of rights regimes to trump, hence to foreclose, collective deliberation. For those who advocate viewpoint-selective bans within public discourse, such laws' legitimacy rests on their acceptance within a collective decision-making procedure.[22] Other republican theorists take the opposite view. They maintain that public deliberation is fair and meaningful only when all views enjoy some opportunity to be heard.[23]

---

[17] European Convention for the Protection of Human Rights and Fundamental Freedoms (as amended by Protocols Nos. 11 and 14), 4 November 1950, ETS 5.

[18] Emphasis added. See Section 3.1, note 4.

[19] See, e.g., Section 1.1, text accompanying note 28.   [20] See Sections 5.1 and 5.3.

[21] See, e.g., Cram, 2006, pp. 5–9.   [22] See, e.g., Cram, 2006, pp. 110–12.

[23] See, e.g., Pettit, 2012, p. 202.

On either of those republican views, what decides the issue is not a canon of higher-law rights, but the criterion of collective deliberation among members of the polity.

Critical theory carries exceptional weight. It has identified central problems and created much of the vocabulary of the hate speech debates. Racist incidents on US university campuses in the 1980s sparked the first blaze of writing by writers like Matsuda,[24] Lawrence,[25] or Delgado and Stefancic,[26] who wrote the phrase 'hate speech' into the legal lexicon.[27] Their views have influenced broader, global debates. Similar to some communitarians, many critical theorists support hate speech bans as part of their comprehensive scepticism towards modern democracies' privileging of liberal rights over the interests of vulnerable groups. They condemn liberal rights for being universal and equal only in abstract principle, while, in practice, being systemically deployed to favour dominant interests, thereby undermining equal citizenship.[28]

Other critical thinkers, such as Judith Butler[29] or Raoul Vaneigem,[30] condemn speech bans. They accuse bans of inhibiting social processes that need to take place, indeed most importantly for the most vulnerable, as a means of empowering them. Vaneigem in particular opposes bans on expressly democratic grounds. Like other writers, however, they both fail to distinguish among various types of democracies. Some *feminist* theorists argue that rights-based models of democratic deliberation assume a traditionally individualist, male socialization, which overlooks relational interactions that are equally constitutive of society and politics.[31] Butler reminds us, however, that feminist opinion remains divided.

2.3 Democracy as Consensus Versus Hatred as Extremism

From a variety of perspectives, then, authors approach hate speech from standpoints that challenge classically liberal, rights-based assumptions. Yet none of them seriously challenge democracy as such. As recently as the Cold War, democracy had throughout history been seen as only one of several types of legitimate government. Since the collapse of the Soviet Union, by contrast, challenges across the political spectrum are waged not in the name of overthrowing democracy but in the name of improving it. That situation is somewhat surprising. In the twentieth and twenty-first centuries, democracies have lurched from crisis to crisis. They have played some role in atrocities, at home and abroad, from controversial wars,

---

[24] See, e.g., Matsuda, 1993   [25] See, e.g., Lawrence, 1993.
[26] See, e.g., Delgado, 1993; Delgado & Stefancic, 1999; Delgado & Stefancic, 2004; Stefancic & Delgado, 1992–93.
[27] See, e.g., Cortese, 2006, pp. 1–2, 60–1; Greene, 2012, p. 99; Jacobson & Schlink, 2012, pp. 232–7; Lawrence, 1993; Lawrence et al., 1993, pp. 1–14; Post, 1995, pp. 291–3; Robitaille-Froidure, 2011, p. 43; Strossen, 1990.
[28] Cf. critically, Heinze, 2008a.   [29] Butler, 1997.   [30] Vaneigem, 2003.
[31] See, e.g., Williams, 2011.

to exploitative trade, to environmental degradation, to immigration or penal practices derogating from the rule of law. Yet criticisms from left to right, barring what come to be defined as extremists, are presented as their authors' attempts not to assail but to enhance democracy.[32]

Today, proposals for 're-thinking' or 're-inventing' (with or without the adverb 'radically') democracy may be easy to come by; but proposals for eliminating it outright remain scarce. For the first time in history, anti-democratic stances can no longer easily co-exist with pro-democratic ones as of equal or even superior status. Democracy, itself once an extremism, has emerged in the West as an antinomy to 'extremism', with which hate speech is commonly associated. That which opposes democracy by definition becomes extremist, and that which most credibly opposes extremism is democracy.[33] Through democracy's well-known paradox of allowing the expression of ideas that would overthrow or weaken democracy,[34] the sheer spontaneity of speech bred within complex, pluralist democracies can lead to hateful expression. When such expression assaults values of equal citizenship, a ban can appear as a necessary balancing tool. The rejection of pluralist democracy embodied by hateful expression stands as extremism. On that view, rejection of extremism, through bans, vindicates democracy.

It is easy enough to challenge bans on classical liberal assumptions, but then only insofar as those assumptions are shared. Such a challenge can preach only to the converted. It persuades only those who are already committed to prevailing liberal rights provisions, and indeed to particular, and in most democracies hotly disputed interpretations of them. Under this book's model of democracy, by contrast, I shall argue that bans undermine precisely those democratic principles which are now so widely shared, indeed as distinguished from liberal and rights-based principles. The liberal, rights-based case against hate speech bans has some strengths, but the democratic case is stronger.

The democratic model proposed here aims at nothing so complicated as a full-scale purge of our current rights regimes. To the contrary, it will certainly *align* with customary liberal rights of free speech. It will urge commensurate revisions to the rights regimes currently dominant within most democracies.

---

[32] See, e.g., Amin & Thrift, 2013; Rancière, 2005; Unger, 1998; Vaneigem, 2003.

[33] See, e.g., Kailitz, 2004, pp. 15–16 (discussing Sartori and Butterwegge). The idea of extremism and democracy as mutually excluding and thereby mutually defining each other underpins the very notion of 'militant democracy' as theorized particularly in post-war Germany. See Section 5.2. The political scientist Hans-Gerd Jaschke argues: 'Democracies without extremist currents are as unimaginable as a society without crime. Extremism is a … pathological component of modern democratic societies. Yet it forms part of society, and holds a mirror to it. The study of extremism allows insights into the defects of political and social development and into the current state of democratisation. The science of extremism [*Extremismusforschung*] is always simultaneously an applied science of democracy [*Demokratieforschung*]' (Jaschke, 2006, p. 12). But see, e.g., Kailitz, 2004, pp. 12, 18–22 (noting the problematic boundaries between 'democratic' and 'extremist'). Kailitz instead distinguishes between 'extremist' and 'pluralist', defining 'extremist' as 'anti-pluralist'. Kailitz, 2004, p. 21. Insofar as such dualisms tacitly equate 'democracy' or 'pluralism' with 'justice', and 'extremism' with 'injustice', they necessarily remain contingent. Cf. Heinze, 2013a.

[34] See, e.g., Wassermann, 2002, pp. 99–100 (discussing Kelsen); Rancière, 2005, p. 15.

However, the model will *derive* not from assumptions about liberalism as such, or about rights as such, but from assumptions about democracy's *legitimating expressive conditions*. By 'legitimating expressive conditions', I mean not 'ideal speech situations',[35] but only those free speech conditions without which democratic processes cannot be said to be fully in place; and which therefore, when only partly fulfilled, point to some measure of illegitimacy within the democratic process.

2.4 Freedom and Liberalism

A democratic model can best be developed by distinguishing it from the liberal, rights-based models. I shall use the terms 'liberal' and 'liberalism' in a classical, juridical sense, to denote *the presumption of individual autonomy protected through legal rights*. ('Liberalism' in that sense becomes articulated in early modernity[36] and the Enlightenment[37] in opposition to monarchical despotism. In the twentieth century, it is construed in opposition to right- as well as left-wing collectivist regimes, such as fascism or state-monopolized socialism.)[38] That element of legal 'presumption' is crucial. Presumptions are ordinarily rebuttable in law. The presumption in favour of expression is routinely overcome in order to avoid such harms as commercial fraud, courtroom perjury, treason in wartime, defacing of property, and the like. Within the dominant value-pluralist proceduralism[39] of most democracies today, a human or civil *right* supplies a legal presumption favouring free expression as part of the weighing and balancing of the totality of competing interests.

Given that purely presumptive character of the right, it yields no uniform position towards speech bans. In advocating 'almost absolute protection of free speech',[40] for example, Edwin Baker construes the right as demanding the strongest possible presumption in favour of that individual freedom. That same juridical liberalism can, however, be invoked just as persuasively to support bans. Steven Heyman[41] and Jeremy Waldron[42] do, for example, affirm the presumption of free expression within liberal rights. They nevertheless deem it to be, under some circumstances, overridden by what they present as an equally liberal interest in maintaining citizen dignity and equality. They would tip the balance away from free speech when it menaces that interest.

---

[35] See, e.g, Habermas, 1973, p. 255. Habermas joins a long line of Western political thinkers who can be read in conflicting ways as to the legal norms that ought to govern expression. For a similar divergence in reading Rawls, see, e.g., Waldron, 2012a, pp. 70–1, 249–50.
[36] See, e.g., Locke, [1689] 1988.
[37] See, e.g., Montesquieu, [1748–49] 1993; Voltaire, [1763] 1961.
[38] See, e.g., Popper, [1945] (2002a).
[39] As captured, e.g., by Parekh. See Section 1.1, text accompanying note 29.
[40] See, e.g., Baker, 2009, p. 139; Baker, 2012, p. 57.
[41] See Section 5.6, text accompanying notes 184–8.
[42] See Section 3.2, text accompanying note 24.

By adopting that juridical definition of 'liberal', we avoid two others, which contradict both it and each other. We avoid, on the one hand, a more absolutist, 'libertarian'[43] sense, which would fail to account for liberalism within the many democracies that maintain speech bans. On the other hand, we avoid the more popular sense of 'liberal', common in English-speaking societies, as connoting overall support for progressive social policies,[44] and commonly construed as requiring at least minimal hate speech bans.

Freedom and liberty. Within traditional political theory, the concepts of *liberty* and *freedom* have often been deemed 'virtually interchangeable'.[45] As a practical matter, I shall generally use the term 'freedom', given its continuity with the phrases 'free expression' and 'free speech'. The choice between the Germanic and the Latinate certainly offers a luxury missing from other Western languages.[46] Some writers treat 'freedom' as the broader, background term, to connote absence of legal restraint. A 'liberty', by contrast, would be said to ensue in function of, hence defined by, the particular regime that creates it.[47] My legal 'freedom' to move my body extends as far as the law forbids me from hitting others, from stealing others' goods, and so forth. By contrast, my legal 'liberty' to marry, and thereby to assume all legal duties and rights of marriage, is not just limited by, but rather its entire scope is created and defined by law.

Such differences between freedom and liberty can certainly be borne in mind. My general preference for 'freedom' hints at the broader, background notion. We shall see that 'free' expression ends up being defined in one way as a liberty created by a rights regime, yet in another way as a freedom inherent within a necessary prerogative of democratic citizenship. Be that all as it may, any distinction between 'freedom' and 'liberty' must remain loose. I shall not rely on it to distinguish between liberal rights and democratic citizenship, nor to elicit any other important concepts. The two terms are, after all, rooted in a history of blended usage. Unlike specialist legal terms absent from the vernacular (like 'contributory negligence' or 'contractual consideration'), they both remain commonplaces within a popular discourse that has always merged them.

2.5 Speech and Expression

The term *expression* covers many activities. Posting a pool-side selfie, secretly passing a message to a schoolmate, shouting a crude insult, throwing a kiss to a stranger, writing vague terms into a contract, publishing *The Communist Manifesto*, whispering classified government secrets to a foreign agent, posting 'White Only' at water fountains or 'Cleansed of Jews' (*Judenrein*) in town squares, staging a

---

[43] See, e.g., Caine, 2004–05.   [44] See, e.g., Dworkin, 1996, pp. 2–3.
[45] Cranston, 1967, p. 32. Cf. Berlin, 1969, p. 121.
[46] See, e.g., Pitkin, 1988 (discussing Arendt).
[47] Cf. Section 3.6, text accompanying note 87.

silent vigil against police violence, scrawling graffiti over a public building, gunning down random individuals to protest against their leaders' politics, or shouting 'Kill the Hutus!', are all 'expressive' acts.

'Expression' includes oral as well as printed words. It also includes pictorial or other non-verbal manifestations of ideas, as witnessed in controversies involving fascist salutes or emblems.[48] Many authors use the concepts of 'free expression' and 'free speech' interchangeably.[49] Although 'free speech' and 'hate speech' are the more usual phrases, I shall generally favour the broader terms 'free expression' and 'hateful expression', which more clearly include non-verbal as well as verbal acts. I shall generally retain the phrase 'hate speech bans', as it remains in wide use. But I shall construe it to mean, as it often means in practice, 'bans on hateful (both verbal and non-verbal) expression'.

Hateful expression and hate crime. Some acts are expressive in themselves, but also constitute independently illegal acts, such as a political murder or a philosophical refusal to pay tax. If I type out on Facebook 'Down with the state!', I commit a primarily expressive act. If I type out that message and send it to the government revenue service in lieu of my expected tax payment, then that refusal to pay tax contains both a primarily expressive element, and an independently unlawful element, namely, the withholding of the tax payment. Any penalty then attaches solely to the non-payment, not to the dissident message, although the latter, like countless lawful communications, may well end up filed away with the state security services, or may serve as evidence of my intent to withhold payment, as opposed to my sheer negligence or confusion. When an independently illegal act, such as a murder, battery, or rape, is motivated by hate, then it can be distinguished as a 'hate crime', although, like hate speech, 'hate crime' remains a disputed concept. Moreover, distinctions between 'hate crime' and 'hate speech' (or 'hateful expression') are not always observed. States maintaining hate speech bans often classify hate speech as one form of hate crime, suggesting that hateful expression itself already constitutes a harmful act without having to attach to any further material harm.

2.6 Content and Viewpoint

A democracy, on the view to be developed in this book, must not impose *viewpoint-selective* penalties on expression within public discourse. Weinstein distinguishes the element of 'viewpoint' not only from 'content', but also from the notion of viewpoint-neutral, 'time, manner, and place'[50] restrictions:

Content-based laws are ones in which the government seeks to regulate expression because of the message it conveys. *Content-neutral* regulations, in contrast, regulate speech for some

---

[48] See, e.g., German penal code, StGB § 86(a) (forbidding the distribution or display of symbols of constitutionally prohibited organizations). See also, e.g., Nowak & Rotunda, 2009, pp. 1476–87.

[49] Cf. Belavusau, 2013, pp. 10–11; Pech, 2003, p. 23; Robitaille-Froidure, 2011, p. 16; Schrank, 2006, pp. 16–31. See also, on 'expressive conduct', Nowak & Rotunda, 2009, pp. 1475–6; Sunstein, 1995, pp. 180–1; Weinstein, 1999, pp. 33–4.

[50] See, e.g., Brown, 2015, pp. 38–48; Nowak & Rotunda, 2009, pp. 1447–74; Baker, 1989, pp. 125–37, 162–3, 173–4.

reason unrelated to the message, such as the time, place, or manner of the speech. A law forbidding anyone from speaking about abortion is content-based; one prohibiting the use of loudspeakers in residential neighbourhoods after 10.00 pm would be content-neutral. [...] The most 'egregious' type of content regulation is *viewpoint* discrimination. Viewpoint discriminatory regulations ... are ones based on 'the specific motivating ideology or the opinion or perspective of the speaker . . .'[51]

A ban, for example, on all discussion of abortion rights, either opposing or supporting them, would be content-based, entailing obvious problems of democratic legitimacy. By contrast, wide expressive freedom for anti-abortionists, within a jurisdiction punishing abortion procedures, and with no comparable freedom granted to pro-abortionists, would raise a further, distinct question of legitimacy. Expression would then be free only to the extent that it echoes the state's view. Within full-fledged, pluralist democracies, bans on hateful expression grant freedom to the state-approved viewpoint—it is admittedly the moral view[52]—but penalize at least some forms of expression of a contrary viewpoint. That is why Weinstein identifies viewpoint-based penalties imposed within public discourse as exceptionally objectionable. After all, many content-based bans are undisputed, again, against commercial fraud or disclosure of security secrets during wartime.

Penalties imposed for courtroom perjury are content-based, and are ordinarily accepted as such. However, a penalty imposed on one witness for committing perjury on grounds of a particular philosophy (such as revolutionary Marxism), while no such penalty is imposed on another speaker who commits perjury on grounds of some other philosophy (such as Christian conscience), would raise a far graver problem of legitimacy for being viewpoint-selective. Moreover, for the purpose of evaluating hate speech bans as they are formulated and applied in many democracies, it makes no difference whether any given expression takes the specific linguistic form of alleging 'fact', 'opinion', 'doctrine', 'belief', or 'interpretation'. All of those can serve to convey some viewpoint.

Some supporters of bans refuse to recognize hateful expression as part of any viewpoint, philosophy, or worldview. They equate at least 'hard core' invective ('Dirty Jews!', 'Kill the Faggots!') with the kind of fortuitous, 'inarticulate grunt', or 'low-value speech'[53] that can legitimately be banned. It forms, to cite one formulation, 'no essential part of any exposition of ideas'.[54] But that objection undoes itself. However low the intellectual or linguistic value one might place on hateful expression, it is the bans themselves that confirm such utterances' ideational content. It is the bans themselves that elevate mindless growls into expression of an

---

[51] Weinstein, 2009b, pp. 82–3 (quoting *Rosenberger v. Rector and Visitors of the University of Virginia*, 515 U.S. 819, 829 (1995)) (emphasis added). See also Weinstein, 2009b at pp. 86–7, 91. Cf. Molnar & Malik, 2012, p. 83; Sunstein, 1995, pp. 11–12, 167–80.

[52] Cf. Section 4.8.

[53] *Texas v. Johnson*, 491 U.S. 397, 432 (1989) (Kennedy, J., concurring) (examining provocative expression in public discourse). Cf., e.g., Sunstein, 1995, pp. 3, 8–9 (distinguishing between 'high-value' and 'low-value', or between 'core' and 'peripheral' expression).

[54] *Johnson*, 491 U.S. at 430 (Kennedy, J., concurring).

identifiable worldview. They do so through their customary, black-letter formulations, and through the broader motives invoked for combating hateful expression. Both of those elements identify within such expression some message that is intelligible *as* hateful or discriminatory.

A wholly inarticulate content would be a lack of meaningful content. It could, by definition, convey neither a hateful, nor a loving, nor any other message. There would be nothing in it either to praise or to condemn. If it were devoid of meaning, there would be no basis for comprehending it, let alone banning it.[55] A partially fortuitous or inarticulate content is still content. It is not meaningless insofar as its hateful content, hence a dangerous or hateful worldview, is communicated. A worldview becomes identifiable without having to extend to a detailed vision of social life, although some prohibited hate speech does that as well. In 1971, during the Vietnam War, the US Supreme Court ruled[56] that the Constitution had to protect, as meaningful political speech, the petitioner's public display even of the 'absurd and immature'[57] message 'Fuck the Draft', inscribed on a citizen's outer garment. Many advocates of bans therefore refrain from distinguishing among levels of articulation. Defenders of German bans, for example, rarely distinguish modes of expression with respect to levels of articulation. German bans can apply to boorish Hitler salutes or slogans just as they can apply to theorized neo-Nazi treatises.[58]

Penalties. Penalties on expression take various forms, all of them assumed in this book. Penalties might take patently illegitimate forms, such as harming a family member who is uninvolved in the impugned expression. But that kind of punishment is disallowed under any liberal or democratic construction of the rule of law, irrespective of the content of an illegal act. As to democratically authorized penalties, they can work retrospectively by imposing, for example, fines or prison sentences for completed expressive acts. Another penalty would be loss of employment, although employment contexts are not entirely co-extensive with contexts of democratic public discourse.[59] Penalties also work prospectively through active or threatened[60] censorship, hence through prior prohibitions to the performance or dissemination of expression.

Non-viewpoint-punitive expression. Every legal norm presupposes some viewpoint, if only in the minimal sense that it promotes some interest, however grand or trivial. The more important the norm in social terms, the greater the weight it imputes to the viewpoint it promotes. A legal norm counts as *non-viewpoint-punitive* not by abstaining from a viewpoint, but when, taken within the legal system as a

---

[55] Cf., e.g., Rachedi, 2014.   [56] *Cohen v. California*, 403 U.S. 15 (1971).

[57] 403 U.S. at 27 (Blackmun, J., dissenting). Cf. Strossen, 1990, pp. 547–9; Weinstein, 1999, p. 172. Cf. also Section 4.10, text accompanying note 129.

[58] See Section 2.5, note 48. As to whether certain elements of expression, even admitting that they express a viewpoint, can nevertheless be deemed non-essential because of their hatefulness, see Section 4.10, text accompanying notes 129–35.

[59] See Section 2.8, text accompanying note 101.

[60] On the problem of self-censorship as a secondary effect of speech regulation, known as the 'chilling effect', see Section 2.9, text accompanying notes 114–15.

whole, it entails *no penalty for the expression, within public discourse, of some contrary viewpoint*. For example, a norm forbidding the production or distribution of cannabis is non-viewpoint-punitive if neither it nor any norm within the legal system imposes any penalty upon persons advocating the legalization of producing or distributing cannabis. Similarly, constitutional separations of powers promote the aforementioned 'less is more' viewpoint about democracy. They presuppose that certain limits on democracy serve to safeguard democracy. But those limits are non-viewpoint-punitive. Neither they nor any norm within the legal system imposes any penalty for the expression of dissent from those constitutional arrangements.

Through anti-discrimination laws, policies, or educational regimes a state can legitimately express and indeed may non-viewpoint-punitively enforce[61] pluralist values. Again, such measures remain non-viewpoint-punitive as long as citizens may, within public discourse, and however crudely, freely express views hostile to that viewpoint. Hate speech bans go a step further. They impose viewpoint-selective penalties on citizens who, within public discourse, express certain forms of hostility towards the state-proclaimed pluralist values represented *by* the bans.

Errors have arisen because the non-viewpoint-punitive state is taken to be a *value-neutral* state. The difference between the two is enormous. As mentioned earlier, there never was nor ever could be any such thing as a value-neutral state: even a 'pure libertarian' regime would, through its sheer operation, promote libertarian values. The term 'non-viewpoint-punitive' will be used, then, instead of 'non-punitive'. After all, a democracy can legitimately impose certain punitive measures to enforce equality, such as through customary anti-discrimination laws applied to the delivery of goods, services, education, or employment, or through mandatory school curricula promoting social pluralism. But its measures must, on the theory to be developed in this book, remain non-viewpoint-punitive. To anticipate the thesis more fully: democracy's legitimating expressive conditions derive from the *citizen's prerogative of non-viewpoint-punitive expression within public discourse*.

2.7 Hate Speech and Hateful Expression

For Parekh, the term 'hate speech' is 'unsatisfactory because it stresses hatred, an extremely strong emotion.'[62] Some provocations indeed speak not in a hot rant, but with cool calculation, including tracts of Holocaust denial or 'scientific' racism. For Barbara Perry, the term 'hate' misleadingly stresses subjective moods. It distracts us from the politics of disempowerment.[63] Weinstein and Hare propose

---

[61] See Section 4.11.   [62] Parekh, 2012, p. 40.
[63] Perry, 2005. See also Brudholm, 2014 (examining difficulties with a distinct concept of 'hatred').

the broader notion of 'extreme speech',[64] although they are aware that it covers very different situations, and, at any rate, 'extreme expression' may be the more accurate, yet still indeterminate notion. Jeremy Waldron rightly warns against the 'futile attempt to define "hatred",'[65] but retains the phrase 'hate speech'. For all its shortcomings, it remains, in Parekh's view, 'widely used and there is no obvious alternative.'[66]

Some definitions focus on what is widely thought to be the primary legal task of hate speech bans. In their post-Second World War formulations, the aim[67] of bans is, above all, to protect vulnerable racial, ethnic, religious, national, linguistic, sexual, or other subordinated or otherwise similarly situated minorities or groups.[68] But such classifications generate as many questions as answers.[69] The Danish or *Charlie Hebdo* cartoon controversies show how the boundary between assailing a religion's ideas and its members remains controversial.[70] Holocaust denial or 'scientific racism', too, stake out tenuous boundaries between fact and opinion. Scholars have certainly unmasked Holocaust denial as a mere re-packaging, beneath a façade of factual claims, of age-old anti-Semitic ideas.[71] Questions also haunt a category like 'glorification of terrorism'. Is it hate speech at all? Does its advocacy of violence distinguish it from other revolutionary politics throughout history, much of which we find in our educational curricula?

'In its purest form', write Weinstein and Hare, 'hate speech is simply expression which *articulates hatred* for another individual or group, usually based on a characteristic (such as race) which is perceived to be shared by members of the target group'.[72] That admittedly circular definition is, strictly speaking, extra-legal. It captures an element identifiable among a range of expressive acts, regardless of which of them may be banned. It does not distinguish between powerful and powerless groups, nor between numerical majorities and minorities.[73] One way to understand 'hate speech' or 'hateful expression' is to examine the various positions taken on it with the aim of formulating legal norms. I shall now begin that task by distinguishing between the positions favouring hate speech bans and the positions opposing them, although, as we shall see, that distinction further sub-divides.

[64] Hare & Weinstein, 2009, p. 4. In other Western languages, the phrase 'hate speech' is sometimes appropriated as a neologism, such as *discours de haine*, *discurso del odio*, or *Hassrede*, although continental writers often retain terms already established in their languages, denoting, e.g., 'incitement' or related concepts.
[65] Waldron, 2012a, p. 36.
[66] Parekh, 2012, p. 40. Cf. Belavusau, 2013, pp. 40–2; Boyle, 2001, p. 489; Nancy, 2013, p. 3; Waldron, 2012a, pp. 33–6. On the phrase's novelty, see Nancy, 2013, p. 1.
[67] On misuses of bans, see Section 6.1, text accompanying notes 41–5.
[68] See, e.g., Bleich, 2011, p. 4 n. 8; Noorloos, 2012, p. 4.   [69] See, e.g., Heinze, 2009b.
[70] See, e.g., Cram, 2009; Hare, 2009b.
[71] See, e.g., Benz, 2005; Imbleau, 2003; Taguieff, 2002; Taguieff, 2004.
[72] Weinstein & Hare, 2009, p. 4 (emphasis added). Cf., e.g., Rosenfeld, 2012, p. 242.
[73] Cf., e.g., *Otto-Preminger-Institut v. Austria*, ECtHR, Ser. A, No. 295-A [1994] (approving penalty on a film deemed offensive to religious beliefs of Austria's Roman Catholic majority).

Prohibitionism. I shall refer to defenders of bans as *prohibitionists.* That term is not ideal,[74] as it sounds highly intrusive. Liberal defenders even of broad bans by no means view such measures as boundless.[75] Another problem is the term's historical link to conventional moralisms, such as those regarding alcohol consumption. The term 'prohibitionist' may also, conceptually or historically, spark criminal law associations. But since hate speech bans can be enforced through both public and private law,[76] the term will denote here acceptance of bans irrespective of their criminal, civil, or administrative law quality.

Proceduralist prohibitionism. I shall use the term 'prohibitionist' to include purely *proceduralist* theories, which I shall also refer to as *value-pluralist proceduralism.* Value-pluralist proceduralists, whom I shall sometimes just call 'proceduralists', do not unequivocally favour or oppose bans. They generally acknowledge fair arguments on both sides, given what they see as the competing and often incommensurable values at stake. Value-pluralist proceduralism commonly arises among scholars of comparative law or politics. For them, the inherent flexibility and cultural specificity of democracy often mean that different democracies can with equal legitimacy adopt different free speech norms.[77]

Why call them prohibitionists? Proceduralists adopt not a compulsory, but nevertheless a permissive stance. They do not claim that a democracy *must* have bans to assure citizen dignity and equality. They nonetheless maintain that a democracy *may* legitimately adopt bans, as long as the norms and procedures followed are otherwise lawful, and no gross abuses result.[78] For *substantive* (or 'compulsory' or 'necessitarian') prohibitionism, hate speech bans are democratically legitimate because they are democratically necessary. For *procedural* (or 'optional' or

---

[74] Randall Kennedy uses the words 'eradicationists' (Kennedy, 2003, p. 36) and 'regulationists' (Kennedy, 2003, p. 124). 'Eradicationist' creates problems of its own. It risks overstating the approaches of writers who advocate only narrow or largely symbolic bans, hence nothing so ambitious as a project of 'eradication' of intolerant expression through legal constraints. By contrast, a 'prohibition' certainly counts as one type of 'regulation'. However, the looser term 'regulationist' risks understating the salient, and problematic, element of hate speech bans, even of narrow ones. Insofar as bans are viewpoint-based, they are categorical prohibitions, and not a question of 'regulation' in any partial sense, e.g., in the sense of least restrictive, non-viewpoint-punitive, 'time, manner, and place' limitations.

[75] See Section 3.2, text accompanying notes 17–26. See also, e.g., Strossen, 1990, pp. 490–1 (discussing Lawrence); Waldron, 2012a, p. 126.

[76] See Section 2.8.   [77] See Sections 3.6–3.7.

[78] See, e.g., Bleich, 2011. In an influential article Cass Sunstein contrasts two models of democratic deliberation. 'Interest-group pluralism' depicts democracy as an arena in which rival factions bargain in their own self-interest to a collectively adopted result. Under a 'civic republican' model, those factions join together in the democratic forum in order to deliberate about collective welfare. See Sunstein, 1988. Value-pluralist proceduralism neither equates, then, with interest-group pluralism nor does it oppose civic republicanism. It stands not temporally, but rather conceptually prior to both. At that conceptually prior moment, we must first pose the threshold question about the extent to which any given interest, such as expression within public discourse, stands as a legitimate object of democratic regulation. Only once that determination has been made can we then meaningfully proceed to pit, respectively, the model of communal deliberation against the model of factional self-interest.

'facultative') prohibitionism, hate speech bans are democratically legitimate because they are democratically permissible.[79]

Even substantive prohibitionists do not always agree with each other on questions of content and scope. They raise a variety of grounds for justifying bans. Some of them reason among more empirical lines, pointing to the social harms of hate speech.[80] Others prefer arguments of principle, citing dignity or equality as inherent values, to be respected regardless of whether speech leads to further harms.[81] Those two approaches are not mutually exclusive. Many prohibitionists adopt both. Their various approaches nevertheless remain united insofar as they would admit some viewpoint-selective regulation of expression within public discourse.

Oppositionism. I shall apply the term *oppositionists* to those who challenge hate speech bans. Prohibitionism's division between substantive and procedural versions knows no analogue among oppositionists. For oppositionists, bans are impermissible hence *a fortiori* unnecessary. Like 'prohibitionist', the term 'oppositionist' admittedly has pitfalls. The phrase 'free speech advocate'[82] fails, since, again, leading prohibitionists do otherwise endorse strong freedoms of expression. The phrase 'free speech absolutist' brings problems of its own, which I shall explore in Section 3.2.

Another problem is the lack of lexical symmetry between 'oppositionist' and 'prohibitionist'. That pair does not offer us a tidy 'for' and 'against'. Both are negatively defined, in terms of what each is against, and not what either is for. The prohibitionist would require or allow hateful expression to be assailed through a ban; the oppositionist assails the ban itself. Yet that pairing is probably as accurate as we can get. There is no more unity among oppositionists than among prohibitionists.

---

[79] In addition to either admitting or opposing bans, many authors adopt the traditionally scholarly stance characteristic of standard treatise writing. They review pros and cons of various norms and procedures in a descriptive vein. They abstain from any final position, although several of them do tacitly embrace a proceduralist stance, presenting viewpoint-selective penalties within public discourse as compatible with democracy as long as the bans are adopted with adequate institutional controls and no evidence of systemic abuse. See, e.g., Josende, 2010; Nieuwenhuis, 2011; Noorloos, 2012; Pech, 2003; Robitaille-Froidure, 2011. Waldron, by contrast, although not undertaking that more traditional brand of systematic, case-by-case doctrinal analysis, nevertheless claims to adopt a more 'modest intention', eschewing any categorical prohibitionism. He states not a 'wish to persuade' his audiences of hate speech bans' 'wisdom and legitimacy', but only a hope that his readers should better 'understand' the bans' rationales. See, e.g., Waldron, 2012a, p. 10; cf. pp. 11–12; Waldron & Weinstein, 2012, minute 48:04–48:59. That purportedly neutral ambition becomes difficult to reconcile, however, with Waldron's substantive arguments, which can only ever be construed as, to some greater or lesser degree, prohibitionist, even accepting his presumption in favour of free expression in hard cases (see Section 3.2, text accompanying note 24), which is the norm among more or less all prohibitionists who otherwise recognize some higher-order entitlement to free expression (and even accepting the qualification that his claims are directed at a strain of American anti-ban scholarship; after all, writers within various national contexts may remind their readers about under-represented positions without deploying them against contrary positions, as Waldron does). Waldron remains unequivocally prohibitionist in the proceduralist sense of finding bans *admissible*. Arguably, however, he proceeds further, into substantive prohibitionism by insisting that some regime of bans is *preferable* and even *necessary* to protect human dignity. See Heinze, 2013b, pp. 602–15.

[80] See Sections 5.1–5.3.   [81] See Section 5.6.   [82] See, e.g., Sunstein, 1995, p. 15.

Some oppositionists are dogmatic libertarians. Others oppose bans on pragmatic grounds, doubting their effectiveness and suggesting that law enforcement could more effectively direct its resources elsewhere. We can only pinpoint the debate's decisive schism by examining what each side is against, as there is too much divergence on each side as to what it is *for*. Despite the surface asymmetry, then, the terms 'prohibitionist' and 'oppositionist' most succinctly characterize the two core positions. For purposes of the theory to be developed in this book, we achieve the best possible symmetry by recalling that 'prohibitionism' denotes support for viewpoint-selective bans within public discourse, while 'oppositionism' denotes rejection of them.

2.8 Public Discourse

'The most stringent protection of free speech', writes Oliver Wendell Holmes, Jr. in 1919, in one of legal history's vintage quotes, 'would not protect a man in falsely shouting fire in a theatre and causing a panic.'[83] No epigram has been repeated in such disproportion to the insight it offers, as confirmed by any number of popular quips: 'No rights are absolute!' 'Rights entail responsibilities!' 'Your rights end where my rights begin!' Those largely interchangeable claims are all correct, but only as the tautology[84] that, within any legal system, freedoms by definition presuppose limits. They merely rebut a straw-man absolutism. Holmes's dictum was certainly understandable, as the US Supreme Court confronted a First Amendment containing no express limitations clause.[85] Like its vernacular analogues, however, it is too readily misconstrued to confirm the legitimacy of full-blown government balancing of interests in the regulation of public discourse.

The dictum in no way supports that conceptual leap, as Holmes's later writings make clear.[86] Underlying the error is an inductive fallacy. Having correctly shown one expressive activity that legislatures and courts can legitimately restrict, free speech then erroneously becomes seen as legitimately subject to legislative and judicial balancing *generally*. That error becomes reinforced by the many regulations of expression—against wartime treason, courtroom perjury, commercial fraud, etc.—that are accepted with the same self-evidence. Each of those restrictions is non-viewpoint-punitive, i.e., imposed regardless of any worldviews which such acts may be undertaken to express. Citizens remain perfectly free to advocate that wartime treason, courtroom perjury, or commercial fraud ought not to be punished.

'Typically,' writes Thomas Scanlon, 'the acts of expression with which a theory of "free speech" is concerned are addressed to a large (if not the widest possible) audience, and express propositions or attitudes thought to have a certain generality

---

[83] *Schenck v. United States*, 249 U.S. 47, 52 (1919) (Holmes, J.)   [84] See Section 3.2.
[85] See Section 3.1, note 7.   [86] See Section 6.1, text accompanying note 25.

of interest.'[87] Scanlon's account works better in a loose than in a literal sense. It is not strictly true, since free speech theory as a whole must encompass situations such as private or confidential communications.[88] We can, moreover, best understand Scanlon's references to audience size and to generality of interest as referring to what phenomenologists would depict as the 'intentional structure' of expression, defined neither solely by fixed, objective criteria nor solely by subjective experience.[89] Public discourse is identifiable as being *of a type* such that the message could plausibly be directed towards a sizeable audience, even if the actual audience in a given situation is small; and *of a type* such that its content might extend to some sector of the population, taking account, of course, that what may specifically 'interest' any random listener is never wholly predictable. Those loose and sometimes debatable contours of public discourse pose problems in particular cases, but do not undermine the notion in general terms. It suffices for democratic legitimacy that there be *some* sufficiently recognized sphere of public discourse, even if disagreement as to its reach will breed doubt at the margins. Within that sphere, I shall argue, the state can never legitimately impose viewpoint-selective penalties on democratic grounds.

Public versus political expression. The concept of 'public discourse' must not be narrowed to encompass only commentary on conventionally political matters. In some settings, a same-sex kiss intrinsically exhibits political dissent, indeed irrespective of the individuals' motives.[90] That political gesture may arise with undeliberated spontaneity. It qualifies as expression within public discourse, without a word uttered 'about' politics, as 'audiences will autonomously query [its] meaning'.[91] Public discourse, by extension, 'unquestionably' encompasses 'Jackson Pollock's art and Arnold Schoenberg's music'.[92]

---

[87] Scanlon, 1977, p. 155. Cf., e.g., Post, 1995, pp. 7, 134–77; Post, 2011a, pp. 483–4; Molnar & Post, 2012, pp. 12–17, 21; Weinstein, 1999, pp. 168–76; Weinstein, 2011a, pp. 495–6.

[88] See Section 4.4.   [89] See, e.g., Merleau-Ponty, 1945, pp. 203–32.

[90] Other kinds of expressive eroticism, by contrast, raise distinct problems. Live and full-on sexual activity by one or more individuals is barred from otherwise open, 'Hyde Park Corner' types of public forums. Staunch libertarians might challenge those limits (although they spend little time on the point), and democracy-based theorists like Dworkin, Post, and Weinstein largely accept them, though also with little discussion. Scholarly writing on pornography, by contrast, has been copious because of its more exclusively expressive, hence more controversial character, as opposed to a live, publicly performed sexual act, which entails a stronger conduct element. Prohibitionists can, however, accuse the more moderate oppositionists of inconsistency. How can it be legitimate to ban public love-making yet to permit public hate-making? Just as conduct-based sexual expression is banned, however, so is conduct-based hatred, such as physical violence or intimidation. Nudity, moreover, be it sexual or non-sexual, raises routine regulatory concerns around public hygiene. Persons maintaining poor personal hygiene, or seized, e.g., with sudden incontinence can create sanitation risks far beyond any state's monitoring capacities. To that extent, restrictions confining public nudity to designated parks, beaches, or camping sites can be justified on grounds other than conventional morality, since, as noted in Section 5.7, expression within public discourse cannot plausibly be restricted on grounds of sheer moral distaste. Phenomenology and socio-linguistics, as noted in Section 5.3, do indeed break down conventional distinctions between speech and conduct; yet, however formalist or artificial those distinctions may be, any plausible conception of the rule of law in a democracy necessarily presupposes them.

[91] Post, 1994–95, p. 1254. Cf., e.g., Majed, 2013.

[92] Baker, 2011, p. 516. Cf. Belavusau, 2013, pp. 10–11; Schrank, 2006, pp. 16–31; Schauer, 1982, p. 13.

Examining US Supreme Court jurisprudence, Post makes that 'personal is political' observation. 'Although the Court has sometimes attempted to define public discourse by distinguishing speech about "matters of public concern," it is evident that this definition is conceptually incoherent. [...] [E]very issue that can potentially agitate the public is also potentially relevant to democratic self-governance, and hence potentially of public concern. The distinction between "matters of public concern" and "matters of purely private concern," insofar as it is used to exclude speech from public discourse, is therefore incompatible with the very democratic self-governance it seeks to facilitate.'[93]

Public versus interpersonal expression. Oppositionists are sometimes asked, 'Are you truly happy for people to shout out racist insults on the street, in school, or in the workplace?' In contrast to staunchly libertarian positions,[94] the sphere of democratic public discourse can be distinguished from face-to-face encounters, such as individually targeted stalking, trespass, assault, harassment, or 'fighting words' situations. The US Supreme Court has observed that everyday language includes 'words and expressions which by general consent are "fighting words" when said without a disarming smile', and which can so suddenly 'cause a fight'[95] when 'directed to the person of the hearer',[96] that the state would be unable to provide protection for participants or bystanders.[97]

Not all such incidents will lead to further disruption. But law cannot foresee every permutation in immediate, inter-personal situations, in which individuals are specifically targeted, as on the street, in the pub, or in routine stalking or harassment types of scenarios. That 'fighting words' doctrine has nevertheless been challenged by both prohibitionists and oppositionists. Some oppositionists argue that certain targets would be unable to fight, such as persons who are ill or disabled, making the restriction arbitrary, and therefore worthy of being dropped, with the result of permitting such speech. Some prohibitionists invoke the same kind of example to argue that the law is actually protecting a broader kind of human dignity—a rationale that would more broadly justify hate speech bans. In either case, legislators and courts can legitimately, outside public discourse, ban speech because of its likelihood of provoking immediate violence in many typical cases, without such likelihood being present in every imaginable case.[98]

---

[93] Post, 1995, p. 194. Cf. Post, 1995, pp. 111, 166–9; and Post, 1994–95, pp. 1253–5. Cf. also Barendt, 2007, p. 189. Some writers would still limit the 'justification' of protected speech within democracy to Alexander Meiklejohn's untenably restrictive 'town hall' model (see, e.g., Rosenfeld, 2012, pp. 250–1), to which Post alludes here. That model has often been invoked to deny protection to speech within public discourse that is not about issues deemed 'political' in a conventional sense. Few social theorists today, however, would circumscribe 'political' discourse so narrowly. Feminist scholars have shown how issues not conventionally political become central within public discourse, and then central to defining what later becomes political.

[94] See, e.g., Caine, 2004–05.

[95] *Chaplinsky v. New Hampshire*, 315 U.S. 568, 573 (1942).

[96] *Cohen v. California*, 403 U.S. 15, 20 (1971).

[97] See, e.g., Post, 1995, pp. 114, 194; Weinstein, 1999, pp. 26–7, 72, 74, 76.

[98] See, e.g., Molnar & Post, 2012, p. 22; Robitaille-Froidure, 2011, p. 40; Weinstein, 1999, pp. 26–7; Weinstein, 2009a, pp. 30, 53; Weinstein, 2009b, p. 82; Weinstein, 2011a, pp. 491–2.

Both public- and private-sector employment create spheres of routinely regulated expression,[99] as does the sphere of primary education.[100] Employers legitimately discipline their employees' expressive conduct in countless ways, for example, for failing to speak courteously or professionally to clients or colleagues, or to draft correspondence or memoranda within prescribed forms and conventions. As workplace speech is not, or at least not principally, public discourse, hate speech bans within ordinary employment contexts pose no threat to democratic legitimacy. Again, leaving aside libertarian extremes, no serious opponent of hate speech bans has challenged regulations granting employers such authority, indeed under well-established anti-discrimination principles. In 2014, a group of British boys returning from a Jewish school were accosted with cries of 'No Jews! No Jews!' by a shop security guard. Such speech distinguishes itself doubly from public discourse. Not only does it spew face-to-face fighting words, but also breaches norms of employee conduct.[101] Hate speech bans limited to those contexts would be wholly legitimate, although they would add little or nothing to already existing and largely undisputed law in most Western democracies.[102]

Public discourse and public law. The distinction between public discourse and targeted harassment does not mean that public discourse must be shielded only from public, as opposed to private law. In the US Supreme Court, a number of landmark cases have arisen out of civil, rather than criminal cases,[103] as the Court has recognized that a government would be tempted to boast of refraining from criminal prosecutions, only to allow civil penalties to do their censoring through the back door. States often penalize dissidents by imposing civil damages on spurious defamation claims.[104] Hate speech bans, moreover, do not necessarily limit acceptable penalties on hate speech to the criminal law.

Public discourse and public places. In a pre-industrial era, public discourse denoted, along Scanlon's lines, speech addressed in general terms to general audiences within forums such as town halls, town and market squares, public parks, and the like.[105] But not everything uttered in a public place need count as public discourse; nor, today, is all public discourse necessarily to be found in traditionally or physically public places. Through electronic media, today's public discourse, although it may still often be associated with activities occurring in conventionally public places, is not itself altogether geographically defined. In addition, its physical manifestations can take place in venues, such as a borrowed or rented assembly

---

[99] See, e.g., Dworkin, 2009, p. viii; Jacobson & Schlink, 2012, pp. 219–27; Molnar & Post, 2012, pp. 11–15; Weinstein, 2009a, p. 30; Weinstein, 2009b, p. 83; Weinstein, 2011a, pp. 491–5.

[100] See Section 4.11, text accompanying notes 154–7. On higher education, see Section 5.10.

[101] Withnall, 2014.

[102] On line-drawing between that expression which may and that which may not count as public discourse in circumstances such as those of employment or primary education, see Section 4.4.

[103] See, e.g., *New York Times v. Sullivan*, 376 U.S. 254 (1964); *Hustler Magazine, Inc. v. Falwell*, 485 U.S. 46 (1988).

[104] See, e.g., Heinze, 2015a; Sim, 2011.

[105] See, e.g., Nowak & Rotunda, 2009, pp. 1449–74 (on the concepts of public and quasi-public forums).

hall, which hosts public discourse in some situations, such as a political meeting, but not in others, such as a confidential drug rehabilitation group. By extension, verbal harassment, stalking, or 'fighting words', targeted at identifiable individuals do not become public discourse simply by being uttered in public places. Public discourse is determined not so much by geography as by its medium or forum,[106] which is itself an historical product: electronic media now stand at the forefront of such communication in ways unthinkable in earlier times.

Imminent lawless action. Just as most leading oppositionists do not object to 'fighting words' restrictions, nor do they go so far as to seek protection for immediate criminal solicitations to commit ascertainable acts of hate-motivated violence or material damage[107] (e.g., 'Hey Jack, go get that brick, and let's kill that faggot now!'), as opposed to wholly vague and open-ended appeals,[108] for example, to 'Overthrow tyranny' or 'Overthrow the agents of capitalism', which would require us to censor an entire history of revolutionary texts.[109] On that view, even advocacy of violence does not in itself justify censorship. As with the fighting words doctrine, the question is whether 'such advocacy is directed to inciting or producing imminent lawless action and is likely to incite or produce such action',[110] such that the state would lack the ordinary resources necessary to protect targeted or vulnerable citizens.

2.9　Defamation: Public Figures and Groups

'Defamation' denotes reputationally detrimental communication to third parties of allegations about specifically identifiable individuals, which, on the preponderance of the evidence, can be called *factually* false, and have been made with inadequate care by the speaker as to the truthfulness of the alleged facts.[111] Consider an ordinary example. Imagine a man, we'll call him Joe, and will assume him to be, on a legal standard, of sound mind. Joe bears a grudge against Dr Bright, his town dentist, for making him wait too long for his root canal surgery. Dr Bright is neither famous nor well known for anything at all. He's just the local dentist. Incensed, Joe runs around hanging notices on buildings and trees, writing on his Facebook page and telling the townspeople that Dr Bright has been secretly administering cyanide to his patients, which Joe knows to be false.

Defamation laws include both libel, if written, and slander, if spoken. Joe has done both. Such misinformation could harm Dr Bright's career, in part because

---

[106] See, e.g., Nowak & Rotunda, 2009, pp. 1441–75.

[107] See, e.g., Molnar & Post, 2012, pp. 22, 23; Weinstein, 2009a, pp. 53–5; Weinstein, 2009b, p. 82.

[108] On distinctions between specific scenarios of criminal solicitation or conspiracy, and more sweeping crimes of 'incitement' to hatred or to violence, including the 'clear and present danger' standard, see Section 5.9.

[109] See Section 5.9. See also Heinze, 2008a, pp. 139–41.

[110] *Brandenburg v. Ohio*, 395 U.S. 444, 447 (1969).

[111] Cf., e.g., Nowak & Rotunda, 2009, pp. 1389–404.

Dr Bright may have no easy means for refuting Joe's lies. Dr Bright is entitled to show actual or prospective loss of earnings in court as part of a damage award. There are, moreover, two important things to note about Joe's conduct. First, he is in no sense aiming to promote general public dialogue on the current state of dental medicine. Second, Joe has not voiced a mere opinion, a sheer value judgement, about Dr Bright. He has not simply told people he thinks Dr Bright is a bad dentist. He has spread allegations amenable to factual refutation on the preponderance of the evidence.

In 2015, the firebrand British Member of Parliament George Galloway threatened to sue the *Guardian* journalist Hadley Freeman. Galloway had previously rejected charges that his anti-Israel stances amounted to anti-Semitism. Freeman tweeted her scepticism, suggesting that some of Galloway's remarks could indeed be construed as anti-Semitic. After Galloway threatened to sue not only her, but anyone who re-tweeted the remark, Freeman announced she would delete the message, which she immediately did.[112]

Not all criticism of Israel, of course, is anti-Semitic. Jewish Israelis, and their friends, publicly criticize the Israeli government every day. Nor is it seriously disputed that some criticism of Israel is anti-Semitic, as witnessed in incidents throughout the world.[113]

Much debate about Israel or about Jews does not take place at those obvious, all-or-nothing extremes. It takes place on a vast and murky middle ground. The question as to whether a borderline criticism of Israel, or indeed of Jews, counts as anti-Semitic is not a matter of demonstrable fact. It is a matter of interpretation and judgement. People will disagree. The organization Media Lens jumped to Galloway's defence, asking if Freeman could cite examples of Galloway's anti-Semitism. But any example she could cite would persuade some and not others, precisely because of the room for meaningful interpretation lurking between conflicting views. Even if an overwhelming majority were unpersuaded, a highly popular opinion does not create an objectively verifiable fact.

Yet Freeman deleted her message. Does the dispute then become moot? To the contrary, that is the biggest problem of all. Decades ago, free speech scholars identified the 'chilling effect', which gives the law a double edge whenever it strays into the realm of public debate on controversial issues of the day. To be sure, some experts doubted that Galloway could win. The point of the 'chilling effect' concern here, however, is that, as long as the law draws hazy lines between, on the one hand, verifiable allegations of fact and, on the other hand, expressions of opinion, speakers and writers remain unsure about what they may and may not say. Where clear law silences them directly, unclear law has the same effect by causing them to self-censor, in Freeman's words, 'to save a day in court',[114] which might turn out to be costly both personally and financially.[115] No one manoeuvred the chilling of

---

[112] See, e.g., Dearden, 2015.
[113] See, e.g., Weiss, 2014.
[114] See, e.g., Heinze, 2015a.
[115] See, e.g., Weinstein, 1999, pp. 142–3.

democratically necessary speech better than Galloway. He threatened that 'any trace-able person who repeats her defamation will be added to the legal action'.[116]

Democracies have largely failed to adopt the so-called 'public figure exception'[117] to defamation law, which would further promote vital public debate by creating a stronger presumption of freedom for speakers when they are discussing high-profile politicians, or other persons who have loudly and visibly entered the cut and thrust of politics or the public sphere. Because of their public profile, such individuals often turn discussion about controversial issues into discussions about themselves—about their statements or their actions. When Diana, Princess of Wales, for example, led mediatized campaigns around the problems of landmines, HIV infection, or public health, discussion turned not merely to those issues, but also to her person and actions. Similarly, unlike the forlorn Dr Bright, a figure like Galloway has broad and immediate access to influential media and public forums. He can, with a wide audi-ence, respond to such criticisms immediately, forcefully, and at length. Again, what is crucial is Galloway's taunt directed not merely at Freeman, but at all re-tweeters, hence to the public in general. The ability of public figures to wield law against the views of ordinary citizens expressed within public discourse raises the concerns about political legitimacy that will be central to this book's conception of democracy.

In addition, defamation of the type directed at Dr Bright, like commercial fraud or courtroom perjury, remains legitimately punishable on grounds of immediately personal and targeted harm; however, no such legitimacy can extend to general-ized, so-called 'group defamation'. It is sometimes suggested that if ordinary def-amation causes some measure of harm to one individual, then we can multiply it by thousands or millions to determine the harm of group defamation. However, it is an operation of division rather than multiplication—i.e., a strong *dilution* of harm—that, on the evidence, more accurately accounts for any such effects once we assume the context of full-fledged democracies.[118]

2.10 Deontology and Consequentialism

Arguments for or against bans generally fall under two familiar styles of moral rea-soning, commonly known as *consequentialist* or 'outcome-based', and *deontological* or 'duty-based'.[119] Those two approaches are not mutually exclusive. Writers some-times fail to distinguish them, confusing claims about the inherent *character* either of hate speech, or of regulations of it, with claims about the further *effects* of the speech or the regulations. Consider, for example, the claim 'Fundamental human dignity must be respected in order to avoid violence'.[120] It is surely true under

---

[116] See, e.g., Heinze, 2015a.   [117] Nowak & Rotunda, 2009, pp. 1389–96.
[118] On questions of causation linking speech to harm, see Sections 5.1 and 5.3. On 'group defam-ation', see e.g., Nowak & Rotunda, 2009, pp. 1386–9. Cf. also Section 5.6, note 172; Section 6.1, note 27.
[119] Cf. Alexander, 2005; Richards, 1999, p. 1. Cf. also, Section 4.3, note 49.
[120] Cf. UDHR, G.A. res. 217A (III), U.N. Doc A/810 at 71, art. 19 (1948), preamble, para. 2.

some circumstances. Its truth cannot easily be evaluated, however, unless we distinguish (a) the deontological, dignitarian claim that 'dignity' is 'fundamental' to the 'human'[121] from (b) the consequentialist–empirical claim that certain actions or attitudes can be identified as causally leading to violence.[122]

The deontological claim that 'dignity' is 'fundamental' to the 'human' has, at least on its face, no conventionally empirical foundation. Concepts of 'dignity', of 'the human', or of that which is 'fundamental to the human' remain steeped in language, culture, and history. Arguments about cause and effect, by contrast, at least formally assume causation—'at least formally', in the sense that some arguments may be verbally structured in causal terms, for example, 'Trust breeds hope', without facially lending themselves to criteria of empirical demonstration.

There is nothing necessarily wrong with metaphorical notions of material causation. They may express justified concern about intolerance. Problems arise, however, when rhetorically consequentialist claims tacitly glide into unexamined assumptions of statistical probability. The obstacle is not that metaphorical causation disproves statistical causation. After all, the words 'Truth breeds hope' might indeed be defined so as to translate into a testable claim. The problem is that metaphorical causation does not, without more, establish statistical causation. The claim, 'Hate speech must be banned to avoid violence' may remain as a purely rhetorical consequentialism, signalling justified anxiety about hateful expression, although it can also serve as a causal claim if it rests upon empirical evidence. (Whether or in what senses it can do so will be examined in Sections 5.1 and 5.3.)

Some consequentialist theses, both prohibitionist and oppositionist, are made in *substance*, through empirical claims about links between bans and their respective social benefits or harms. Other arguments are made only in *form*, rhetorically suggesting such causation but without being of the type that is amenable to empirical determinations. Some writers implicitly take one position, without explaining why they ignore the other. Dworkin, for example, failing to distinguish stable from unstable democracies, deontologically aligns political legitimacy with the rejection of bans. But he never indicates whether or how demonstrable links from hateful expression to violence or discrimination might ever enter as a factor. Conversely, when Delgado, Matsuda, Parekh, or Waldron deontologically align political legitimacy, at least in part, with the acceptance of bans, they never indicate whether any empirically demonstrable circumstances, such as the effectiveness of non-viewpoint-punitive measures,[123] or indeed counter-productive effects of bans,[124] might render bans incompatible with democratic legitimacy.

Hence four basic positions, summarized now for convenience in Table 2.1. All four will be further explored in Chapter 5, but their basic differences are worth bearing in mind from out the outset. For *consequentialist prohibitionism* (quadrant [1]), bans are necessary or permissible to avoid unjust effects caused by hate speech,

[121] See Section 4.9, text accompanying notes 115–19.
[122] Cf. Post's criterion of a 'sufficiently close causal nexus' between speech and some further, distinct harm. Post, 1995, p. 109.
[123] See Section 4.11.   [124] See Section 5.5.

Table 2.1 Common positions on hate speech

	Prohibitionism (supports bans)	Oppositionism (rejects bans)
Consequentialist (outcome-based)	[1] *Thesis:* Hateful expression within public discourse can lead to harmful effects, such as violence or discrimination against target groups. *Substantive response:* Viewpoint-punitive bans imposed within public discourse are *necessary* to prevent or to combat those effects. *Procedural response:* Viewpoint-punitive bans imposed within public discourse are *permissible* to prevent or to combat those effects.	[3] *Thesis:* Bans can provoke the very hostilities they are designed to prevent. *Response:* Viewpoint-punitive bans imposed within public discourse are counter-productive.
Deontological (duty-based)	[2] *Thesis:* Hateful expression within public discourse degrades its targets' inherent human dignity or equal citizenship, regardless of whether any distinctly harmful effects can be traced to it. *Substantive response:* Viewpoint-punitive bans imposed within public discourse are *necessary* to prevent or to combat hateful expression per se. *Procedural response:* Viewpoint-punitive bans imposed within public discourse are *permissible* to prevent or to combat hateful expression per se.	[4] *Thesis:* Non-viewpoint-punitive expression within public discourse is a legitimating condition of democracy. *Response:* Viewpoint-punitive bans imposed within public discourse are illegitimate.

The theses and responses appearing on this table are illustrative, not exhaustive. They are examined in closer detail in Chapter 5. Although some provisional credence is lent, in Section 5.5 to oppositionist arguments of the consequentialist type, as summarized here in quadrant [3], the core thesis developed in Chapters 3 and 4 is deontological, as set forth in quadrant [4]. It is from the quadrant [4] perspective, then, that this book's theses primarily differ from the prohibitionist views appearing in quadrants [1] and [2]. While quadrant 4 certainly includes rights-based theories such as Dworkin's or Post's, it will serve in this book to develop a distinctly democratic theory.

such as promoting violence or discrimination against vulnerable target groups. For *deontological prohibitionism* (quadrant [2]), bans are necessary or permissible because hate speech is inherently unjust, inherently denying the equal worth of all citizens, irrespective of whether any further detrimental effects trace back to it. For *consequentialist oppositionism* (quadrant [3]), bans are counter-productive, leading to materially ill effects, such as actively provoking the very hostilities that they claim to combat. For *deontological oppositionism* (quadrant [4]), the bans are wrong or illegitimate in principle, for example, on the liberal principle that they violate an important freedom, or on the principle, to be advanced here, that they violate a condition of democratic legitimacy.

My insistence on distinguishing between different models of democracy will draw upon the view that weaker types or stages of democracies may legitimately rely upon consequentialist rationales, whilst stronger ones become more bound to deontological criteria.[125] Value-pluralist proceduralism will be of particular interest in this book,[126] as it raises the bar for oppositionism. If the oppositionist argues only that bans are not *necessary*, that still leaves open the possibility that they may be *admissible*. If, however, the oppositionist can show that, under certain circumstances, bans are not *admissible*, then that thesis by definition encompasses the further conclusion that bans are, under those circumstances, not *necessary*.

Dignity. The notion of 'dignity', too, can become ambiguous. Both prohibitionists and oppositionists lay claim to it. Oppositionists focus on the dignity of *speakers* and of willing *audiences*, while prohibitionists stress the dignity of the *targets*.[127] To avoid confusion, I shall use other concepts to characterize the interests of speakers and of willing audiences, in particular, as already noted, the notion of an inherent citizen prerogative of expression, which will also include a prerogative to see or to hear others' expression within public discourse. Accordingly, I shall refer to 'dignity' solely to denote the interests of the victims or targets of hate speech. I thereby aim to reflect the trend of characterizing deontological, i.e., non-consequentialist prohibitionism under the mantel of *dignitarianism*.[128]

---

[125] See Section 4.1.   [126] See Sections 3.6–3.7.
[127] See, e.g., Dworkin, 2009, p. vii; Nieuwenhuis, 2011, pp. 23–7; Post, 1995, pp. 21–116; Smolla, 1993, pp. 9–11; Waldron, 2012a, pp. 139–40.
[128] See Section 5.6.

3

Liberalism and Value Pluralism

Far from undermining most democracies' rights regimes, hate speech bans have become integral to them. This chapter begins by revisiting the view within most democracies that speech bans are compatible with individual rights. Oppositionists are sometimes branded, or even brand themselves, as 'free speech absolutists'; yet it soon becomes apparent that no legal system can contain an 'absolute' individual freedom. That obstacle, however, also poses a problem for prohibitionists, as an anti-absolutist view can readily feed into an anti-democratic one. The task of oppositionism is, then, to identify principles of citizenship in terms other than naïvely absolutist ones. Crucial for identifying those principles is to distinguish among legitimating conditions for state security, legitimating conditions for the state as a rights regime, and legitimating conditions for the state as a democracy.

3.1 Prevailing Norms

Its status as a human right confers great weight on free speech. In 1948 the Universal Declaration of Human Rights (UDHR) seemed to give the right a broad scope: 'Everyone has the right to freedom of opinion and expression; this right includes freedom to hold opinions without interference and to *seek, receive* and *impart* information *and ideas* through *any* media and regardless of frontiers.'[1] As was noted in Section 2.8, however, not only Holmes's famous dictum but ordinary folk wisdom immediately inflects that right. Having set forth its charter of fundamental[2] rights, the UDHR admonishes: 'Nothing in this Declaration may be interpreted as implying for any … group or person any right to engage in any activity or to perform any act aimed at the destruction of any of the rights and freedoms set forth herein.'[3]

Most democracies today endorse the 1966 International Covenant on Civil and Political Rights (ICCPR). Article 20(2) provides: '*Any* advocacy of *national, racial or religious* hatred that constitutes incitement to discrimination, hostility or violence shall be prohibited by law.'[4] Yet that categorical 'any' rings alarm bells. When

---

[1] UDHR art. 19 (emphasis added).   [2] See, e.g., UDHR, preamble, para. 5.
[3] UDHR art. 30.
[4] 999 U.N.T.S. 171, *entered into force* 23 March 1976 (emphasis added). For current information on ratification, accession, and succession, including declarations and reservations relevant to articles

the Ghanaian author Nana Darkoa Sekyiamah calls Americans 'arrogant, rude and disrespectful',[5] she might well 'incite' her readers to 'hostility' on grounds of Americans' 'national' identity. But would we want to censor her? The phrase 'any advocacy' surely means something contrary to what it says: some types of advocacy, but not *any* kind.[6]

It is those same Americans who most ardently shield Sekyiamah's right to rail against them. Yet their 'lone ranger' views echo objections to bans now heard in many democracies. Upon ratification in 1992, the US sought to limit ICCPR's scope, insisting that article 20(2)could not be construed to 'authorize or require' the US to adopt laws 'that would restrict the right of free speech and association protected by [its] Constitution and laws'.[7] The UN Human Rights Committee, which monitors ICCPR's implementation, nevertheless

affecting freedom of expression, see 'International Covenant on Civil and Political Rights' (n.d.). Elaborating on the principles set forth in UDHR arts. 19 and 30, ICCPR art. 19 provides general statement of free expression coupled with a limitations clause,

...

2. Everyone shall have the right to freedom of expression; this right shall include freedom to seek, receive and impart information and ideas of all kinds, regardless of frontiers, either orally, in writing or in print, in the form of art, or through any other media of his choice.
3. The exercise of the rights provided for in paragraph 2 of this article carries with it special duties and responsibilities. It may therefore be subject to certain restrictions, but these shall only be such as are provided by law and are necessary:
(a) For respect of the rights or reputations of others;
(b) For the protection of national security or of *public order* (*ordre public*), or of public health or *morals*. (emphasis added)

ECHR art. 10 takes a similar form,

1. Everyone has the right to freedom of expression. This right shall include freedom to hold opinions and to receive and impart information and ideas without interference by public authority and regardless of frontiers. This Article shall not prevent States from requiring the licensing of broadcasting, television or cinema enterprises.
2. The exercise of these freedoms, since it carries with it *duties and responsibilities*, may be subject to such formalities, conditions, restrictions or penalties as are prescribed by law and are necessary in a democratic society, in the interests of national security, territorial integrity or public safety, for the prevention of disorder or crime, for the protection of health or *morals*, for the protection of the *reputation or rights of others*, for preventing the disclosure of information received in confidence, or for maintaining the authority and impartiality of the judiciary. (emphasis added)

On interpretation and application of international and regional provisions within European legal systems, see, e.g., Josende, 2010; Nieuwenhuis, 2011; Noorloos, 2012; Pech, 2003; Robitaille-Froidure, 2011. Cf. the concepts of an 'ever-harmonising "European freedom of expression"' (Belavusau, 2013, pp. 71, 77, 78) and 'Brussels harmonisation' (Belavusau, 2013, p. 77).

[5] Sekyiamah, 2013.
[6] Cf., e.g., Heinze, 2009b (examining difficulties in the identification of groups to be protected under hate speech bans).
[7] See 'International Covenant on Civil and Political Rights' (site regularly updated). According to the US Constitution, Amendment I, 'Congress shall make no law respecting … abridging the freedom of speech, or of the press; or the right of the people peaceably to assemble, and to petition the government for a redress of grievances.' That provision has progressively been interpreted as applying to other branches of government, including governments within the individual states. For a standard exposition, see, e.g., Nowak & Rotunda, 2009, pp. 1252–538.

voices the response still dominant within both democratic and non-democratic governments. The Committee deems article 20(2) '*fully* compatible with the right of freedom of expression'. It rejects any notion of expression as an unqualified good. Free expression must, on its view, cede to certain 'duties and responsibilities'.[8]

Democracies today also overwhelmingly endorse the 1965 International Convention on the Elimination of All Forms of Racial Discrimination (ICERD). Article 4(a) provides that states parties shall punish 'by law *all* dissemination of ideas based on racial superiority or hatred, incitement to racial discrimination, as well as ... incitement to [violence] against any race or group of persons of another colour or ethnic origin.'[9] Upon ratification in 1994, the US again rejected 'any obligation ... to restrict' its 'extensive protections of individual freedom of speech, expression and association.'[10]

The UN Committee on the Elimination of Racial Discrimination, which monitors ICERD's implementation, equally recites a strong global consensus against the US stance. That Committee, too, maintains that 'the prohibition of dissemination of all ideas based upon racial superiority or hatred is compatible with the right to freedom of opinion and expression'. We again find free expression subject to 'duties and responsibilities', including 'the obligation not to disseminate racist ideas.'[11] Like the ICCPR's reference to 'any advocacy', ICERD's reference to 'all dissemination' is vast. If ICERD demands penalties for a reprint of Hitler's *Mein Kampf*, then it robs public discourse of a work of historical stature. If it does not,

---

[8] Human Rights Committee, General Comment 11, Article 20 (Nineteenth session, 1983) (emphasis added), Compilation of General Comments and General Recommendations Adopted by Human Rights Treaty Bodies, U.N. Doc. HRI/GEN/1/Rev.1 at 12 (1994), para. 2. It is crucial to distinguish the Committee, a reputable, expert body, from the similar-sounding but deeply corrupt UN Human Rights Council. See, e.g., Freedman, 2013.

[9] 660 U.N.T.S. 195, *entered into force* 4 January 1969 (emphasis added). For current information on ratification, accession, and succession, including declarations and reservations relevant to articles affecting freedom of expression, see 'International Convention on the Elimination of All Forms of Racial Discrimination' (regularly updated). For critical discussion of art. 4(a), see, e.g., Heinze, 2008a, pp. 120–8; Mchangama, 2011. Cf. UN Declaration on Race and Racial Prejudice, E/CN.4/Sub.2/1982/2/Add.1, annex V (1982), art. 6(1). Similarly, the Committee of Ministers of the Council of Europe has taken a broad view of the scope of hate speech bans. The Committee calls upon member nations to combat 'statements ... which may reasonably be understood as hate speech, or as speech likely to produce *the effect of legitimising*, spreading or promoting racial hatred, xenophobia, anti-Semitism *or other forms* of discrimination or hatred based on intolerance.' Recommendation No. R (97) 20E (1997), Principle 1 (emphasis added). See The Council of the European Union, Framework Decision 2008/913/JHA of 28 November 2008, on combating certain forms and expressions of racism and xenophobia by means of criminal law.

[10] See 'International Convention on the Elimination of All Forms of Racial Discrimination' (regularly updated).

[11] Conclusions and Recommendations of the Committee on the Elimination of Racial Discrimination: United States of America, U.N. Doc. A/56/18, paras. 380–407 (2001), para. 391. See also Conclusions and Recommendations of the Committee on the Elimination of Racial Discrimination: United States of America, U.N. Doc. CERD/C/USA/CO/6, paras. 380–407 (2008), para. 18; Committee on the Elimination of Racial Discrimination, General Recommendation 15: Measures to eradicate incitement to or acts of discrimination (Forty-second session, 1993), U.N. Doc. A/48/18 at 114 (1994), para. 4.

then it, too, means something contrary to what it says, demanding bans on some dissemination of racist ideas, but not all.

3.2 Absolutism

For writers dissenting from those prevailing norms, a beguiling question is whether freedom of speech should be absolute. Too much time is wasted on that question, as it is no way particular to the problem of free expression. No individual freedom of any type can be absolute under any legal system without destroying the entirety of the system. To test that hypothesis, recall that an 'absolute' freedom must by definition supersede all competing interests. UDHR article 18, for example, guarantees 'freedom of … conscience'. As a thought experiment, let's assume an 'Absoluteness Thesis', which holds freedom of conscience to be absolute, on the grounds that one's internal beliefs, unlike their verbal or physical expression, lie beyond the reach of law: I have absolute freedom of conscience because the law remains always outside my mind.

Before proceeding to our test, three incidental objections can be noted in passing. First, totalitarian states pervasively controlling information and the media might be said to exercise that general regulatory power even without immediate access to individuals' thoughts and feelings. Second, questions arise as to whether states could deploy neuro-technologies to the point of exercising a general regulatory power over the mind. Third, under capitalism, it might be claimed that the media only appear free, while in fact controlling our hearts and minds, in the service of hegemonic commercial interests, through the total web of messages to which we are and are not exposed.

Those are familiar concerns, but a bit tricky in their details. Instead, the Absoluteness Thesis can be defeated on purely conceptual grounds. Once we assume any legal system, absolute freedom of conscience becomes a nonsense. It would overturn any legal regime. Individuals would merely need to claim, as acts dictated by conscience, the freedom to kill, to beat, to steal, to breach contracts, to withhold payment of taxes or fines, and so forth.

One way around that result is to circumscribe the freedom's scope. We could construe the freedom as absolute solely as concerns internal thoughts and feelings, such as articles of private religious or spiritual faith. Far from bolstering the Absoluteness Thesis, however, that adjustment would seal its defeat. To circumscribe a legal interest in its initial, verbal formulation is merely to 'build in' its non-absoluteness from the outset. There is no conceptual difference between, on the one hand, first stating an interest in formally absolute terms but then limiting it, and, on the other hand, interpolating the limit into that interest's initial formulation, rendering that formulation overtly non-absolute.

Taking another example, if freedom of bodily movement were absolute, it, in the same way, would overturn all laws on homicides, batteries, trespasses, and the like. Again, to circumscribe our verbal formulation of that freedom from the outset, far from restoring any absoluteness to it, would be to confirm the impossibility of its absoluteness within the confines of any legal system. My 'freedom to give the dog a biscuit this coming Saturday at noon' exercises an absolute freedom of movement only in the trivial sense of already incorporating extensive non-absoluteness within the freedom's formulation. Accordingly, if free expression were absolute, one individual could commit an endless list of destructive acts as long as they were undertaken to make some statement. Two theorists otherwise as opposed as Rousseau and Hobbes agree, then, in defining non-law, the utter absence of law in their so-called 'state of nature', *as* each individual's unlimited, hence absolute right to everything.[12]

Let's now leave aside that thought experiment. Leading oppositionists like Dworkin, Post, or Weinstein acknowledge that free expression fulfils its democratic role without reaching so far as to protect, for example, wartime treason, courtroom perjury, or commercial fraud. Nor does the democratic freedom of expression I am proposing need to protect a 'symbolic' refusal to pay one's taxes, or an 'expressive' trespass to scrawl one's musings on a neighbour's house.[13] The notion of 'free speech absolutism' may work well enough as hyperbole, a mantle donned to make oppositionism appear provocative, but it has no legally plausible meaning. Within ordinary democratic contexts, to call a serious oppositionist a free speech 'absolutist' is as exaggerated as calling a prohibitionist a 'totalitarian'.[14] A plausible oppositionism always assumes legitimate limits on expression. The serious questions concern the criteria for finding particular limits legitimate.

An absolute freedom would preclude, then, the possibility of any legal system. Once we assume a legal system, the fact that the system must limit individual freedoms is not a matter of jurisprudential subtlety or political wisdom. It is a tautology. It is true neither by empirical observation nor by reasoned judgement, although endless examples of legal limits to individual freedom are certainly observable. Rather, it is true by definition, given what it would mean for any individual freedom to form part of any legal system.[15]

Difficult questions arise only about which limits to impose and to what degrees, never about whether freedoms ought to be limited at all. We cannot legitimately limit a citizen's freedoms until we determine how far that limit may reach. Value-pluralist proceduralism captures the response of most democracies, which view the balancing of rival interests as a necessary government task. The problem is not that legislatures or courts may sometimes strike a bad balance. After all, the law, as Parekh reminds us, is always 'a blunt instrument'. All laws are subject to the occasional bad application. That risk, he claims, flows from our inevitable

---

[12] See *Leviathan*, ch. 13, *in* Hobbes, [1651] 1998, pp. 150–3; *Du contract social* book 1, ch. 8, *in* Rousseau, [1762] 1964, p. 364.

[13] On 'expressive' defacement of public property, See, e.g., Post, 1994–95, pp. 1252, 1257.

[14] Cf. Parekh, 2012, p. 52. But on *epistemic dictatorialism* see Section 4.7.

[15] It might seem possible to imagine a regime in which only one individual has absolute freedom, namely, an absolute monarchy or dictatorship. The qualifier 'only one', however, renders the freedom as such drastically non-absolute. Unsurprisingly, those regimes which do vest absolute freedom in one supreme individual or coterie arise above all to curtail general freedoms, not to absolutize them.

human fallibility. Such pitfalls are 'not unique' to hate speech regulation.[16] We avert them, according to prohibitionists, when bans are implemented 'carefully',[17] 'responsibly',[18] 'with great care',[19] 'with sensitivity and good judgment',[20] 'with due regard for their likely results',[21] 'solely in the service of preserving the prevailing liberal democratic order',[22] and indeed even in a 'decidedly liberal'[23] way, with strong presumptions in favour of free speech. To avoid trampling on free expression, according to Waldron, and 'where there are fine lines to be drawn the law should *generally* stay on the liberal side of them.'[24] Supervising that balancing function are democracies' tried and tested institutions: '[a]n independent judiciary, a representative legislature, a popularly accountable government [and] a free press',[25] which offer 'our best protection against misuse'[26] of government powers over individual expression.

The common law world has long vaunted the 'genius' of a system that assures 'useful, just and flexible solutions to individual cases.'[27] That 'genius' of the law indeed speaks more than English. Most established legal orders boast one or another version of it. Comparative scholars identify legal cultures as different as Confucian, Jewish, Roman, African, Islamic, Native American, as well as European civil law traditions, all of which deploy some 'genius' of 'flexibility', for the simple reason that law becomes unmanageable without it. That ubiquitous legal flexibility prompts us to view 'weighing and balancing', 'proportionality', 'assessing the totality of the circumstances', and other such guidelines as enlightened responses to social conflicts. Since a regime of individual freedom by definition entails regulation, balancing between freedoms and limits becomes not so much a lofty achievement as an inevitability.

That panorama of regimes displaying interpretive flexibility indeed proves too much. It shows that many legal systems balance rival interests without being democratic at all. Flexibility is no unqualified good in itself. Flexibility can just as easily flex against values of democracy (or, for that matter, of liberalism, human

---

[16] Parekh, 2012, p. 53.   [17] Bleich, 2011, p. 5.
[18] Thiel, 2003b, p. 18; Waldron, 2012a, p. 203.
[19] Parekh, 2012, p. 53.   [20] Parekh, 2012, p. 53.   [21] Parekh, 2012, p. 53.
[22] Thiel, 2003b, p. 18 ('Das Streitbarkeitsprinzip muß ... ausschließlich der Bewahrung der geltenden freiheitlichen demokratischen Grundordnung dienen'). German scholarship relevant to problems of extremism frequently transposes, either strictly or loosely, the phrase *freiheitliche demokratische Grundordnung* from the text of the German Basic Law. See, e.g., Morlock, 2002, pp. 73–4; Seils, 2002, p. 49; Thiel, 2003c, pp. 136–8. Standard translations cautiously render it as 'free democratic basic order'. See 'Basic Law for the Federal Republic of Germany', 2012. That translation avoids confusion between narrower notions of the 'liberal' free-market order and the Basic Law's provision for a 'social', i.e., social-welfarist democracy. European democratic thought has nevertheless long recognized that 'liberal' and 'social-welfarist' elements co-exist, as in the Basic Law itself. The adjective 'free' ordinarily translates *frei*, a concept not altogether interchangeable with the more ideologically laden *freiheitlich*. Construing the notion of *freiheitlich* as broadly 'liberal', as I shall do in this book, yet in no way contradictory to 'social-welfarist', see, e.g., Tillmanns, 2003, p. 30. On the phrase's problematic character, See, e.g., Dreier, 2002, pp. 83–4.
[23] Tillmanns, 2003a, p. 30.
[24] Waldron, 2012a, p. 126 (emphasis added). Cf. this Section, text accompanying notes 17–19.
[25] Parekh, 2012, p. 54.   [26] Parekh, 2012, p. 54.   [27] Lobban, 1991, p. 15.

rights, or whatever one's favourite conception of justice happens to be) as in favour of them. Flexibility can just as easily flex to promote government power at the expense of essential citizen prerogatives as it can flex to protect those prerogatives from government excess. Flexibility does not provide the aforementioned 'limits to the limits' on individual freedoms. It instead heightens the need to ascertain them.

Famously, in hard cases, with strong arguments on both sides, 'weighing and balancing', 'proportionality', and 'totality of the circumstances' approaches can plausibly favour either side of a dispute. It is a commonplace that lawmakers and judges in controversial disputes can easily reach findings no more grounded in legal or ethical principle than the opposite results would have been, tempting them to bow to political expediency.[28] The present problem will not, however, be the familiar one of malleability or indeterminacy within legal norms, but rather of identifying the correct threshold norms, the limits of permissible balancing of interests affecting individual expression, in the first instance.

3.3 Political Legitimacy

Casting doubt on theories that invoke democratic values to defend free speech, Seana Valentine Shiffrin maintains, 'there is plenty of disagreement' about what democracy is or ought to be, and, in particular 'about the point of democracy, the form democracy must take, and what does or does not further democratic values.'[29] DAJ Richards calls democracy 'a contestable concept if ever there was one.'[30] Shiffrin's and Richards's objections are true enough, in the sense that general commitments to democracy scarcely guarantee identity of aims or outcomes. Any form of government is a form of decision-making. Notwithstanding the attempts of writers from Plato through to Montesquieu to correlate constitutional forms to determinate values, general political forms rarely guarantee the details of the ensuing policies and practices. No two monarchies produce identical laws. No two dictatorships produce identical laws. In that formal, constitutional sense, it is unsurprising that no two democracies would do so.

---

[28] See, e.g., Belavusau, 2013, pp. 64–5 (noting criticisms among experts that the European Court of Human Rights has at times 'disregarded the value of free speech for the sake of the political moment'); Meier, 2002, p. 27 (criticizing arbitrary applications of proportionality principles in German law on speech and assembly). See also, e.g., Seils, 2002, p. 49.

[29] Shiffrin S. V., 2011, p. 551.

[30] Richards, 1999, p. 6. Cf. also pp. 19–22. For example, claims deriving speech prerogatives from democracy, Richards charges, 'can, depending on your view of democracy, be as plausibly used against as for the constitutionality of campaign finance laws.' Richards, 1999, pp. 6–7. Cf. also at p. 19. We cannot, however, assess a given political system solely by collapsing it into its controversial elements. That risk of malleability and internal contradiction will generally haunt any political or ethical ideal pitched at a high level of generality, including Richards's own ideal of tolerance. Cf. Section 4.12, text accompanying notes 183–5. Given the sometimes overlapping, sometimes divergent criteria of 'democracy', 'liberalism', 'republicanism', 'tolerance', 'secularism' (or the related but distinct *laïcité*), 'inclusion', 'pluralism', and other such concepts, the present task is to decide whether it is the ideal of democracy that provides the most appropriate understanding of the role of speech, at least for Western societies.

We fall prey to an untenable particularism, however, if we fail to recognize shared democratic values and culture in spite of such differences. If the meaning of democracy were not just complex, but fundamentally 'contestable', we would lack any criteria for identifying sham democracies or even for imagining such a concept. Yet we immediately recognize Kim Il-Sung's 'Democratic People's Republic of Korea', along with its Cold War cousins ('German Democratic Republic') as sinister mockery. We can recognize variety and divergence, then, among democratic values and constitutions. But those features cannot be wholly open-ended without the concept of democracy becoming vacuous. Democracy must include some minimally necessary attributes and values.

Echoing Shiffrin's and Richards's views about democracy's intractable open-endedness is Waldron's image of the essential open-endedness of democratic 'legitimacy', which, he cautions, 'is a vague term'.[31] 'In social science', Waldron claims, 'legitimacy often means little more than popular support.'[32] Waldron leaves his decisive adverb 'often' unelucidated. That omission begs the question as to when democratic legitimacy means popular support, and when it means something else; and, in the latter case, *what* else. In the Southern US, slavery and then racial segregation once enjoyed 'popular' support in white majority states. Did those institutions therefore become 'legitimate'? The early civil rights movements would have enjoyed little legitimacy on such a crudely majoritarian, 'social science' criterion.

If 'legitimacy' doesn't at least in part entail critical scrutiny *of* popular opinion as reflected in law, if it merely amounts to ratification of the *status quo* then it becomes unclear what independent work it does as a concept. Waldron doesn't really define 'legitimacy'. He eliminates it. Since Socrates, a central role of ethical and political discourses is to question popular beliefs. Western political philosophy altogether begins as a rejection of legitimacy as sheer popularity.[33] 'In social science', the most basic notions of 'good', 'right', or 'just' also 'often mean little more than popular support'. In ethical and political dialectic, however, we view popular opinion not as dispositive, but more as a starting point, which may at times lead to a deeply unpopular, yet more defensible view.

Failing certain criteria, a society remains at best a sham democracy. But legitimacy never equates with popularity, no more than democracy equates with outright majoritarianism. Legitimacy becomes a question as to the degree to which those criteria, which can be called legitimating criteria, are met. In Section 3.6, I shall argue that Rawls and Dworkin do correctly identify the constitutive role of normative criteria of democratic legitimacy, beyond the doubt cast by Shiffrin's, Richards's, or Waldron's surface notions of 'democracy' or 'legitimacy'. Where Rawls and Dworkin err, I shall argue, is in anchoring those criteria within individual rights, instead of anchoring them in democratic citizenship.

---

[31] Waldron, 2012b, p. 332 (disputing Dworkin's theory of political legitimacy).
[32] Waldron, 2012a, p. 184. Cf. Waldron, 2012b, p. 332.
[33] See Section 3.5, text accompanying note 62.

3.4 State Legitimacy and Democratic Legitimacy

Most democracies today maintain value-pluralist proceduralism through the government balancing of rival interests. Human rights law becomes increasingly indistinguishable from other branches of law, except insofar as it inserts greater or lesser legal presumptions into those balancing processes. For legislative, judicial, and administrative bodies, whose everyday tasks consist of balancing any number of interests against any number of competing interests, human rights charters end up as checklists, then, of more or less presumptive interests. To identify some sufficiently strong countervailing interest is to rebut the presumption, and thereby to trump the right, however frequently or rarely that may in practice occur.

Free expression, on that rights-based view, encompasses one 'subset' of presumptive interests among a host of human rights. Those include, for example, protections from unlawful killings, from torture, from arbitrary arrests or detention, from unfair trials, from invasions of privacy, and from other abuses—many of those interests enjoying rather strong presumptions in most modern democracies—in addition, depending on the state, to economic and social entitlements. The category of 'hate speech' covers, moreover, only a small 'subset' of problems arising under the heading of 'free expression'. On its face, hate speech reduces, then, to a 'subset of a subset' of civic problems. Prohibitionists indeed insist that only tiny quantities of speech, containing little public value, are limited by bans. That seemingly secondary nature of the problem might be said to support the view that we should leave hate speech debates to our ordinary legislative and judicial processes.

In a democracy, however, free expression cannot altogether be itemized on a checklist alongside other human rights. Free expression is, again, not more important to individual or collective welfare than a number of other rights or goods. Rather, what I am identifying as a particular manifestation of free expression, *the citizen prerogative of non-viewpoint-punitive expression within public discourse*, is the most distinctly *democratic* of them. Recall that expression within public discourse is *not* non-punitive. Government may impose legitimate restrictions within public discourse where the communication of *content* is liable to cause materially demonstrable harm (commercial fraud, courtroom perjury, disclosure of national security secrets in wartime, etc.); and may impose least-restrictive, 'time, manner, and place restrictions'. Assuming otherwise non-restricted content, however, which includes issues of general social or political concern, a democracy cannot legitimately penalize expression solely on grounds of its odious or dangerous viewpoint. Democratic legitimacy assumes the citizen prerogative of non-*viewpoint*-punitive expression within public discourse.

Many factors legitimate a state as a *state*. Through public discourse, by contrast, a state legitimates itself as a democracy. In examining something as complex as a *state's* overall political legitimacy, we would ordinarily consider a variety of factors. We might scrutinize its commitment to the rule of law by reviewing its record for extra-judicial killings, arbitrary arrests, conditions of detention, or discriminatory practices. Or we might assess its commitment to distributive justice by investigating its record on tax equity, employment opportunity, health care, or child welfare. We could in principle undertake either of those two enquiries for *any* society—an absolute monarchy, a dictatorship, a military junta, a one-party state, as well as a democracy.

Refraining from torturing prisoners, guaranteeing fair trials, or avoiding famines legitimate a state as a state. A state does not need to be a democracy in order to torture less or to assure access to nourishment. Those measures are by no means distinctive of democratic legitimacy per se. If they were, then the leading international human rights documents, such as UDHR, ICCPR, or ICERD, would have to declare that they apply only to democracies. Of course, they proclaim nothing of the kind. They were never adopted on that assumption, nor have they been interpreted in any such way. They were expressly adopted during the Cold War as criteria for assessing the overall legitimacy of state action regardless of a state's democratic or non-democratic constitution or government (even if some of their provisions are more plausibly realized within democracies—at the time, a hotly debated question). Accordingly, rights of political participation[34] ended up as nothing less, but also nothing more, than an item on the human rights 'checklist'. Any number of fundamental interests might be cited to test the legitimacy of states as *states*. It is the citizen prerogative of non-viewpoint-punitive expression within public discourse, along with any necessary derivatives of that prerogative, which legitimates states as *democracies*. By extension, food and water are required for a democratic society to thrive in the truistic sense that they are required for any society to thrive. Food and water are vital for democracy, but not distinctive of it. Adequate access to them legitimates a state as a state, but not specifically as a democracy.

Today's democracies have drifted into an unacknowledged assumption. The state exercises an authority to determine, and thereby to constitute attributes of citizenship as by-products of purely administrative acts. Citizenship is confirmed through birth certificates, identity papers, passports, and the like. But democratic citizenship must surely amount to more than an offshoot of administrative record-keeping. After all, North Korea and Saudi Arabia can print birth certificates as crisp and clean as those of any democracy. Of course, what democracies offer in addition is the vote. Many would maintain that it is not speaking, but voting that distinguishes democracy from other forms of government. Voting, however, is nothing but a formalized procedure for speaking. In most Germanic languages, the customary word for 'vote' derives from the word for 'voice': the German *Stimme*, the Dutch *stem*, the Danish *stemme*.[35] The Latinate 'vote' traces to the solemnity of pledging or 'vowing' (*vovere*), as in the French *donner sa voix*.[36]

---

[34] See, e.g., UDHR art. 21; ICCPR art. 25.

[35] Cf. Kelsen, 1920, pp. 8–9.

[36] Consider *Coriolanus*, Shakespeare's only drama set in a fully republican Rome (recalling that *Julius Caesar* has already shifted to the republic's demise). The play's eponymous hero spits contempt for the people's 'voices' no fewer than ten times. (*Coriolanus*, 2.3.77, 82, 108, 121, 122, 125, 127, 133; 3.1.23, 32, *in* Shakespeare, 1994, pp. 235–47). The word simultaneously signifies the plebeians' informal opinions as well as their formally offered mandates. Coriolanus's disdain of their voices becomes comically metonymic for his disdain of republican citizenship as such, and of its prerogatives

Voting remains derivative of something more foundational, something constitutive of it. It derives from, as a formalized procedure for, expression within public discourse. It remains a vital yet slightly more attenuated prerogative than that foundation itself. A state may, for example, legitimately bar infant children from voting. Or it may legitimately bar them from expressive events on demonstrable health or safety grounds (health and safety forming part of the broader security interest of protecting all or part of the population). But the state can never, on democratic grounds, impose a viewpoint-selective limitation even on a three-year old's expression within public discourse (and even if one were to assume that some children of that age might fail to understand their own words, which may also be true of some adults). It is implausible for democratic citizenship to manifest only once every few months or years, in a fleeting moment, within the polling station's cloistered confines. That modest addition scarcely brings citizenship very far beyond the purely administrative concept.[37] There must be some attribute of citizenship, even more primordial than voting, which we carry around with us always and everywhere within the borders of our democracy. That attribute, the citizen prerogative of non-viewpoint-punitive expression within public discourse, must be such that it cannot legitimately be regulated for the sake of democracy because it signally constitutes democracy.

Dworkin maintains that, 'though majoritarian procedures may be a necessary condition of political legitimacy, they are not a sufficient condition.'[38] He adds, '[f]air democracy requires what we might call a democratic background: it requires … that everyone have not just a vote but a voice: a majority decision is not fair unless everyone has had a fair opportunity to express his or her attitudes or opinions or fears or tastes or prejudices or ideals.'[39] Dworkin emphasizes that parity between 'voice' and 'vote' as pre-conditions of democratic legitimacy. To deny the citizen a voice is tantamount to denying a vote—even more so, I would add, in post-Enlightenment democracies, where voting is both seldom and

---

of expression in the public sphere. The playwright elicits the polity's signally democratic element through a caricature of the anti-democrat, through a mockery *of* the mocking of democracy. The word's parodic repetition suggests at least as much *contempt for the contempt* of citizens' views as Coriolanus's contempt for those views themselves. (This is not to say that Shakespeare discernibly condones or condemns democracy or republicanism per se, no more nor less than the equally precarious and largely arbitrary forms of monarchy or aristocracy that he portrays elsewhere. From the ever-encumbered standpoint of authorial intention, questions about such an artist's 'real' political convictions, although many still hack away at them, are fruitless. See, e.g., Dollimore, 2004; Dollimore & Sinfield, 1994; Hadfield, 2005; Heinze, 2009c; Heinze, 2009d; Heinze, 2012a; Heinze, 2013a, pp. 97–197.)

[37] See, e.g., Kelsen, 1920, p. 6.   [38] Dworkin, 2009, p. vii.

[39] Dworkin, 2009, p. vii, and also at p. viii. Cf. Baker, 2009, pp. 142–3; Barendt, 2007, pp. 18–21; Dreier, 2002, pp. 87–88 (citing *i.a.* Alexy, Toulmin, and Habermas); Dworkin, 1992, p. 56; Dworkin, 1996, pp. 200–1; Haworth, 1998, pp. 174–9 (discussing Rawls); Heinze, 2006, pp. 568–9; Meier, 2002, p. 15; Molnar & Post, 2012, pp. 18–19 (discussing Rousseau and Habermas); Nieuwenhuis, 2011, pp. 21, 34–8; Pech, 2003, pp. 371–4, 381–8; Post, 1995, pp. 7, 119–20, 185 (discussing Kelsen), 192, 273, 286; Smolla, 1993, pp. 12–17; Weinstein, 1999, p. 12; Weinstein, 2009a, p. 25; Weinstein, 2011a, pp. 497–500, 505–14.

indirect. Vote and voice do not compete as constitutive elements of democracy. They become two manifestations of the same legitimating expressive condition.

Together with the panoply of political institutions, a formalized voting procedure is not the origin of, but already the product of an ever self-renewing public discourse, which, as constitutive of such institutional arrangements, can also always move to change them. Vote ensues from voice, but with the instrumentalized role of performing an institutional function within political structures already established through, and contingent upon, public discourse. That more derivative and functional role of voting is further illustrated by the fact that, in some democracies mandatory voting is deemed legitimate to ensure the best possible representation. It would be unthinkable, however, for an LSPD to attach any such compulsory stricture to the more fundamental prerogative of expression within public discourse, which entails the citizen's prerogative not to exercise it. (The exceptional circumstances under which the state may compel speech, like swearing in a trial witness, is not public discourse of the aforementioned general type. Trial procedure entails the pervasively constrained expressive rules of conduct, decorum, and judge-directed speech.)[40]

In order for voting to accomplish its democratic function fairly and effectively, it must be subject to non-viewpoint-punitive rules, regarding means of recording the vote, protection of voter privacy, transparent counting, appeal procedures, and the like. Constitutional separations of powers are similarly essential, yet derivative vis-à-vis the core attributes of citizenship which most fundamentally constitute democracy. They, too, stand as the kinds of non-viewpoint-punitive limits on democracy that safeguard democracy. They certainly reflect and enforce a viewpoint about how government ought to be structured. But, again, they entail no penalties for citizens who, within public discourse, and however crudely, may propose alternative constitutional arrangements or indeed, in a revolutionary vein, abolition of the constitution altogether.

Jacques Rancière questions whether even full-blown representational institutions reflect a distinctly democratic element within the modern Western state. He recalls our various founders' original scepticisms towards popular sovereignty. The ongoing effects of that scepticism surface as constitutional *curbs* on democratic forces.[41] If we entertain Rancière's scepticism, then the more general citizen voice overwhelms even the vote as democracy's pre-eminent feature. States offering votes and parliaments but denying citizens' voices, through murders or persecution of dissidents and journalists and closures of alternative media are autocracies, not democracies. As far back as the Enlightenment, the political role of public

---

[40] That more derivative status of voting also explains why, contrary to findings of the US Supreme Court, it is a mistake to deduce from the citizen prerogative of expression within public discourse a rule barring even-handed restrictions on campaign financing. The US Supreme Court's reduction of the democratic citizen prerogative of expression (a legal interest lying beyond democratically legitimate regulation *only* as to non-viewpoint-punitive expression within public discourse) to a liberal right (a legal interest to be weighed and balanced against competing interests, albeit enjoying a strong presumption in its favour) manifests in the Court's decisions overturning campaign finance reform. See *Citizens United v. Federal Election Commission*, 558 U.S. 310 (2010); *McCutcheon v. Federal Election Commission*, 572 U.S. ___ (2014), 133 S. Ct. 1242.

[41] Rancière, 2005, pp. 79–81 (citing Raymond Aron).

discourse outside formal organs of government has been recognized through the informal, 'Fourth Estate' power of the media; and, since the electronic revolution, through public yet informal networks of social media. During, indeed prompting, the Arab uprisings that began in December 2010,[42] one element that counted as constitutively democratic, even before the vote existed, was public discourse through actual as well as virtual media.

Voting derives, then, from the more fundamental citizen prerogative of expression within public discourse. But voting is not therefore facultative. It is a manifestation of public discourse that remains specifically necessary for democracy, not as a matter of enlightened judgement, but as a constitutional matter—a matter of definition. The problem for a democracy that lacked any form of voting would not be that it is bad, but that it would not exist at all. A 'non-voting democracy' would be, like a 'non-quadrilateral square', words to which nothing material can correspond. A society without voting may be many things, perhaps wonderful things. Whatever it might be, however representative and consultative might be its institutions and officials (representation and consultation being possible and even effective in societies that do not otherwise recognize them as flowing, as a compulsory matter, from citizenship), however much art and culture might thrive in it, it could not be called a democracy. That observation applies *a fortiori* for the prerogative of expression within public discourse, which therefore surpasses even the necessary procedure of voting as democracy's defining element.

A freedom, as we have seen, can be abused. It therefore legitimately remains subject to balancing against rival interests. Essential democratic citizen prerogatives, by contrast, cannot legitimately be subject to balancing in that way. The *prerogative* to vote is, then, the more accurate term, in a democracy, than the 'right' to vote. There is no such thing as limiting one *individual* citizen's prerogative to vote in order to assure other citizens an equal prerogative to vote (even if voting is at times adjusted in *collectively* controversial ways, as by gerrymandering), or in purely incidental ways, as by facilitating disabled voters in ways that may cause other voters to have to wait a few additional minutes. In the same sense, excluding citizens from public expression on viewpoint-selective grounds, however strongly that exclusion may be motivated by the goal of achieving substantive justice, can never render society 'more' democratic.

Despite varying interpretations of the concept of the rule of law, or *Rechtsstaat*, a democratic conception admits state-authorized incursions either on property (fines, civil awards, appropriations, garnishment of wages, maintenance payments, etc.) or on physical freedom (arrest, detention, imprisonment, restraint and prior restraint orders, etc.). No *Rechtsstaat* can legitimately curtail an essential element of citizenship on any democratic rationale.[43] (That is why the death penalty, too, can never be legitimate on democratic grounds.)[44] To claim, by extension, that the prerogative to vote can be 'abused' is conceptually meaningless.

---

[42] See, e.g., 'Arab uprising: Country by country' (n.d.).
[43] See Section 5.3, text accompanying note 89.   [44] See Section 4.6.

There may well be such a thing as limiting one individual's freedom in order to assure some other individual's freedom, hence the intricate jurisprudence of rights. But there is no such thing as limiting one individual's citizenship in order to assure some other individual's citizenship, hence the fallacy both of reducing essential elements of democratic citizenship to a sheer checklist of human rights, and then of subjecting them to a jurisprudence of balancing competing interests.

Whatever legitimacy the state may have in setting limits on freedoms, those limits must themselves remain subject to the limit that they may not, on democratic grounds, be placed on freedoms attaching to any essential element of citizenship. To say the prerogative of non-viewpoint-punitive expression in public discourse can be abused is, then, a purely verbal formulation. It corresponds to no reality. To say citizenship can be abused is an easy error to make when essential citizenship prerogatives are reduced to the status of individual rights, which in turn fall subject to legislative, judicial, or administrative balancing. When we suspect individuals of abusing their citizenship, either we mean that they are abusing freedoms falling outside the necessary attributes of citizenship, and so the democratic state may legitimately intervene, or we mean nothing at all.

The citizen prerogative of non-viewpoint-punitive expression within public discourse cannot admit of degrees,[45] although some of its derivatives do admit of them, such as voting being subject to age or procedural restrictions. That prerogative is conferred not by natural right, not by the sheer fact of belonging to 'the human family',[46] but only insofar as the society is democratic. 'Citizens' (in the purely administrative sense) of a dictatorship may well be 'born' with a natural or human *right* of free expression, notwithstanding the lack of any such effective right within the state's positive law. Whether or not they are born with it depends on one's view of human beings and of rights, but that tenet certainly remains paramount in international law. When we point to international law to attribute to North Koreans, for example, a human right of free expression, we speak in an aspirational or natural law vein. As a practical matter, we do so in order to characterize North Korean violations, but not to identify any positive law rights accruing to individual North Koreans in any effective sense.

Citizens of a dictatorship may, in that aspirational sense, be 'born' with a human right of free expression that is, in a kind of medieval-scholastic sense, yet to be 'actualized'. But they are not born with the citizen prerogative of expression within public discourse, which makes sense only insofar as it is more than aspirational. That citizen prerogative has meaning only as being already effective. Accordingly, for as long as Sweden remains a thriving democracy, the Swede is born into that essential attribute of democratic citizenship; for as long as Saudi Arabia remains undemocratic, the Saudi is not. The Saudi enjoys free expression in a legal sense (as opposed to engaging in clandestinely unlawful communication) solely through the state's forbearance. That is why Sweden cannot legitimately impose

---

[45] See Sections 4.5 and 4.10.   [46] UDHR, preamble, para. 1.

viewpoint-selective penalties within public discourse, as its law currently allows. The question as to whether or not Saudi Arabia may legitimately impose them depends on the prior question as to whether it *ought* to be a democracy, which is an altogether different enquiry.

Saudis may, as a matter of either natural or of positive international law, claim a *human right* of free expression. But they can insist upon a *citizen prerogative* of non-viewpoint-punitive expression within public discourse only by insisting upon democracy as a whole. Swedes arguably do also enjoy, as a matter of positive law, a *right* of free expression as 'humans'. They maintain their democracy, however, only to the extent that they enjoy free expression as a citizen prerogative. That extent certainly reaches far. Overwhelmingly Swedes, like citizens of other democracies, enjoy historically unprecedented expressive prerogatives within public discourse, despite their hate speech bans. A measure of illegitimacy remains insofar as Sweden, with most other democracies, continues to impose viewpoint-selective penalties on expression within public discourse. Still, that illegitimacy is nevertheless residual. It deprives Sweden only of a measure of democratic legitimacy, while most of its democratic legitimacy remains intact.[47]

Some Swedish citizens belonging to disfavoured minority groups may well reap less *profit* from that country as an *economy*, and altogether less *benefit* from it as a *society*, as compared to the ethnically Germanic majority. Those drawbacks are weighty. But members of minorities in no sense reap less *citizenship* from Sweden as a *democracy*. To assert that they do would be not mistaken as a factual matter, but nonsensical as conceptual matter. It is a perennial category error when we assume even a grave substantive injustice within a democracy to display a defect in its securing of citizenship.

That observation applies, moreover, beyond the relationship of the state to individuals or groups. Western democracies have undoubtedly committed or facilitated harmful conduct both within and beyond their own borders. Such conduct, such as harm to many innocents in Afghanistan, Iraq, or Guantanamo Bay in the early twenty-first century, diminishes those democracies' achievement of justice. Not only survival and security, but justice must remain the highest aim of political conduct if we are to assume any serious conception of ethics at all.[48] Such conduct does, then, diminish those Western democracies' achievement of justice, but not their legitimacy *as* democracies, except in those instances where such harm specifically diminishes democracies' legitimating conditions. (The age-old error of confusing imperfect justice with imperfect democracy renders no succour to those whom we would wish to help. It becomes easily fuelled by Foucauldian theories of power, which, admittedly persuasive, would render *any* constitutional form a sheer arena within which 'real' power then becomes systemically deployed in the service of dominant interests. Anticipating Vaneigem, Foucault not only refrains from advocating

---

[47] On degrees of legitimacy, see Sections 4.5 and 4.10.
[48] Cf. Section 4.8, text accompanying note 91.

speech bans within Western democracies, but holds up Socratic *parrhesia* or frankness as the exemplar of politics through public discourse.)[49]

Few important laws within a value-pluralist democracy will create only winners. Most laws entail winners and losers, which will indeed issue from the overall dissemination of power, at the expense of the vulnerable. Losers under any socially important law may suspect injustice to the extent that some alternative law might have made them lose less, or might instead have made them winners. That suspicion may, in turn, point to a substantive injustice, but not necessarily a failure of democratic citizenship, barring material destruction of the exercise of some essential attribute of citizenship.

Substantive injustice may indeed emerge out of democratic failure, but the straightforward inference of democratic failure solely from an actual or presumed injustice misconstrues the mandate of democracy as a constitutional form. We can call that inference the *legitimacy fallacy*. Every failure of democracy may entail injustice. That does not mean that every injustice *within* a democracy amounts to a failure *of* democracy. Substantive injustice may diminish the legitimacy of the state *as* a state, i.e., as guarantor of certain legal interests; but it does not diminish the legitimacy of the state as a democracy. Or, again, it does so only insofar as harm is caused to essential attributes of citizenship, or to rules governing the state's democratic institutions, such as election rigging.

Distinctions between necessary elements of humanity and necessary elements of citizenship are complex, given important overlaps between them. That obstacle mirrors our difficulties in distinguishing between rights regimes and democratic regimes. The enormous expansion of human rights, encompassing wide-ranging sets of civil, political, social, economic, cultural, and other types of rights, arises from the ambition of human rights law to define necessary attributes of human beings as such. On that view, rights against torture or rights to food inhere in humans regardless of whether they live in a democracy, an absolute monarchy, or a dictatorship. The very specific task of identifying democracy's legitimating features, by contrast, must seek the necessary attributes only of humans as citizens. That enterprise does not require that we posit democracy as superior to other forms of government or society. It asks only which norms must obtain *if* a society is to be democratic. (It requires not, to phrase the point in Kantian terms, that democratization be construed as a categorical imperative, but only as a hypothetical one.)[50]

A tacit syllogism is built into the politics of human rights. The syllogism's major premise is that respect for human rights legitimates the state. That premise might

---

[49] See Foucault, [1983–84] 2009. *Parrhesia* can include forgiveness requested for one's candour. Yet that does not mean regret about frankness as such, but only about the fact that listeners may feel disarmed. Hateful expression may rarely count as parrhesiac in any politically useful sense. The point, however, remains that, in themselves, objectionable manifestations of democratic citizenship do not indicate failures either of democracy or of citizenship.

[50] See, e.g., *Grundlegung zur Metaphysik der Sitten* BA40-45, *in* Kant, [1785] 1968, pp. 43–5.

well be debated even on its own terms,[51] but our present problems remain even if we do accept it. The syllogism's minor premise is that democracy counts as one form of state. The conclusion is that human rights therefore legitimate democracy. Assuming both premises, the syllogism works indeed. But it applies only insofar as a democracy is a state, in the same way as it would apply to any other state. It bypasses any requirement for legitimating a state as a democracy.

That conceptual misstep emerges through logic, but also through history. The aim of the post-UDHR, Cold War-era human rights movement was to identify overriding norms of state conduct irrespective of the world's clashing political systems. That conventionally humanist quest to seek 'what unites us rather than what divides us'[52] posited human rights above politics, as apolitical. The idea of a complete system of norms deployed to assess the legitimacy of all political systems, while itself remaining otherwise impartial to any of them, might well have baffled most pre-twentieth-century political theorists—at least within the Western secular tradition (it is a curiously Christian–universalist idea, though arguably common to some other faiths).

For centuries, political theorists had enquired into the best political norms, while it was lawyers who had asserted their vocation to administer law 'irrespective' of its background politics. With the international human rights movement, that relationship between law and politics inverts. Human rights deliver a politics as if designed by lawyers: a panoply of norms, obedient solely to a formally universalist ideal of the rule of law. Such norms emerge as 'fundamental' while remaining 'equally' applicable to 'all' states 'irrespective' of their regimes. For decades, lawyers signed up to the human rights movement while political scientists found it at worst risible, and at best something that could not literally mean what it says.

For decades, particularly during the Cold War, political scientists ignored the international human rights movement entirely, or dismissed it as a by-product of power politics. Their own intellectual traditions could scarcely take seriously the idea of something expressly presenting itself as *both* politically foundational *and* politically neutral. (To this day the political scientist is still inclined to take human rights, if perhaps more seriously, yet still largely as a strategic or rhetorical tool for making claims about the exercise of power. In their more honest, off-the-record moments, some lawyers will say the same.) It was, by contrast, lawyers and even legal academics who far more eagerly embraced the human rights ideal on its own terms, often embarking upon human rights activism as an activity wholly embodying their conventional professional activity. Lawyers had, after all,

---

[51] A long line of radical critiques of modern theories of human rights begins with Marx, [1844] (1976) and continues still. See also Section 3.6, text accompanying note 75.

[52] See, e.g., US Bureau of Public Affairs, 2007, p. 221 (quoting Soviet foreign minister Andrei Gromyko in meeting with Richard Nixon, 22 October 1970); US Bureau of Public Affairs, 1971–72, p. 484 (quoting US Secretary of State Henry Kissinger in meeting with Soviet General Secretary Leonid Brezhnev, 21 April 1972).

traditionally tended to norms that were presented just as the international and regional corpuses present them—as distinct from politics, administered within the rule of law. Even their 'over coffee' nuances that supposedly 'universal' human rights law *really is* about politics or strategy, or *really needs* to accommodate local differences, or *really tries* to push for democracy despite the *Realpolitik* of tip-toeing around despotism and corruption, in no way impairs their face-value deployment of its fundamentally universalist norms and assumptions.

Official inter-governmental bodies like the aforementioned UN committees, as well as flagship non-governmental organizations (NGOs) like Amnesty International, Human Rights Watch, Oxfam, or Save the Children, stake their authority on being *un-political*, yet authoritative in pronouncing upon massive and complex political situations.[53] Human rights NGOs proceed along conspicuously 'lawyerly', cosmetically neutral models of activism, presented as an improvement upon models that would publicly announce a preference for one type of political regime over another. Politics, on that view, 'work' better 'on the ground' when presented apolitically, presented as *not* politics. It is no accident that such an inversion between law and politics occurs precisely as politics witness the rapid 'juridification' or 'judicialization' characteristic of democracies since the late twentieth century. To be sure, I am not condemning any of those approaches or understandings per se. To the contrary, if our concern is simply to assess the legitimacy of states *as* states, human rights provide criteria as serviceable as any others. Democracies *as* states can still remain subject to them. But any peremptory choice *for* democracy and *against* non-democracy is flagrantly political and can in no serious sense be rendered un-political. The contemporary human rights corpus does not provide, then, nor was it conceived to provide, specifically legitimating conditions for democracy.

The end result simmers with irony. Since antiquity, everyday politics come time and again to be viewed as value-relativist power-mongering, cynically parading partisan interests in the guise of the common weal.[54] The aim of the human rights movement is to transcend that political cut-and-thrust by identifying universal values. However, values purporting to apply indifferently to all states, 'irrespective' of their particular political regimes, become not politically neutral, but politically relativist. Purporting to apply equally to all constitutional forms, they distinguish none. The judgement that Saudi Arabian politics are inferior to Swedish politics becomes not a conceptual matter of principle, but rather collapses at best into a purely empirical observation, and at worst into a matter of sheer opinion.

That is where the aforementioned syllogism kicks in. That indifferent vein of being equally applicable to all states, regardless of politics, does not strengthen, but rather dilutes human rights as criteria of political legitimacy—again applying, at best, to states as states, but not sufficiently to states as democracies. The same irony dictates that the only norms that would have any hope of claiming universality would be ones that, from the outset, precisely renounce any such claim to

---

[53] Cf. Heinze, 2008b, pp. 14–15.   [54] See Section 3.5, text accompanying note 62.

transcendental universalism, emphatically proclaiming that they do *not* apply 'equally' to 'all' systems, 'irrespective' of their institutional realities, instead expressly favouring those politics which promote the best norms, and denouncing those which run contrary to them.

What are the 'best' norms? The perennial controversies surrounding that question are not to be resolved here. They instead bring us back to our starting point. For purposes of examining democratic legitimacy, I am, again, assuming a democratic order as a hypothetical, and not as a categorical political imperative. The task is then to enquire into democracy's legitimating conditions, not contrary to or suspicious of human rights, and yet independently of them. My aim is not to discredit certain achievements of the human rights movement. Nor is my point the old and distinct one, which I shall not examine further here, that rights undermine democracy by withdrawing 'too many' problems from legislative deliberation. I am challenging human rights not as legitimating elements of states, but as legitimating elements of democracy. Whether or to what degree human rights are required or desirable within a democracy, or rather within a democratic state, are important but distinct questions. Human rights offer limited authority in drawing limits to democracy—not despite, but precisely because of their universalist pretensions.

3.5 The Dual Character of Democratic Law

The conventional wisdom of human rights law is that it is anti-relativist. We have just seen, however, that it does in fact presuppose and continue to promote political and ethical relativism. That relativism arose during the Cold War not despite, but as a product of the universalist conception of human rights. It was common to compare the relative advantages and disadvantages of, respectively, democratic and dictatorial systems. On the side of democracy lay, in addition to free expression, other civil liberties, like freedom of religion or immunity from *ex post facto* crimes. But democracies, it was argued, had their drawbacks, such as job insecurity or opportunity based on status or wealth.

Those sorts of comparisons maintained free speech as just one interest on the checklist of important interests—fair trials, protection from torture, access to food and water, and other such desiderata. Each such interest was to be assessed on its own merits. Britain may well have given people *a*, *b*, and *c*, but, it was countered, the USSR gave people *d*, *e*, and *f*. Free expression is, again, not more *humanly* important than food, water, housing, or job security. Within the corpus of post-Second World War international law, free expression is certainly not more important as a human right.[55] That view of expression as just one among many important interests

---

[55] According to para. 5 of the Vienna Declaration and Programme of Action, adopted by the World Conference on Human Rights in Vienna, 25 June 1993, 'All human rights are universal, indivisible and interdependent and interrelated. The international community must treat human rights globally in a fair and equal manner, on the same footing, and with the same emphasis. While the significance of national and regional particularities and various historical, cultural and religious backgrounds must

on the human rights checklist sows confusion about what democracy is and requires. The fault lies not with any Cold War dictatorship, but with the dominant liberal, rights-based tradition itself.

Under a totalitarian regime all non-trivial laws or policies, and many trivial ones—irrespective of the area of law that they regulate, and therefore cutting across all spheres of life—tacitly entail a distinct, concomitant rule, namely, that such law or policy is not to be publicly criticized. In most of the Soviet sphere, for example, it was generally mandatory for competent adults, in the domain of acts, to participate in a command economy managed through state-installed hierarchies. On its surface, that injunction appears relevant only to economic interests, which appear on the checklist as interests distinct from the interest in free expression. But attached to that policy—nowhere formally enshrined, yet binding in any legal realist sense[56]—was a further requirement making it unlawful, in the domain of words, for the policy to be challenged. The interdiction of free expression persisted not as one distinct area on a checklist of legal regulations; it attached throughout the system to all areas of regulation. Public discourse as the essential medium for examining alternative politics was not, as it often is in democracies, merely encumbered; it was annihilated. Copious state television, radio, print media, and indeed high art and literature could certainly generate enormous quantities of public expression, often of high quality, but they created no public discourse (even if we read masterpieces by figures such as Elem Klimov or Miklós Jancsó, if and when they managed to pass through the censors, as politically pregnant, as full of winks and nods).

The totalitarian state entails, then, a regime of dual legality. In the first instance, it commands, either *de jure* or *de facto*, certain acts and omissions. But then, in addition, the state attaches to all non-trivial commands, and usually to some trivial ones, a tacit prohibition on views expressed contrary to those commands or to the values or policies motivating those commands. Such a state vindicates a given policy, such as a programme for publicly honouring certain political leaders, not only substantively—many democracies do the same—but also, in Dworkin's words, 'further upstream',[57] by viewpoint-selectively penalizing expression contrary to the policy. Totalitarianism entails that dually compulsory regime throughout the whole of law, and not merely limits on expression as one particular point on a checklist of legal interests. Those living under such a regime are certainly *homo*

---

be borne in mind, it is the duty of States, regardless of their political, economic and cultural systems, to promote and protect all human rights and fundamental freedoms.'

[56] 'Already in Stalinism,' notes Slavoj Žižek, 'it was not only prohibited to criticise Stalin and the party publicly, it was even more prohibited to announce this prohibition publicly. If someone were to shout back at a critic of Stalin, "Are you crazy? Don't you know that we are not allowed to do this?" he would have disappeared into the Gulag even faster than the open critic of Stalin' (New Statesman, 2015). Moreover, although the present focus is on public discourse, even private dissent, the mildest gripe among friends or family, is perilous. Spying networks delve deeply into private and family life: children are trained to inform on parents; teachers on pupils; and spouses, cousins, friends, or co-workers on each other.

[57] See Section 4.5, text accompanying notes 55–6.

sapiens, hence 'human' insofar as that term bears meaning in international law; yet their citizenship is nothing but the administrative by-product of birth certificates and passports.

My aim is not to resort to the cowboy libertarianism of accusing democracies that maintain hate speech bans, like France or Sweden, of being dictatorships, or even of being, as a whole, of a 'less democratic cast'. Such hyperbole misconceives the complex and comprehensive character of democratic legitimacy.[58] My aim is only to illustrate how democracy requires the opposite duality. Democratic law, too, commands certain acts and omissions. But it requires that each such command—even the most salutary, such as anti-discrimination policies—be entirely subject to non-viewpoint-punitive rebukes, even utterly repulsive ones, within public discourse.

Such duality, one might argue, is by no means exclusive to free expression. The need to eat also persists not in isolation, but throughout all of life, equally attaching to any other law. One can obey tax laws, traffic laws, or zoning laws in any durable way only if one can eat. But that duality characterizes the law of any society. The need to eat constitutes humanity, indeed all living beings, and not specifically democracy.[59] To make all such vital interests not just legitimating conditions of the state as a state, but additionally legitimating conditions of the state as a democracy would be to take the politically relativist step of rendering the legitimating conditions of non-democracies identical to those of democracies, as international human rights law does, at least in its immediate post-Second World War conception. We can leave aside for now the broader question of whether it is *humanly* misconceived to view free expression as but one item on a checklist of things prohibited under totalitarianism, counter-balanced either by the goods or services any such regime does provide, or by democracies' respective failures to achieve other interests on the list. From the democratic standpoint, that checklist approach is in any event *politically* misconceived.

Through that dual character of democratic free expression, verbal violence is the gadfly clinging to every socially conscious law, policy, or practice. Tens or even hundreds of thousands of people in some democracies depend on basic social services. An economic libertarian who advocates abolition of those services, perhaps hatefully sneering at those recipients as 'lazy' or 'parasites', disseminates a view that, if influential, places some socio-politically vulnerable people and their human dignity at risk. The physical or emotional welfare of countless women is promoted through the freedom to choose abortion. A traditionalist who advocates abolition of that service, perhaps hatefully branding the women as 'sluts' or 'baby murderers', disseminates a view that, if influential, places those socio-politically vulnerable women and their human dignity at risk. Abolition of the death penalty has humanized punishment and can spare the

---

[58] See Sections 4.5 and 6.1.

[59] Cf. Nicomachean *Ethics* 1.5.1097^{b}11 (reading πολιτικὸν as 'civic' and not just 'social'), 1097^{b}34-1098^{a}21, *in* Aristotle, [4th century BCE] 1984, vol. 2, pp. 1734–5. Cf. also Section 4.12, text accompanying notes 173–82.

lives of those wrongly convicted. A retributionist advocating its reinstatement, perhaps hatefully labelling all convicts as 'scum', places them and their human dignity at risk. Global warming risks havoc for hundreds of millions, including socio-politically vulnerable people living in poor countries, yet climate-change denialists place all those people at risk. Which of those positions, all potentially lethal or brutal ones, all stacked against the socio-politically vulnerable, shall we penalize or censor? If none of them, then it becomes difficult for prohibitionists to justify maintaining hate speech bans solely on grounds of protecting the vulnerable or disempowered,[60] although I shall also be examining other prohibitionist positions.

Controversial speech by definition places some people's welfare, even millions of people's welfare, at risk when it is voiced to endorse a policy that, if influential, might leave those people worse off, and might either crudely or—even worse, subtly[61]—demonize them. The very origin of the systematic, programmatic strand of Western political philosophy traces back to anxiety about the abuse of democratic public discourse through dangerous viewpoints expressed to further the speakers' interests at the expense of others. Despair about democracy in Plato's *Gorgias* is nothing but despair about the subversion of ethics, and then of law, through public discourse.[62] Despair about democracy *is* despair about public discourse. More than two millennia later, Carl Schmitt's rejection of parliamentary democracy, wedding Schmitt to a dictatorship vastly more atrocious than anything in Plato, becomes a categorical rejection of politics as public discourse.

The more politics is theorized as deriving its legitimacy from public discourse, the more it will be deemed vulnerable to hijacking, at the expense of the vulnerable. That fear surfaces in radical right- and left-wing currents of the post-Enlightenment. The more suspicious one becomes towards alternatives to one's own politics—even when that suspicion, as with hateful expression, is ethically compelling[63]—the more hostile one becomes towards a fundamentally discursive politics.

More than Machiavelli's *The Prince*, more than Hobbes's *Leviathan*, Plato's *Republic* is Western philosophy's blueprint of despair about politics as public discourse. Leaving aside the specifics of the *Republic*'s prescribed norms, consider its basic premise: 'in establishing our city, we aren't aiming to make any one group outstandingly happy but to make the whole city so, as far as possible.'[64] Plato plans a government that proceeds directly to substantive justice, unburdened by the risks of interest group factions.[65] Assuming the ideal of that harmonized society, censorship, the 'upstream' prevention of contrary views expressed in public discourse, becomes not just a policy, but an imperative. Plato limits the advocacy of bad views in order to safeguard good ones.

---

[60] Cf., e.g., Heinze, 2009b.   [61] See Section 5.5, text accompanying notes 131–5.
[62] See, e.g., Corcoran, 1989; Weinrib, 1989.   [63] See Section 4.8.
[64] *Republic* 4.420b, *in* Plato, [4th century BCE] 1997, p. 1053.
[65] See, e.g., Heinze, 2013a, pp. 50–60.

3.6 Value Pluralism and Liberal Theory

Value-pluralist processes of legislative and judicial balancing display the humanist aspirations of classical liberalism, its vaunted spirit of tolerance and diversity.[66] A robust democracy, on that view, can never represent only one group. There must be freedom for speakers, but also social inclusion for the disempowered. Oppositionists, however, lay the opposite claim to liberal philosophy. They argue, with John Stuart Mill: 'If all mankind, minus one, were of one opinion, and only one person were of the contrary opinion, mankind would be no more justified in silencing that one person, than he, if he had the power, would be justified in silencing mankind.'[67]

Such contradictions are familiar within liberalism. Liberalism, writes Gerald Gaus, 'fractures into a variety of types and competing visions'.[68] As Shiffrin, Richards, and Waldron remind us, democracy often appears similarly Protean, seemingly relativist in its values insofar as it seems to resist fixed criteria. Given that apparent mutability, a refusal to compromise on expression within public discourse can make oppositionists seem illiberal, even fanatical.[69] While effectively rejecting Waldron's 'popular support' criterion of *legitimacy*, Weinstein does duly note that 'restrictions on extreme speech in democratic societies are often imposed not by some executive decree or police action, but by legislation truly expressing the will of the people.'[70] For many prohibitionists, those restrictions maintain their legitimacy through democracies' legislative and judicial balancing processes.

Jeremy Bentham counts among the first Enlightenment figures to construe law's task as concerned with systematically weighing up and balancing the kinds of rival interests that divide mass societies. That modernist approach stood as an innovation in an era when individual rights regimes still cloaked class privilege behind a legalist apparatus. Bentham introduces his utility principle, which 'approves or disapproves of every action whatsoever according to the tendency it appears to have to augment or diminish the happiness of the party whose interest is in question.'[71] By, extension: 'A measure of government … may be said to be conformable to or dictated by the principle of utility' when 'the tendency which it has to augment the happiness of the community is greater than any which it has to diminish it.'[72]

Not all legislative, let alone judicial balancing today proceeds along rigorously utilitarian lines, although broadly consequentialist reasoning abounds.[73]

---

[66] See, e.g., Locke, [1689] 1983; Voltaire, [1763] 1961. Cf. Waldron, 2012a, pp. 204–33.
[67] *On Liberty*, ch. 2, *in* Mill, [1869] 1991a, p. 21.   [68] Gaus, 2010.
[69] See, e.g., Waldron, 2012a, p. 10.   [70] Weinstein, 2009a, p. 26.
[71] An Introduction to the Principles of Morals and Legislation I:3, *in* Bentham [1789] 2001, p. 88.
[72] Id. I:7, *in* Bentham [1789] 2001, p. 89.
[73] Utilitarianism represents a particular type of consequentialism—or types, given that there are various utilitarian schools. Consequentialism stands more generally for the proposition that goods are measured by their effects, rather than by any inherent qualities or by any principles or intentions that might motivate them. Utilitarianism represents methods for assessing those effects in terms of overall benefits procured in the light of overall costs or risks.

Arguments about the individual or social effects of expression, or of its regulation, have dominated the hate speech debates. As those are considered on their merits in Chapter 5, the aim for now is to consider utilitarianism more generally, simply as an historically influential defence of the proposition that value-pluralist balancing stands as a central and legitimate task of government. Only after first examining a rigorous defence of value-pluralist balancing will we then be able to enquire into its limits—into those areas that guarantee its democratic legitimacy precisely through immunity from it.

In the nineteenth century, Mill would amend those elements of utilitarianism which had been understood to reduce human problems, for balancing purposes, to material and measurable quantities. In *Utilitarianism*, Mill aims to reconcile utility with something unquantifiable, which we today call deontological, and which he describes as 'a sense of dignity, which all human beings possess'.[74] By the mid-twentieth century, we find utilitarian theory still progressing beyond its more materialist, eighteenth-century origins. Even certain higher-order 'rights'—construed as interests not straightforwardly amenable to outright legislative or judicial balancing, hence once blasted by Bentham as 'nonsense upon stilts'[75]—come to be embraced within an emerging 'rule utilitarianism'.[76]

With Rawls's *A Theory of Justice* in 1972, value-pluralist proceduralism certainly maintains a strong role, hence Rawls's overall faith in democratic processes. For Rawls, however, it fails in itself to supply legitimating conditions for democracy as the arena within which the balancing of values occurs.[77] Dworkin's *Taking Rights Seriously*, only a few years later, reaches a similar conclusion. Higher-order 'rights' are, for Dworkin, meaningful only through law's recognition of certain principles as standing at least presumptively above balancing processes, legitimating those processes precisely insofar as they enjoy that higher-order status.[78]

Democratic legitimacy, on Rawls's and Dworkin's views, derives not merely from conformity to prescribed procedures, but also from adherence to substantive norms.[79] Those norms cannot derive their *constitutive* authority solely from the very kinds of balancing procedures which they constitute. It would be incoherent, for example, to maintain that the authors even of a given society's founding constitutional act or document can wholly decide or vote upon what democracy 'is'. Otherwise they could call any constitutional form at all a democracy, emptying the word of all meaning. If the word 'democracy' is not endlessly malleable, any founding constitutional act must already presuppose some notion of what democracy

---

[74] *Utilitarianism*, ch. 2, *in* Mill, [1861] 1991b, p. 140. Cf. Mill at p. 189 (justifying rights on utilitarian grounds).

[75] Anarchical Fallacies (§ Article 2), in Bentham, [1843] 2001, p. 405.

[76] See, e.g., Nathanson, n.d.

[77] See Rawls, 1999, pp. 19–24 (on utilitarianism); and pp. 30–6 (on balancing of interests within schools value-pluralist intuitionism). On optimizing versus legitimating elements of democracy, see Section 4.12.

[78] Dworkin, 1977.

[79] Cf. Farrell, 2006 (rejecting an overly 'thin, procedural conception of democracy' (criticizing Alexander, 2005)).

must necessarily be, even if its authors maintain latitude in determining many of the particulars of their nation's institutional arrangements.[80]

Writers like Dworkin or Rawls challenge, then, the assumption that democratic legitimacy rests entirely upon adherence to duly constituted legislative, adjudicative, or administrative procedures. After all, even the crudest majoritarianism, the 'tyranny of the majority',[81] can supply purely procedural legitimacy.[82] Parallel to the aforementioned split in liberal philosophy, we witness a split in democratic theory. For some writers, adherence to value-pluralist balancing means 'trusting the *democratic* aspect of a liberal democracy'.[83] For theorists like Rawls or Dworkin, by contrast, those processes cannot be entirely self-legitimating. In order to claim legitimacy, balancing processes must respect certain substantive, higher-order norms standing outside and immune from those processes. Those norms set limits to the balancing that can legitimately be thrust upon individual freedoms.

In identifying what Dworkin calls legal 'trumps', he and Rawls do not seek to undermine the integrity of democratic decision-making, nor the value-pluralism that nourishes democracy. They wish only to ground democracy as a sphere within which legislative and judicial balancing can claim a legitimacy greater than the sheer positive law conventionalism of conformity to formally sanctioned procedures. In that necessary effort, they make a big mistake. In order to strengthen democracy, they seek to strengthen liberalism. They root much of that 'greater claim' in higher-order rights. Since the late twentieth century, in an era of centrifugal expansion both of rights and of regulations,[84] Rawls's and Dworkin's rights-based foundations face ever steeper objections as to what count as higher-order interests, and whether those interests can remain as insulated from rival claims—of the type that we find urged within prohibitionism—and from concomitant balancing processes as their liberal theories promise. Dworkin replies only in brief, anecdotal terms to the objection that democracies other than the US, through their hate speech bans, interpret at least some rival claims as trumping the 'right' to free speech on solely viewpoint-selective grounds.[85] Rights, then, are not the solution. They are part of

---

[80] See Section 3.3, text accompanying notes 29–32.

[81] See Section 1.1, text accompanying note 25.

[82] Cf. Carl Schmitt's critique of *Scheinkompromisse*, i.e., formal expressions of compromises of contradictory policies struck more with the effect of postponing than of resolving the substantive incompatibilities. See, e.g., Schmitt, [1928] 1993, pp. 31–6. Schmitt refers to purely 'formal compromises' achieved, e.g., by placing rights alongside their restrictions in conventional constitutional or human rights instruments, not by virtue of having established, but simply by virtue of uncritically assuming that all such conflicts fall indifferently (*unterschiedslos*) within the domain of legislative or judicial balancing.

[83] Bleich, 2011, p. 153 (original emphasis). Cf. Section 3.7.

[84] Cf. preminitorily, e.g., Schmitt, [1928] 1993, p. 163. We could arguably take that observation one step further, although my argument in this book does not require that additional step. We could surmise that as rights expand, their higher-order status dilutes. That ubiquity increasingly demotes human rights to the status of routine statutory, administrative, or judicial rules, with their higher-law claims becoming little more than rhetorical, or only weakly presumptive. If that is the case, then this book may strengthen the cause of re-establishing a limited, but higher-order citizen speech prerogative on democratic, as opposed to rights-based, grounds.

[85] See Section 2.1, text accompanying note 6.

the problem that Rawls and Dworkin had originally sought to redress. Even assuming their presumptive weight, rights end up subsumed within the very balancing processes from which they had demanded some clear immunity.

Recall the wording of UDHR article 19: 'Everyone has the right to freedom of opinion and expression'.[86] It first presents a *right*. It then states that the right protects a *freedom*, namely, the '*freedom* of opinion and expression'. Rawls observes that, in a legal sense, individuals can be said to enjoy the liberty (or freedom) 'to do something' under two conditions: first, 'when they are free from certain constraints to do it or not to do it'; and, second 'when their doing it or not doing it is protected from interference by other persons',[87] including interference by agents or institutions of government.

That two-pronged definition of freedom can be re-phrased. First, to say that individuals enjoy the freedom to do something 'when they are free from *certain* constraints to do it or not to do it' is to say that they enjoy that freedom *to the extent* that they are *free from constraints* to do it or not to do it. Second, they enjoy that freedom *to the extent* that their doing it or not doing it is protected from interference by other persons. Rawls's point is not that a freedom exists only when it is absolute, but that it exists *to the extent* that those two conditions are fulfilled. Freedoms are subject to limits which determine that 'extent'. Those limits establish the degree to which an individual's choice to do or not to do something enjoys legal protection from interference by other individuals or by the state.

How do liberal rights set those limits? In his 1859 essay *On Liberty*, Mill answers with his famous harm principle: 'the only purpose for which power can be rightfully exercised over any member of a civilized community, against his will, is to prevent harm to others'.[88] We can set aside for now the reams of scholarship which have elicited vagaries, contradictions, or shortcomings in that principle, notably surrounding the concept of 'harm' (and any attendant concepts of 'freedoms', 'rights', or 'liberalism').[89] Within the everyday practice of legislatures, courts, and international bodies, the *formal* presence of Mill's principle is manifest. Those institutions routinely reach determinations—however persuasive or unpersuasive we may find them as a *substantive* matter in individual instances—as to harms actually or potentially caused by the exercise of individual freedoms. They do so regardless of the debatable interpretations of 'harm' which they sometimes assume, and which might well pale under more probing critical scrutiny, for example,

---

[86] See Section 3.1, text accompanying note 1.

[87] Rawls, 1999, p. 177. That definition contains a surface circularity, as it employs the concept of being 'free' to define 'liberty'. But that circularity is not structural. It can be overcome if the clause 'when they are free from certain constraints to do it or not to do it' is replaced by a clause such as 'when nothing constrains them to do it or not to do it'. We again see, moreover, that the terms 'freedom' and 'liberty' tend to overlap.

[88] *On Liberty*, ch. 1, *in* Mill, [1869] 1991a, p. 14. Cf. Déclaration des droits de l'homme et du citoyen (1789), art. 4.

[89] Cf., generally, Heinze, 2003, pp. 117–82; Heinze, 2005, pp. 39–60; Heinze, 2012b; Kelly, 2003. Cf., with specific reference to speech, Molnar & Post, 2012, p. 31; Nieuwenhuis, 2011, pp. 28–32.

along philosophical, sociological, or empirical lines. They then proceed, expressly or tacitly, to balance those freedoms against such evaluated risks.

Irrespective of their final assessments' substantive strengths or weaknesses, such weighed and balanced results become adopted via those bodies' sheer institutional authority. Any problems attending a *substantive harm principle*, regarding ultimate determinations about the cause or content of 'harm' in any given instance, give way to what we can call a *procedural harm principle*. Government determinations of harm come to be accepted through its various institutions' established powers, which always remain subject—or so it is traditionally explained—to democratic controls and revisions. Whatever Mill's vague concept of 'harm' may lack, the authority of democratic processes is supposed to supply. Our familiar catalogues of human rights enumerate norms in bare-bones language, with or without correlative restrictions, of the types set forth in the various ICCPR or ECHR limitations clauses. A liberal rights *regime* must therefore encompass the totality of norms and processes by which empowered bodies balance rights against restrictions.

Mill introduces his harm principle (as liberal philosophers from Locke and Kant through to Rawls and Dworkin, as well as modern human rights corpuses, often introduce such principles)[90] as a tool for resolving certain controversies on 'transcendental' premises, which claim some universal or foundational validity, beyond the machinations of partisan politics. There is some irony, then, in the shift from substantive to procedural means of identifying harm within value-pluralist proceduralism, i.e., the shift from a substantive to a procedural harm principle. Once determinations about harm flow from government balancing, that claim of transcendence *over* balancing processes dissolves back into them.

Hate speech reveals the problems of anchoring the citizen's prerogative of expression within a liberal right. Instead of balancing speakers' *interests* against the concerns of vulnerable groups, legislatures and courts balance speakers' *rights*, their *presumptive interests*, against those concerns. Public discourse ends up being protected solely by such a right. It fails to supply a norm constitutive of, and thereby itself legitimating, value-pluralist balancing processes. That failure emerges through a bevy of comparative studies undertaken across Western democracies.[91] Such works reveal the divergent, scarcely reconcilable interpretations applied to otherwise similar democratic principles within conventional liberal rights frameworks. Their authors devote several hundred pages to reaching the only conclusion that could ever be possible from the purely tautological limiting principle that demands nothing more than 'Freedoms must have some limits', even assuming the application of that principle 'carefully', 'responsibly', 'with great care', and in a 'decidedly liberal' way.[92]

---

[90] See Section 6.2.

[91] See, e.g., Josende, 2010; Nieuwenhuis, 2011; Noorloos, 2012; Pech, 2003; Robitaille-Froidure, 2011. As those studies contain a strong focus on European jurisdictions, the indeterminate or contradictory results they uncover stem not merely from national law, but also from international and European sources of law.

[92] See Section 3.2, text accompanying notes 16–24.

Despite their wealth of insightful analysis, the studies all (a) begin by assuming value-pluralist proceduralism, i.e., by assuming that each democracy may *in principle* balance free expression against rival interests, as long as it generally respects prescribed democratic and constitutional norms and procedures. They then (b) observe that each democracy does *in fact* balance free expression against rival interests, by generally respecting prescribed democratic and constitutional norms and procedures. Hence the inescapable 'conclusion' that (c) each democracy *can legitimately* balance free expression against rival interests, by generally respecting prescribed democratic and constitutional norms and procedures.[93] Seemingly questionable laws or cases are cast, as Parekh casts them, as the usual aberrations and imprecisions that are inevitable in law.

References to history and culture are invariably invoked to explain discrepancies not only across but even within various jurisdictions. Given that most Western democracies have known histories of freedom as well as histories of conflict, both factors can be cited to justify any result, thereby robbing both historical narratives of the authority they are meant to provide. British lawmakers or judges, for example, can cite a British history or culture of free speech to favour permitting a particular offensive statement, while their Dutch counterparts may invoke a Dutch history or culture of social conflict to penalize a similar statement.[94] Yet those British officials could just as readily locate a British history or culture of social conflict, which would justify penalizing the statement, while the Dutch officials might just as easily locate a Dutch history or culture of free speech which would allow it. Similarly, German officials might cite their Nazi past in order to ward off the dangers of hate speech, yet can just as plausibly cite that same past to ward off the dangers of state control over speech.[95] We can translate such pervasively equivocal results into the language of the procedural harm principle, which displays the impasses of conventional liberal, rights-based approaches. The harm of hate speech

---

[93] As an exceptional example of value-pluralist proceduralism within comparative legal theory, Lauriane Josende's *Liberté d'expression et démocratie: Réflexion sur un paradoxe*, lifts the tension between permitting and restricting speech from the sphere of routine balancing to philosophically rigorous ground. Josende structures her enquiry around the paradox of democratically enacted restraints on democratic public discourse, rather than, as many jurists have done, uncritically deeming such restraints to be justified solely by virtue of their origin in democratically established processes of legislation or adjudication. See Josende, 2010, pp. 11–15. Cf., e.g., Post, 1995, pp. 8, 147–8. Josende draws a problematical inference, however, from the correct premise that democratic forums must presumptively host anti-democratic speech, to the proceduralist conclusion that democracies legitimately overcome that presumption, and thereby resolve the dilemma by restricting public discourse through their balancing processes. Josende rightly elicits the paradox of the premise, then, but errs in assigning any such normative necessity or institutional inevitability to her conclusion. The error arises in part from assuming a positivist distinction between the 'philosophical' and the 'juridical' elements of the problem (See, e.g., Josende, 2010, p. 13) as two 'contradictory logics' (Josende, 2010, p. 414, and generally pp. 411–16). Once democratic legitimacy offers a normative criterion for assessing law, positive law reference to the 'juridical' only begs the question, which I am examining in this book, as to whether either legislatures or courts are adequately respecting the necessary elements of democratic citizenship.

[94] Cf., e.g., the comparative discussions in Noorloos, 2012.

[95] On similarly spurious deployments of history, see Section 5.7, text accompanying notes 194–8. See also, generally, Section 5.2.

is deemed sufficient to justify a ban when construed with reference to a history of injustice; yet that harm is just as plausibly deemed insufficient when construed with reference to a history of free speech. We witness Gaus's observation of the internal contradictions within liberalism entirely mirrored in such jurisprudence.

The present question is not the perennial one as to whether law becomes illegitimate through inconsistent or indeterminate interpretations. To the contrary, like Parekh, those comparative scholars rightly join an age-old tradition in observing that law is complex and textured. Law often reflects human fluidity and fallibility more than it reflects systemic coherence.[96] Our question still remains: are there any circumstances that demand an exception to the general rule, i.e., an exception to that rule of normative and institutional flexibility which is invoked to justify value-pluralist balancing processes? With reference to the problem of hate speech, that question can be phrased, from a liberal and rights-based standpoint, in terms of the substantive harm principle: are there any circumstances under which hate speech can never legitimately be said to cause a harm sufficient to justify bans on it? It can likewise be phrased in terms of the procedural harm principle: are there any circumstances under which hate speech can never legitimately be deemed, by those duly empowered to make such assessments, to cause a harm sufficient to justify bans on it?

Those liberal formulations do not, however, mean that the problem is best resolved on liberal, rights-based principles. Assume that we can identify circumstances under which hate speech cannot legitimately be judged—either substantively, in material terms; or procedurally, through institutional authority—to cause a harm sufficient to justify bans on it. Those circumstances must, then, necessarily be governed by principles other than the traditionally liberal ones, which must always admit the possibility of such harm. Such principles must stand as conceptually prior to those liberal ones such that they preclude, from the outset, any finding of a harm that can be deemed sufficient to justify viewpoint-selective bans imposed within democratic public discourse.

That is where democracy enters, as it is now worthwhile re-phrasing those two Millian questions in a third, non-Millian way: Are there any circumstances under which principles other than conventionally liberal ones must resolve the hate speech controversy? If it turns out to be democracy itself which offers such circumstances, then the question now becomes: when, if ever, must democratic principles categorically override—or even *within* liberalism's own rights-based frameworks, must always conclusively decide—that standard liberal calculus which would otherwise have to balance *rights* of speech against determinations as to the risks or harms of that speech?

Rawls's and Dworkin's attempts to ground the legitimacy of balancing processes within higher-order principles immune from those processes are correct, despite the failure of ('human', 'constitutional', etc.) rights to supply such principles. My aim is not to amend their theories root-and-branch, but only to renew the attempt

---

[96] Cf. Section 3.2, text accompanying note 27.

to identify elements that legitimate democratic processes precisely because they do not issue from those processes. That will be the task of Chapter 4.

3.7 Value Pluralism and Empirical Social Science

Value-pluralist proceduralism finds support not only within various strands of legal reasoning along Parekh's lines, or of liberal philosophy along Waldron's lines, but also within empirical political science. In a study entitled *The Freedom to be Racist?*, the political scientist Erik Bleich, albeit through a different method, ends up adopting a procedural prohibitionism similar to those of the aforementioned comparative scholars.

Bleich argues that several democracies, such as Austria, Canada, France, or Germany, have successfully implemented their hate speech bans without having 'trampled upon liberal rights'.[97] For Bleich, those countries maintain democratic legitimacy by ensuring that 'multiple perspectives have been articulated and factored in to the process',[98] and that the social and political 'trade-offs are fully recognized and openly debated'.[99] Through hate speech bans, several democracies, with ample popular approval, therefore seem to vindicate essential values of human dignity.

Bleich's method is more rigorously consequentialist. He certainly recognizes deontological rationales within both prohibitionism and oppositionism. But he does not resolve the problem through any dialectic of transcendent ethical, legal, or political axioms. He does not ask whether viewpoint-selective bans within public discourse are admissible or inadmissible in principle. He instead pursues the hypothesis-formulating, hypothesis-testing, and hypothesis-confirming method of empirical social science as follows.

First, from the outset, and again like the legal-comparativists, he bypasses those thickets of dialectical reason through a *prima facie* presumption of value-pluralist proceduralism. His strategy is to treat that presumption as sound as long as subsequent empirical study can conclude that the balancing processes which weigh up the competing interests do not produce results that would endanger essential democratic institutions and practices. Second, his empirical survey is then introduced to *confirm* that value-pluralist balancing has indeed eschewed any such abuses. For Bleich the empirical political scientist, as for Parekh the common lawyer, or Waldron the liberal theorist, hate speech bans implemented under normal democratic controls have not generally led to such extremes as excessive censorship, overly harsh punishments, or sweeping incursions into civil liberties. Third, given that very high threshold criterion—nothing less than serious damage to democratic institutions or practices—it comes as no surprise that the analysis

---

[97] Bleich, 2011, p. 153.
[98] Bleich, 2011, p. 152. Cf. p. 153 (discussing democratic and republican deliberation theories).
[99] Bleich, 2011, p. 5.

would end up with a conclusion affirming the original hypothesis of the legitimacy of value-pluralist balancing, again strikingly similar to the methods and conclusions of the comparative legal writers. After all, no leading oppositionists reproach bans for causing that kind of grave damage. Their criticisms are of an altogether different order. They object to bans through precisely that deontological dialectic of democratic principle that Bleich's empirical method is constructed to avoid.

Bleich delivers, then, an empirically validated model of a fundamentally self-legitimating democratic process, as adopted also by the comparative scholars. As long as no grave abuses can be demonstrated, that approach must inevitably end up ratifying value-pluralist proceduralism. Its consequentialist criteria are curbed only by the extreme deontological criterion of 'serious abuse'. That criterion certainly does admit a few minimally fixed requirements of democratic norms or institutions. Because no abuse of them has been detected, however, they are not examined in detail. Since the starting point never emerges as the product of a normative, i.e., deontological dialectic about democratic legitimacy, but is rather adopted to avoid that dialectic, it finds its justification in the consequentialist rationale of locating insufficient abuse in practice.

Leading oppositionists have never waged the contrary consequentialist claim (although they do counter some consequentialist prohibitionisms with contrary consequentialist arguments),[100] because their core claim about democratic legitimacy is not the sheer product of consequentialist reasoning. They do not object to viewpoint-selective bans on grounds of gross damage to democracy. Together with Rawls or Dworkin, they criticize proceduralism as a matter of principle, as a matter of fundamental legitimacy, and not because only severe harm caused to democracy would challenge proceduralist assumptions.

But why get hung up on principles and dialectics, if, as Bleich and the comparativists rightly observe, no serious abuses arise? What more legitimacy do we need? All manner of aberrations may be illegitimate in principle without grievously endangering democracy in practice. On a strictly consequentialist rationale, for example, forging one or two ballot papers, among tens of millions, leaves a democracy effectively untainted if, as will invariably be the case, it bears no immediate impact upon an electoral outcome. As a matter of democratic principle, however, there is no imaginable sense in which even the most trivial voter fraud thereby becomes *legitimate*. (In Kantian terms, at least if we assume democracy, the injunction against voter fraud becomes categorical, a postulate of sheer reason, and not merely an evil if it can be traced to some empirically demonstrable harm. This book's remaining task is to determine circumstances under which the citizen prerogative of expression within public discourse, at least on that assumption of democracy, may claim the same categorical status.) I shall henceforth reject, then, Parekh's, Bleich's, and other consequentialist assumptions that lack of overall abuse in practice suffices to establish the democratic legitimacy of viewpoint-punitive penalties within public discourse.

---

[100] See Section 5.5.

Like Parekh's more traditionally juridical reasonableness criterion, the empirical approach retains the seductive appeal of dodging thorny philosophical debates through its initial—attractive and, under the reigning dictatorship of empiricism within political science, seemingly self-evident—presumption of value-pluralist proceduralism, hence a presumption of self-legitimating democratic process confirmed by the relatively remote danger of severe abuse. That is always the appeal of empiricism, namely, the appearance of an objective, neutral, fact-driven basis for superseding controversial, normative dialectics about founding principles. But such empiricism in social science is not normatively neutral. (Nor indeed does Bleich suggest otherwise. He expressly presents his project as a quest to assess the relative merits of various approaches with an eye towards informing future policy.)

In seeking to bypass that necessary normative dialectic, both the empirical and the traditionally lawyerly foundations for value-pluralist proceduralism end up in a vicious circle. By setting the mere criterion of gross abuse as the normative outer limit, they necessarily assume *some* distinction between respect for and abuse of democracy. That distinction, in turn, assumes its authors' own normative criterion, namely, the criterion of serious abuse—no excessive censorship, no excessively harsh sentences, etc. Yet how are we to know that *those* are the only normative assumptions about regulating speech that we ought to make? How are we to know whether democracy also requires any further legitimating expressive conditions, since that is precisely the question which the empirical or the lawyerly reasonableness models end up skipping? Insofar as both the empirical and the traditionally lawyerly approaches eschew a normative dialectic that would put to the test their model's assumed criteria governing respect for or abuse of democratic process, they end up circular, i.e., self-constituting and self-affirming as to the specific status of viewpoint-selective penalties imposed within public discourse.

4

Democracy and Citizenship

Alexander Meiklejohn calls free speech within public discourse 'a deduction' from core democratic principles.[1] Hans Kelsen maintains that '[a] democracy without public opinion is a contradiction in terms'.[2] The Australian High Court has found a constitutionally protected freedom of speech to be 'implied', even if not expressly stated, in a democratic constitution.[3] According to Ulrich Preuß, 'the police-like repression of dangerous ideas' can 'scarcely be reconciled with the self-conception (*Selbstverständnis*) of a liberal democracy'.[4] The citizen's prerogative of expression in public discourse stands, for Lauriane Josende, as an 'ontological principle of democratic organisation'.[5] We have seen that the dominant liberal and rights-based doctrines, rooted in value pluralism, can be cited just as plausibly to oppose or to support speech bans. But democratic values are equally broad. They boast that same pluralism. Wouldn't they line up just as readily behind either position? The aim of this chapter is to examine a more concrete model of democracy than the abstractly universalized ones that both prohibitionists and oppositionists often assume. That model must be grasped within history, and not merely at the level of formal constitutional law.

4.1 Longstanding, Stable, and Prosperous Democracy (LSPD)

The weekly periodical the *Economist* publishes an annual *Democracy Index* to evaluate levels of democracy throughout the world.[6] Such a project might certainly be challenged with regard to that publication's traditional political stances, or to the project's broader philosophical assumptions or particular applications.[7] But it does

---

[1] Meiklejohn, 1948, p. 27. [2] Kelsen, [1949] 2005, p. 288.
[3] See *Australian Capital Television v. Commonwealth* (1992) 177 CLR 106.
[4] Preuß, 2002, p. 112. [5] Josende, 2010, p. 1.
[6] See, e.g., Economist Intelligence Unit, 2013. For periodically updated individual state reports, see http://www.eiu.com/. Other organizations also issue annual or periodic reports relevant to democratic operations. See, e.g., Reporters Without Borders (n.d.); Transparency International (n.d.) Studies placing greater stress on social and economic progress offer useful comparators, although they do not purport to focus specifically on democratic culture or institutions. See, e.g., Social Progress Imperative, 2015.
[7] The leading positions of Northern European social democracies, not only in 2013 but in other years, nevertheless undermines any suspicion that the *Economist* would be assuming excessively de-regulatory criteria. While the particular indices applied by the report are broadly compatible with those of, e.g., Gilens & Page (2014), those authors' findings challenge the *Economist*'s qualification of the US as a top-tier democracy, in view of the powers of wealthy elites. Conversely, the *Economist*'s

sketch the kinds of factors that commonly inform decision-makers' evaluations as to any given democracy's norms, institutions, and practices. It points towards what I shall call the model of the *longstanding, stable, and prosperous democracy* (LSPD). Tracing back no further than the 1960s, the LSPD is an historically recent political form.[8] As I am arguing, the citizen's prerogative of non-viewpoint-punitive expression in public discourse must stand outside value-pluralist proceduralism, being itself one of the latter's legitimating criteria. However, many democracies cannot fulfil all criteria of political legitimacy at all times in their histories. Some are newly emerging, or face foreign aggression or internal conflict. Societies unable to fulfil certain legitimating criteria may be democracies, but cannot count as LSPDs.

In the 2013 *Democracy Index* report, only twenty-five states rate as 'full democracies', similar to what I am calling LSPDs, according to such indicia as: 'electoral process', 'functioning of government', 'political participation', 'political culture', and 'civil liberties'. Those criteria included *respect* for human rights, but, like the LSPD model, without assuming rights as the defining basis of democratic legitimacy. Ranked starting from the highest scores, they are: Norway, Sweden, Iceland, Denmark, New Zealand, Australia, Switzerland, Canada, Finland, Luxembourg, the Netherlands, Ireland, Austria, the United Kingdom, Germany, Malta, Uruguay, Mauritius, the USA, Japan, the Czech Republic, South Korea, Belgium, Costa Rica, and Spain. To classify such states as LSPDs is to suggest that they maintain sufficient legal, institutional, educational, and material resources to admit all viewpoints into public discourse, yet remain adequately equipped to protect vulnerable groups from violence or discrimination. The number of LSPDs may be small, but is not so marginal as to render the model utopian for purposes of identifying a plausible sense of democracy's legitimating expressive conditions.

---

exclusion of France from the topmost category, due largely to a surge of the far-right *Front National* during the period covered (although France does appear there in other years) may raise further questions as to the application of democratic indicators in particular cases. Over a course of years, some states may tend to migrate back and forth between the bottom of the top tier and the top of the second tier.

[8] See Section 6.1. One might push the point further by arguing that democracy in its modern sense does not really begin at all until that time. It could be maintained that modern Western European history shifted in the first instance from feudal, aristocratic, and monarchical regimes into hybrid societies blending a bourgeoning liberalism with residual hierarchies, even while invoking democratic values and instituting electoral and parliamentary constitutions. That 'partial', 'embryonic', or 'gestating' pre-LSPD form of democracy arguably better explains exclusions on grounds of class, ethnicity, or sex. Our ongoing tendency to collapse democratic values into liberal ones can be explained as our failure to appreciate the historical transition, beginning only after the Second World War, from those admixtures of liberalism and hierarchy into steadily yet distinctly democratic expectations, even despite certain concurrent de-democratizations within modern post-industrial, administrative states. We commonly acknowledge momentous cultural changes occurring in the second half of the twentieth century, but rarely explain them as products of a specific transition from that earlier hybrid of liberalism and hierarchy, i.e., from quasi-democracy, into an expectation of full-fledged democracy, not least because liberalism by no means displaces democracy within the LSPD. It continues to flourish, even as the hierarchies within which it had emerged become more fluid. Perhaps a patriotic nostalgia assigns modern democracy an older age than it deserves. Cf. Section 5.2.

The model indicates that, as a matter of social and civic awareness, plurality of opinion is, in LSPDs, robust enough to enable counter-speech[9] and scrutiny of hate speakers and groups. That is why prohibitionists have failed[10] to substantiate the kinds of empirical links from speech to violence or to discrimination that can more easily be adduced within non-LSPDs. Hans-Gerd Jaschke enumerates no fewer than seven contributing factors now relevant to Western democracies, each highly complex, suggesting only limited possibilities for a distinctly causal distillation of the role of hate speech.[11]

The category 'non-LSPD', assumes no further commonality among the states concerned, which may include states well on their way to strong, pluralist democracy as well as brutal dictatorships. That variety of non-LSPDs emerges in the *Democracy Index*'s remaining tiers. The *Index* describes the second, larger tier of states as 'flawed democracies'. Many of the country assessments under that heading confirm them as democracies, yet as non-LSPDs. Such democracies may lack adequate resources to assure protection for vulnerable groups. Hate speech bans *may* be appropriate—again never as democratizing but, where appropriate, as security measures—as those states cannot always be expected to fulfil the totality of their legitimating conditions as easily as LSPDs. Individuals living within LSPDs can readily gain an impression of ordinary criminal law and national security as distinct spheres. Under circumstances of instability and unrest, that distinction blurs. For a society otherwise committed to pluralist democracy, protecting the vulnerable remains as vital a security interest as protecting the population generally.

The third tranche encompasses 'hybrid' states, including non-LSPDs with limited and deeply defective democratic processes. The fourth covers 'authoritarian' states, which are, at most, democratic in name only. To be sure, hate speech bans become democratically meaningful only against a weighty presumption of free speech. For those third- and fourth-tier states, bans become shams as to their intentions or significance, as they form no serious rebuttal to any such presumption. Even for non-LSPDs—that is, the states falling short of the top tier—it is by no means clear that hate speech bans are always justified. Non-LSPDs are known to abuse bans, enforcing them *against* vulnerable groups to silence opposition to the dominant powers or social groups.[12] The non-LSPD nevertheless stands as a political entity for which hate speech bans may be justified, given the legitimate security concern of protecting vulnerable groups.

For an LSPD, inability to fulfil such criteria would arise only within the security-driven contexts of states of emergency scenarios.[13] Under those

---

[9] See Section 4.11, text accompanying notes 161–2.   [10] See Sections 5.1–5.3.
[11] See Jaschke, 2006, pp. 9–12.   [12] See Section 6.1, text accompanying notes 41–5.
[13] That national security and emergency power, and scepticism about controls over it, has bred famous doubts about the legitimacy claims of liberal democracies. Schmitt endeavours to undermine assumptions of popular sovereignty by reducing the sovereign function to whichever individual or agency monopolizes the power to call a state of emergency (Schmitt, [1922] 2009, p. 13), and thereby to suspend the democratic constitution. That problem need not be settled for present purposes. Democracy being postulated here only as a hypothetical, and not as a categorical imperative (see

circumstances, in which all sorts of liberal, rights-based as well as democratic foundations—in other words, all sorts of politically legitimating criteria—may be at least partly suspended, an LSPD might show persuasive reasons for imposing hate speech bans as expressly extraordinary security measures. To suspend an LSPD's legitimating criteria is to declare that, to the extent of the suspension, a state stops *being* an LSPD. For either entity, be it a non-LSPD or an LSPD invoking emergency powers, this book's central point is that viewpoint-punitive penalties imposed within public discourse must always be acknowledged as categorical flaws within democratic processes. Viewpoint-punitive bans must never be understood in the way that international and European norms and many experts currently present them: they must never be understood as necessary or desirable enhancements of democracy, as 'less democracy for the sake of more democracy', except again in the truistic sense that a democracy, like any state, lays claim to security interests.

The distinction between LSPDs and non-LSPDs owes to the LSPD representing an historically distinct form of society. Hatred and its expression by no means disappear. But a sufficiently (which does not mean 'fully', as that would be a more elusive idea) democratized society turns hate speech into a different type of phenomenon. Prejudice continues to work its way through society, but in tandem with multilateral counter-forces, both official and informal, which can be more effectively harnessed against hatred without the state needing to diminish citizens' speech prerogatives within public discourse. The LSPD model assumes a range of factors, both material and cultural, indicating a democracy's ability to protect vulnerable groups without having to impose viewpoint-selective penalties within public discourse. It draws upon evidence about the comparative effects of hate speech within various types of societies in ways that independently confirm social differences between LSPDs and non-LSPDs, beyond sheer black-letter norms governing hate speech.[14]

With those preliminary accounts of the LSPD in mind, we can now examine its components. The term *longstanding* denotes a society functioning democratically not merely because it has adopted an 'on paper' constitution, or because its citizens drop an occasional ballot in a box, or because it contains nominally parliamentary, representative, or consultative institutions. It is a society in which a large portion of the population has been educated over time with attitudes of social and political pluralism. Those attitudes include expectations that citizens possess prerogatives of autonomous and effective civic participation, and of individual legal protections.

The term 'longstanding' is as much qualitative as quantitative. It denotes no fixed period of time, but rather an era during which norms, practices, and expectations of democratic citizenship penetrate a substantial portion of the population. An LSPD is founded not just on democratic rules, but on a democratic culture. Such education becomes nurtured progressively, from the youngest ages. Since the Second World War, it has been honed through anti-discrimination policies in

---

Section 3.4, text accompanying note 50), the possibility of genuine democracy is assumed from the outset. It is not a premise to be independently established for present purposes.

[14] See Sections 5.1–5.3.

education, employment, and the delivery of goods and services. That remains an ongoing state duty. It includes the efforts of state institutions, which, far from being 'value neutral', maintain, through anti-discrimination regimes, enforceable policies of civic and social pluralism, beyond purely ritual or opportunistic lip service (and notwithstanding utopian libertarian visions of such populations emerging spontaneously, free of any but minimal state presence—utopian at least in the sense that such aspirations lack any historical precedent or sociological self-evidence). Far from assuming neutral or libertarian government, advances in these areas have been achieved in Western democracies through massive state intervention.[15]

By *stable*, I refer to a democracy able to police itself, according to independently (e.g., judicially) reviewable criteria. Acts of violence or discrimination against vulnerable groups or persons can then be reliably combated, and victims of hate crime protected, without the state having to impose viewpoint-selective penalties within public discourse. Those alternatives include, for example, safety for vulnerable individuals during such public events as political demonstrations,[16] as well as non-viewpoint-punitive 'time, manner, and place' regulations on speech imposed equally on all speakers.

By *prosperous*, I refer not to a society that has eliminated all political, economic, or social inequities, but to one sufficiently wealthy to assure adequate measures against violence and discrimination, as well as means of combating intolerance and protecting vulnerable individuals. Such practices mean, for example, that controversial political or cultural events can proceed, with speakers, audiences, and dissenters alike protected from violence. That concept of 'prosperity' assumes no judgement about the means by which wealth has accumulated (although such a judgement informs the enquiry into other problems of political legitimacy). Crises of legitimacy have, since ancient Athens, arisen from democracies' capacities to generate wealth, often entailing widespread exploitation and other social imbalances and conflicts. It is an old paradox that we expect even wealth unjustly gained to fund, in part, our civic and social supports. For example, even a company involved in political corruption or in exploitation of labour or resources, either at home or abroad, we would expect to pay at least some level of its domestic taxes, with any further breaches of law or professional ethics treated as a separate matter.

To illustrate the point, assume a large crowd of protesters against global capitalism in Sweden. The demonstrators may advocate the outright elimination of neo-liberal economic and political arrangements; but, as a matter of modern democratic principle, such participants can expect the state—and national law legitimately requires the state—to draw upon its treasury, funded largely through capitalist enterprise, to provide such guarantees as a police force trained in methods of non-violent crowd management; arrestees' individual opportunities to receive competent, state-appointed legal counsel; appropriately managed judicial procedures; adequate appeal and review procedures; humanely and hygienically

---

[15] See Section 4.11.

[16] See, e.g., *Plattform 'Ärtze für das Leben' v. Austria*, Judgment of 21 June 1988, Eur Ct Human Rights, Ser. A, vol. 139, § 32. Cf. *Feiner v. New York*, 240 U.S. 315, 326–27 (1951) (Black, J., dissenting). Cf., e.g., Ash, 2015 (distinguishing between violent and non-violent expression).

maintained detention facilities, including reasonable accommodations of special needs; and other such services.

Those guarantees add up to a sizeable public cost. That is one reason why old distinctions between, on the one hand, 'cheap' civil and political rights, and, on the other hand, 'expensive' social and economic rights have long been challenged, rendering Isaiah Berlin's well-known distinctions between 'negative' and 'positive' concepts of liberty blurrier than is often thought.[17] Traditional civil liberties remain purely formal without those extensive protections, which render them effective by supplying an entire, expensive background machinery of law.

Some might argue that our democracies, or 'post-democracies',[18] propagate mythologies of 'stability' or 'prosperity', goods enjoyed by the well-off, while unleashing socio-economic de-stabilization and impoverishment upon the disempowered, both at home and abroad, and which can in turn trigger resentment, along with the very forms of intolerance at issue in the hate speech debates. It might then further be argued that hate speech bans become necessary responses to democracies' failures. Yet no such conclusion follows either in theory,[19] or in terms of practical remedies for intolerance. In his tract *Rien n'est sacré, tout peut se dire* (*Nothing is sacred, everything can be spoken*), Vaneigem, as part of his decades-old challenges to prevailing neo-liberal policies, and in a vein otherwise rooted in vintage Francophone leftism, nonetheless rejects viewpoint-punitive bans within public discourse. Vaneigem wants us to overcome what he portrays as the illusory freedoms of late capitalist societies, which generate cultural commodification and homogenization.[20] There may be endless problems with liberal, market-driven societies; but, for Vaneigem, the citizen's chance to speak is not one of them. He casts such participation as a weapon against capitalism's excesses, a weapon he deems most effective within a culture in which it is assumed no views are barred.

Post makes the same point within a conventionally liberal framework. The debilitating effects on public discourse of 'overpowering corporations, media moguls, and gaping class divisions'[21] neither justify, nor are they defeated by laws designed to 'excise speaker autonomy'.[22] As Vaneigem's Foucauldian insights suggest, views

---

[17] Berlin, 1969, pp. 121–31. To be sure, Berlin's critique of positive rights does not focus primarily on their cost. Discussions about the distinction do nevertheless often characterize 'negative' rights as sheer abstentions, and therefore effectively cost-free.

[18] Cf. Section 2.4, text accompanying note 40.   [19] See generally, e.g., Post, 1996–97.

[20] Vaneigem, 2003. Although Vaneigem does not frame that point in broader historical terms, it is of older lineage. Following similar ideas in Rousseau and Hegel, Marx famously critiques a fatal tension between the individual as a *bourgeois* and as a *citoyen*. That clash mirrors a tension between the individual as a liberal and the individual as a democrat. As a liberal or *bourgeois*, a person enjoys freedom to pursue purely private interest, irrespective of that collective good with which the democrat or *citoyen* is charged. Public and private good then come into a conflict reflected within the divided self, split between opposing loyalties. In that sense, Vaneigem joins a tradition concerned that our societies are heading so far down the path of liberal rights as to neglect democracy, under the misapprehension that, as long as we secure individual rights, democracy will take care of itself.

[21] Post, 1996–97, p. 1527 (discussing Fiss). Cf. Sunstein, 1995, p. 17.

[22] Post, 1996–97, p. 1528, cf. at p. 1533.

about the diluted quality of modern citizenship, far from diminishing, more urgently press the question about our attitude of either resistance or capitulation towards ever-weakening citizenship.[23] In societies where we risk becoming 'just a number', problems arising from the exercise of citizenship can and should be met by a number of means other than viewpoint-punitive attenuations of citizenship within the public sphere.

Opposition to bans, as is being argued, need not perforce fall under the heading of classical liberalism; conversely, on the pro-ban side, advocates of viewpoint-based speech bans throughout history have, overall, rarely been political progressives. Viewpoint-selective penalties have overwhelmingly been imposed to stifle, not to promote critical thought.[24] Marx's rejection of Prussian censorship[25] admittedly targets, in part, a rejection of private monopolies on the press; and Marx certainly insists on the tendency of oppressive ideas to mirror the injustice of the prevailing political order. However, he by no means identifies the expression of particular viewpoints per se as dangerous. As Vaneigem would later do, Marx sees the suppression of injustice lying elsewhere than in the outright stifling of unjust expression on grounds of its viewpoint.

From the standpoint of a substantive harm principle, routine personal injury or breach of contract can be identified as causes immediately traceable to damaging effects. Within non-LSPDs, hate speech may, depending on the place and time, pose a similar type of problem, as an evil provoking some of history's worst atrocities. Within LSPDs, by contrast, asserted links from hate speech to broader abuses such as violence or discrimination have, over decades, lacked any reliable support,[26] reflecting LSPDs' different political and social dynamics.

Some febrile theorizing has taken place to confront that anomaly of a noxious cause which, within LSPDs, lacks any statistically confirmed link to a damaging effect. Such projects include phenomenological, socio-linguistic, or deconstructionist attempts to bypass questions about material causation by depicting hate speech as its own harmful effect. Those approaches often claim to challenge standard liberal approaches, such as the harm principle's recipe of limiting a freedom by identifying a harm that it causes. The Millian approach frustrates even mainstream experts and lawmakers when an undeniably revolting cause traces to no confirmed or predictable effect. Yet those supposedly alternative theories, far from overthrowing the standard liberal view, emphatically re-affirm it. They may indeed identify alternative starting points, by challenging liberal, 'sticks and stones' assumptions about the speaker's peremptory autonomy. But they in no way overturn the core liberal project of delineating concepts of freedom with reference to limiting concepts of harm. Instead, they merely end up doing what their run-of-the-mill liberal nemeses do: when dissatisfied with one account of the freedom–harm relationship, they propose another, i.e., an alternative schema about what freedom and harm 'really' are.[27]

---

[23] Cf. Josende, 2010, p. 11; Post, 1995, pp. 278–9, 282–6.
[24] See, e.g., Hare, 2009b; Rohrßen, 2009.   [25] Cf. this book's epigraph.
[26] See Section 5.1.   [27] See Section 5.3.

The lack of causal evidence linking expression to violence or discrimination is not accidental. It reflects LSPDs' historically distinct social dynamics. Empirical evidence of harms that manifestly cannot be countered without viewpoint-selective bans would not provide an 'exception' or a 'limiting case' to the LSPD model. As the LSPD is being defined here, such evidence would instead show that one or more LSPD criteria have at least provisionally failed, i.e., that the society, even if only temporarily, is not an LSPD at all, or, as was the case of Britain as to Northern Ireland over many decades, is not one with respect to all of its territory. Such a situation can arise if an LSPD is unexpectedly hit by outbreaks of social conflict plausibly linking to factors of discrimination or intolerance.

Within liberalism's standard rights jurisprudence, balancing between, on the one hand, deontological matters of principle and, on the other hand, consequentialist, empirically determined elements of harm has become routine. For a distinctly democratic model, by contrast, empirical factors enter only the threshold determination of any given democracy's qualification as an LSPD through its capacity to fulfil its legitimating conditions. Hence this book's assumption that it is entirely coherent within moral reasoning to make two assertions. First, under some empirically determinate conditions (a society not achieving or not maintaining LSPD conditions) factors may justify viewpoint-punitive bans on public discourse, on the legitimate security grounds of protecting the vulnerable. Second, under contrary, empirically determinate conditions (a society achieving and maintaining LSPD conditions), factors no longer legitimately justify such a finding. That second scenario arises not only (a) because of lack of causal evidence reliably linking hate speech within LSPDs to further harms, but also (b) because, as will be noted in Section 5.5, some evidence works in the opposite direction, suggesting that, within LSPDs, bans serve to aggravate rather than ameliorate hateful expression. In a nutshell, empirical factors may well establish the legitimacy of bans, on *security* grounds, for non-LSPDs; however, for societies that fulfil the threefold empirical criteria of being longstanding, stable and prosperous, it is deontological criteria which then become dispositive of *democratic* legitimacy.

Although fulfilment or failure of at least some LSPD criteria (such as availability of resources to protect targets of hatred without requiring viewpoint-selective bans) draws equally upon *threshold* empirical determinations, central to the LSPD model is the principle that, once its criteria are fulfilled, i.e., *within* the LSPD framework, no empirical criteria can play any such limiting role. Recall the UN Human Rights Committee's view that 'the exercise' of the 'right of freedom of expression … carries with it special duties and responsibilities',[28] insofar as those 'duties and responsibilities' are assumed to have legally binding effect. On the Committee's own rights-balancing criteria, that requirement can correspond only to 'duties and responsibilities' *not* to cause some legally cognizable harm sufficiently grave to justify abridgement of the right, and to be determined either on a substantive or a procedural harm principle. Such a limit may indeed apply straightforwardly to some

---

[28] See Section 3.1, text accompanying note 8.

non-LSPDs. Within an LSPD, by contrast, it would be a contradiction in terms to assume that any exercise of the citizen prerogative of non-viewpoint-punitive expression within public discourse *could* cause any legally cognizable harm sufficiently grave to justify abridgement of that prerogative.

Again, the LSPD model does not preclude a legitimate domain of non-viewpoint-punitive regulation of public discourse. Notwithstanding the illegitimacy of viewpoint-selective balancing within public discourse, a broad range of expressive activities legitimately remain within the ambit of routine government balancing. For non-viewpoint-punitive regulations, Bleich's recommendations of testing for overall abuse of democratic norms and institutions are entirely sound. Non-viewpoint-punitive regulations reflect the legitimate balancing of freedoms against restrictions within conventional, procedurally Millian, rights-based frameworks. Holmes's 'fire' scenario, then, merely dramatizes Mill's harm principle in the patently uncontroversial, non-viewpoint-punitive context of manifest risk to health and safety.

By definition, as was noted in Section 3.2, no legal freedom can be absolute. The veneer of absoluteness emerges only when non-absoluteness is incorporated *ab initio* into a given interest's verbal formulation. While the citizen prerogative of participation within public discourse engenders an expressive freedom, that freedom too, *as a freedom*, is not absolute. What can be called absolute, by contrast, because it is a fixed status that requires certain freedoms without itself being a freedom, is the citizen prerogative of non-viewpoint-punitive expression within the public discourse of an LSPD. What emerges is not 'free speech absolutism' but rather *viewpoint absolutism*,[29] as no conceivable abridgement of that citizen prerogative could ever be deemed to promote democracy.

Attributions of obsessive 'individualism'[30] are fair enough as applied to extreme libertarian positions, which would admit hate speech even in non-public, interpersonal contexts, such as 'fighting words'. However, to ascribe excessive individualism to viewpoint absolutism is to misconstrue democracy altogether. To find 'too much' individualism within public discourse would be to find 'too much' citizenship there. One may legitimately wish to rescue democracy from too much individualism in the sense of, say, consumerism or selfishness. But there is no such thing as rescuing a democracy from too much citizenship. Any incursion into citizenship itself, the essence of which lies in non-viewpoint-punitive expression within public discourse, never enhances democracy, but only erodes it as part of a trade-off against competing state interests.

Even if many problems remain to be examined, a preliminary statement of this book's primary theoretical claim can now be attempted: *A longstanding, stable, and prosperous democracy can fully be held to its legitimating expressive condition, which requires the citizen's prerogative of non-viewpoint-punitive expression within public discourse.* That claim's assumption of viewpoint absolutism derives from an account

---

[29] Cf. Heinze, 2006; Heinze, 2007, pp. 299–305.
[30] See, e.g., Tillmanns, 2003, p. 29.

of general *democratic* normativity. Its limitation to LSPDs, by contrast, reflects the *historicist* recognition that not all democracies are alike, nor are they equally able, throughout all moments of their history, to fulfil their legitimating conditions. Notwithstanding that theoretical claim, public discourse continues in practice to be regulated within rights regimes. For LSPDs, those processes retain legitimacy as long as the democratic imperative governs public discourse, so as always to preclude viewpoint-selective penalties. The citizen prerogative of expression does not derive, then, from assumptions about liberalism or about rights, but does remain compatible with them. It otherwise leaves legislative and judicial balancing processes intact. It confirms those processes' democratic legitimacy by forbidding them from 'balancing away' the viewpoints of citizens within that selfsame public discourse which first—not perforce temporally, but rather conceptually—constitutes those processes.[31]

4.2 Derogations Jurisprudence and the Limits of the LSPD

The qualifiers 'longstanding', 'stable', and 'prosperous' may still appear too politically mutable to yield politically precise or legally justiciable criteria. Those three attributes, however, distil concepts long implicit in the jurisprudence assessing states' capacities to fulfil democratic and rights-based mandates, such as the derogations jurisprudence of bodies like the European Court of Human Rights or the United Nations Human Rights Committee.[32] National and international judicial or quasi-judicial bodies always effectively consider those factors, even when they do not use those three adjectives. Both of those bodies have been willing to assess responsibility for ensuring human rights in view of a state's ability to fulfil such obligations in terms of historical obstacles, demographic conflicts, and available resources.

While Britain, for example, counts as an LSPD in general terms, the European Court has legitimately scrutinized elements of stability and available resources during declared states of emergency in Northern Ireland to assess the state's duties within that territory.[33] Similarly, bans within public discourse can be justified in a state like Israel, where the UN Human Rights Committee has found states of emergency to have been legitimately declared,[34] and which may depend on bans in

---

[31] See Section 5.5, text accompanying note 130.

[32] See, e.g., UN Human Rights Committee, *General Comment 29: States of Emergency (article 4)*, U.N. Doc. CCPR/C/21/Rev.1/Add.11 (2001).

[33] See generally, e.g., *Lawless v. United Kingdom*, Eur. Ct. H. R. Series A, No. 3, Judgment of 1 July 1961; *Ireland v. United Kingdom*, Eur. Ct. H. R. Series A, No. 25, Judgment of 18 Jan. 1978; *Brogan v. United Kingdom*, Eur. Ct. H. R. Series A, No. 145-B, Judgment of 29 Nov. 1988; *Brannigan & McBride v. United Kingdom*, Eur. Ct. H. R. Series A, No. 258-B, Judgment of 26 May 1993.

[34] Concluding Observations of the Human Rights Committee, Israel, U.N. Doc. CCPR/C/79/Add.93 (1998); Concluding Observations of the Human Rights Committee, Israel, U.N. Doc. CCPR/CO/78/ISR (2003); Concluding Observations of the Human Rights Committee, Israel, U.N. Doc. CCPR/C/ISR/CO/3 (2010).

view of material difficulties in assuring safety for individuals and groups of various ethnicities or identities; or a state like India with its own ongoing trouble spots, in which reliable material protections for the vulnerable may prove difficult to secure.[35]

The respectively liberal and democratic approaches partly overlap, but also partly diverge in their limiting conditions. Both of those approaches will, to some degree, draw upon empirical determinations, sometimes admittedly subject to differences of opinion—in the case of democracy, to determine its 'longstanding', 'stable', and 'prosperous' character; in the case of liberalism, to determine whether any actual or likely harms justify a limit on the right. The two approaches do converge, then, insofar as determinations of 'harm', on the one hand, and, on the other hand, determinations of available resources for countering such harm amount to a substantive enquiry.

We can debate such findings in their details, but, under international and European principles, the LSPD model certainly accommodates bans during legitimately declared and independently reviewable states of emergency—which, partly confirming the integrity of the LSPD ideal, have been rare despite rapidly shifting, often inflammable demographics and social conditions. The German term for 'state of emergency', *Ausnahmezustand*, literally 'exceptional circumstance' better captures the idea—an 'exception', for purposes of the present discussion. Leaving aside the specifics of actual German law, which hosts broad bans, that concept would, on the LSPD model, mean that the state's duty to refrain from viewpoint-selective penalties within public discourse ought to remain the norm. By contrast, bans subject to independently reviewable criteria might be legitimate either for a non-LSPD, or for an LSPD under a legitimately declared and independently assessed state of emergency. The latter, again, amounts to a declaration that the state has stopped *being* an LSPD to the extent that democracy's legitimating criteria are suspended.

Derogations jurisprudence displays the exceptions that prove the rule. Aside from Northern Ireland, no intergovernmental or non-governmental human rights organization has suggested, for example, that Britain or most other Western European democracies have lacked adequate resources to qualify as LSPDs in any way that would render them unable to preserve public discourse while protecting vulnerable persons. Those bodies err, then, in deeming bans compatible with the requirements of public discourse[36] for those

---

[35] Parekh slips, then, into a one-size-fits-all model of democracy. He extrapolates from bans justified within exceptionally turbulent democracies to bans justified for democracies with vastly different socio-political climates. He turns the exception into the rule, citing Israeli and Indian hate speech bans among those which serve as examples generally for Western democracies. Parekh, 2012, p. 37. Cf. Post, 1995, p. 306. His reference to India is particularly questionable, given that 'more than 600,000 lives having been lost [there in] communal violence.' Abrams, 2012, p. 118. Seeking to reconcile the contradictory approaches of two otherwise constitutional democracies, the US and Israel, Reichman concludes that 'passion, not merely reason … organizes the realm of public discourse'. Reichman, 2009, p. 351. That descriptive, sociological observation has merit, but begs the question as to the law's normative criteria. The LSPD concept supplies those criteria in view of the instability which, in the late twentieth and early twenty-first centuries, has legitimately relieved India, Israel, and Northern Ireland from a rigorous LSPD standard.

[36] See, e.g., Nieuwenhuis, 2011, pp. 305–41; Noorloos, 2012, pp. 57–119.

LSPDs that enjoy ample alternative means to combat intolerance. Persistence in that error becomes acute when European institutions include bans within a one-size-fits-all, 'ever-harmonising "European freedom of expression"'.[37] That approach may, at best, serve transitional or weaker democracies,[38] but lacks legitimacy for LSPDs. The fact that bans may legitimately be introduced as derogations from expressive freedoms under extraordinary conditions of social or political upheaval does not mean that they should remain as routine 'public order' or 'morals' exceptions in LSPDs.[39]

It might be objected that the LSPD standard is too high, embracing only a handful of states. My aim is not, however, to oppose bans in societies where they may be a necessary evil, such as societies with active inter-group rivalries and inadequate means to pacify them. I oppose only the widespread view that bans are a necessary norm even for LSPDs. The LSPD conception might seem to warrant a green light for the great numbers of states that do not meet an LSPD threshold. That conclusion follows, however, neither in logic nor in practice. *If* a society is an LSPD, *then* viewpoint-selective penalties within public discourse become illegitimate. In logic, it would be the fallacy of 'denying the antecedent' to extrapolate that bans are *therefore* legitimate for non-LSPDs. Whether bans are legitimate for non-LSPDs becomes a state-specific enquiry. More importantly, in practice, for non-LSPDs, there can be no rule quite so obvious or universal as Dworkin might suggest, in view of the variety of social and political forms that *not* being an LSPD can take.

A similar concern arises around the emergence of global media. The Danish cartoon controversy dramatized the speed with which speech in one country can inflame violence in others.[40] It is sometimes asked whether Denmark ought to have imposed restrictions not merely for its own sake, but for the sake of citizens of other states with different cultural attitudes. However, states cannot on democratic grounds abridge a core element of citizenship in view of hostilities that might be stoked beyond their borders. In some non-Western societies, photographs of scantily clad women may be deemed offensive or sinful. But European women cannot be asked to button up in order to avoid transmissions of such images into cultures likely to revile them.

One might be tempted to ask: 'What conclusion ought we to reach if, contrary to the claims thus far made, empirical evidence were to emerge showing that hate speech in the public discourse of an LSPD does indeed trace to such otherwise unlawful material harms as violence or acts of discrimination, in more than random, i.e., in statistically decisive ways?' But that query would commit a category error. If, as in certain periods of Northern Irish history, empirical evidence plausibly links hate speech to such acts, then we are presented with a situation in which

---

[37] Belavusau, 2013, pp. 71, 77, 78; see also at p. 77 (discussing *inter alia* 'Brussels harmonisation').
[38] See generally, Belavusau, 2013.
[39] See Section 5.7.
[40] See Chapter 1, text accompanying notes 1–2.

that overall LSPD which is the United Kingdom fails in at least one of the LSPD criteria with respect to one of that state's regions. As a result, Northern Ireland, during those historical periods, is not an LSPD which 'contradicts' the criteria thus far set forth; rather it is not an LSPD *at all*. Nor is Britain, during those periods, an LSPD which 'contradicts' the criteria thus far set forth, but rather is a democracy fulfilling LSPD criteria over some, or most, but not all of its territory.

The challenge might even be pushed further. 'What', it might be argued, 'should be our response if statistically reliable causation could be traced from hate speech to broader social harms not merely for trouble spots like Northern Ireland, but for some or all LSPDs generally?' Such an objection would, of course, under-mine the LSPD model outright. A model maintains credibility only if it sets forth the conditions under which it fails. That said, it is not merely happenstance that hate speech within public discourse has shown nothing like the snowball-ing effects witnessed in Weimar Germany, Rwanda, the former Yugoslavia, and other non-LSPDs. The LSPD paradigm serves as an explanatory device to suggest that both the LSPD's 'active state' and the efforts of independent and individual counter-forces within civil society generally become sufficiently disseminated to offset such effects. Non-viewpoint-punitive approaches can proceed not only with greater democratic legitimacy, but with greater efficiency. Empirical evidence to the contrary, then, would have to be statistically credible. It would shatter not merely the LSPD model, but, as will be suggested in this and the next chapter, any number of sociological and political observations about contemporary societies. One aim of the LSPD model is, then, to synthesize the deontological viewpoint absolutism inherent by definition in the concept of democracy with materially de-terminate criteria governing any given democracy's ability to fulfil its legitimating expressive criteria in light of its state of historical development.

4.3　The 'Pre-legal' Element of Public Discourse

The citizen's prerogative of non-viewpoint-punitive expression within public dis-course stands not as a sufficient condition, but only as one necessary condition for democratic legitimacy. By extension, killing[41] or torturing[42] citizens, whatever se-curity interests may be served—and bearing again in mind the exceptional justifica-tion required to impose security at the expense of democracy—could never serve a democratic interest. Democracy's expressive conditions, like (at least some readings of) Hobbes's social contract, might at first seem to be 'pre-legal' in the sense of being a pseudo-historical one-off, exercised in a postulated past, to form a body of law which would *then* maintain the authority, through its sovereign powers, to extinguish

---

[41]　On the democratic illegitimacy of killing a citizen through the death penalty, see Section 4.6.

[42]　Despite serious doubts (see e.g., Posner 2002 (discussing Alan Dershowitz's 'ticking bomb' scen-ario)), international law deems certain protections to be non-derogable, even under states of emer-gency. See ICCPR art. 4(2). Cf. ECHR art. 15(2).

or to abridge those self-same speech conditions. We mostly live, however, within already-constituted states, and not states still—like that of the *Leviathan*'s fictional fugitives from the 'war of all against all'—in gestation. Viewpoint absolutism precludes any suggestion that non-viewpoint-punitive expression in public discourse, as a criterion of legal legitimacy, *eo ipso* confers legitimacy on any democratically enacted law, including a law that curbs that selfsame access to public discourse.[43] The citizen's prerogative of non-viewpoint-punitive expression within public discourse certainly includes the prerogative to plead for abolishing the prerogative itself, just as a law prohibiting cannabis production correlates with the freedom to advocate legalization. That possibility, however, merely instantiates the age-old point that democracy must tolerate the views of those who would overthrow it.

Hence the—not literally or temporally, but conceptually and normatively—pre-legal character of non-viewpoint punitive expression within democratic public discourse. For Post, 'it is precisely because absolute agreement can never actually be reached that the debate that constitutes democracy is necessarily "without any end," and hence must be independently maintained as an ongoing structure of communication.' Post adds, 'I call this structure of communication "public discourse."'[44] To that sociological account, we must add the formal, legal status of public discourse as something that is necessarily presupposed as the original and ongoing source of the constitution, as the 'constitution of the constitution'. Recall that that status is confirmed by the very possibility of abolition or amendment within the democratic framework. The ascription of a pre-legal prerogative to viewpoints uttered within public discourse might seem like reinventing higher-law human rights under a different name. To the contrary, a 'pre-legal' status preserves the LSPD's distinctly democratic character in an age of ballooning catalogues of legislatively and judicially regulated higher-law interests.

The overlap between the present notion of pre-legal legitimating conditions and more familiar theories of higher-law rights nonetheless raises questions about whether any of the familiar criticisms of rights apply equally to democracy's pre-legal legitimating conditions. Susan Williams challenges references to democratic citizenship as a foundation for free speech, since it entails the 'distinction between the realm of public democratic discourse and other speech'. Williams's scepticism echoes ancient Greeks', as well as Rousseau's, Hegel's, Marx's, or Heidegger's concerns about normatively untenable and politically damaging divisions between the public and the private self:

This distinction ... rests on a division between different models of the person, each of which applies in a different realm. In the realm of public discourse, persons are (and must be treated as) autonomous; outside of this realm, persons are (and may be treated as) constituted by community-based norms and understandings and [are] therefore ...

---

[43] See, e.g., Kelsen, 1920, pp. 8–9, 36. Cf. Frank Michaelman's notion of the conceptually pre-legal as a 'jurisgenerative politics', in Michaelman, 1988, p. 1527. Cf. also Post, 1995, pp. 133, 186. 'Responsive democracy', observes Post (at 194), 'requires that public discourse ... will necessarily precede and inform government decision-making.'

[44] Post, 1995, p. 186 (quoting Lefort). Accordingly, 'responsive democracy is inherently incomplete.' Post, 1995, p. 189. See generally, Post, 1995, pp. 134–50. See also Weinstein, 2009a, pp. 26–9 (discussing Dahl and Kelsen).

non-autonomous. … [T]his dividing line between public discourse and the rest of life … rests on and institutionalizes the idea that these two different models of the person (as autonomous, on the one hand, and as constituted by social connections, on the other) can and should be separated into different realms of life. We are autonomous in the realm of public discourse, but are socially constituted in other aspects of life.[45]

That challenge also recalls ongoing doubts about conventional liberal rights regimes, as voiced within various feminist, communitarian, post-Marxist, and post-structuralist perspectives. Those voices query liberal rights, just as Williams queries concepts of pre-legal democratic prerogatives, for assuming reductionist models of 'atomised' individuals as society's constitutive units—outmoded, patriarchal models of the autonomous citizen interacting in a public sphere, surgically removed from private, familial, or socially interconnected spheres:

It is because autonomy is seen as threatened by the imposition of community norms that this division becomes important, and the boundary of the public domain must be defended. If autonomy were understood in a more relational way, then the contribution of communal norms to the creation and maintenance of autonomy would be clearer. I would argue that autonomy is dependent upon our relations to others at three levels: causally (we learn to be autonomous from others), substantively (the substance of our choices/stories is a product of communal norms and understandings), and conceptually (the very meaning of autonomy—in terms of its relation to self-respect, integrity of the person, responsibility and so on—cannot be understood separate from our relations to others).[46]

Williams joins in with Steven Shiffrin's[47] and Eugene Volokh's[48] observations that not all speech requiring strong protection arises within public discourse, including, for example, certain intimate conversations among family members. Williams, Shiffrin, and Volokh direct that objection against attempts to ground the entirety of the free speech *right* in a concept of public discourse. The crucial point, however, for the purposes of assessing bans imposed on hate speech within public discourse, is that no such all-encompassing foundation for expressive freedoms is required. To theorize about speech *insofar* as it arises within public discourse does not equate with assuming that *all* speech prerogatives derive from the status of speech within public discourse.[49]

The postulate that expression within public discourse precludes viewpoint-selective punishment, as a legitimating condition of democracy, does not mean that all speech deserving protection claims that foundation, nor does it deny the facts or contingencies of our socialization. Democratic theory can postulate a status for the citizen as a public self, which citizens will express in very different ways, without assuming a reductionist schism between a public and a private self. Such a schism might certainly arise through other forces of political modernity, but not from the concept of democratic public discourse.

---

[45] Williams, 2011, pp. 610–11.   [46] Williams, 2011, pp. 614–15.
[47] See Shiffrin, S., 2011, pp. 559–62.   [48] See Volokh, 2011a.
[49] See, e.g., Greenawalt, 1989b, pp. 125–54 (expressing 'great scepticism' towards any 'singly unifying justification for freedom of speech').

4.4 Residual Liberal Domains Within and Beyond Public Discourse

Viewpoint absolutism bars legislatures, courts, or administrative agencies from penalizing expression within public discourse on viewpoint-selective grounds. That condition of democratic legitimacy still leaves those bodies with strong latitude in other areas concerning speech and expression. Time, manner, and place regulations represent, again, an area within public discourse in which value-pluralist rights regimes legitimately balance competing interests. By extension, even if democratic legitimacy requires that viewpoints within public discourse must lie beyond those strictures, government balancing of competing interests is still left with legitimate roles to play in the inevitable hard cases as to whether a peripheral situation counts as public discourse. Official bodies must still arbitrate matters of speech falling *squarely* outside public discourse, such as private commercial and contractual language or indeed everyday stalking, harassment, or fighting words. Those official processes will also be required to arbitrate legal complexities as to the *boundaries* demarcating the 'inside' and 'outside' of public discourse, as in employment situations.

Delineating the boundaries of public discourse will reveal much expression falling both inside and outside. As to that falling outside, including content that has nothing to do with hate speech, different questions arise as to grounds for legal protection. In those areas, specifically democratic principles will not necessarily have any role to play. The traditional rights-based principles then remain intact. As this book is not about regulation beyond hate speech, I shall not examine those principles further. Regulation of expression outside public discourse may raise questions about *state* legitimacy, but not necessarily about democratic legitimacy. The concept of public discourse serves only as one necessarily protected sphere of speech, of particular concern in view of the wording and application of most hate speech bans, even though other spheres of speech may deserve legal protection on grounds—of liberal rights, or ethics, of public policy, etc.—other than their specific relationship to democratic public discourse.[50]

Borderline difficulties arise around such matters as informal workplace conversation, such as chats around the water cooler. Such situations do not inherently convert an otherwise routine workplace environment away from its primary function into a full-fledged forum of democratic public discourse. The employer may legitimately enforce rules of professional conduct, but the employee does not lose all expressive freedoms. This is the more appropriate domain of rights-based, value-pluralist balancing on the part of legislatures and courts.

Democracy requires a wide sphere of public discourse, but, given different democracies' divergent institutional arrangements, for example, for regulating speech in public parks or shopping centres, that sphere need not take precisely the same

---

[50] See, e.g., Shiffrin, S., 2011, pp. 559–62 (endorsing eclectic over comprehensive theories of free speech); Volokh, 2011a (examining limits on the concept of public discourse); Williams, 2011, pp. 610–11 (agreeing with Shiffrin and Volokh).

forms throughout all democracies. A British court, for example, has upheld a man's freedom to post, in his private time, his opposition to gay marriage on a restricted-access internet site, after the man incurred disciplinary action from a public sector employer whose management believed he had violated its equality principles.[51] Translating that result into the terms of the present analysis, it can be said that the court maintained democracy's recognition of that sphere of public discourse within which speech must not be censored solely on grounds of the view-point it expresses.

A question then arises as to whether employees can ever legitimately face dis-missal on grounds of views expressed outside work. But that question, arising in contexts not strictly limited to public discourse, entails more general elements of employment law, concerning the ways in which suitability or character may legit-imately be assessed. May a pro-feminist organization dismiss an employee who expresses anti-abortion views? May a social services department dismiss an em-ployee who criticizes lifestyle habits of the poor? Such line-drawing complexities may differ from one democracy to another, and indeed from one situation to an-other, but in no way diminish the core proposition that, in each LSPD, there must remain some genuine public sphere within which citizens may speak without fear of viewpoint-selective penalties imposed by the state, hence upon an individual as a *citizen*.[52]

For Kant, one's necessarily limited prerogatives of speech in the exercise of certain professional functions cannot abrogate one's prerogatives as a citizen. To cite his example, one's duty as a soldier to obey commands does not erode one's prerogative, as a 'member of a whole community, indeed of the world citizenry (*Weltbürgergesellschaft*)' to challenge errors of military judgement, at least when it becomes safe to do so.[53] For one and the same utterance, and for one and the same individual, Kant recognizes a speech-restricted, duty-bound sphere, from which the utterance may legitimately be barred; but also a public sphere, in which it must be permitted. Difficulties in delimiting those spheres in particular instances—at what point or to what extent, for example, does it become 'safe' for the soldier to speak?—do not erase them as a general matter. Here too, legislators and judges are by no means exiled from borderline cases.

We have observed three domains, then, for the regulation of expression within the LSPD.[54] In the first, the state pursues national *security*. It may legitimately impose bans in situations of conflict as warranted under a standard derogations jurisprudence. In the second, the state pursues *liberalism* in the juridical sense of a presumption of individual autonomy protected through legal rights. Insofar as regulation does not entail viewpoint-selective penalties within public discourse, for example, as to time, manner, and place restrictions, the state may pursue value-pluralist balancing, which includes special weighting for higher-order expres-sive rights, such as those protecting confidential communications. In the third, the state pursues *democracy*. Although the liberal rights should certainly tip the balance

---

[51] 'Christian wins case against employers over gay marriage comments', 2012.
[52] Cf. Section 2.8, text accompanying note 105.
[53] See Post, 1994–95, pp. 1274–5.   [54] See Section 1.2, note 41.

in favour of non-viewpoint-punitive expression within public discourse, such expression remains a democratic citizen prerogative independent of such rights.

4.5 The *Pro Tanto* Character of Legitimating Conditions

'The temptation may be overwhelming', according to Dworkin, 'to declare that people have no right to pour the filth of pornography or race-hatred into the culture in which we all must live.' He continues,

We may and must protect women and homosexuals and members of minority groups from specific and damaging consequences of sexism, intolerance, and racism. We must protect them against unfairness and inequality in employment or education or housing or the criminal process, for example, and we may adopt laws to achieve that protection. But we must not try to intervene *further upstream*, by forbidding any expression of the attitudes or prejudices that we think nourish such unfairness or inequality, because if we intervene too soon in the process through which collective opinion is formed, we spoil *the only democratic justification we have for insisting that everyone obey these laws, even those who hate and resent them.*[55]

Waldron helpfully re-phrases Dworkin's idea as a terse maxim: 'if we interfere coercively upstream, we undermine political legitimacy downstream.'[56] When a democracy bars a citizen from public discourse, it loses, for Dworkin, a measure of legitimacy in imposing upon that citizen a duty of obedience to law. Having correctly formulated Dworkin's view, however, Waldron still rejects it. He spurns Dworkin's assumption that democratic legitimacy stands as a deontological principle. Waldron substitutes that assumption with his 'social science' notion of legitimacy as 'popular support'. Yet that rebuttal, as we have seen, in no way discloses a superior criterion of legitimacy. It altogether jettisons legitimacy, collapsing it into the very *status quo* that it is supposed to be examining.[57]

Hate speech bans admittedly raise questions about legitimacy, but democracies have loads of questionable laws and practices. It seems odd to suggest that a citizen whose views are penalized under such a ban becomes ethically un-bound by law. Can Dworkin seriously mean that German neo-Nazis or Islamist hate preachers ought to enjoy immunity from law until the bans are abolished?

The inevitable imperfections of legal norms and institutions mean that democracy's legitimating conditions do frequently falter. But that defect by no means obliterates citizens' duties to obey law within an LSPD. If the police physically abuse an ordinary street criminal, for example, a democracy's duty to provide an adequate remedy remains intact; yet, even in that case of extreme abuse, it does not follow—assuming at least a case in which some genuine remedy is provided—that the victim would additionally be justified in committing generally lawless activity. Similarly, democracy's legitimating expressive

---

[55] Dworkin, 2009, p. viii (emphasis added). Cf. Dworkin, 2012.
[56] Waldron, 2012b, p. 331.   [57] See Section 3.3, text accompanying notes 31–2.

conditions remain tenable without requiring an all-or-nothing application. Viewpoint-punitive bans within public discourse certainly diminish an LSPD's legitimacy, but do not utterly destroy it. Hate speakers win no prerogative of general legal disobedience if democracies fail to repeal such bans. Politically legitimating elements apply *pro tanto*. LSPDs lose some margin of legitimacy *to the extent* that they abrogate certain legitimating conditions, but still retain legitimacy when other such conditions are generally upheld.[58]

For Post, a viewpoint-selective ban 'prevents persons from participating in a process of public-opinion formation in ways that would make the law responsive to them. With respect to such persons, the state has *pro tanto* ceased to be legitimated because it has excluded them from the process of public-opinion formation.'[59] Viewpoint absolutism furnishes democracy's signally defining ingredient, but that does not mean that democracy ceases when viewpoint absolutism is less than perfectly achieved. Several Northern European democracies impose hate speech bans within public discourse, but otherwise maintain robust democratic and rule-of-law standards.

Waldron rightly observes that democratic '[l]egitimacy is not an all-or-nothing matter.' He errs, however, in drawing from that premise the relativist conclusion that legitimacy is therefore '*all* a matter of degree'.[60] Some questions of political legitimacy may entail borderline matters of judgement, but others are patently all-or-nothing. Notwithstanding borderline cases, there are plenty of unambiguous infractions under normal hate speech bans. An individual then either unambiguously *does* or unambiguously *does not* enjoy a legally protected freedom to express a given worldview in public discourse. In those uncomplicated cases, that freedom is in no way relative. It is patently all or nothing. Questions as to its legality must then be decided by democracy's legitimating expressive conditions, which, within any LSPD, must be construed as viewpoint-absolutist.[61] That instance of the citizen prerogative of expression is emphatically not a matter of degree, even if democracy's *overall* illegitimacy, in excluding certain speech acts on grounds of viewpoint, does remain *pro tanto*, and in that sense a matter of degree, thereby disallowing the banned speaker's general lawlessness.

A democracy's illegitimacy in banning the expression of a viewpoint in public discourse remains absolute, even if any given hate speech ban's absolute illegitimacy diminishes the democracy's *overall* legitimacy only to a small degree, i.e., only *pro tanto*. Bans become, then, absolutely illegitimate within LSPDs, and yet only *pro tanto* illegitimate for those democracies *as a whole*. At its core, democracy's legitimating expressive condition of non-viewpoint-punitive expression within public discourse remains indivisible and unquantifiable.[62] The legitimacy of the

---

[58] See, e.g., Post, 1995, pp. 273, 275.

[59] See, e.g., Molnar & Post, 2012, p. 25.

[60] Waldron, 2012b, p. 334 (emphasis added).

[61] If, alternatively, the ban retains deep ambiguity even as to its central applications, then it entails the equally grievous illegitimacy of 'chilling'. See Section 2.6, note 60, and Section 2.9, text accompanying note 114.

[62] See Section 4.10.

entire democracy is not overcome by one defect. Nor, however, does a democracy's overall legitimacy suffice to overcome the defect.

4.6 Demarcating Liberal and Democratic Spheres

In order to distinguish between, respectively, liberal and democratic criteria for evaluating free speech, it helps to distinguish those two strands more generally. The *liberal* strand, or the strand of *liberal rights*, endows each citizen with some set of government abstentions, such as not being tortured, as well as performances, such as receiving a fair trial. We have seen that there is nothing irreducibly democratic about those guarantees. Non-democracies can in principle secure many of them, as international human rights law demands. The second, distinctly *democratic* strand, embraces each citizen's prerogative to participate both in the state's formal political life, such as through voting or seeking elective office, and in its informal political life, such as through conversation and debate. As a prerogative, rather than a government dispensation, we find it only in states effectively functioning as democracies.

The liberal and the democratic strands often overlap, but are not interchangeable. Protections from torture and fair trials could certainly be justified on democratic as well as liberal grounds. Much free speech, too, can plausibly fall under either heading. The two headings nevertheless offer different foundations for free speech, hence divergent theories for its protection and its appropriate limits. As we have seen, value-pluralist proceduralism within liberal rights regimes may or may not legitimately construe 'harm' to include hate speech. Legitimacy criteria within an LSPD, by contrast, preclude that determination.

The two strands become difficult to distinguish because each is presented as entailing the other. Democracies today widely recognize catalogues of fundamental rights and liberties as politically constitutive, on the assumption that there can *be* no democracy without fundamental rights and freedoms. Conversely, those rosters commonly include the same rights of speech and of political participation which allow democratic government to proceed on the assumption that there can *be* no fundamental rights and freedoms without democracy. Western democracies emerged largely within cultures of pre-existing liberal values that had gained force within what were still constitutionally monarchical and aristocratic power structures. Britain had Whigs before it had democrats; France had liberals before it had Jacobins.

Yet one strand by no means requires the other.[63] For thinkers as different as Hobbes and Montesquieu, an enlightened monarchy could certainly offer broad

[63] Cf., e.g., Schmitt, [1928] 1993, pp. 36, 49. As we have seen, those are not the only two political or legal components of liberal democracies. They nevertheless provide much of the vocabulary of the more controversial free speech debates, which are commonly framed either in classical liberal terms, as evaluations of the appropriate extent of individual rights; or in democratic terms, as evaluations of the appropriate frameworks of citizen participation within public discourse.

protections without being a democracy. For ancient Athens or for Rousseau, conversely, a society could be democratic without a fixed or comprehensive charter of higher-law rights. The at least partial separation between liberalism and democracy arises, then, both conceptually and historically. On the one hand, while admiring a culture of critical thought under Louis XIV,[64] more fruitful than in many democracies,[65] Voltaire never advocates democracy. Kant, too, pens one of history's strongest theories of liberalism despite, or rather because of the fact that the theory does not conceptually require democracy. Early twenty-first-century China can grant its citizens a pound of economic and social freedoms without according them an ounce of democracy.[66] Several differences persist, then, between higher-order rights of expression and democracy's legitimating expressive conditions.

First, both in the secular natural law tradition and in contemporary international law, higher-order rights are themselves posited as foundational. They do not derive from anterior norms. Nor, again, do they conceptually presuppose democracy, even if some enumerated rights appear to be best realized in a democratic order (and even that was a controversial suggestion during the formative, Cold War era of the modern international corpus). By contrast, the politically legitimating conditions examined under the LSPD model are derived from the assumptions of a democratic order.

When a democracy assumes solely rights-based criteria of legitimacy, then rights, far from proving their functions as the limits on democracy that 'really' strengthen democracy, wholly defeat that aim. Democracy then exists only instrumentally, as a means to the greater end of achieving rights, which, themselves, have never been manifestly conceived as requiring democracy. From the standpoint of democratic legitimacy, by contrast, rights and freedoms exist as tools, along with democracy's distinct legitimating criteria, to safeguard and to continue to improve[67] a society as a democracy.

The LSPD model could be called 'neo-Rousseauian'. It admittedly departs from Rousseau in crucial respects. It entails neither Rousseau's opposition to the post-Westphalian state nor his collectivist alternative. The LSPD model does therefore admit higher-order individual or human rights to legitimate the state as a *state*. It nevertheless assumes that the state becomes legitimated[68] as a

---

[64] *Le Siècle de Louis XIV* ch. 1, *in* Voltaire, [1751] 1957, pp. 616–20.

[65] See Section 1.1, text accompanying note 25. In their gestating years, modern liberal *versus* democratic worldviews clash nowhere more vividly than in the volleys between Voltaire, liberal rather than democratic, and Rousseau, democratic rather than liberal. Similarly, Foucault notes Aristotle's praise for the pre-democratic Athenian *tyrannos* Pisistratus, whose rule was 'more like constitutional government than tyranny', *Constitution of Athens*, in Aristotle XVI:2, [4th century BCE] 1984:2, p. 2350 (citing also an example of Pisistratus's tolerance of citizens' free speech at XVI:6). Foucault, 2009, p. 56. Foucault also mentions Plato's praise for Cyrus. Foucault, 2009, p. 57.

[66] Cf. Heinze 2015b (identifying domestic democratic public discourse as a prerequisite for global leadership on human rights).

[67] See Section 4.12.

[68] See, e.g., *Le Contrat social* 1.1, 1.3, 1.4, 1.9, 2.6, 3.1, 3.10, *in* Rousseau, [1762] 1964, pp. 352, 355, 356, 367, 380, 396, 423 (on political legitimacy).

democracy through constitutive citizenship. That is the soul of Rousseau's *Contrat social*.[69] The public discourse of the citizenry[70] stands as the constitution of the constitution[71]—democracy's *Urverfassung*.

Second, both in their black-letter and in their interpretation by international bodies, *human* rights are, again, exhibited to the world as applying to non-democracies and to democracies alike. The LSPD model, by contrast, suspends any investigation into whether democracy's legitimating conditions also supply legitimating conditions for actual, historical, or hypothetical non-democracies. Recall the question that arose for Dworkin's approach: does justified opposition to hate speech bans within some democracies necessarily presuppose justified opposition to bans in all of them?[72] Within our prevailing human rights regimes, the question must be posed another way, namely: does the requirement of hate speech bans within some states presuppose a requirement of them for all states? Provisions like International Covenant on Civil and Political Rights (ICCPR) article 20(2) or International Convention on the Elimination of All Forms of Racial Discrimination (ICERD) article 4(a) compel an affirmative reply. International law leaves little 'margin of appreciation' on the question, but rather presents at least minimal prohibitionism as necessary in view of the very nature of the universal 'human', irrespective of any given society's democratic or non-democratic character.

Third, higher-law rights are often presented as 'inherent' within human beings as such.[73] Democracy's legitimating expressive conditions, by contrast, might certainly be construed in such ontological terms. On that view, prerogatives of citizenship, which can only be fully realized in an LSPD, would inhere essentially within human nature. But that view is in no way compulsory for purposes of the purely hypothetical conception being assumed here, which enquires only into politically legitimating conditions *if* democracy is assumed. For present purposes, then, we need assume no view about the ultimate existential status of democracy's legitimating expressive conditions.

Fourth, a rights corpus can remain limited to a discrete set of individual interests only by assuming fixed assumptions about human traits, needs, desires, and aspirations. The more incomplete such assumptions come to appear, the more the corpus must expand to embrace alternatives. Indicia aiming at the totality of important human traits, needs, desires, and aspirations offer few obvious stopping points. The transformation of a given interest *x* into a human right then becomes a formal matter, requiring two elements: first, some threshold consensus that *x* inheres within that which counts as 'human'; and, second, some linguistic

[69] *Le Contrat social* 1.7, 2.7, 3.1, 3.9, *in* Rousseau, 1964, pp. 363, 382, 396, 419 (on constitutive citizenship).
[70] *Le Contrat social* 1.5, 1.7, 2.3, *in* Rousseau, 1964, pp. 359, 362, 371 (on public deliberation). Cf. Section 4.12, text accompanying notes 186–8.
[71] *Le Contrat social* 1.8, *in* Rousseau, 1964, p. 365 (on the relationship between freedom and obedience to law). Cf. Section 4.12, text accompanying notes 186–8.
[72] See Section 2.1.   [73] See, e.g., UDHR, preamble, para. 1.

formulation in passably general terms, such as, 'Everyone has a right to *x*'. Criteria of democratic legitimacy, by contrast, demand attention not to those traits, needs, desires, and aspirations necessary to constitute the human, but only to those elements necessary to constitute democracy.

Fifth, as we have seen, and notwithstanding international and regional human rights treaties' non-derogation clauses, it is of the essence of higher-order rights regimes that they routinely and comprehensively balance rival interests. Rawls and Dworkin stumble, then, in their attempts to legitimate democratic balancing processes by rooting them within rights regimes. Higher-order rights are not just incidentally, but are rather fundamentally relative, and only incidentally absolute, i.e., where their conceptual formulations already include built-in limitations. Democratic citizenship is the opposite. The freedoms which flow from it are limited, as freedoms must always be within any legal system. But citizenship itself makes sense only as absolute in its defining elements. Higher-order rights concern, at least in large part, individuals' relationships to their governments. Democratic citizenship, by contrast, concerns citizens' relationships to, as constitutive members of sovereignty itself through public discourse.

A human right must routinely be modulated in terms of its greater and lesser exercises. Rarely if ever can it make sense that democratic citizenship could be modulated in that way. It is a conceptual impossibility, a conceptual nonsense, that one could ever abuse or misuse one's citizenship, no matter how hard one tries to do so. My liberty to swing my fist may stop at your nose, but there is no such thing as swinging one's citizenship in any such way. When we metaphorically accuse people of abusing their democratic citizenship, by affronting others in word or deed, what we mean is that they are abusing their individual freedom, which *is* amenable to degrees of more and less, hence to necessary limits as with 'fighting words' or commercial fraud.[74] But freedom must remain *viewpoint*-absolute within the public discourse of an LSPD precisely on grounds of the democratic citizenship which establishes the LSPD.

Consider again the claim that there must be attributes of citizenship which cannot be constituted through democratic norms and processes wholly because it is they that constitute, and thereby lend necessary legitimacy to, those democratic norms and processes. Imagine that the 90 per cent ethnic majority of a state seeks, through a binding referendum, to nullify the citizenship of the state's

---

[74] See Section 5.6. It is on those grounds, e.g., that an LSPD may legitimately punish criminals only through deprivations of freedom. They can only conceivably be defined as criminals through their abuse of individual freedoms, and not through any concept of abuse of democratic citizenship, which, again, like a non-quadrilateral square, would be an empty verbal formulation. A democracy cannot legitimately deprive them of essential elements of citizenship, such as voting rights, which indeed ought, for all of us, to be grasped as constitutionally pre-legal voting *prerogatives*, derivative of the citizen prerogative of non-viewpoint-punitive expression within public discourse. They cannot conceptually be amenable to degrees of more and less on democratic grounds. Nor *a fortiori* can any state destroy any individual's citizenship entirely, i.e., through the death penalty, on any conceivable democratic grounds. Kant's justification for the death penalty, even leaving aside its questionable derivation from the categorical imperative, might at best be reconciled with theories of liberal freedoms, also a debatable point, but can in no way be reconciled with any notion of democratic citizenship.

10 per cent ethnic minority. That measure can be deemed undemocratic despite its majoritarian voting procedure. But why? Some observers might call such a measure unethical on its face. The precise question is not, however, whether the vote is unethical, but whether it is undemocratic, even though it can, of course, be both. Others might call the vote grossly unlawful. They might, for example, condemn it as a violation of the human right to non-deprivation of nationality.[75] But nor is the present question whether such a vote in one or another sense violates current, positive law, be it national or international. The question is only whether the vote is unlawful *insofar* as a given legal system is democratic.

In a democracy, citizenship must, again, entail some legally protected interest beyond sheer administrative recognition. Routine democratic processes must certainly constitute some attributes of citizenship, but, by definition, cannot constitute all of them. One way of setting limits upon democratic processes is, admittedly, to ascertain who may participate by determining attributes of citizenship. Citizenship may, for example, be acquired by non-nationals only on certain conditions, or may be exercised through the vote only after a certain age, and so forth. As the present hypothetical scenario nevertheless illustrates, a democracy cannot legitimately extend limits on citizen prerogatives so far as to authorize outright retraction of citizenship even through an otherwise duly conducted voting procedure. To do so would be to reduce democratic citizenship to the purely administrative by-product of birth and naturalization certificates.

That is why no state can legitimately maintain the death penalty on democratic grounds, even leaving aside the familiar ethical and pragmatic objections to it. Whatever claims might be voiced to support capital punishment on retributive, religious, or other classical moral grounds; whatever justifications it may claim within non-democracies, such as ancient Biblical societies; and whatever support it may in the past have enjoyed among democracy's founders, it contradicts the very idea of democratic sovereignty. Any notion of the citizens as sovereign must reserve some minimum attributes of citizenship as constitutive of, and not constituted by, the state, which at the very least would include the citizen's very existence. A democracy may legitimately abridge a liberal interest, such as freedom of movement through incarceration, or free disposition of private property through imposition of a criminal fine. Those, again, are the purely liberal freedoms that are constantly weighed and balanced through the conventions of value-pluralist proceduralism and including limits imposed by tax laws, health and safety laws, zoning laws, and the like. In no way can those routine regulations of liberal freedoms be casually extended to encompass any element of citizenship by which the democracy is itself constituted. The death penalty is not just an incrementally greater penalty. It is not just a logical next step after a life sentence. It is a categorically different, and in that sense democratically infirm penalty. To be sure, the international and European human rights movements have been strongly abolitionist,[76] but, here too, not as

---

[75] See, e.g., UDHR art. 15(1) and (2).
[76] See, e.g., ICCPR art. 6(2)–(6); ECHR art. 2(2); Protocol No. 6, 28 Apr 1983; Protocol No. 13, 3 May 2002.

a matter of specifically democratic legitimacy but solely on abstract 'humanist' or purely pragmatic grounds.

Sixth, a question arises about the democratic citizen as a legal subject. Central to classical liberalism is the abstract, universal legal subject, formally equal to all others. That liberal subject is already evident in Locke, and becomes axiomatic for Kant, the exemplary theorist of the liberal subject. Hegel in turn critiques liberalism in general, and Kantianism in particular, rejecting them as ahistorical, de-contextualized formalisms, which implausibly assume law to exist irrespective of culture. That critique resurfaces, albeit, to say the least, on more questionable political assumptions, in Heidegger and Schmitt.[77] In our own time, Rawlsian theory faces similar challenges. The legal interests that it defines for the liberal subject are reproached for recapitulating the identities of self-interested, white, heterosexual males.[78] That critique remains vital for prohibitionists within critical theoretical schools, who advocate bans as tools for restoring balance within societies stacked against the interests of vulnerable groups.

Democracy is a system of political participation that certainly entails essential exercises of freedom. Yet even that tall order pales in comparison to the ambitions of liberalism, which promises nothing less than a total system of human freedom—a project even further complicated in view of liberalism's many, often mutually incompatible variants.[79] Accordingly, those critiques of the legal subject reach far further into liberalism than into democracy. If the liberal is feeling exasperated by the countless critiques of the legal subject, one can only respond: *You asked for it.* Yet theorists who critique liberal formalisms in a realist vein generally propose not their elimination, but their more effective realization for those traditionally disadvantaged within law and society. Many of them advocate elimination of dominant liberal models, but, as was noted earlier, few if any of them aim to eliminate democracy. Those challenges to liberalism are generally presented as efforts to strengthen democracy.

How much liberalism is necessary or optimal for democracy is a vast question, central for political theory today. The abstract universalism of the legal subject may indeed reach far too broadly to sustain some version of liberalism as a total system of freedom. But democracy cannot be theorized at all without some general concept of equal citizenship and of its necessary prerogatives. Those necessary prerogatives cannot be even minimally 'reformed' or 'adjusted' without decaying democratic legitimacy. Any communitarian or critical theorist who challenges the liberal subject, in order not to eliminate but to strengthen democracy, already necessarily presupposes some element of abstract, formally equal citizenship.

Some might worry about transferring expression from the human rights framework to the democratic framework. That shift might seem to disempower dissenters in non-democratic societies, confirming free expression as a peculiarity of

---

[77] Cf. Section 6.2.

[78] The literature, from various theoretical perspectives, is legion. See generally, e.g., Cornell, Rosenfeld & Carlson (eds.), 1992; MacIntyre, 2007; Norrie (ed.), 1993; Sandel, 1998; Taylor, 1992.

[79] See Section 3.6, text accompanying note 68.

democracy, unsuited to other constitutional forms. That concern can be answered on both logical and practical grounds. From a logical standpoint, the premise 'Puppies are mammals' in no way entails the conclusion 'Kittens are *not* mammals.' The premise 'Puppies are animals' entails nothing at all about kittens. It leaves their status as a separate enquiry. Nor does the premise entail the conclusion that puppies are not *animals*. It wholly allows the proposition that puppies, as mammals, are also animals. Similarly, the premise that democracy presupposes a citizen prerogative of expression does not entail the conclusion that other constitutions do *not* presuppose it. It leaves their relationship to speech as a separate enquiry. Nor does the premise entail the conclusion that free speech is not *also* a human right. It can be both a democratic citizen prerogative and a human right.

From a practical standpoint, dissenters in non-democracies would be of various types. If they dissent with a view towards genuine democratization, then, on the present analysis, they do indeed presuppose the citizen prerogative of non-viewpoint-punitive expression within public discourse, hence viewpoint absolutism. If, by contrast, they dissent with a view towards replacing one non-democratic constitution with another, then, whatever their human rights may be, no democratic basis for the citizen prerogative of non-viewpoint-punitive expression within public discourse ever arises. A democratic system must—not merely as a policy choice, but by definition—extend that prerogative even to those whose politics are non-democratic, which includes those who would deprive certain fellow citizens of citizenship, being itself an anti-democratic stance.[80]

4.7 Democratic Versus Liberal Conceptions of Freedom

Denying that free speech perforce entails democracy, the former German Constitutional Court judge and publicist Dieter Grimm refers to 'countries that recognize *and respect* a *fundamental* right of speech without being democracies'. That is a spectacular claim, particularly because he cites no examples.[81] Grimm may have

---

[80] See Section 5.2.

[81] Grimm, 2009a, p. 12 (emphasis added). Grimm does cite some purely black-letter provisions, which we might indeed deem to be 'recognized' within the Chinese Constitution and by '[m]any Islamic countries', but never enquires into their actual status at the time of his writing. Grimm, 2009a, p. 11. Publishing his views well before the Arab uprisings that began in December 2010, Grimm certainly cannot be assuming countries such as those, not least because those movements began as *democratizing* ones, with free speech a key aspiration. That highly doubtful premise is nevertheless, for Grimm, 'of some importance because it shows that freedom of speech does not derive its *raison d'être* from democracy.' Grimm, 2009a, p. 12. Even if Grimm did cite examples of non-democracies that materially (and not just on paper) 'respect' a 'fundamental' (which means not just 'important', but legally 'foundational' or 'constitutive') right of free speech, his logic runs in the wrong direction. There is no such thing as a state which is first (not perforce temporally, but conceptually) democratic and *then* decides whether or not to 'respect' free speech. The logic is precisely the opposite. A state becomes democratic on the conceptually prior *assumption* that it must necessarily respect free speech. And yet even if we overlook that flaw, and instead assume Grimm's premise *arguendo*, he commits an even more basic logical fallacy, unsurprisingly lurking behind the phrase *raison d'être*. It is certainly true that one might identify lots of reasons—*raisons d'être*—why free speech is good. Among them Grimm includes 'individual self-determination' and 'personal dignity'. Grimm, 2009a, p. 12. It by no

some of our aforementioned historical precedents in mind. Voltaire praised Louis XIV's absolute monarchy for robust speech and expression,[82] which he also found in Prussia under Friedrich the Great. Neither Voltaire nor we, however, could contend that any such regime pre-supposed a politically legitimating citizen prerogative of speech. Such monarchs or dictators readily loosen their grip, then just as easily tighten it, with neither warning nor recourse for speakers who overstep what may, moreover, be indiscernible bounds.[83] Viewpoint absolutism entails not a discretionary privilege, which either the citizenry or its senior officials may grant or withhold from any given citizen willy-nilly. It entails not the kind of liberty that old monarchies or modern dictatorships, even if they grant it, retain the prerogative to rescind. In a democracy, as Philip Pettit observes, citizens' participation is not 'granted as an indulgence of the Government'.[84] What Voltaire praises is indeed a freedom of expression under Louis XIV, but not a politically constitutive one. *L'État, ce n'est pas vous.*

For argument's sake, we can read the assumption of—something like—an LSPD context into Post's or Weinstein's views, since, unlike Dworkin, they concede that oppositionism may be inappropriate for weaker democracies. Accordingly, they both maintain (although this phrasing is not theirs) that the citizen's prerogative of non-viewpoint-punitive expression within public discourse stands as democracy's legitimating expressive condition. For them, however, that legitimating condition enters as decisive factor only *within* a pre-established framework of liberal, rights-based jurisprudence.

Recall that the LSPD model aims to mediate between Dworkin's ahistoricist political universalism and Post's historical and political relativism. On the one hand, from a universalist perspective on democracy, we can accept that democratic legitimacy entails the citizen's prerogative of non-viewpoint-punitive expression in public discourse, *regardless* of the origin, text, or interpretation of this or that particular constitutional act or document. On the other hand, from an historicist standpoint, societies cannot always, at all stages of their histories, fully be held to their legitimating conditions. Only when a democracy, as an LSPD, can reliably protect and empower vulnerable groups can it fully be held to that legitimating expressive condition.

Post and Weinstein do nevertheless show us how democratic principles can be incorporated into the liberal right of free speech, without being theorized as

---

means follows, however, that other reasons for speech being good, or even 'fundamental', willy-nilly remove its role as a legitimating element of democracy. (To spell out that second logical defect in simple terms: it is no argument that we do not need to drink water simply because some people may have other reasons for drinking it, such as a feeling of pleasure.)

[82] See Section 4.6, text accompanying note 64.

[83] Shakespeare dramatizes the perils of pre-democratic liberalism. In *Richard II*'s opening trial scene, free speech is invoked, calling attention to a principle deemed politically or at least ethically imperative, and weighty, as it involves speech prerogatives of a nobility often at odds with the monarchy. *Richard II*, 1.1.55, 123, *in* Shakespeare, 2011, pp. 137, 140. It is precisely that reiteration which, with standard Shakespearean irony, confirms the freedom as a sham. One of the trial's central objects, the murder of the Duke of Gloucester, although mentioned, cannot be discussed freely because it traces to the king himself.

[84] Pettit, 2012, p. 202.

something conceptually separate. So why create that separation? Recall that liberal rights serve as limits to dangers such as brute majoritarianism. Liberalism's background assumption is that those rights must be balanced against legitimate competing interests—limits *to* the limits. The rights-based approaches are then left with no alternative but to carve out the protection of viewpoints within public discourse as, themselves, limits to that background assumption of legitimate balancing. From that conventional liberal, rights-based perspective, then, what is supposed to be a categorical democratic imperative ends up as something glaringly derivative, at three removes from democracy, being nothing more than *a limit to a limit to a limit* upon democratic government. The democratic citizen prerogative, by contrast, when grasped independently of rights regimes, remains foundational and unequivocal. However persuasively Post or Weinstein may insist on the constitutive role of expression within democracy, it is precisely their aim of doing so as part of the interpretation of a liberal right formalized within an already existing constitution which precludes that possibility.

In many democracies, notably the US, the jurisprudence of speech is altogether the jurisprudence of a liberal or constitutional right. For First Amendment experts like Post or Weinstein, the democratic imperative of free speech is certainly strong, but arises only within, necessarily subordinate to, that constitutional, rights-based framework. Under their approaches, democracy may indeed dictate the rules governing public discourse, but it is the written constitution which first dictates the content and structure of democracy: it is the on paper constitution, however that instrument may then be interpreted, which is ultimate and foundational. Far from being foundational for democracy, however, the status of public discourse within the standard liberal rights frameworks ends up as altogether derivative, at three removes from democracy, and that becomes, unsurprisingly, how all value-pluralist proceduralisms treat it, be they American or European.

To be sure, the prohibitionist position, at two rather than three removes from democracy—i.e., as the limit upon that individual right which supplies a limit to majoritarian democracy—is no more persuasive. Two removes from democracy are not more democratically legitimate than three. In either case, such a fastidious casuistry does not necessarily end up 'wrong'. Any tax lawyer can confirm that much of our law flows from circuitous strains of reasoning, including exceptions to exceptions, i.e., limits upon limits. On questions of legal legitimacy, however, what matters is not only concrete results, but the reasoning by which they are attained. That necessarily attenuated process for arriving at the status of public discourse from 'inside' existing liberal rights jurisprudence is entirely satisfactory for case-by-case problem-solving conceived solely as arising within that already-established, positive law context, i.e., 'How is the US First Amendment to be applied in this or that particular case?'. But that approach admits only the established on paper constitution and its subsequent interpretation as foundational of democracy. It precludes from the outset precisely what Post and Weinstein seek, even once they claim to have found it, namely, an identification of the citizen's prerogative of expression in public discourse as foundational.

We can now further establish that viewpoint absolutism provides a conception superior to that of Millian liberty. We can again leave to one side the perennial problem of indeterminacy in substantive Millianism, i.e., the problem of substantive indeterminacy in Mill's concept of harm. Let us simply assume some interpretation of harm under Mill's principle such that it safeguards non-viewpoint-punitive expression within public discourse. Even on that concept of harm, recall that nothing in Mill's principle presupposes democracy (irrespective of the quasi-democratizing policies he advocates elsewhere). A monarchy could, in theory, just as easily and plausibly apply that construction of harm as a democracy might do. Nor does that restrictive reading of the concept of harm into Mill's harm principle politically or normatively presuppose a specific sphere of public discourse, even if we admit the purely sociological likelihood that such a sphere inevitably arises *incidentally* to that liberty—for the simple reason that people like to talk. By failing, then, to entail any conceptual necessity of democracy or of public discourse, that construction of the harm principle fails to supply standards for identifying public discourse as that sphere which distinctly legitimates democracy.

Once again, the distinction between, on the one hand, a generally liberal freedom of expression, and, on the other hand, the citizen's prerogative of non-viewpoint-punitive expression within public discourse bars us from rejecting democratic free speech as 'too individualist'. Communitarians ask whether the pervasively rights-based and concomitantly 'litigious' society elevates individual interests above relationships and communities. Prohibitionists, targeting the conventional notion of a free speech 'right' raise the same concern, whether or not they expressly identify as communitarian. They ask whether the speaker's interests ought to be able to trump the interests of those whom their speech demeans.[85]

That question overlooks the distinction between the democratic freedom of speech and the liberal one. *To the extent* that a liberal 'right' to free speech is construed in the classically liberal terms of a sheer 'negative liberty',[86] i.e., a duty upon the state to refrain from interference where the speech causes insufficient 'harm', it becomes indistinguishable from any other individual liberty. It swims in that pool of countless other actions—eating, drinking, shopping, playing—that one can undertake *to the extent* that government does not interfere on grounds of 'harm' ensuing from such acts. That freedom tells us something, perhaps everything, about a traditionally liberal, harm-based conception of free speech, but nothing about a distinctly democratic conception. Under a democratic conception, speech in public discourse is not merely an indifferent exercise of liberty, formally interchangeable with eating or shopping. A principle of democratic legitimacy distinguishes the irreducible status of non-viewpoint-punitive expression within public discourse, even in facially trivial contexts like, for example, student union debates about legalizing cannabis or late-night internet debates about global warming. Unlike the liberal freedom, the democratic citizen prerogative does not

---

[85] See Section 5.6.   [86] See Section 4.1, text accompanying note 17.

merely amount to a few hours spent chatting which might just as freely be spent eating or drinking.

However stupidly or ineptly it may be undertaken, non-viewpoint-punitive expression within public discourse is always a qualitatively different exercise of freedom. It is informally but nevertheless politically constitutive in a way that eating or drinking, although necessary to survive, and playing other important socializing roles, can never be in themselves. A regime of sheer, harm-based 'negative freedom' fails to distinguish among the uses to which freedom is put, except perhaps in subjective terms, such that whether one chooses to drink or chooses to engage in public discourse becomes merely a matter of private preference.

Many prohibitionists counter that democracy encompasses not only citizens' freedom, but also citizens' dignity. That calculus would re-introduce government balancing of competing interests. Instead of government balancing within the register of liberal rights, we would end up importing the same balancing into the register of democratic citizenship. We would then need a viewpoint-selective assessment about what kind of free speech, or 'how much' of it,[87] is to be permitted in view of countervailing dignitarian interests. That dignitarian view, then, does not raise an objection *within* the bounds of democratic legitimacy. It instead collapses democracy back into a sheer assumption of government-directed, value-pluralist proceduralism. It is obvious where that step would lead. The routine doctrinal and policy arguments would again line up on each side of that citizenship calculus, precisely as they currently line up on each side of the rights-based, value-pluralist calculus. That new calculus would be identical to the one it had replaced.

Liberalism posits freedom as constitutive of law's legitimacy and citizenship as derivative of it; democracy posits citizenship as constitutive of law's legitimacy and freedom as derivative of it. Hence two spheres which cannot wholly reduce to each other. Conceptual and historical overlaps between liberal and democratic movements mean that there is often no need to distinguish the two strands for many everyday problem-solving purposes. Only, as with the present problem, where the two strands yield divergent outcomes must they be distinguished as a practical matter.

Hence the triad of democratic, liberal, and security domains. *As a democratic state*, a democracy cannot legitimately impose viewpoint-selective penalties within public discourse on democratic grounds. Only *as a security state* may a democracy regulate speech as required, even viewpoint-selectively, to ensure the lives or safety of some or all of the population. But it then, like Britain in Northern Ireland, disqualifies itself as an LSPD throughout the territory in which it authorises viewpoint-selective penalties. *As a liberal state*, a democracy may subject all expression outside public discourse to its familiar, value-pluralist balancing regimes,

---

[87] See Section 4.10.

within which expression enjoys the strong legal presumption provided by an individual civil or human right.[88]

4.8 Democratic Freedom Versus Epistemic and Ethical Claims

The citizen's prerogative of non-viewpoint-punitive expression within public discourse strikes a mean between two extremes. The freedom it entails avoids, on the one hand, expanding so widely as to encompass non-viewpoint-punitive freedom beyond the bounds of public discourse (e.g., to primary schools, workplaces, or interpersonally targeted 'fighting words' scenarios).[89] On the other hand, we can now consider how, within public discourse, that freedom avoids narrowing to the point of being superseded even by the most compelling truth claims. Mill rejects any power to censor expression on the grounds that an idea is false:

> [T]he opinion which it is attempted to suppress by authority *may possibly be true*. Those who desire to suppress it, of course deny its truth; but they are not infallible. They have no authority to decide the question for all mankind, and exclude every other person from the means of judging. To refuse a hearing to an opinion, because they are sure that it is false, is to assume that their certainty is the same thing as *absolute certainty*. All silencing of discussion is an assumption of infallibility. Its condemnation may be allowed to rest on this common argument, not the worse for being common.[90]

That passage's first sentence recalls classical liberalism's ontological and epistemic scepticism. It evokes the privileged Victorian gentleman sitting in an armchair by the fireside, disposing of endless leisure to accept or reject propositions as and when his mind ambles upon them. It is the epistemology of the trial and error chemistry lab. That Baconian model of testable and ever-accumulating truth may persist today in the empirical sciences (even that point is debatable). In politics and ethics, however, it no longer commands easy acceptance. An idealistic 'marketplace' rationalism might certainly still hold that racist, xenophobic, anti-Semitic, sexist, homophobic, or other such prejudices, because their content is either factually or ethically wrong, will ultimately succumb to truth by being put 'to the test' within public discourse. Prohibitionists nevertheless rightly challenge any suggestion that such bigotries deserve freedom on grounds of the assumption that 'they may possibly be true'. In the aftermath of the Holocaust, colonialism,

---

[88] Post identifies, respectively, 'managerial', 'community', and 'democratic' domains distinguishable within an overall regime of constitutional rights. See generally, Post, 1995. By contrast, I am identifying the domain of democracy as, along with the domain of security, bound to yet distinct from the domain of rights. What Post deems to be the 'democratic' domain *within* rights is, rather, the domain of *individual* interests, merely taking democracy into account. Our two schemas can then be reconciled as follows. As a state, a democracy broadly maintains the three, often overlapping domains of security, rights, and democracy. The domain of rights, in turn, subdivides into managerial, community, and individual sectors.

[89] It must again be emphasized that such a limitation does not destroy that freedom entirely outside public discourse, but merely leaves it within the familiar sphere of liberal rights balancing.

[90] *On Liberty*, ch. 2, *in* Mill, [1869] 1991, p. 22 (emphasis added).

trans-Atlantic slavery, and regimes of lawful racial segregation, prohibitionists rightly doubt whether ethical reason—if the concept of 'ethics' is not to languish into absurdity—can seriously be said to assume classical liberalism's neutral, empiricist model of a blank slate upon which reasoned conclusions always ultimately remain up for grabs.

Either slave plantations and Auschwitz are absolutely unethical, demonstrating a moral certainty from which we proceed to develop further ethical notions (including the far more complex ones, e.g., about the rights and wrongs of legalizing drugs or of assisted suicide), or else we dispense with any serious notion of ethics entirely, and conceive of humanity in determinist or mechanistic terms. But to suppose some hypothetical 'ethics' in which crudely racist, anti-Semitic, or other prejudices 'may possibly be true' (except, perhaps, for a classroom-type thought experiment)[91] is not to 'open up' onto some innocently 'pluralist' concept of ethics. It instead eviscerates the project of ethical reason entirely.

Life, the prohibitionist reminds us, exists beyond the seminar room. A democracy, on that view, may legitimately penalize expression that *could* never reconcile with any plausible ethics at all.[92] That prohibitionist stance adopts, then, a persuasive premise. The classical liberal 'blank slate' theory of knowledge, according to which *anything* 'may possibly be true' misconceives the character of ethical reasoning and practice, as if there were no difference between reasoning processes of ethics and those of the chemistry lab.

That prohibitionist premise is sound. The widely shared conclusion which is supposed to follow from it does not, however, logically or ethically follow at all. The citizen prerogative of non-viewpoint-punitive expression within public discourse does not just slightly diminish, as if it were a quantitative measure, when it becomes abridged on the grounds that some subset of attempts at persuasion must from the outset be doomed by an ethical insight that has been recognized in advance to be greater or better. In a word: the problem is about citizenship, and not, as Mill maintains, about epistemic or ethical rightness. Nor does that kind of exception entail, as prohibitionists often suggest, a *de minimis* adjustment.[93] It undermines the citizen's democratic prerogative at the core. Mill's conclusion is correct, but he reaches it incorrectly. Contrary to his starting point, we ought indeed to assume certain ethical absolutes. But they in no way confer upon a democracy any legitimate censorial power over even the crudest dissent from them within public discourse.

The citizen's democratic prerogative cannot coherently depend on some conceptually antecedent criterion of either truth or value. Socrates's prerogative

---

[91] After all, to articulate, in a seminar-room sense, and against any and every conceivable challenge, *why* genocides or plantation slavery are categorical evils can be tricky, which is one reason why few of our intellectuals and none of our students are able to do it. The Greeks recognized that kind of pure disputational exercise as a 'debater's argument' (literally, 'thesis' or 'position'). See, e.g., *Meno* 80e, 81d, *in* Plato, [4th century BCE] 1997, p. 880; *Nicomachean Ethics* 1.5.1096ᵃ1-3, *in* Aristotle, [4th century BCE] 1984, vol. 2, p. 1732.

[92] Cf., e.g., Thiel, 2003a.   [93] See Section 5.8.

to talk like a philosopher is a prerogative to talk like a fanatic, a lunatic, a subversive, an ignoramus, or a bigot. '[T]rue statements and false statements, useful opinions and harmful or hurtful opinions—all becomes juxtaposed and blended in the tumble of democracy.'[94] The citizen prerogative does not expand so widely, even beyond public discourse, as to entail the undifferentiated licence yielded by a restrictive, libertarian interpretation of 'harm' under Mill's principle; but nor can the prerogative legitimately be narrowed even in the face of factual or ethical certainty (at least, not without a demonstrable link to harm, as with commercial fraud). By extension, 'marketplace' theories of free speech, rightly challenged by prohibitionists, do indeed add little to the oppositionist cause. Contrary to widespread belief, leading oppositionists like Baker, Dworkin, Post, or Weinstein have mostly abandoned any serious reliance on marketplace rationales.

The marketplace model is already anticipated before the ascent of modern free-market economics, for example, in John Milton's famous mid-seventeenth-century injunction: 'though all the winds of doctrine were let loose to play upon the earth, so Truth be in the field, we do injuriously, by licensing and prohibiting, to misdoubt her strength'.[95] Two centuries later, Europe, and particularly Britain, witness the rise of three mutually reinforcing social developments. One is the rise of *scientific positivism*, which views the best idea as emerging from the free competition of conflicting hypotheses. Another trend is *Darwinism*, notably as translated into overtly social terms by figures such as Herbert Spencer. 'Social Darwinism' presents individual competition as salutary and 'natural' for human progress. It views the best product as emerging from the interplay of, respectively, conflicting natural or social forces. A third influence is laissez-faire economics, which views the best product as emerging from the free competition of rival market forces.

The second chapter of Mill's *On Liberty* reflects those nineteenth-century currents. For Mill, truth emerges from the clash of opinions. Classical economic theory, however, predicts a socially beneficial distribution of resources through apolitical assumptions about marketplace actors' equal bargaining positions. Similarly, Mill's theory tacitly assumes the de-politicized, 'gentlemen's club' context of a Victorian elite, for whom ideas are entertained in sedentary removal from the hierarchies of socio-economic life. That marketplace theory does not merely advocate a random freedom to exchange ideas. It takes Mill's further leap of faith that the best product will result from such clashes.

The marketplace theory assumes a criterion as to the character of truth and of how we acquire it. It betrays its historical roots in those various nineteenth-century intellectual trends. The US Supreme Court is still a decade before the great Wall Street crash of 1929 when Holmes echoes Mill's discursive optimism, joined by Louis Brandeis, that 'the best test of truth is the power of the thought to get itself

---

[94] Foucault, 2009, p. 36.
[95] Milton, [1644] 1991, p. 269. Milton, as it happens, had no intention of admitting Catholics.

accepted in the competition of the market'.[96] With the serendipitous hand often allowed by a dissenting opinion, Holmes fibs, 'That, at any rate, is the theory of our Constitution'.[97] The late eighteenth-century framers of the Bill of Rights had not in fact justified protection of speech in such specifically epistemological terms. Holmes's rapidly industrializing, pre-Depression, Anglo-American world could nevertheless confidently ascribe the power of markets to laissez-faireism, trusting that marketplace evils would steadily self-correct.

As the twentieth century progressed, laissez-faireism, social Darwinism, and scientific positivism would face growing challenges.[98] Today, they can scarcely be embraced on face value, even if they still boast eager disciples. Holmes's view reflects, if not an American jurisprudence, then certainly an American folklore. Given America's free market ethos, it is tempting to take this Holmesian dictum, too, on face value. Even after shifting towards Holmes's viewpoint-absolutist stance in the 1960s, the US Supreme Court never adopts a marketplace epistemology test in any rigorous sense. It remains at the level of metaphor. For cases involving hateful or hurtful speech, the Justices invoke their various 'vagueness', 'overbreadth', 'underinclusiveness', or viewpoint-neutrality principles,[99] but rarely suggest any epistemologically rigorous view that such criteria necessarily favour truth. Notwithstanding Holmes's Damascene conversion to epistemological optimism,[100] his successors on the Court certainly adopt no detailed 'theory' of the constitution which would protect hate speech on the specific grounds of its defeat through competition with tolerant ideas.[101]

Comparative scholars sometimes cite Holmes's and Brandeis's marketplace analogies,[102] while overlooking important caveats. Originating in a pre-Great Depression world, those dicta do capture a social aspiration, a popular mythology, in impressionistic terms. But they never induce the US Supreme Court to develop a systematic technique for comparing the truth-seeking consequences of upholding any given speech regulation with the consequences of striking it down. Nor would most judges deem themselves trained or competent to perform that task. As to hate speech, rules on Holocaust denial might admittedly form an exception. Legislators and judges in Europe do indeed posit a body of factual assertions to be immune from popular or scholarly challenges, in what might be called a vein of marketplace-epistemological scepticism. That exception cannot, however, be called distinctly representative of the 'European' model. It arises only

---

[96] *Abrams v. United States* 250 U.S. 616, 630 (1919) (Holmes, J., dissenting). See critically, e.g., Richards, 1999, pp. 16–17; Sunstein, 1995, p. 25.

[97] Abrams, 250 U.S. at 630.   [98] Cf., e.g., Sunstein, 1995, pp. 25–6, 29–32.

[99] See, e.g., Nowak & Rotunda, 2009, pp. 1274–81.   [100] See Healy, 2013.

[101] In an influential dissenting opinion in the landmark McCarthy-era case of *Dennis v. United States*, Justice Douglas invokes a marketplace aspiration. By allowing pro-Soviet speech, he argues, 'the ugliness of Communism is revealed, its deceit and cunning are exposed, the nature of its activities becomes apparent, and the chances of its success less likely.' *Dennis v. United States*, 341 U.S. 494, 582 (Douglas, J., dissenting). But Douglas neither cites precedent to suggest that the Court has generally adopted a view that the best ideas will prevail, nor has his view subsequently been recognized by the Court as establishing such a criterion.

[102] See, e.g., Belavusau, 2013, pp. 83–4.

in some democracies, and then more on the view of Holocaust denial as thinly disguised anti-Semitic hate speech than on thoroughgoing epistemological grounds. Accordingly, even in those states, the principle has not generally been extended to other factual scenarios of equal certainty, underscoring its *sui generis* character. The same observation applies to leading US oppositionists. Baker's, Post's, and Weinstein's painstaking analyses of the case law disavow marketplace theories as either descriptively or prescriptively adequate accounts of US law.[103]

Rob Wijnberg's 2008 manifesto *In Dubio: Vrijheid van meningsuiting als het recht om te twijfelen* (*In Dubio: Freedom of opinion as the right to doubt*) nonetheless offers an ideal example of the resilience of Mill's marketplace view. The Dutch publicist sticks closely enough to Mill to commit the same error—still reaching a defensible conclusion, but still for the wrong reasons. Wijnberg derives the necessity of a free play of ideas from Mill's epistemological scepticism,[104] in a vein reminiscent of Cartesian radical doubt,[105]

[O]nly an unshakeable definition of the Good ... can create a definitive basis for limiting freedom in a generally valid sense. It is no surprise, then, that nearly the entire history of thought consists of a search for precisely that definition: the irrefutable formula for distinguishing between Good and Evil—without success.[106]

For Wijnberg, 'unshakeable' notions of 'the Good' remain elusive. Only a Millian type of unhindered debate provides the best answers. That confidence bears, in turn, the hallmarks of Enlightenment rationalism.[107] A crucial point of post-colonial and post-Holocaust moral theory, however, and which challenges the older sceptical tradition assumed by Mill, is that an 'infallible definition of the Good' is not required to comprehend categorical evil.[108] Wijnberg may well embrace the view that a moral judgement is 'never definitively true',[109] but many prohibitionists rightly view condemnations of the Holocaust or trans-Atlantic slavery as 'definitive' for any discourse that does not reduce the concept of morality to a nonsense,

---

[103] One obstacle confronting some of the Euro-American comparisons, such as those of Belavusau, Pech, or Robitaille-Froidure, is the formidable obstacles they confront in the secondary literature on the US First Amendment, and on US constitutional law more generally. That shortfall surely arises from the sheer volume of literature, which leaves foreign scholars scarcely equipped for the necessary triage. Scholars unfamiliar with that corpus run the risk of construing too literally, hence too sweepingly, dicta such as Holmes's or Brandeis's marketplace epistemology credos. Impressionist metaphors come to appear as doctrinal imperatives. As I have noted, the same problem in reverse afflicts US-based prohibitionists who praise the black-letter of non-US bans with no enquiry into those bans' political or legal contexts. See, e.g., Heinze, 2008a.

[104] Cf., e.g., Wijnberg, 2008, p. 101 (citing Russell). Although Wijnberg rejects the label of 'scepticism', he does so only to distinguish his view, which certainly does fit the tradition in its prevalent philosophical sense, from one that would reject a specifically doctrinaire ethics, i.e., from an 'unqualified denial (*ontkennen*) of the existence of a definition of the Good.' Wijnberg, 2008, p. 42.

[105] Cf., e.g., Wijnberg, 2008, p. 127.

[106] Wijnberg, 2008, p. 24, see also at pp. 31–2, 43.

[107] Cf. Wijnberg, 2008, pp. 83–4, 126.

[108] See, e.g., Heinze, 2013a, pp. 13–49; Zwagerman, 2009, pp. 8–14. Cf. *Die Welt als Wille und Vorstellung* §§63–68, *in* Schopenhauer, [1819] 1996, pp. 487–540.

[109] Wijnberg, 2008, p. 43. Cf. Wijnberg, 2008, p. 44 (citing Mill's thesis, 'The usefulness of an opinion is itself a matter of opinion'.) Cf., e.g., Schauer, 2012 (critically discussing Mill's epistemologically grounded defence of speech).

hence Theodor Adorno's cognitivist view of the immorality of such atrocities as epistemically constitutive, and not morally speculative.[110]

Free expression requires a justification stronger than the possibility that a democratic majority might someday be persuaded to vote for a new Auschwitz. Viewpoint absolutism lies in democracy's legitimating condition of allowing one's worldview to be expressed in public discourse not because that worldview 'may possibly be true', but also when there can be no question that it is heinously wrong. An LSPD cannot legitimately impose viewpoint-selective penalties within public discourse on grounds of that idea's inferior ethical value. It must preserve all ideas' *civic* equality, irrespective of intellectual inequality.[111] Einstein's theory of relativity remains democratically equal to L. Ron Hubbard's theory of 'Scientology', even while the two are, we can only hope, intellectually unequal.[112] That civic equality 'attaches to persons', as citizens, and 'not ideas'.[113]

Again, accusations of 'dictatorialism' or 'totalitarianism' misrepresent prohibitionism, as most prohibitionists, even those favouring broad bans, support the overwhelming freedom of expression which remains beyond bans. We end up with two clashing intuitions. On the one hand, the oppositionist suspects that viewpoint-selective penalties within public discourse represent a rejection of democratic principles. Even the narrowest ban makes no sense except on the inadmissible assumption that officials may exercise a legitimate power to penalize the expression of certain views within the public sphere. Once the power to ban is assumed in principle it knows no *inherent* limits—which is the essence of dictatorial government—even if it is, as a practical matter, exercised 'carefully', 'responsibly', 'with great care', and 'with sensitivity and good judgment'.[114]

On the other hand, the accusation of dictatorialism seems overblown, not only in view of the bans' scope or their dignitarian or egalitarian rationales, but because bans do generally fall well within the bounds of democratic controls. The question is not about whether, but rather about the sense in which such accusations are exaggerated. Viewpoint-selective penalties within public discourse diminish democratic legitimacy even when we unreservedly recognize that hateful expression is wrong. Hate speech bans within LSPDs are in no serious sense politically dictatorial, but are nevertheless *epistemically dictatorial*.

---

[110] See, e.g., Adorno, 1971, p. 88.

[111] See Post, 1996–97, p. 1530; Post, 2011a, pp. 484–5.

[112] The political equality of ideas—the disaggregation of intellectual and political status—is what Plato notoriously condemns in those of his writings which expressly reject democracy. The *Republic* derives political value from intellectual value. Precisely by rejecting the political parity of ideas for the *Republic*'s idealized society, Plato confirms such parity as a defining feature of democracy. Never does Plato seek to *reform* democracy by coercively eliminating bad opinions, because that would not be democracy at all.

[113] Post, 2011a, p. 479 (comparing Kant and Meiklejohn). See also Post, 2011a, pp. 479–80 (distinguishing autonomy from democratic citizenship as a basis for the civic equality of speakers); Post, 1996–97, pp. 1531–2; and generally, Post, 2006. Cf. Post, 1996–97, p. 1531 (discussing Fiss).

[114] See Section 3.2, text accompanying notes 17–20.

The moment in which a state suspends democracy in favour of what is an essentially dictatorial power, as in a declared state of emergency, is the moment in which it pursues security interests, and not democratic ones. Prohibitionists see hatred as an extremism, an exception to the rule of democracy, for which a commensurately exceptional and extreme response becomes justified. Accordingly, a viewpoint-selective ban within public discourse may not be politically dictatorial; but, however minimal it may be, it adds to its epistemic dictatorialism the coercive force of the state.

4.9 Autonomy and Personhood

Having distinguished a democratic foundation for public discourse from rights-based approaches and from epistemological, truth-based approaches, we can also distinguish it from *personhood* or *autonomy* theories, for which expression remains an essential mode of human existence.[115] That overtly individualist stance presents an ontologized liberalism, in contrast to the Millian tradition of ontologically sceptical or agnostic liberalism. On the personhood theory, censorship on grounds of sheer viewpoint, absent compelling evidence of harm beyond the idea's inherent odiousness, negates what is distinctly human about the speaker. In de-humanizing any speaker in that way, even a speaker whose ideas de-humanize others, far from overcoming the logic of hate speech, the state perpetuates it. By analogy, in most Western democracies, it has long been thought that A torturing or beating B does not justify the state in torturing or beating A.

C. Edwin Baker refuses to derive prerogatives of speech from assumptions about political legitimacy, such as those discussed thus far. Baker views expression not merely, as I do here, as conceptually pre-legal. He takes a giant step further, deeming it to be existentially pre-political, i.e., as primordially constitutive of the human being, irrespective of social or political contexts.[116] Although Baker does not expressly cite Aristotle, an Aristotelian perspective sheds light on that kind of personhood theory. Aristotle examines the distinct 'function' (ἔργον) of the human as such. That function is not the sole thing that humans are or manifest. It is what they are or manifest such as to be distinguished from other animals or from plants.[117] He famously identifies the distinctly human function as 'an activity of soul (ψυχῆς) in accordance with reason (κατὰ λόγον)'.[118] That view has been thought to reduce human subjectivity to abstract, individual rationalism, which deeply misreads Aristotle and most other Greeks. That *logos* entails both *reason* and *speech*. Reason manifests not merely through solitary thought processes, but

---

[115] See, e.g., Baker, 1989, pp. 53–4; Baker, 2009; Baker, 2011; Baker, 2012; Emerson, 1963, pp. 879–81; Josende, 2010, pp. 6–11; Nieuwenhuis, 2011, pp. 23–4.
[116] Baker, 2012.
[117] *Nicomachean Ethics*, 1.7.1097ᵇ32-98ᵃ3, *in* Aristotle, [4th century BCE] 1984, p. 1735.
[118] *Nicomachean Ethics*, 1.7.1098ᵃ8, *in* Aristotle, [4th century BCE] 1999, p. 9.

also through interactive process of communication. We do not ban, but rather entertain even the worst ideas to safeguard our vigilance in refuting them. To that foundation we can add later theories of communication as something not merely attributable to, but constitutive of the human, from Herder or Hegel through to Wittgenstein or Merleau-Ponty. Personhood theories identify semiotic complexity and polysemic texture as foundational for the human. Accordingly, our humanity becomes diminished, if not erased, when expression, however trivial or repulsive, is coercively silenced to achieve collective aims. Such theories become long and complex. They reach far beyond any summary I can offer here.

One problem in moral reasoning poses an obstacle for personhood theories. Even if we accept a descriptive 'is' of humans as constitutively communicative, such theories risk mistaking a culturally determinate prescriptive preference, an observed 'is', for a universal value or 'ought'. Baker's ambitious ontologizing of free expression, in contrast to the restricted role of political legitimation solely within the bounds of the LSPD model, would tacitly absolutize liberal freedom to a quasi-libertarian extreme, losing any distinction between, on the one hand, fighting words or primary educational and workplace situations, and, on the other hand, public discourse. (Again in Kantian terms, Baker strives for a categorical imperative where a hypothetical imperative more plausibly performs the task of identifying the legitimating expressive conditions for modern democracies.)

Many an anthropologist would argue that, from the observed phenomenon of humans' constitutive expressiveness, there by no means follows a universal *norm* elevating that value above other recognized human attributes or values. It remains controversial to recognize as universal or essential a social value that few cultures throughout history or today have unequivocally embraced. A gap between the sociological and the normative, between that which describes and that which pre-scribes the human, widens here to the hilt. One drawback is that advocates of the personhood or autonomy theories have not taken anti-essentialist or social constructionist objections into account, nor is it obvious how they might do so. We stray too close to heralding as universal a value that has rarely if ever been adopted throughout most human cultures and histories (some have argued that we face such hurdles with notions of higher-order individual interests or rights al-together, but that is another long debate).[119] Dworkin runs into similar problems. He argues that free speech is, without qualification, a universal right, required not only in democracies, but everywhere, 'even in non-democratic societies'.[120] He performs that sweeping claim in a few lines, as if such a vast universalism, covering incalculable and often inscrutable cultural and historical situations, is trivially—in his words, 'plainly'[121]—obvious. Such formulaics fall too far short on crucial details of culture and history.

---

[119] For other criticisms of autonomy or personhood theories, see, e.g., Post, 2011a, pp. 479–82; Weinstein, 2011a, pp. 502–4, 506–11. But see Williams, 2011, pp. 607–10 (examining 'narrative autonomy').

[120] Dworkin, 2009, p. ix.

[121] Dworkin, 2009, p. ix. Cf., critically, Holmes, 2012, pp. 345–6.

4.10 Citizenship Unmodified

Bleich begins and ends his empirical study by asking, 'Just how much freedom should we *give* to racists?'[122] Yet that formulation of the debate raises several problems. First, there can be no democratically legitimate 'we', independently constituted in some conceptual antechamber to the polity, and charged with 'giving' out those attributes which constitute individuals as citizens. To the contrary, as we have seen, a state draws democratic legitimacy from the assumption of individuals already constituted as citizens. Second, nor does any such 'we' take the form of that legislature or judiciary, or other responsible institutions, which are themselves legitimately created only *by* full-fledged citizens, who are *always first exercising* those democratic attributes in both formal political and informal social settings. Third, those attributes are not quantities to be measured out, either literally or figuratively, in terms of 'how much' is to be accorded to each citizen, in proportion to each citizen's worldviews, let alone as the object of outright 'trade-offs'[123] consigned to legislators or judges.[124]

Such legislative or judicial parcelling does not promote, but rather erodes democratic legitimacy. The citizen's prerogative of non-viewpoint-punitive expression within democratic public discourse—unlike, for example, least-restrictive, non-viewpoint-punitive, 'time, manner, and place' limitations—cannot be the state's to give or to withhold *in part*, through government balancing, for the same reason that it is never the state's to give or to withhold *in full*.[125] Advocates of 'narrow' hate speech bans, as the adjective suggests, often speak in such literally or figuratively quantifying terms. They argue that 'very little' speech will be affected, being, moreover, speech of very 'low' grade, with vast freedoms of speech still left intact. On that view, any philosophy or worldview may be presented in public discourse, as long as its articulation is not excessively provocative. Presumably, although they rarely state their case in such explicit terms, they would legalize, for example, T.S. Eliot's upmarket anti-Semitism,[126] and even Brigitte Bardot's mid-market Islamophobia,[127] but not Omar Bakri Mohammad's downmarket homophobia.[128]

I shall examine the notion of 'incitement', i.e., the risk of translation into violent or discriminatory action, with which narrow bans are often concerned,

---

[122] Bleich, 2011, p. 5 (original emphasis) and pp. 133–55. By 'racists', Bleich means racist *speakers*. As to racially motivated murders, beatings, vandalism, etc., see Section 5.9.

[123] Bleich, 2011, pp. 5, 6.

[124] Bleich's, Delgado's, Matsuda's, Parekh's, or Waldron's approaches, and the quantifying concept which such weighing and balancing notions expressly or implicitly entail, become typical specimens of Rancière's view that apprehensions about democracy are constantly expressed as a fear of democratic 'excess' (*démesure*) or 'limitlessness' (*illimitation*) (Rancière, 2005, pp. 26, 36, 38, 41, 48, 70), which we could call the fear of democracy's quantitative boundlessness, tracing as far back as Plato's *Gorgias* or *Republic*.

[125] Cf. Narr, 2002, pp. 126–7.   [126] See, e.g., Wynne-Jones, 1996.

[127] See, e.g., Bleich, 2011, pp. 17–18.   [128] See, e.g., Dodd, 2013.

in Section 5.9. As to viewpoints themselves, however, narrow bans in no way avoid the problems posed by broad ones, because citizenship does not exist in parcels, in the way that freedoms must do by definition (as was noted in Section 3.2). Elements such as speech duration, or speech volume, which may be routine time, manner, and place elements, can certainly be quantified. But non-viewpoint-punitive expression in public discourse cannot be quantified and apportioned because viewpoints as such do not exist in either literal or figurative quantities.

For Waldron, 'there is a lawful way of expressing something like *the propositional content* of views that become objectionable when expressed *as vituperation*.'[129] We can certainly identify materially quantifiable linguistic signifiers (e.g., phonemes)—loud or soft, or of long or short duration.[130] However, the opinions or meanings (e.g., morphemes) they signify[131] are not materially quantifiable. Opinions cannot be viewpoint-neutrally divided into component ingredients. Viewpoint-punitive bans within public discourse are not suddenly rendered legitimate simply because—to quote more of the customary quantifying formulas—there are only 'very few prosecutions',[132] or because those prosecutions are 'relatively low-profile',[133] or because only a 'fairly small fine'[134] is imposed on offenders, or because 'enforcement has not been heavy-handed'.[135]

That public discourse which is democracy's distinctly legitimating medium is not a cake for the state—a state which public discourse itself constitutes—to measure out and to slice up; nor are its citizens so many children sitting around the kitchen table to be awarded larger and smaller slices in function of their good or bad opinions. Our analysis becomes misbegotten when, from the outset, the question of hate speech is formulated as 'How much freedom should we *give* to racists?', as if one class of citizens can formally resolve, through a fully constituted legal procedure, to degrade the co-equal citizen attributes of another class.[136] That approach resumes the instrumentalist calculus assumed by a purely managerial concept of citizenship, as an effluence of bureaucratic record-keeping (birth certificates, passports, and the like), within which government distributes goods in quantified terms.[137]

Debates in the West surrounding gay marriage, for example, mean that opponents must by definition assert the inferiority of gay unions vis-à-vis heterosexual ones, even if they staunchly insist that such inferiority does not extend to any broader, human inferiority.[138] We must, for example, apply the core values of ICERD article 4(a), beyond their specific application to race, unless non-discrimination

---

[129] Waldron, 2012b, p. 335 (emphasis added).
[130] Cf., e.g., Martinet, 2008, pp. 79–114; Saussure, 1981, pp. 44–113.
[131] Cf., e.g., Martinet, 2008, pp. 115–52; Saussure, 1981, pp. 141–92.
[132] Bleich, 2011, p. 27. Cf., e.g., Thiel, 2003b, pp. 21, 22.
[133] Bleich, 2011, p. 29.   [134] Belavusau, 2013, p. 67.
[135] Bleich, 2011, p. 27.   [136] Cf. Foucault, 2009, p. 43.
[137] On the quantification of citizen attributes as commodification, see, e.g., Rancière, 2005, p. 25 (discussing Marx).
[138] See, e.g., Matussek, 2014.

instruments are themselves to become instruments of discrimination. But then any public debate on gay marriage becomes impossible, as we would then have to 'declare an offence punishable by law *all* dissemination of ideas' based on hetero-sexual 'superiority'. One might seek to avoid that result by distinguishing sexual orientation from race as a targeted classification. A threshold obstacle, however, is the implausibility of the ways such a distinction between sexual and ethnic minor-ities, as vulnerable social groups, is to be drawn.

The universalist phrasing of hate speech bans in terms of protected classifi-cations means either that democratic public discourse, as in the gay marriage debate, becomes undermined, or that hate speech bans become vehicles of the very discrimination they purport to combat, by distinguishing between more and less protected categories of target groups. We end up with a new kind of quantification, as two classes of targeted groups now emerge: first, groups who qualify as targets of discrimination, and who receive greater legal protection; and second, groups who qualify as targets of discrimination, but who receive some lesser legal protection. (A third group, not qualifying as targets of discrim-ination, hence receiving no protection, such as, under most current bans, per-sons physically overweight, may entail yet further inconsistencies.) Hate speech bans, designed to combat discrimination, then generate their own discrimin-atory categories, their own categories of greater and lesser protection of targeted groups, hence their own categories of greater and lesser viewpoint expression. The proceduralist myth of moderation and balancing turns precisely into its opposite—an unavoidably arbitrary regime of protected and unprotected tar-gets of hate speech.[139]

It might be objected that *any* legal restriction on freedom in some sense dimin-ishes citizenship. But that objection, too, would conflate citizenship prerogatives with liberal rights. In practice, much of what happens in the day-to-day life of democracy can indeed be understood in procedurally Millian terms of government demarcating freedoms with reference to harms. Many generally liberal freedoms can be cast in quantifying terms of more and less. Democracy's legitimating expres-sive conditions, by contrast, are fulfilled by admitting all viewpoints into public discourse, thereby precluding either qualifying or quantifying distinctions between admissible and inadmissible viewpoints.

In 2014, the French Conseil d'État upheld the prohibition of an anti-Semitic performance by the entertainer Dieudonné M'bala M'bala. Endorsing the deci-sion, leading French officials and intellectuals rehearsed an epigram popular among French supporters of bans, namely, in the words even of *Le Monde*'s editors, that such 'systematic provocations' are 'not opinions, but crimes'.[140] That assessment

---

[139] Cf., e.g., Heinze, 2009b.

[140] *Le Monde*, 2014 ('Les provocations systématiques de M. M'bala M'bala ne sont pas des opin-ions, mais des délits, punis par la loi.'). Senior officials employing such a maxim on that or related issues include former Prime Minister Jean-Marc Ayrault and former Justice Minister Christiane Taubira (Ms Taubira, too, has been the target of racist slurs). Cf. Faux, 2014; *Le Nouvel Observateur*, 2013; Gonzalvez, 2014. Cf. also Rachedi, 2014.

might at first be construed as rhetorical hyperbole, a catchy phrase to emphasize outrage at ongoing anti-Semitism or racism. Any such offhand quip readily merges, however, into legal literalism.

Consider an analogy. A ban on heroin obviously cannot warrant us in declaring, 'It is not a drug, but a prohibited substance'. Heroin is banned not despite its failure to be a drug, but precisely because it is a drug. Law does, of course, operate through linguistic 'performatives'. To cite a famous example, a duly empowered individual does not merely recapitulate the social world, but transforms it, creating a state of marriage, by uttering the words 'I now pronounce you man and wife'.[141] To extrapolate, however, from that function of law to an unbridled metaphysics—a collapse of social phenomena into the after-effects of legal rules—would be to load the theory of linguistic performatives with a greater weight than it can bear: 'I now pronounce you no longer an opinion'.

It is easy enough to understand why French history, including the Dreyfus affair or complicity with Nazi Germany, induces public figures to condemn anti-Semitism, particularly in view of its rapid rise throughout the early twenty-first century.[142] Anti-Semitism does not, however, lose its character as an opinion by falling under the magic wand of a ban, as if *ab initio* the only opinions which remain opinions are those which evade bans. Even in cases of doubt as to the content of an expressive act, it is the ban itself which confirms a hateful opinion as, by definition, an opinion.[143] Whatever French officials may purport to be doing, they ban intolerant expression not because it fails to communicate an opinion, but because of the opinion it communicates. (To be sure, bans remain disputed in France, as in other democracies. While resolutely condemning intolerance, many French public officials have challenged the country's bans on speech, as we equally discover in the pages of *Le Monde*.)[144]

In modern times, French democracy has never sat comfortably with the notion of 'crimes of opinion' (*délits d'opinion*)—a discomfort indeed in a state both celebrating its revolutionary and republican heritage, and high intellectual achievements, while maintaining exceptionally broad bans. The strategy behind the 'not an opinion, but a crime' mantra is obviously to surmount the contradiction between democratic expression and hateful opinion by defining the latter as 'not opinion'. Of all possible resolutions to the problem of hate speech, that abracadabra is the least credible. The second best solution, if an LSPD refuses to embrace non-viewpoint-punitive expression within public discourse, is to declare honestly that it does indeed punish the expression of certain worldviews, and that it openly renounces that measure of democratic legitimacy, for whichever historical or cultural reasons it then wishes to state. The least legitimate solution for any democracy is to justify a ban through an Orwellian re-defining of undesirable viewpoints as *not* viewpoints.

---

[141] Austin, 1962, pp. 8–9.   [142] See, e.g., Taguieff, 2002; Taguieff, 2004.
[143] See Section 2.6, text accompanying notes 53–7.
[144] See, e.g., Wieder, 2014. Cf. Section 5.7, text accompanying note 209.

4.11 The Active Democracy

It is illegitimate, then, for an LSPD to impose viewpoint-punitive bans within public discourse. That measure of illegitimacy casts no shadow, however, over the state's non-viewpoint-punitive measures for promoting civic and social pluralism. The LSPD must remain ideologically neutral (or, if one prefers, the LSPD must maintain the ideology *of* ideological neutrality) solely in the sense of avoiding viewpoint-selective penalties within public discourse. That imperative entails no further requirement of neutrality as to non-viewpoint-punitive measures. Of course, such measures *can* be non-punitive by facilitating diversity without imposing punishments. However, as with anti-discrimination laws they can also impose punishments without violating any criterion of democratic legitimacy. Both types of rule flow legitimately from decisions reached within value-pluralist processes precisely insofar as no viewpoint has been barred from the public discourse that surrounds those processes. Both types promote democratic participation, having been decisive for the historical emergence of the LSPD model.

The perennial mistake of extrapolating *from* the imperative of non-viewpoint-selective access to public discourse *to* an assumption of overall state neutrality categorically misstates democracy's legitimating expressive conditions. Among US writers, that mistake often arises from superficially literal readings of the First Amendment. Writers err in reading 'the American' approach as requiring, unlike 'the European' approach, strict government neutrality.[145] Post replies, 'The American state takes substantive positions [against intolerance] all the time.' He asks us to '[c]onsider', for example, concrete measures, such as 'regulation of workplace actions and speech' or 'the rules and regulations that the American state imposes on the army, on government institutions, on contractors, and so on', as well as established statements of adopted policy, including 'the ongoing expression of American government officials about issues of race and tolerance.' Post concludes that '[n]o one should confuse the American state with a neutral state'. Contrary to common opinion, the contrast between the US and even, for example, the strongly prohibitionist German or French states is, in that respect, 'much smaller' than has been suggested.[146]

The model of a democracy constituted through public discourse does not collapse into schemas of a 'libertarian', morally abdicated 'night watchman state'. It does not force upon us a crude choice between, on the one hand, criminally punishing intolerant expression, or, on the other, remaining 'morally neutral', even callously indifferent. Waldron mistakenly assumes that model of law—already outmoded with Hart's *The Concept of Law* (1961), though arguably well before—when

---

[145] See, e.g., Belavusau, 2013, pp. 109–10; Pech, 2003, pp. 422–4; Robitaille-Froidure, 2011, p. 48.
[146] Molnar & Post, 2012, p. 26.

he charges that, for opponents of bans, intolerance is 'no concern of the law'.[147] While not explicitly denying alternative approaches, Waldron never examines any concept of law's approach to hate speech beyond that reductively punitive model of law as coercive rules.[148] He wrongly attributes to oppositionists the belief that, as far as law is concerned, the 'people who are targeted' by hate speech 'should just learn to live with it'.[149]

Writers at the strongly libertarian end may take such a stance.[150] Oppositionists, however, along with a prevailing US Supreme Court position, have long made clear that they presuppose no such view either of the law or of its underlying ethics.[151] The countries that Waldron identifies as 'advanced'[152] democracies have long taken a varied range of steps against hatred. As Baker reminds us, the debate has never seriously been between 'uncaring "liberal" defenders of free speech and fierce opponents of the worst forms of racism.'[153] Primary school curricula entail government-directed choices (including private schools, which require accreditation), allowing states to implement comprehensive education in pluralist policies and practices. States can and ought to strengthen that curriculum.

Those censorial choices within, for example, education or employment do entail punitive or disciplinary measures. Staff must comply, and parents must send their children to school.[154] *Any* ideological grounds, or none at all, for derogating from state-prescribed primary education, or for denying it to one's own children, may legitimately be penalized. There is no such thing as non-censorial primary education, as there is no such thing as wholly child-controlled education. The state-authorized curriculum constantly makes value-laden selections for teaching civics, arts, humanities, and social sciences. LSPDs frequently voice their own pluralist philosophy within public discourse. They may implement it by assessing penalties for non-compliance outside public discourse, for example, in schools or employment situations, without imposing viewpoint-selective penalties within public discourse.

The democratic state maintains a duty to pursue a censorially ethical agenda by promoting pluralism, and indeed ought to enhance its ways of

---

[147] Waldron, 2012a, p. 3. Cf., e.g., Parekh, 2012, p. 50. But cf. also, e.g., Strossen, 1990, pp. 489–90 (criticizing a similar 'straw civil libertarian' view expressed by Lawrence).

[148] Cf. Hart, 1994, pp. 7, 20–5. One might argue that Waldron's only interest is in bans per se, which are by definition punitive. However, no serious legal analysis can so narrowly circumscribe a legal interest when its very essence is its broad social and symbolic scope. The crux of Waldron's 'slow-acting poison' thesis is his insistence upon a broadly sociological view of the effects of hate speech, and his urging of a legal-realist sensibility. See Section 5.3, text accompanying note 71; and, critically, Heinze, 2013b, pp. 607–9.

[149] Waldron, 2012a, p. 3. To be fair, Waldron takes his view in response to the equally reductionist oppositionist view of Anthony Lewis. See, e.g., Waldron, 2012a, pp. 32–3.

[150] See, e.g., Caine, 2004–05.

[151] Waldron discusses both at some length. See Waldron, 2012a, pp. 36–7, 157–8, 197–201; Waldron & Weinstein, 2012.

[152] Waldron, 2012a, p. 29. Cf. Section 5.4, text accompanying note 102.

[153] Baker, 2009, p. 149. Cf. Brettschneider, 2010, pp. 1005–6 (comparing Dworkin and Waldron).

[154] Home schooling remains too rare to have a general social impact, and, at any rate, remains subject to curricular requirements.

doing so, albeit without imposing viewpoint-selective penalties within public discourse.[155] The mission of primary education in a democracy is certainly to initiate pupils into critical thinking, but by no means on an assumption of value neutrality. On the one hand, '[i]t can hardly be argued that either students or teachers shed their ... rights to freedom of speech or expression at the schoolhouse gate'.[156] On the other hand, it remains appropriate for primary schools to enforce pluralist values through measures more stringent than would be acceptable within public discourse generally, just as we might hope parents would do at home.[157] Banning hate speech within early education, like banning it from workplaces, forms part of the *active democracy*'s prerogative to promote pluralist values. That curricular choice helps to empower vulnerable groups, as they learn the techniques of counter-speech: it teaches them to 'answer back' in public discourse, with the views of a pluralist state backing them.[158] Indeed, through general education as well as electronic media, the burden of counter-speech need not fall on victims alone. On any given mainstream media website, for example, discriminatory remarks, if not voluntarily removed by monitors, will be bombarded with rebukes from disgusted readers from all backgrounds.

For educational campaigns beyond the classroom, within familiar arenas of public discourse, it would be silly to imagine that routine government-sponsored messages urging people to avoid drugs, or smoking, or unsafe sex, or battering women, must, to preserve viewpoint neutrality, be balanced, either by a government-sponsored or—depending on the forum, such as a poster in a train station or on the side of a publically operated bus[159]—even a privately funded message urging people to take drugs, to smoke, to engage in unsafe sex, or to beat women. Democratic governments rightly can and do sponsor 'one-sided' messages promoting pluralism, with no democratic imperative to 'balance' those messages through messages of hatred.[160] Government's duty not to punish odious speakers does not equate with an affirmative duty to facilitate them.

Given the state's legitimately censorial role to choose primary educational curricula, or to undertake public interest campaigns, it would be equally silly to require strict neutrality for state-led anti-hate campaigns. A government-sponsored message urging tolerance need not be balanced by a government-sponsored message urging racism, sexism, or homophobia; nor must a state-sponsored programme of Holocaust education be balanced by a state-sponsored programme of Holocaust denial. Katharine Gelber notes that the state's efforts can include measures to empower marginalized groups, supporting them in 'speaking back'[161]—not, as is

[155] See, e.g., Molnar & Post, 2012, pp. 32–4 (discussing Amy Gutmann).
[156] *Tinker v. Des Moines Independent Community School District*, 393 U.S. 503, 506 (1969).
[157] See, e.g., Post, 1994–95, p. 1274.
[158] See later in this Section, text accompanying notes 161–2.
[159] See, e.g., Molnar & Post, 2012, p. 22; Raz, 1994, p. 108.
[160] See, e.g., Brettschneider, 2012; Evans, 2009, pp. 368–73; Malik, 2009, pp. 105–20.
[161] Gelber, 2012a; Gelber, 2012b, pp. 54–6 (contrasting 'speech-enhancing' or 'speech-enabling' with 'speech-limiting' policies). Cf. Molnar & Strossen, 2012, pp. 392–3.

sometimes confusingly argued, within face-to-face, fighting words situations,[162] but rather within arenas of public discourse.

Ian Leigh equally observes the state's peremptory power as a speaker. In scarcely a generation, religiously motivated anti-gay opinions in the UK, which used to be common, have been pushed to the margins, partly through the weight of changed state norms, policies, and practices.[163] For Leigh, bans on those who publicly challenge gay rights are neither required nor are they democratic.[164] Nor *a fortiori* need privately operated media or forums be obliged to host all viewpoints, and many will remove hate speech, which may feel subjectively punitive to the speaker, but in no way amounts to a state-authorized penalty in any criminal or civil sense.

How is the state to choose which stands it will and will not take? Jacob Mchangama rightly asks, 'should governments condemn cartoons of the prophet Mohammed as intolerance?' He concedes 'very obvious cases like Nazism, support for Al-Qaeda style fundamentalism, and overt racism' which governments readily condemn. However, 'once we move into greyer shades it becomes more problematic'.[165] Value-pluralist proceduralism retains a legitimate role in response to those types of questions, as such choices involve no viewpoint-selective penalties within public discourse. If, moreover, a government finds a category of intolerance too problematical to protect under non-discrimination law or under pro-tolerance education or campaigns, then that category would make a bizarre candidate for protection under hate speech bans, punishing the speaker's views, while the state abstains from declaring a contrary view. Nor does any LSPD reveal evidence of such an anomaly, for example, extending speech bans to protect groups that are deemed unworthy of protection in those other areas of law. (Admittedly, even non-viewpoint-punitive non-neutrality, such as official state proclamations and enforcement of non-viewpoint-punitive pluralist policies, offers no cure-all.[166] Wolfgang Benz warns that ceremonially solemn state pronouncements often betray a hollow, ritualistic quality.[167])

A further dilemma is posed by foreign hate speakers. If viewpoint absolutism guarantees the citizen's prerogative both to express and to receive views, does it guarantee a prerogative to invite non-citizen speakers? No—precisely because the prerogative inheres not in the human as such, but in the human as a democratic citizen, and therefore not in any non-citizen. The non-citizen may certainly enjoy all prevailing human rights, as provided within international law; however, it is inherent to the standard notion of state sovereignty, as an established principle of international law, that individuals have no general right to immigrate. Refugee or

---

[162] Lawrence, 1993, pp. 67–71.

[163] On the role of the mass media within LSPDs in challenging stereotypes, see, e.g., Weinstein, 1999, pp. 111–12.

[164] Leigh, 2009, pp. 379–98. Cf., e.g., Molnar & Strossen, 2012, p. 395 (on fundamentalist Christians as a minority).

[165] Private communication of 14 December 2012 (on file with author).

[166] See, e.g., Cram, 2006, p. 5 (noting limits to 'civil society' and to non-state entities, including 'the market, schools, private associations and religious organizations as pre-existing *loci* of civic virtue').

[167] Benz, 2005, p. 13.

asylum situations based on well-founded fear of persecution or imminent danger fall into a different category than an invited speaker. Refugees and asylum seekers are the exceptions that prove the rule, namely, of states' ordinary discretion in matters of inward migration, as they would be unnecessary if there were already a general universal right to migrate either permanently or even for a few hours.[168] Ordinary immigration decisions are matters of standard state policy.[169] Although questions may arise under distinct, internationally agreed or recognized norms, for example, against racial discrimination or separation of families, a state may generally exclude non-citizens for virtually any reason. It may therefore legitimately exclude foreign hate speakers on viewpoint-selective grounds, even if there may be good policy reasons to admit some of them, such as an opportunity for the media or members of the public to 'grill' them.

It is fallacious, then, to extrapolate from a non-viewpoint-punitive public sphere to an ethically neutral state. It is equally fallacious to extrapolate from a non-viewpoint-punitive public sphere to a presumption of state approval. Within LSPDs, public discourse invariably overflows with multifarious and conflicting ideas. As an active democracy, the state must perforce choose some above others. The LSPD can promote tolerant ideas over intolerant ones with an institutional authority and power that dwarfs any stature held even by well-organized hate groups. It is erroneous to reason that abstention from banning a viewpoint equates with affirmative state approval of it, or that ordinary people will be unable to draw that distinction, a common error among those who claim that failing to ban, for example, a far-right political party would equate with 'promoting and accepting it like any other party'.[170] By promoting non-viewpoint-punitive pluralism, while refraining from viewpoint-selective bans, the LSPD no more endorses intolerance than it endorses other unprohibited expression, such as astrology or Ouija boards.

Oppositionists risk exaggerating their own position not only by calling it 'absolutist', but also when they claim to insist on a 'state neutrality', which, on closer inspection, they do not, and cannot support at all. We can concede to oppositionists who call themselves 'absolutists' the correct premise (even if they phrase it differently) that an LSPD must admit non-viewpoint punitive expression into public discourse. It is a false step, however, to deduce that the rejection of viewpoint-punitive bans within public discourse must therefore entail the state's *total* viewpoint neutrality,[171] a 'night watchman state'[172] in the realm of ideas.

---

[168] See, e.g., Mowbray, 2004, pp. 110–28.

[169] See, e.g., Malanczuk, 1997, pp. 75–7. A difficult question would arise as to the status of legally resident aliens, but not, in practice, any more in this area than in other areas of law. Legal aliens are admitted into LSPDs on an assumption of treatment equal in most areas of law to that of citizens. Questions also arise as to dual nationals, e.g., whether a democracy can withdraw a second citizenship on viewpoint-selective grounds. But dual nationality is a convenience. There is no sense in which *democracy* requires it. The fact that a democracy may refuse it entails a painful individual choice, but scarcely a violation of democratic legitimacy. As states are not bound to accord dual nationality, nor can there be any right to it, beyond the rights granted by statute.

[170] Buntenbach & Wagner, 2002, p. 133.

[171] See, e.g., Pech, 2003, pp. 401–2.

[172] Cf., e.g., Nozick, 1977, pp. 26–7.

Prohibitionists then easily tumble into a straw-man argument. They end up criticizing oppositionists for advocating an absolutism which few if any have seriously advocated, except in a figurative sense.

There is no such thing as state neutrality because countless state norms and practices represent moral or philosophical choices. Total state neutrality would preclude even viewpoint-selective intervention within public discourse which does *not* penalize opposing views. That logical fallacy appears to have been easy for many writers to miss, but it is no small one. However cumbersome the phrase may sound, *non-viewpoint-punitive non-neutrality*—in other words, a non-neutrality that warrants the state to promote one viewpoint (such as pluralism and tolerance) without punishing contrary ones—has offered the most important means of state intervention within public discourse for purposes of promoting civic pluralism.

An historically unprecedented feature of a number of post-Second World War democracies is that their public education, media, and civic life have promoted critical enquiry into their historical abuses, including ethnic discrimination, sexism, normative heterosexuality, colonialism, the Holocaust, or the trans-Atlantic slave trade. They do so not merely in offhand ways, but in ways that have progressively nurtured more inclusive concepts of citizenship. Far from a stark choice between punishing hate speech and ignoring it, democracies' arsenals against intolerance have long boasted a variety of means for supporting democratic pluralism. Such approaches include constructive means of giving voices to minorities—programmes which are still far from perfect, but which reflect the active democracy, being both a product of and an ongoing support for modern democracies.

4.12 Legitimating and Optimizing Conditions

In the *Rhetoric*, Aristotle supports robust public discourse as a means to promote citizen awareness and vigilance. Seeming at first to have only the devil's advocate's skill in mind, he writes: 'we must be able to employ persuasion … on opposite sides of a question'.[173] Aristotle envisages a truth-seeking function that anticipates (or perhaps already fully states) Mill's. Truth is acquired, on that view, not merely through private contemplation, but via interpersonal and public exchange, by which we hone the ability to defeat unjust views. Aristotle anticipates 'counter-speech': 'if another man argues unfairly, we on our part may be able to confute him'.[174] He envisages, of course, two full-fledged males of equal standing as citizens, unhindered by power differentials. Prohibitionists today, often failing to appreciate the non-viewpoint-punitive alternatives available through the active state, cast doubt on counter-speech strategies, calling them unrealistic as between members of a privileged majority and members of an historically subordinated minority or outsider group.

---

[173] *Rhetoric* 1355ᵃ29-31, *in* Aristotle, [4th century BCE] 1984, vol. 2, p. 2154.
[174] *Rhetoric* 1355ᵃ33-34, *in* Aristotle, [4th century BCE] 1984, vol. 2, p. 2154.

Recall that Aristotle condemns those who 'speak evil'.[175] Yet that passage refers to a 'fighting words' context, distinct from public discourse. In the same breath he abhors 'striking another' (τύπτειν).[176] For Aristotle, a central role of law as νόμος (*nomos*), which encompasses citizens' broader ethics, attitudes, customs, and habits, is to strengthen social bonds. Generations of readers remain impressed by the peripatetic view that amity (φιλία, *philia*) among citizens must count among lawmakers' chief concerns.[177] Such a view, recurring in Rousseau and Hegel, has motivated the post-Rawlsian communitarian renaissance, which would seem scarcely hospitable to hate speech in public discourse. Which, then, is the real Aristotle? The Aristotle of robust speech or the Aristotle of civic bonds?

In the *Nicomachean Ethics* and the *Politics* Aristotle seeks the ultimate or greatest good (τὸ ἄριστον) for humans in society.[178] He seeks the best, the optimal, beyond political society's minimal, legitimating conditions. The teleological character of his quests for optimal political conditions generally prompts him to focus more on the best possible substantive outcomes, and not on minimal legitimating conditions. That emphasis distinguishes late classical Greeks from seventeenth- and eighteenth-century contractarians, such as Hobbes, Locke, Rousseau, and Kant. Both sets of writers philosophize precisely contrary to their background circumstances. Plato and Aristotle write against the backdrop of an all-too grossly proceduralist democracy, which will resolve even to kill a Socrates, and which had also voted to pursue Athens's militarism and economic domination in Greece. In their political philosophy, Plato and Aristotle seek alternatives through a politics conducive to the best substantive outcomes. By contrast, in an aristocratic Europe claiming, with declining credibility, to be legitimate by delivering the best substantive outcomes, Hobbes, Locke, Rousseau, and Kant seek a politics grounded in foundational and procedural legitimacy.

Aristotle does not justify robust oratory, then, through any detailed analysis of the problem of legitimating political conditions. But, strongly contrary on this point to Plato of the *Republic* or the *Laws*, his philosophical context strongly warrants that interpretation. In works expressly sceptical of democratic practices, notably *Gorgias*, Plato had condemned democratic public discourse altogether. Like prohibitionists today who warn of the dangerous potential of hate speech to convince people of prejudiced views, *Gorgias* deems any argument endorsing the constructive uses of public oratory[179] to be nullified by its potential to manipulate and misguide people who lack facility in critical reason.[180]

[175] See Section 1.1, note 19.
[176] *Nicomachean Ethics* 5.2.1129ᵇ23, *in* Aristotle, [4th century BCE] 1984, vol. 2, p. 1782.
[177] See *Nicomachean Ethics* 8.1.1155ᵃ24-29, *in* Aristotle, [4th century BCE] 1984, vol. 2, p. 1825. Cf., e.g., *Politics* 2.4.1262ᵇ6-10, *in* Aristotle, [4th century BCE] 1984, vol. 2, p. 2003.
[178] See *Nicomachean Ethics* 1.2.1094ᵃ22, *in* Aristotle, [4th century BCE] 1984, vol. 2, p. 1729. Cf., e.g., Heinze, 2009e, pp. 34–5.
[179] See, e.g., *Gorgias* 452e–457c, *in* Plato, [4th century BCE] 1997, pp. 798–802.
[180] See, e.g., *Gorgias* 461b–522b, *in* Plato, [4th century BCE] 1997, pp. 805–65. Cf., e.g., *Apology* 18a-e, *in* Plato, [4th century BCE] 1997, p. 19.

Aristotle aims to avoid both the extreme of unbridled speech and the extreme of abolishing the politics of public discourse. He seeks a fundamental shift, closer in that respect to Mill, refining oratory as a truth-seeking tool by urging an engaged citizenry to overcome manipulative expression by mastering dialectical and rhetorical, hence counter-speech techniques—to learn, as many a US First Amendment scholar would later phrase it, how to counter bad ideas through better ones.[181] In contemplating the *best* that society can achieve, by contrast, Aristotle rightly proceeds to emphasize harmonious and respectful relationships, *philia*, among citizens. That tacit distinction between minimal and optimal conditions[182] sheds light on the legitimate measures democracies can take to promote civic pluralism. A problem for modern communitarians is that they have celebrated the optimizing conditions of Aristotle's *Ethics* and *Politics*, ignoring the legitimating ingredients of the *Rhetoric*.

The failure to distinguish between elements essential for a society to be a democracy at all, and those necessary or desirable for it to be a *good* democracy weakens attempts by prohibitionists to root modern bans in the views of classical liberal figures, such as Locke, Bayle, Voltaire, and Diderot,[183] or in Hegel's views about mutual respect.[184] There can be no doubt that those thinkers, like Plato and Aristotle, recognize the overall importance of respect among citizens, including the identifiable inscription of that value within much of our law. The same aim is shared by oppositionists who advocate democracies' 'active' albeit non-viewpoint-punitive drives for pluralism.[185] That oppositionist alternative differs starkly from any view that seventeenth- through nineteenth-century philosophers specifically theorized *democracy*'s legitimating elements, not least because most of them were not democrats.

To the degree that such figures contemplate future republics or democracies *at all*—which the admittedly liberal but nevertheless royalist Voltaire, for example, does not do; or which Diderot or Bayle do in no exhaustive or systematic way—it remains far from their minds to be formulating democracy's legitimating conditions with the precision we demand today. Waldron rightly observes those philosophers' overall concern with human dignity; but we would need to reach almost Nietzschean extremes to find political theorists, ancient or modern, who do not share that *general* concern in one or another form. Such an insight ends up more question-begging than conclusive as to the legitimating role of public discourse within post-industrial democracy.

Rousseau poses a greater problem—not without interest given his status as the Enlightenment's towering democratic theorist. Perhaps influenced on this, as on other points, by Plato, Rousseau advocates censorship for purposes of promoting

---

[181] Cf. *Whitney v. California*, 274 U.S. 357, 375 (1927) (Brandeis, J., concurring) (famously arguing that 'the fitting remedy for evil counsels is good ones').

[182] See, e.g., Barendt, 2007, pp. 13–18; Dworkin, 2009, p. ix; Haworth, 1998, pp. 70–117; Post, 1995, pp. 293–4, 304; Weinstein, 1999, pp. 13–16.

[183] See, e.g., Waldron, 2012a, pp. 204–33.   [184] See, e.g., Heyman, 2009, p. 168.

[185] See Section 4.11.

good values.[186] He suggests that the *volonté générale*, the General Will, would make such choices wisely. The legitimating processes by which a democracy would achieve, and could know it had achieved, an authentically General Will nevertheless remain notoriously ambiguous in Rousseau's writings,[187] as are democracy's legitimating conditions generally throughout the early modern contractarian tradition. (That is surely one reason why Rawls later seeks to revisit and to sharpen contractarian foundations, even if his resort to rights poses the problems that were noted in Section 3.6.) At the very least, if some form of General Will is not, as some critics of Rousseau would have it,[188] to be dictatorially imposed, then it can hardly emerge except through a public discourse in which all citizens maintain equal expressive prerogatives. That observation, moreover, applies just as plausibly to public discourse within Locke's rights-based constitutionalism if it is to be adapted to politically legitimating conditions, and in no way contradicts Locke's politically optimizing exhortations in his famous *Letter Concerning Toleration*.[189]

We must distinguish, then, between the inherently relative, 'more or less' character of optimizing conditions and the categorical, 'all or nothing' character of legitimating conditions. (The distinction is trickier than it may seem, since, again, the state's failure in fully realizing its legitimating conditions de-legitimate its democracy only *pro tanto*.) Politically optimizing conditions retain a 'more or less' character because even partial advances towards them can count towards their partial fulfilment, and partial retreats from them, towards their partial failure. Assume, for example, an optimizing condition of age-15 literacy rates for all 12-year-olds by year 10 under a particular educational plan. Assume further a starting point of age-12 literacy rates for all 12-year-olds in the first year of that plan. At year 5, age-14 rates for 70 per cent represent partial fulfilment.

A legitimating condition cannot be of that type. Either it utterly succeeds or utterly fails, albeit only with a *pro tanto* de-legitimating effect. If the name of a duly registered voter fails to appear on the voters list, thereby barring the individual from casting a vote, and indeed irrespective of whether the omission is intentional or negligent, the illegitimacy towards the voter is absolute, even if it de-legitimates the democracy as a whole only relatively, only *pro tanto*. If such incursions into essential citizen prerogatives remain generally rare, then the democracy remains intact, any *pro tanto* de-legitimacy being minimal, yet without abrogating the absolute illegitimacy vis-à-vis the barred voter. If, by contrast, such incursions into essential citizens' prerogatives emerge as systemic, then the *pro tanto* de-legitimating effect becomes appreciable.

Failure of an optimizing condition may, under some circumstances, constitute an injustice, or may de-legitimate some other element of the state, but does not

---

[186] See Cram, 2012, p. 476.
[187] See, e.g., Fetscher, 1975, pp. 119–33; Qvortrup, 2004, pp. 65–70.
[188] See, e.g., Russell, 2000, p. 660.
[189] Locke, 1983. Similar observations can be made about writers like Rawls and Habermas, whose views are cited by oppositionists and prohibitionists alike. Cf. Section 2.3, note 35; and Section 6.2, text accompanying note 78.

de-legitimate the state as a democracy, not even *pro tanto*. Recalling the argument outlined in Section 3.4, even if members of ethnic minorities can justly point to failures in the equal enjoyment of Sweden's optimizing opportunities or benefits, that does not necessarily entail failures of democratic legitimacy. To argue otherwise is to commit the 'legitimacy fallacy' described in that discussion. Within an LSPD, failures of legitimacy are always failures of substantive justice, but not all failures of substantive justice are failures of legitimacy.

As noted earlier, reasoning about democracy as only a hypothetical, and not a categorical good[190] would have remained question-begging at any time in history until the fall of the Berlin Wall. After all, why bother reasoning about a system's legitimating conditions without first asking whether it is the system we want? Today, the necessity of that first step, establishing whether democracy is even our objective, may seem less pressing. Yet humanity's long history of non- and indeed anti-democratic government, and the ongoing vitality of anti-democratic movements into the twenty-first century, cannot leave us complacent. By the second half of the twentieth century, the Cold War was still teaching us how readily many intellectuals would deem non-democratic regimes as being at least equal in legitimacy to democratic ones if they appear to promise certain elements of substantive justice that are deficient or uncertain in democracies.[191] We must not forget that famines were still occurring well into the twentieth century (leaving aside controversies as to the boundaries between their political, economic, and agricultural causes), making concern about immediate livelihood more urgent. That concern remains crucial, given the broader preoccupations with equality underlying disputes about the seemingly narrow problem of hate speech.

Rawls, writing in that Cold War context, proposes the 'maximin' principle of distributive justice. On the maximin principle, all of us would choose economic inequality if it left even those who are worst off in a better condition than they could be under any competing regime.[192] Simplifying for the moment to assume a choice between only *two* possible regimes (in reality, there would be more), we would choose to be the poorest citizens of a democracy, if that situation left us with greater freedom and overall purchasing power than enjoyed by the bulk of citizens within a command economy. Yet the choice for democracy is not merely a choice in favour of *formally* equal rights and liberties within a liberal democracy, even if it could achieve those maximin conditions within the economy. Ethnic minorities in Sweden do not just wish to collect social-welfare benefits. They want genuine, substantive equality in the material enjoyment of rights and liberties. They want more than just legitimate democracy, even if they do accept the democracy's legitimacy.

A maximin principle would need to apply, then, not only to distributive justice, but also to the background regime of rights and liberties. A choice in favour of democracy demands that all of us would accept not merely economic inequality, but also inequality in the overall material enjoyment of rights and liberties if that

---

[190] See Section 3.4, text accompanying note 50.   [191] See Section 3.5.
[192] Rawls, 1999, pp. 132–5.

latter inequality, too, left those who are worst off in a better condition than they could be under any competing regime. It is by no means clear how many people would make that choice, even if we were to assume it to be the most rational in principle. But that is an altogether different enquiry. For present purposes, then, we can continue to assume democracy solely as a hypothetical imperative.

4.13 Egalitarianism and Social Welfarism

Comparisons between US and European approaches to hate speech often proceed by attributing 'liberty over equality' to US law and 'equality over liberty' to European law.[193] Cass Sunstein takes up that problem, albeit not through any detailed comparative analysis. Sunstein draws an analogy between President Franklin D Roosevelt's New Deal of the 1930s, commonly perceived as a movement from liberty towards equality in the economic sphere, and what Sunstein calls his own 'New Deal' for the regulation of speech. Roosevelt's New Deal had certainly transformed entrenched assumptions about law, politics, and society. Roosevelt had encountered opposition to legislative reforms aimed at redressing economic damage wrought during the Great Depression. That calamity had, in turn, arisen within a legal culture committed to quasi-absolute property rights, founded on natural law rights discourses. Mass poverty, unemployment, and exploitation were surfacing to challenge laissez-faire myths that humans' 'natural' economic behaviour proceeded in its own pristine state, below the surface of law.

That free market ideology, naïve and yet abetting a status quo of stark disparities of wealth, imagined law as a largely obstructive artifice. State regulations, on that view, would distort the supposedly natural play of market activity, often conceived by early twentieth-century conservatives in the naturalist terms of social Darwinism. The New Deal challenged that increasingly implausible rights-based naturalism, spurring the growth of American legal realism.[194] Legal realists did not wholly abandon the view that law in the form of excessive regulation can stifle fruitful economic activity; but they rejected the myth of 'natural' economic life which proceeds quasi-independently of law. Law taking the form of a sheer reification of markets' power relationships was a force that could actively generate poverty, with severe economic and social consequences.

Sunstein's strategy is to compare what he—as we have seen, somewhat misleadingly—calls America's dominant, post-1950s 'free speech absolutism'[195] to America's pre-Depression, laissez-faire economics protected by speciously naturalized property rights. He proposes a second 'New Deal' to re-conceive free speech along the contemporary lines of the modern regulatory state, just as property rights came to be re-formulated to mirror the material realities of relationships between legal norms and economic processes. That modernizing of rights entails, on

---

[193] See, e.g., Belavusau, 2013, p. 9; cf. pp. 87–8.
[194] See, e.g., Feldman, 2000, pp. 105–15.   [195] Sunstein, 1995, p. 5.

Sunstein's analysis, a shift from classical theories of rights as ends in themselves to theories of rights as instrumentalized means to broader social ends. Free expression must be viewed not as the object of a free floating, quasi-natural 'right', but as a means to the distinct end of promoting democratic public discourse.

Framed in those terms, my own break from a rights-based foundation may seem similar. Sunstein's approach, however, persists in the assumption of higher-law (in his case, American constitutional) *rights* as the foundation for protecting speech, rights which must *then* be integrated into—in order to serve—the public discourse of an already-constituted democracy. Sunstein can certainly use rights discourse, extrapolating straightforwardly from property rights to speech rights, in order to re-formulate a generally *liberal* theory of speech, a theory in which speech rights *qua* rights would share a higher-law status with property rights *qua* rights. By contrast, as for the distinctly *democratic* theory which his analysis promises, no such historical or conceptual analogy holds from property to speech.

In a nutshell, it is correct to argue that *liberalism* underwent a full-blown crisis in its theory of property, or that the *state* underwent it. However, whatever other changes *democracy* may have undergone, it would be misleading to suggest that democracy as such underwent *that* change. It may well be liberal rights that, very rightly, underwent the change, but not democratic citizenship. By extension, within a longer history, some nations had once recognized only property-based voting rights. However, universalizing the franchise, while changing the material *outcomes* of voting, in no way changed the *conceptual* relationship between voting and democracy in the thoroughgoing way that the New Deal, or European social democracy, transformed the relationship between property and liberal rights.

Like other US constitutional scholars, Sunstein fails to distinguish the liberal strand from the democratic strand of the liberal–democratic state. His otherwise plausible theory of the instrumentalization of *rights*, insofar as it is applied to *private* property, stumbles into a far less credible instrumentalization of democratic citizenship itself. To instrumentalize the property right, as social democracy has done, is simply to recognize the defects of a regime which excessively protects *purely private* interests. But to instrumentalize a core prerogative of citizenship is altogether different: it does not somehow render *more* public an attribute that was otherwise private. It does the opposite. It erodes, it renders *less* public, the one element of our individual political existence which is already *wholly public*, the citizen's prerogative of non-viewpoint-punitive expression in public discourse.

Sunstein's proposal had in fact become reality long ago in Western European social-welfare systems. Although the existence or scope of the social-welfare state (*l'État social*), has always had Western European sceptics, advocates of hate speech bans have characteristically argued within egalitarian[196] and social-welfarist assumptions about the state's role in avoiding excessive socio-economic disparities. Discrimination, of course, scarcely helps vulnerable minority groups out of poverty; poverty entrenches their socio-political disempowerment. It is important,

---

[196] Cf., e.g., Belavusau, 2013, pp. 9, 91.

however, to maintain some boundary between the theory and the folklore of the social-welfare state. Questions as to the foundations or future of the redistributive state remain separate from the hate speech debates. Under the notion of the active democracy, as was set forth in Section 4.11, viewpoint-punitive bans within public discourse can be altogether abolished without affecting the principles or practice of social welfarism, or the benefits and opportunities it offers, and therefore without requiring a full-blown debate about the virtues or vices of social welfarism.[197] Indeed, some social welfarists have argued that hate speech bans easily become gesture politics—symbolic means of simulating a concern for vulnerable groups through laws which place little practical burden on the state (indeed earning it kudos through occasional, high-profile prosecutions), while allowing governments to sidestep more comprehensive strategies for empowering vulnerable groups.[198]

[197] Cf. Heinze, 2006, pp. 569–81.
[198] See Section 5.5, text accompanying note 149.

5

The Prohibitionist Challenge

The citizen prerogative of non-viewpoint-punitive expression within public discourse has thus far been presented as a higher-order legal interest. A higher-order interest is legitimately overridden only by an interest of similarly higher-order stature, severe security emergencies being a dramatic example. An LSPD can claim no rival *democratic* interest of equal stature to that citizen prerogative on any consequentialist or deontological rationale.

The viewpoint absolutism presented in the preceding chapters is deontological. It admits harm-based, consequentialist reasons for imposing viewpoint-selective penalties within the public discourse of non-LSPDs, but not of LSPDs. It further assumes that threshold determinations as to the achievement of LSPD status are themselves subject to consequentialist criteria. However, insofar as those criteria remain fulfilled, consequentialist rationales have no further role to play. The citizen's expressive prerogative must then prevail.

The LSPD model assumes the absence of statistically demonstrable causation tracing hateful expression to distinct acts of violence or discrimination within those societies that meet its criteria. But the model still faces further challenges. Particularly influential have been views that harm is caused indirectly, diffusely, or symbolically, in ways powerful in their impact, even if inaccessible to demonstrable causation. Those are the various consequentialist challenges that viewpoint absolutism must face. Equally important, however, is deontological prohibitionism, which deems at least some forms of hateful expression to be a *malum in se*, a harm in itself, such that it may legitimately be penalized irrespective of whether it entails any further harms, either through direct or through indirect causation. In addition we must ask whether oppositionism must rely solely on the deontological claims adduced thus far, or whether it, too, can find further support through consequentialism.

5.1 Direct Consequentialist Prohibitionism

One way of showing that a rival interest of equal, higher-order stature must override the citizen's expressive prerogative is by showing some risk of harm caused by the exercise of that prerogative to another individual or to the state. Such an argument would take the form of what we can call *direct consequentialist prohibitionism*.[1] It is with that kind of risk in mind that the US Supreme Court long ago adopted the 'fighting words' doctrine.[2] 'Fighting words' situations stand apart from the generality of forum, audience, or subject matter that typically characterizes public discourse. For the Court, government can legitimately deem such words sufficiently likely to 'cause a fight',[3] when 'directed to the person of the hearer'.[4] The state would have no time or means to intervene so as to avert violence.[5] Legislators and courts can legitimately ban speech because of its likelihood of provoking immediate violence in many typical cases, without such likelihood being present in every imaginable case.[6]

Personal injury caused by hate speech, such as infliction of psychological harm, arises in those sorts of immediate, interpersonal contexts, as distinguished from the ordinarily general character of public discourse. The problem with countless prohibitionist writings is that they start with those empirically demonstrable harms of immediate, interpersonal situations, which the more studious oppositionists like Post or Weinstein have never questioned, but then extrapolate straightforwardly from them to a purely rhetorical empiricism, lacking any empirical references, about equivalent harms putatively caused by hatred expressed within public discourse.

In Section 2.10 that strategy was identified as 'rhetorical consequentialism'. Recall the two main types of rhetorical consequentialism. Some claims take the verbal form of empirical causation, but without any evidence adduced through standard empirical criteria (e.g., 'Even an LSPD must ban hateful expression in order to avoid violence'). Other claims cannot even lend themselves to empirical study, at least not without more precise verbal formulation to refine their operative terms (e.g., 'Fundamental human dignity must be respected in order to avoid violence').

As was noted, rhetorically consequentialist claims are not in themselves infirm. They may metaphorically articulate a genuine fear. They may more pithily state what is really a categorical, deontological claim. They may seek to ban hateful expression as inherently harmful, as a *malum in se*, irrespective of any legally cognizable evidence of harm, and yet are worded for effect in the language of material causation. Such rhetorical leaps are customary within countless types of social controversies and across the political spectrum. They become more precarious when they leak into government and scholarly discourses. Academic analysis within the social sciences always maintains a fluid rapport with the vernacular, yet must also demand greater precision.

LSPDs are the most empirically surveyed societies in history. Eating, sleeping, smoking, drinking, running, sitting, standing, jumping, and everything else we do

---

[1] Direct consequentialist prohibitionism is one, but not the only type of claim falling within quadrant [1] in Table 2.1 (see Section 2.10). Section 5.3 will focus on indirect consequentialism.

[2] See Section 2.8, note 95.

[3] *Chaplinsky v. New Hampshire*, 315 U.S. 568, 573 (1942).

[4] *Cohen v. California*, 403 U.S. 15, 20 (1971).

[5] Cf., e.g., Post, 1995, pp. 114, 194; Weinstein, 1999, pp. 26–7, 72, 74, 76.

[6] See also, e.g., Molnar & Post, 2012, p. 22; Robitaille-Froidure, 2011, p. 40; Weinstein, 2009a, pp. 30, 53; Weinstein, 2009b, p. 82; Weinstein, 2011a, pp. 491–2.

are constantly canvassed for evidence of their harmful effects. No previous societies would have had the means to produce the volumes of social dissection generated within LSPDs, including ongoing studies about violence and discrimination against the vulnerable. Despite decades of pro-ban law and policy, however, no empirical evidence has, in any statistically standard way, traced hatred expressed within general public discourse to specifically harmful effects.

Horst Meier illustrates that failure. His conclusions are probative, as German practice is widely admired by prohibitionists, largely through rather off-the-page readings[7] of the 'dignity' provision of the *Grundgesetz*.[8] In 2001 the German Constitutional Court (*Bundesverfassungsgericht*) was charged with examining whether the far-right German National Democratic Party (*Nationaldemokratische Partei Deutschlands* (NPD)) could be banned. The government's 585-page 'paper flood' lacked any evidence linking the NPD's expressive conduct within public discourse to materially harmful effects. Such an exercise 'compensates for implausibility through sheer volume'.[9]

The government memorandum cites copious examples of the NPD's aggressive and anti-democratic rhetoric, but 'no concrete incitements to violence (*Aufforderungen zur Gewaltanwendung*)' nor 'a single example of "hate propaganda"' that could be shown to have provoked any 'concrete act'.[10] Instead of a 'rational' risk assessment, as would have been 'normal in a democracy', and expected from a document strong on consequentialist formulas, one typical government argument casually shifts gears to a deontological claim, with no explanation as to why it had relied so heavily on suggestions of empirical harm: 'Whether the NPD's aspirations ... currently show any likelihood of success, whether a concrete danger exists for the liberal–democratic order, is *irrelevant* (*belanglos*)'.[11]

US-based prohibitionists have similarly lanced rhetorically consequentialist claims without citing evidence on point. To overcome the citizen's prerogative of non-viewpoint-punitive expression in public discourse, the prohibitionist would have to offer statistically reliable evidence adequate to indicate some generality of risk over a vulnerable population. Non-statistical, anecdotal evidence, for example, of one-off copycat incidents, can indeed indicate plausible causation in random episodes. But countless activities may impair citizenship in that incidental sense, such as road accidents (which indeed demonstrably cause thousands of deaths and injuries in the West) or workplace accidents.

A serious problem is that the evidence thus far supplied by US-based prohibitionists has been published in twentieth- or early twenty-first-century in-house university law journals (or in spin-off book publications and reprints from those

[7] See Section 5.6, text accompanying notes 170–1. See also, e.g., Waldron, 2012a, pp. 39–40, 149.
[8] See Section 5.6, text accompanying notes 166–72.   [9] Meier, 2002, p. 17.
[10] Meier, 2002, p. 22. Cf. Neumann, 2002, p. 363; Preuß, 2002, pp. 110–11 (questioning the causal link between viewpoint-punitive bans and broader social harms).
[11] Quoted in Meier, 2002, p. 18 (emphasis added). In December 2015, the German Constitutional Court announced a new enquiry to begin in 2016. Of course, evidence of criminal activity since 2001 would in no way impact upon the lack of evidence as to the effects of expression within general public discourse, absent a heretofore unprecedented showing of specific causation to that effect.

original pieces), which, throughout those years, have lacked standard scholarly peer review.[12] That defect becomes decisive as to details of empirical or statistical method.[13] Several studies include credible claims of psychological injury suffered by victims of immediate racist, sexist, homophobic, or other such attacks or assaults—i.e., of the stalking, harassment, or 'fighting words' types which, as we have seen, are generally distinct from public discourse. Those copious publications fail to cite statistical data that would trace causation from hateful expression within public discourse to cognizable social harms.

Reviewing several issues relevant to hate speech bans, Stefancic and Delgado, for example, reach the conclusion that European bans are generally justified, delivering a better and more legitimate result than the US First Amendment regime.[14] They then cite empirical evidence to argue that racism has dramatically *increased* in Europe throughout the period they examine.[15] That surface anomaly turns out to assume two unstated premises. First, if evidence shows that rates of discrimination in Western Europe are steady or are increasing, then bans are required in order to combat it. Second, if evidence shows that discrimination is decreasing or has ceased, that proves the success of bans, so they must be maintained in order to preserve that achievement. In other words, bans are required not as a result of empirically contingent facts, but regardless of them. An empiricist discourse is invoked, then, to lend authority to an inherently non-empirical argument, conceived from the outset to yield only one possible conclusion under all empirical circumstances, irrespective of specific findings. An empirical method can only play an operative role for choosing legal rules when we assume a variable outcome contingent on the data being measured. If that outcome remains fixed irrespective of any such measurement, then the language of empiricism was, all along, purely rhetorical. No data-contingent assessment was ever really being taken.

The lack of demonstrated causation between bans within public discourse and hate-based discrimination or violence by no means removes immediate harm as a ground for restricting speech where such harm can be demonstrated, as with the regulation of child pornography. The demonstrated harm caused to child victims of sexual contacts with adults[16] justifies rules precluding a child's capacity to give informed consent. Those rules presume criminal liability for adults who undertake such contact, regardless of any consent that might appear to be displayed by the child (and regardless of the fact that such rules might historically have arisen

---

[12] See, e.g., McCormack, 2009 (surveying debates and current reforms relevant to US law journals). That defect has, moreover, been misrepresented. As of this writing, the Ex Libris Primo electronic search engine, e.g., lists many of those US law school journals as having been peer reviewed throughout their existence. Non-US readers are then misled to believe that such journals, often carrying the names of established and prestigious institutions, must therefore be peer reviewed, hence their failure to notice that scholarly fault in citing US prohibitionists. We end up with truth manufactured through sheer reproduction and proliferation.

[13] See, e.g., McCormack, 2009, pp. 61–2.

[14] Stefancic & Delgado, 1992–93, pp. 741–4 (published in a non-peer-reviewed journal).

[15] Stefancic & Delgado, 1992–93, p. 745.

[16] See, e.g., Paolucci, Genuis, & Violato, 2001.

from principles other than the protective ones that we cite today). Once the child's non-consent becomes irrebuttably presumptive, any adult breach incurs liability for inflicting harm.

Child pornography exemplifies causation between, on the one hand, sexual activity which might, in turn, become the object of communicative production and representation, and, on the other hand, harm legitimately deemed grave as a matter of legal presumption. That causation, in turn, justifies measures for suppressing markets or networks dealing in materials linked to child sexual abuse.[17] Within the LSPD, an individual or a group (such as a paedophile organization) agitating for the repeal of protective laws nevertheless retains the same freedoms of non-viewpoint-punitive expression within public discourse, but would be no more entitled to use such imagery as part of such advocacy than business people would be, claiming some expressive prerogative to pollute the environment, to discriminate in hiring, or to withhold tax payments.

If LSPDs can combat discrimination without viewpoint-selective bans on public discourse, how shall we account for periodic rises in intolerance? Viewpoint-punitive bans work in the classical legal mode of individualized, retrospective criminal or civil sanctions. Non-punitive educational and social policies, by contrast, work in a prospective and collective mode, over populations; their results cannot realistically be absolute. They will not succeed at all times with all citizens. Crucial to the four LSPD elements is their combined effect to produce a society in which such causal links nevertheless appear to become attenuated.[18] That arguably occurs for various reasons (inherently speculative, since we face having to explain the negative of a causal link ordinarily *not* existing in a statistical sense), but apparently because, in LSPDs, and particularly through electronic media, such views become defused through a population habituated through cultural practice to overkill, counter-speech, effective debunking, parody, and other such, often highly informal means.

5.2 Militant Democracy and the 'Weimar Fallacy'

In the aftermath of the Second World War, Western European politics became dominated by memories of totalitarianism, and the propaganda that had fuelled it. In West Germany, an imperative of 'militant democracy' (*wehrhafte* or *streitbare Demokratie*)[19] recalled the French revolutionary Saint-Just's maxim, 'No liberty for

---

[17] See, e.g., *New York v. Ferber*, 458 U.S. 747 (1982).

[18] See Section 4.1, text accompanying note 11.

[19] See BVerfGE 2, 1 (SRP-Urteil); 5, 85 (KPD Urteil). See generally, e.g., Leggewie & Meier, 2002a; Thiel, 2003a. See also Fennema, 2009, pp. 18, 26; Günther, 2000; Hoppe, 2008; Nieuwenhuis, 2011, pp. 143–5; Noorloos, 2012, pp. 225–8, 319–22. Cf., critically, Baker, 2009, p. 144; Schrank, 2006, p. 100; Weinstein, 2001; Weinstein, 2009a, pp. 37–8. In post-Second World War Germany, which has maintained a consensus favouring hate speech bans, the problem of militant democracy has arisen with respect to bans on extremist political parties—a formally different matter, yet generally overlapping in terms of substantive arguments for or against such measures.

the enemies of liberty'.[20] That ideal arose to protect democracy not only as a constitutional regime, but also as a form of pluralist society that had been abused on the path to dictatorship.

Parallel debates have proceeded in leading democracies for decades, often unaware of each other. Post-colonial or post-segregationist countries like the US, UK, and Australia, have focussed largely on the oppression of minorities by majorities, but within a tradition that has remained generally confident about democracy as such (the resilience of that English democratic aspiration persists even in more precarious settings, as in India, Israel, or South Africa). Germans, by contrast, have traced atrocities in their recent history, despite the obvious oppressor–oppressed dynamic of the Holocaust, to weaknesses of democratic structure as such, and of the Weimar Republic above all. Where English-speaking prohibitionists emphasize the interests of minorities per se, German prohibitionism focuses on preserving democracy per se: two different sets of concepts and vocabularies for a very similar discussion, which may explain the limited scholarly cross-fertilization, beyond superficial references to Americans' supposed primacy of 'liberty over equality' or Germans' supposed emphasis on 'dignity'. Over decades, massive quantities of literature have taken scarce notice of each other, although that is perhaps a constant problem for comparative law, given the difficulties of analysing elements of a legal system in abstraction from solid training in the whole of the system and of its historical context. Prohibitionists constantly cite—often with a curious blend of literalist Kantianism and quasi-romanticism—the Basic Law's reference to human dignity as if it captures an obvious and absolute value (always a mistake with broad concepts enshrined within documents of constitutional stature), yet with no attention to its jurisprudence or to critical commentary surrounding it.[21]

Within German constitutional law, 'militant democracy' remains, as Ralf Dreier notes, 'unclarified in its theoretical content and in its doctrinal scope'.[22] Its principles are 'ambivalent'[23] and 'far from obvious'.[24] In terms echoing those of Parekh, Waldron, and others, Tillmanns nevertheless defends that ideal. The 'liberal–democratic order', he claims, 'presupposes a responsible use of

---

[20] 'Pas de liberté pour les ennemis de la liberté'. See, e.g., Dreier, 2002, p. 85; Neumann, 2002, p. 155; Wassermann, p. 101.

[21] See Section 5.6, text accompanying note 167.

[22] Dreier, 2002, p. 81. Cf., Thiel, 2003b, pp. 5–6 (noting divergent concepts of militant democracy).

[23] Dreier, 2002, p. 85. Cf. Groh, 2002, p. 95.

[24] Dreier, 2002, p. 84. Crucial to the immediate post-Second World War concept of militant democracy was the view that 'only a metaphysical and value-absolutist epistemological and moral theory, not a positivist and value-relativist one, could legitimate a material and value-bound theory of democracy and constitutionalism'. Dreier, 2002, p. 87 (discussing Steinberger). Cf. Groh, 2002, p. 91 (on Weimar's clashes of political values); Wassermann, 2002, p. 102 (on democratic relativism). For a continued affirmation of that anti-relativist view, see Tillmanns, 2003. See also, e.g., Thiel, 2003b, p. 14; Thiel, 2003c, p. 129. For Dreier, however, 'the current state of debate on the foundations of scientific and moral theory renders obsolete the dichotomy between "metaphysical and value-absolutist" and "positivist and value-relativist" theories'. Dreier, 2002, p. 87.

freedom'.[25] For Markus Thiel, 'even the most modern concept of democracy cannot forego institutions' to protect the state from 'enemies of the constitution (*Verfassungsfeinde*)'.[26] 'Democracy', he argues, 'has therefore adopted limits, and does not permit that its own protections be abused for purposes of eliminating it. That implicit self-limitation forms a genuine component of any modern understanding of democracy.'[27] At no point, however, does Thiel distinguish between 'enemies' in word and 'enemies' in deed, as if material causation plays no important role in determining a risk attributed to the exercise of higher-order rights or prerogatives.

Thiel holds that an illegal 'combat (*Kampf*)' against the liberal–democratic order' consists not merely of traditionally criminal acts of terrorism, sabotage, or syndicalism, but also stretches to include 'intellectual combat' (*geistiger Kampf*),[28] with the customary caveat that such determinations are to be made judiciously so as to avoid punishing 'occasional offensive remarks or substantive criticism',[29] hence a standard, value-pluralist theory of legislative and judicial balancing of interests. 'To ensure that citizens enjoy their constitutional protections, the state can and must fend off aspirations (*Bestrebungen*) aimed at endangering or abolishing the liberal democratic order'.[30] Questions as to whether such 'aspirations' must manifest through materially demonstrable acts of 'endangering or abolishing the liberal democratic order' become wholly neglected. The aspiration, the *Bestrebung*, becomes its own materialized or threatened harm, a *malum in se*.

Democracy certainly remains legitimate in banning conduct aimed at materially impairing democratic institutions. It is always 'militant' in the truistic sense of preserving its national security. An LSPD cannot, however, coherently turn a security threat into a democratic threat simply by dubbing a philosophy, worldview, or viewpoint 'anti-constitutional' (*verfassungsfeindlich*).[31] 'By definition', Dreier reminds us, a 'democracy cannot be militant against [political] aims, but only against the means for their realisation, namely, against violent means.'[32]

One prohibitionist fallacy is, then, to extrapolate, without empirical support, from evidence about face-to-face, 'fighting words' situations to general expression within public discourse. A similar error, which I shall call the 'Weimar fallacy', is to extrapolate, similarly lacking empirical support, from evidence about non-LSPDs to LSPDs. The phrase 'Weimar fallacy' carries European connotations, but the error of generalizing from conditions in weak democracies or non-democracies, reaches further.

Although pervasive within European prohibitionism,[33] several US-based prohibitionists also commit the mistake. In *Destructive Messages: How Hate Speech*

---

[25] Tillmanns, 2003, p. 29 ('Die freiheitliche demokratische Ordnung des Grundgesetzes setzt einen verantworteten Freiheitsgebrauch voraus.'). Cf. Tillmanns, 2003, p. 33. Cf. also Section 3.2, note 22.
[26] Thiel, 2003b, p. 19. Cf. this Section, note 31.   [27] Thiel, 2003b, p. 20; cf. p. 23.
[28] Thiel, 2003c, pp. 137–8.   [29] Thiel, 2003c, p. 138.   [30] Thiel, 2003b, p. 23.
[31] Morlock, 2002, p. 69.   [32] Dreier, 2002, p. 86.
[33] See, e.g., Günther, 2000; Thiel, 2003a.

Paves the Way for Harmful Social Movements, Alexander Tsesis extrapolates to LSPDs from observations about hate speech not only in the Weimar Republic, but even in world history's paradigm case of non-democracy, Nazi Germany,[34] as well as the US in a dramatically different era.[35] That study supplies no evidence empirically documenting even remotely comparable patterns of causation within LSPDs. It, too, falls back upon the rhetorical consequentialism of harm attributed to hate speech not as the kind of causative agent that such empirical discourse would suggest, but instead as a *malum in se*. Delgado,[36] Cortese,[37] and Waldron[38] similarly aggregate Rwandan Hutus' 1994 calls for Tutsi genocide with extreme utterances in the US, with no discussion of those societies' divergent socio-political backgrounds. Delgado links the Rwandan history with the earlier 'extermination of Native Americans',[39] yet, as mentioned earlier, that past, along with its history of slavery and racial segregation, *ipso facto* precludes the US, taken as a whole, from having been an LSPD from its colonial period through to the mid-twentieth century.

The Weimar Republic, albeit constitutionally democratic, was certainly not longstanding, having emerged, out of disastrous military defeat, as an historical novelty largely unwelcome among Germans. The Weimar constitution was implemented in spite of a population untrained in practices of democratic norms and institutions. By the 1920s, no large-scale adult German population (trade unions representing only partial exceptions) had been raised or schooled in generations-old habits and traditions of open and candid civic dissent, debate, and political participation.[40] Weimar's political parties reflected, and pursued, a popular majority sentiment aiming to eliminate democracy altogether. Hence the Weimar Republic's famous epithet, 'the democracy without democrats'.[41] Nor was that democracy stable, hovering between two world wars in one of the most socially toxic environments of modern history.[42] And nor did it know any period of durable prosperity, having plunged into hyperinflation in what still remains one of modern economists' textbook examples.

Kathrin Groh recalls West Germany's post-war 'constitutional founders' distrust towards the people of the untutored republic', and the founders' 'absolute' determination 'to prevent a repeat of history'.[43] The post-Second World War Federal Republic could not immediately have sprung into an LSPD. During that period as a transitioning democracy, speech bans may well have played a security role and even the educational, 'tutoring' role of teaching pluralist values to a people alienated from them, but cannot in themselves be called affirmatively *democratizing*. Implicit within the LSPD model is that such a democracy becomes not merely

---

[34] Tsesis, 2002, pp. 11–27.

[35] Tsesis, 2002, pp. 28–65. Cf. Altman, 2012, pp. 38–9 (criticizing Tsesis on overbreadth grounds).

[36] Delgado, 2006, pp. ix, xi.   [37] Cortese, 2006, pp. 38–52.

[38] Waldron, 2012a, pp. 34, 71.   [39] Delgado, 2006, p. ix.

[40] Cf. Nieuwenhuis, 2011, p. 143 (noting the continued absence of civil rights in the constitution of 1871).

[41] Groh, 2002, p. 93; Wassermann, 2002, pp. 100–1 (discussing Joseph Goebbels).

[42] See, e.g., Thiel, 2003b, p. 3.   [43] Groh, 2002, p. 91.

an incrementally different, but a qualitatively different type of society—not one in which hatred disappears, but one in which means proliferate for countering it. Far from being a minor variant, which would differ from the democracies of Weimar, the former Yugoslavia, or Rwanda only in details, the LSPD stands as an arch-opposite to those democracies. They lacked not one, but all three of the qualifications, 'longstanding', 'stable', and 'prosperous'.

'Every idea is an incitement', Holmes famously observed. 'Eloquence may set fire to reason.'[44] Holmes was responding to an anxiety still voiced, often with reference to Weimar, namely, that hateful expression must be nipped in the bud, lest it lead to atrocities that can no longer be controlled (the Weimar fallacy can also be called the 'snowball' argument). We end up with legal penalties on grounds of sheer speculation as to harmful effects—always illegitimate as grounds for overcoming a higher-order legal interest, be it a citizen prerogative or even, more conventionally, a human or civil right. Such derogation can be questionable even as a security rationale, but fails by definition as either a democratic or a liberal rationale for penalizing expression. Contrary to any notion of a democratic rule of law, the state punishes people because their expressive activity *may* provoke social harms through an unspecified chain of material causation.[45]

Challenging the persistence of German bans on extremist political parties, Preuß distinguishes between forms of social mobilization before and after the Second World War,

[Germany's current] ban on political parties responds to the challenge of [early twentieth-century] mass democracy, i.e., against the experience of large masses mobilised through centralised party apparatuses, organised in quasi-militarist fashion against (liberal) democracy. The masses allowed themselves to be mobilised by those party apparatuses. They were compliant, disciplined, and often ideologically schooled ... and wedded to ideals of collective emancipation, as embodied by 'their' party.[46]

The point, then, is not that LSPDs eliminate organized parties or groups that incubate dangerous ideas. Rather, their populations' earlier disposition towards uncritical obedience to such movements changes markedly under the circumstances of post-Second World War democracies. People confining themselves over time to fascist or quasi-fascist types of group organization are today often as loud as they ever were, but proportionally far fewer in number within nothing like the vast mobilizations through which their numbers can suddenly increase, as we witness in non-LSPDs. Post-Second World War, LSPDs have promoted, on the one hand, individualism, and, on the other hand, simultaneously fluid and diverse forms of social association differing starkly from those which had powerfully fuelled Nazi support under Weimar,

We witness a clear shift in the loci of political opinion and will formation (*eine deutliche Schwerpunktverlagerung der Orte der politischen Meinungs- und Willensbildung*) and of

---

[44] *Gitlow v. New York*, 268 U.S. 652, 673 (1925) (Holmes, J., dissenting).
[45] See Section 5.9.   [46] Preuß, 2002, p. 114.

citizens' fundamental social orientations ... towards the variety of social and employment contexts within civil society, such as grassroots movements, professional networks, self-help groups, as well as social, cultural, athletic, religious, and other organisations.[47]

Preuß recalls the 'loosening or even dissolution of traditional social milieus and collective loyalties',[48] which is often condemned within critical and communitarian theories. Yet that social transformation also bears fruit in the struggle against hatred. We witness 'growing social resistance to hierarchical–centralised models of social and political organisation. Large-scale organisations are being replaced by a more multifaceted "associative infrastructure", characterised more by horizontal than by than vertical networks.'[49] Preuß concludes: 'What apparently follows is by no means social or political disintegration, but rather a different mode of integration of citizens into the institutional and normative frameworks of the political order.'[50]

A marketplace model comes into play after all, albeit not in the rationalist ways envisaged by Mill, Holmes, or Brandeis. Consumers of popular ideas and passions, like consumers of goods and services, are not necessarily guided towards the best choices. People still fall for marketing scams, and may also 'purchase' prejudices over reason. A preponderance of the population, in the manner of neither wholly uninformed nor optimally informed consumers, will not always choose the best goods and services nor the best ideas. But nor will people be as easily seduced by the crudest, as we witness in non-democracies or weak democracies. As Wayne Sumner observes, 'advocacy is one thing and successful advocacy quite another.'[51] Hate groups continue to form, yet without the spontaneous snowballing effects displayed in Weimar Germany, Rwanda, or the former Yugoslavia.

The point is not, then, that democracies' current forms of social and political integration proceed seamlessly or without inequality; nor that today's democracies have become immune from committing or overlooking group-based injustices. Rather, patterns of communication and socialization have shifted away from the potential for politically orchestrated conformity that we witness in the orchestrated atrocities that draw on considerable popular participation. Hateful ideas caught fire immediately in Weimar Germany and ushered in Nazism within a few brief years. Those same types of ideas also spread widely and easily today, and have done so for decades, particularly through electronic media, yet without any comparable effect within LSPDs, even taking our current terror networks or far-right movements into account.

The Weimar fallacy—that the snowballing of hatred in some democracies proves the vulnerability of democracies as such—mirror-images the one-size-fits-all

[47] Preuß, 2002, p. 115.   [48] Preuß, 2002, p. 115.
[49] Preuß, 2002, p. 115 (discussing Elias and Habermas).
[50] Preuß, 2002, p. 115 (discussing Elias and Habermas).
[51] Sumner, 2009, p. 210 (observing that 'no serious scientific attempt has been made to factor out and measure the extent' to which hate speech contributes to violent or discriminatory conduct). See also, e.g., Sumner, 2009, p. 211 (discussing studies of hate crime by Perry, Levin, & McDevitt, and Levin, McDevitt, & Bennett); Weinstein, 1999, p. 138.

assumption about democracy that trips up Dworkin. Any such evidence of comparable causative forces currently appears 'too remotely and speculatively linked to harm to minorities'[52] in LSPDs. To be sure, and in contrast to Tsesis, many prohibitionists today do not present arguments of Weimarian direct causation. We need not trivialize the ongoing dangers of intolerance, but need only to consider that the LSPD requires an 'altogether different'[53] understanding of the context and effects of hate speech. Our democracies marked by that progression of both individualism and mutable forms of socialization remain by no means immune, then, from the dangers of intolerance. But as Preuß suggests:

That kind of collectivity … is vulnerable to dangers facing its functional foundations (*Funktionsvoraussetzungen*) in a way different than under the model of organisation-mediated mass democracy familiar to us from the Weimar Republic. Weimar's—sadly too tardily detected—dangers lurked in the possibility of democratic *self*-destruction through the anti-constitutional militancy of parties, which, seeking to conquer state power through legalist forms, could organise and tether broad masses of people.[54]

Not only questions of legitimacy in principle, but also questions of efficacy in practice arise around the strategies of prevailing hate speech bans. 'The "society of individuals"', Preuß continues, has brought about the 'de-centralisation and autonomisation of its enemies'.[55] Hate groups do, then, continue to thrive. However:

A glance at the daily newspaper items shows that insults, hate crimes and affronts particularly against foreigners, the spreading of racist slogans and displays of Nazi symbols take place, on all appearances, in uncoordinated, decentralised, spontaneous and 'self-organised' ways, and are only in small numbers of cases organised by a party.[56]

For Jamal Greene, '[t]he standard European argument in favor of [hate speech bans] may easily be characterized as anti-democratic: Restrictions on hate speech protect unpopular minority groups from *democracy run amok*.'[57] That 'anti-democratic' argument, can be cast in dignitarian terms: a limit on democracy serves to strengthen democracy by protecting its vulnerable members. In a fleeting reference to 'the self-destruction of Germany's democracy in 1933',[58] Grimm, writing in 2009, praises as ethically self-evident Germany's penalties on hateful expression, and thereby the exclusion from public discourse of a—certainly vile, because often neo-Nazi—sector of the population. The Weimar fallacy arises through Grimm's unstated assumption, common within consequentialist prohibitionism, that democracy per se is nothing more than a protean, ahistorical formalism: a danger that once arose in one democracy automatically becomes an intractable risk to

---

[52] Sumner, 2009, p. 220.   [53] Mommsen, 2002, p. 148.
[54] Preuß, 2002, p. 116 (original emphasis).   [55] Preuß, 2002, p. 118.
[56] Preuß, 2002, p. 118.   [57] Greene, 2012, p. 92 (emphasis added).
[58] Grimm, 2009a, p. 14. Grimm's statement of German law is misleading. He suggests a limited scope to German law, arguing that the Grundgesetz arts. 18 and 21 apply only to 'a party's or a person's attempt to overthrow the system.' With respect to right-wing extremism, that observation is deceptive without express reference to further criminal law prohibitions, notably § 86, § 86a, and § 130 StGB, which regulate speech more broadly. See, e.g., Schrank, 2006, pp. 16–56.

any democracy, regardless of any further historical or cultural factors. On that one-size-fits-all prohibitionist concept of democracy, mirroring Dworkin's oppositionist one, no further distinction becomes relevant between Germany anno 1933 and Germany anno 2009.[59]

In the West, we must view the formally democratic *non*-LSPD as distinguishable from our present historical era. It forms a historically prior period, alongside the Roman Empire, medieval aristocracies, and early modern monarchical absolutisms. The history of seventeenth-century to early twentieth-century colonialism, imperialism, and slavery is a history of that pre-LSPD era, and not of the post-1960s LSPD period, which is normatively defined in opposition to those.

A similar thesis often refers to German humanism. It warns that even a high culture which had produced Dürer, Lessing, Kant, Goethe, Schiller, Beethoven, Herder, Hölderlin, or Heine could, without vigilance, end up deifying a Hitler. Elite eighteenth- and nineteenth-century circles, however, had never represented average levels of popular German political consciousness, no more than cultural elites at the time represented their overall populations in Britain or France. The LSPD model is in no way a proxy for some free-floating notion of 'civilization', a term rightly problematized in twentieth-century post-colonial theory.[60] It is neither more nor less than a particular historical stage within democratic societies. The inductive, Weimar fallacy is to deem concrete dysfunctions of societies formally designated as democratic to inhere within democracies generally.

Weimar Germans, as Heinrich Mann so vividly evokes,[61] had still mostly descended from generations schooled in hierarchy, prejudice, and obedience, not in any broad culture of democratic norms, values, institutions, or practices, just as their white cousins in the American South would take doctrinally elaborated notions of white supremacy as self-evident. No generalized claim of 'civilization' can be casually equated with a specifically democratic culture. Their upbringing was authoritarian, patriarchal, Euro-centric, and often patently racist, scarcely stressing what LSPDs today recognize as pluralist values concomitant with open, active, critical debate. Weimar arose in the dying days of a Concert of Europe world, in which a rigorous culture of individual rights and liberties stood more as an ideal nurtured by relatively small numbers of Enlightenment-style intellectuals than as the reality of the workaday world or of popular consciousness.

Germany's historical injustices are manifold, but its unjust Nazi past discloses no single, unequivocally opposite set of speech norms to be just, except through a question-begging negation. A just government certainly *refrains* from committing genocide—it is, in that sense, easy to ascertain what that government does *not* do—but what coercive legal elements it additionally requires, in controversial

[59] Cf. Schrank, 2006, p. 96.
[60] See, e.g., Cornell, Rosenfeld, & Carlson, 1992; Derrida, 2005; Norrie, 1993.
[61] See Mann, 2010. Works of figures like Hašek, Kafka, or Musil also sketch that era.

contexts, remains less obvious.[62] The equally negatively defined 'Never again!' injunction[63] is by no means as self-evident as many would like to think. Nazism was manifestly unjust. A just society does not include Nazi elements. But what does it mean 'not to include' Nazi elements? What is 'included' instead? One Nazi atrocity was indeed hateful expression, but an equally odious one was the totalitarian suppression of public discourse. What, then, is the 'opposite' of Nazi policy on speech? Does that opposite admit viewpoint-punitive bans within public discourse, or does it lead down precisely the opposite road? If we seek a just society through elements that represent the negation of the ultimate, unjust society, it may certainly be democratic and pluralist. But to say that it must also repress expression within public discourse is another matter entirely,[64] and by no means follows any obvious logic of 'negating' Nazism. It only begs the question as to which element of Nazism is more legitimately negated: the hate speech or the suppression of speech.

5.3 Indirect Consequentialist Prohibitionism

A trend that we can call *indirect consequentialist prohibitionism* has arisen, arguably in response to the absence of statistically reliable evidence of direct causation from hate speech in public discourse to ascertainable harms. That theory of indirect effect rejects notions of language as a sheer medium of otherwise immaterial ideas, which would then culminate in materially distinct social harms. Writing from phenomenological, socio-linguistic, and deconstructionist perspectives, such theorists deem hate speech to have harmful albeit diffusive effects. The harm of hate speech, they suggest, qualitatively differs from that which can be demonstrated empirically.

That strand emerges in the 1980s and 1990s with the feminist approach of Catharine MacKinnon,[65] the linguistic philosophy of Rae Langton,[66] or the phenomenological approach of Charles Lawrence.[67] Langton, synthesizing feminist insights with the theories of linguistic philosophers J.L. Austin and Charles Sanders Pierce, examines hateful expression as *illocutionary*, i.e., not merely, in Saussure's sense, 'signifying' hatred but enacting it,[68] and as *perlocutionary*, disseminating adverse psychological effects regardless of any materially evident impact. Anthony Cortese describes a 'cultural transmission theory',[69] whereby broadcast or other popular media 'pass hate on to each succeeding generation', making intolerance 'normal or conventional'.[70] Waldron, although writing in a more established

---

[62] See, e.g., Heinze, 2013, pp. 22–8.   [63] See Section 1.1, text accompanying note 21.
[64] Cf. Wijnberg, 2008, p. 61.
[65] MacKinnon, 1996. Cf., e.g., Cortese, 2006, pp. 77–101.
[66] Langton, 1993. See also Langton, 2012.   [67] Lawrence, 1993.
[68] Cf. Greenawalt, 1989a, pp. 57–63; Nancy, 2013, pp. 9–10.
[69] Cortese, 2006, pp. 3–4; cf. pp. 4–6 (adopting a 'group-identification' theory) and pp. 7–9 (adopting a 'stage-developmental model of hate-speech severity').
[70] Cortese, 2006, p. 4. Cf., e.g., Günther, 2000, p. 65.

liberal vein and therefore not expressly identifying with those movements, does cite some of its exponents in condemning the 'ugliness' and 'slow-acting poison', which 'become a disfiguring part of the social environment.'[71]

These theorists focus on the intangible yet pervasive power of language. Hate speech, they argue, germinates cultures of intolerance, not always through discrete, causally traceable chains of events, so much as through gradual and cumulative effects. Violence and discrimination, on that view, arise within LSPDs not through clockwork mechanisms triggered in each case by discernible speech acts, but through an entire culture to which those acts individually and cumulatively contribute. Such theories challenge classical, Cartesian notions that language would serve to represent purely mental acts and would therefore remain neatly severable from the material world of action and physical causation.[72]

Critical race theorists[73] have joined Lawrence[74] in describing hateful expression as a weapon delivering a blow as harsh as a physical assault. Such invective does not convey information or invite discussion. It serves only to attack. The difference between fists and words becomes immaterial. These theorists, here too, cite empirical evidence arising from acts of immediate harassment or 'fighting words', though not necessarily to extrapolate directly onto hate speech in public discourse. Their aim in this context is rather to dramatize the overall detriments of hate speech, as instantiations of broadly ambient social evils. Through the more diffuse yet thereby all the more insidious mechanisms of illocution and perlocution, hate speech powerfully constructs and entrenches social structures of superiority and inferiority.

A threshold problem with those theories arises from the transition from a direct to an indirect model of harm. The model of direct harm had presupposed a dual causation: first, hateful expression in public discourse produces harmful effects; second, a hate speech ban will not only redress that harm retrospectively through penalties imposed on hateful expression, but will also prospectively reduce those effects by deterring hate speech. The second assumption, as we have seen, fails because the first assumption lacks evidence. A model of indirect harm fails for the opposite reason. The first assumption becomes more secure, by defining harmful effects in broader terms, but, by definition, at the expense of any remedial or deterrent solution in the form of viewpoint-selective regulation of speech. It is precisely by including indirect harm, that any residual notion of causation destroys a consequentialist rationale for seeking recourse in a ban. A ban makes *consequentialist* sense only on an assumption of sufficiently *direct* causation.

We end up on the horns of a dilemma which is unsatisfactory at both ends. If we take indirect causation literally, banning all expression which might pervasively feed into broader patterns of intolerance, then bans must sweep far more broadly than

---

71 See Section 1.3, text accompanying note 43.
72 Cf. Williams, 2011, pp. 603, 606–7.
73 See generally, e.g., Matsuda et al. (eds), 1993; Delgado & Stefancic, 2004.
74 See Section 1.1, text accompanying note 17.

even the most zealous prohibitionist could ever seriously propose. By contrast, if we narrow that scope, which we would have to do not marginally but dramatically even to reflect the broader French, German, or Scandinavian types of bans, then much of the speech covered by theories of indirect causation remains, and it becomes unclear what distinct contribution those theories can be making. Indeed we end up back at square one, since, at that point, it is really some other criterion that is being used to decide which of the types of expression falling under those theories are to be banned, and then *that* is the criterion which must truly be examined.

Leaving aside those questions of principle, concrete observation does little to support such theories. Nowhere, for example, have hate speech bans with respect to anti-Semitism been stronger, over decades, than in Germany, yet during the Gaza conflict of 2014 no LSPD witnessed more potent demonstrations of anti-Semitism.[75] More generally, despite comparable levels of intolerance across democracies, irrespective of the existence or extent of bans,[76] the LSPDs with the strongest bans have tended to witnesses conspicuous consolidation of extremist political parties.[77] Even taken on their own terms, and even accepting many of their findings, theories of indirect causation end up proving far more than any conception of democratic legitimacy could support. To designate the illocutionary, perlocutionary, or culturally transmissive force of utterances as a legally cognizable harm would reach so far into speech, including violence or offence in countless works of film, music, art, literature, or colloquial speech, as to turn public discourse within LSPDs into the wholly subordinated object of a government-operated licence, along the lines of the aforementioned 'How much free speech shall we "give" people?' paradigm.[78] (Everyday sexist expressions like 'bitch', or idioms diffused into public thought so as to denigrate disabled or otherwise different persons, such as 'idiot', 'moron', or 'fatso', make the point starkly. What kind of penalty shall we impose on someone uttering those words within public discourse, or a phrase like 'dialogue of the deaf', thereby socially constructing the mental inferiority of a group far more vulnerable than many of our currently protected groups? Those who would distinguish such speech as 'normalized' or 'innocuous' serve more to confirm than to undermine the arbitrariness of viewpoint-punitive measures within public discourse.)[79] Commenting on mainstream German broadcasting, Alexander Kühn and Marcel Rosenbach write,

German television viewers are surely monsters. Sunday upon Sunday, they demand a human sacrifice: shot, strangled, drowned, poisoned, pushed down the stairs, driven to suicide, frozen, or burned. A few weeks ago in [the police series] *Tatort* … the murder victim even had his fingernails ripped out. Nine million people watched.[80]

---

[75] See, e.g., Weiss, 2014.   [76] See Section 6.1.

[77] See, e.g., Backes, 2011; Freitag & Thieme, 2011; Jesse, 2011; Lucardie, Voerman, & Wielenga, 2011; Schubert, 2011.

[78] See Section 4.10. We need not, then, decide on any *legal* conclusions which might follow from Butler's socio-linguistic oppositionism, Butler, 1997, which goes further than I do here, in eroding lines between public discourse and other speech situations beyond what is strictly required for an LSPD to maintain democratic legitimacy.

[79] See, e.g., Heinze, 2009b.   [80] Kühn & Rosenbach, 2013.

Other weekdays, the authors note, include similar items, as part of a long-term increase in violent shows. The authors nonetheless go on to observe that the programming 'reads like the inverse of [recently] published criminal statistics, which show a nationwide decrease in murders and physical assaults'.[81] Taken together with the aforementioned displays of anti-Semitism, it appears that, within that LSPD context, indirect consequentialist prohibitionism bears little resemblance to social trends. A normative theory of indirect causation deliberately circumvents empirical method. We must instead construe such broadcasts not as, so to speak, 'indicative', but as 'performative'. In other words, they convey not, or not only, inert or neutral Saussurian signifiers, indifferently transmitting one set of messages just as any other show would transmit other messages; rather, the broadcasts systemically construct and even exalt violence as a social norm.

Butler challenges various critical schools, rejecting their view of a one-sided, wholly disempowering social construction of inferiority through hate speech. She admittedly fails to distinguish between the different effects of speech within LSPDs and non-LSPDs;[82] but, to ponder her argument in its best light, we can easily take her to be assuming LSPDs. Butler argues that such provocations cannot be construed as generating purely passive victims. In her view, they serve as a mobilizing force.[83] For example, calls for suppressing the publication of cartoon images of the Prophet Muhammad loudly followed the 2005 Danish cartoon controversy. The familiar prohibitionist claim was made that such expression silences disempowered groups. Cram, however, confirms Butler's view, observing the opposite,

[A]llowing the offensive expression appeared to embolden a number of those who claimed to be offended. Public discourse in Europe was inundated by a range of Muslim perspectives and responses to the cartoons. Indeed, far from alienating Muslims from the state, or silencing them in public discourse, it could be argued that these participants in public debate demonstrated a healthy commitment to the idea that they could shape the contours of public policy. In so doing, those protesting against the right to engage in speech offensive to particular religious communities ironically revealed the fortitude that can be demanded of all of us in a pluralistic liberal democracy.[84]

Instead of construing literally the marketplace analogy,[85] Vaneigem welcomes the marketplace of speech to subvert social and political effects of the market-driven economy. He opposes viewpoint-selective bans, not to enhance our post-industrial marketplace ethos, but to assail it. Again, reading an LSPD assumption into his view, what emerges is not a liberalism of expression straightforwardly aping the liberalism of the marketplace, but rather a democracy of expression as a check and balance against excesses of marketplace liberalism. 'Free expression gives life to language, in contrast to a [capitalist] economy that produces a dead, desiccated language, composed of interchangeable grunts, [an economy] that makes language an object of trade.'[86]

---

[81] Kühn & Rosenbach, 2013.
[82] That lapse may explain some of the ambiguities in Butler's view. Cf. Howe, 1998, pp. 102–4.
[83] Butler, 1997.   [84] Cram, 2009, p. 310.   [85] See Section 5.5.
[86] Vaneigem, 2003. p. 23; cf. pp. 30, 56, 78. Cf. also Rancière, 2005, pp. 62–3.

Prohibitionists ordinarily concede that not all indirectly harmful expression, such as every violent television programme, can legitimately be banned. What they instead defend is bans on the most extreme, crudest forms, entailing the most vulnerable targets. That objection, however, far from refining the phenomenological, socio-linguistic, or deconstructionist starting points, renders their insights superfluous. The whole point of distinguishing indirect effects is to highlight attitudes conveyed amorphously, as a subtle and pervasive whole. If we are now to add independent criteria as to what qualifies as 'extreme and crude' from within that fluid mass, then the identification of indirect effects again loses its purpose as a distinct foundation for bans. Suddenly we are back to square one, simply making straightforward viewpoint-selective judgements, for which theories of indirect causation cease to play any distinct role.

Theories of diffuse effect do plausibly defeat the traditional separation of expression and action as applied to fighting words, harassment, and other such legally cognizable harms, already agreed on all sides (again, barring a libertarian extreme) as legitimately subject to regulation. For public discourse, by contrast, their own arguments underscore the imperative of maintaining that distinction. Its undoing would prohibit anything from hard-hitting fiction through to more radical Marxists' calls for revolution,[87] entailing not slight, but colossal overbreadth.[88]

Meindert Fennema links the speech–conduct distinction, supporting the presumption of free speech within public discourse, to the classical 'requirement of the rule of law (*Rechtsstaat*) that criminal prohibitions must relate directly to actions or behaviours.'[89] However cogently phenomenological or socio-linguistic theory may dissolve conventional formalisms, law by definition never gets beyond them. A world beyond formalism is a world beyond law (not by accident, Hitler, Stalin, or Mao saw no obstacles in legal formalism, which they, to the contrary, heartily mocked). Along with Stanley Fish's challenges to classical liberal assumptions about a realm of distinctly 'free' speech,[90] he recognizes that 'theoretical assaults on the speech–action distinction', as cogent as some of them are, cannot 'disable' the speech–conduct distinction for legal purposes. 'If you want the benefits you believe [free speech] brings, then you must presuppose the distinction, although, in the afternoon, when you are doing philosophy and not democracy, you can deconstruct it all you like.'[91] Democracy certainly grants us the freedom of rejecting Cartesian ontologies, but must nevertheless, in the area of speech, maintain to an important degree that admittedly reductive Cartesian distinction between attitudes and conduct. Democracy is precariously, in some senses unfairly, yet irretrievably Cartesian. We cannot overthrow democracy's Cartesianism without overthrowing democracy itself.

---

[87] See Section 5.9. See also Heinze, 2008a, pp. 139–41.

[88] Cf. Strossen, 1990, pp. 542–3; see also pp. 544–6 (examining the public–private distinction).

[89] Fennema, 2009, p. 17. Cf. Preuß, 2002, p. 11.   [90] Fish, 1994.

[91] Private communication of 30 December 2012 (on file with author). The speech-conduct distinction is certainly not absolute in law. Elsewhere I have proposed a refinement of it to assess the extent to which democratic law can legitimately target subjective attitudes. See Heinze, 2016b.

The 'sticks and stones' adage turns out to be not so much correct as irrelevant. *Of course* vulnerable individuals and groups will often feel hurt by hatred, even when it takes the general form of expression within public discourse. The present writer can attest as much from personal experience. The active LSPD rightly adopts strong and ongoing policies against such discrimination. However, within that LSPD context—the context of a democracy fully situated to fulfil its legitimating expressive criteria—it remains doubtful that consequentialist rationales can override those criteria's deontological foundations.

5.4 Consequentialist Prohibitionism and Public Discourse

In addition to questions about the effects of bans on targeted groups, a question arises as to their effects on the quality of expression, for all of us, as a component of collective self-government. If black-letter law reflected material causation within everyday reality, then the contrast between, on the one hand, France's, Germany's or the Netherlands's extensive penalties for bans, and, on the other hand, the strong protections afforded by the US First Amendment,[92] would mirror a stark contrast in the broad character of public discourse within the respective societies. Consequentialist prohibitionism, whether it be based on a theory of direct or of indirect causation, would mean that French, German, or Dutch bans would curb rising intolerance, and American rejection of bans would foster it. It would mean that French or German bans would hinder robust public debate, while American freedoms would promote it. Yet neither comparison can boast much evidence.

Differences in public discourse across democracies are surely noticeable. But those differences emerge against backdrops of open debate that are, taken solely as *democratic* public discourse, scarcely distinguishable. Taking demographic differences and local cultures and histories into account, all four democracies have, over decades, witnessed comparable levels of racist, anti-Semitic, Islamophobic, homophobic, sexist, and other intolerant speech.[93] Their respective climates of speech and expression are not as divergent as their black-letter differences, on any consequentialist reasoning, would suggest. All four nations arguably generate similar levels of intelligent or stupid, original or repetitive, and creative or bland speech, on topics ranging from the political to the personal, from the tawdry to the sublime. Dutch, French, and German speech and debate remain diverse and robust, although intolerance persists, under legal regimes that some regard as excessively regulatory of expression. American speech and debate remain diverse and robust, although intolerance persists, under a regime often viewed as unfeeling towards traditionally disempowered groups.

In any given LSPD, we can always find some example of either formally or informally policed speech; yet we can always match it with a counter-example of unconstrained speech. French primary education, for example, or its cultural

---

[92] See generally, e.g., Nieuwenhuis, 2011; Pech, 2003; Robitaille-Froidure, 2011.
[93] Cf. Section 5.5, text accompanying note 159.

broadcasting, routinely includes not just moderately centre–leftist, but expressly Marxist and anti-capitalist perspectives on history and current affairs, in ways unknown among their American counterparts. Yet in 2007 France prosecuted an elected member of the National Assembly for stating, with no crude invective, opposition to gay rights, indeed at a time when gay rights had moved into the French political foreground, prompting public discussion across the political spectrum. Although the sentence was later reversed,[94] the sheer prospect of purely viewpoint-punitive intervention in democratic political discourse, leaving speakers uncertain about the legality of their speech, raises questions about 'chilling', and about the integrity of political debate.[95]

Americans, by contrast, have relished a far fuller freedom to air every imaginable view about gay rights, including hostile voices from some Christian or traditionalist quarters. Yet the most dedicated, accomplished, and patriotic American would seriously risk any hope of high elective, and even some non-elective, public office by avowing even a marginal appreciation for Marxism, let alone atheism—a wholly informal constraint, yet betokening an impoverished range of critical perspectives within culture, within society, and therefore within public discourse. In recent years, the monitoring group Reporters Without Borders (RWB) has ranked the US behind many Western European states in view of measures taken that are perceived as inhibiting public dissent.[96] I shall not undertake a detailed assessment of that claim, but it casts doubt on any suggestion that overall public discourse has been freer *in practice* in the US than in Western Europe since the mid-twentieth century, even if it enjoys greater formal freedom there from the standpoint of black-letter rules. We can multiply such imperfections and such comparisons ad infinitum, yet only with the ultimate effect of confirming the lack of trans-Atlantic differences in the overall levels of democratic public discourse.

The problem is not that, beyond the black-letter texts, continental Europe and the US somehow present socio-political extremes, for which an intermediary option might offer the right compromise. If it is only in their formal law that Western Europe and the US represent opposites—if, in the everyday character of public discourse, they are not opposites at all—then nothing requires compromise. We can add other LSPDs, with their own histories of constitutional or demographic pluralism, such as Australia or Canada. Once demographic differences are taken into account, we still find an overall comparable quality of background public discourse. (Or at least, on this point, too, no empirical study has ever been cited in the comparative free speech literature to suggest the opposite.) Differences arise at more specific levels, such as the quality of print or broadcast journalism, but it would certainly be difficult to correlate such discrepancies to respective differences in viewpoint-based regulation.

---

[94] Cour de cassation, criminelle, Chambre criminelle, 12 November 2008, 07-83.398.

[95] Cf. Section 2.9, text accompanying notes 114–15.

[96] See, e.g., Reporters Without Borders (2014). That assessment will surprise readers who judge free expression in the US predominantly on Supreme Court decisions, which represent only a fraction of situations posing threats to expressive freedom in the US. Indicia examined by RWB include, e.g., government responses to organized protests and dissent.

If otherwise incompatible regimes of formal law, the continental European and the American, lead to similar socio-political circumstances—if it just does not matter to overall levels of public discourse whether LSPDs do or do not ban hate speech within that sphere—then it again becomes unclear whether we ought to worry about bans one way or the other, and should revert to value-pluralist proceduralism after all. Could it be that, as long as most people are happy with, or oblivious to, their national laws, it makes no difference whether or not they have bans?[97]

Black-letter differences obviously affect the experiences of particular speakers. Individual Holocaust deniers enjoy freedoms in the US denied to them in France or Germany. That difference certainly raises questions as to whether hate speakers' citizen prerogatives ought to trump the dignity of historically persecuted groups, or the views of democratically elected lawmakers, and in some states the popular majorities, who favour bans. The debate matters, then, with respect to hate speakers and with respect to their targets, but not necessarily with respect to one of the chief aims of free speech, namely to keep civic discussion dynamic. The hate speech debate, in other words, is about political and legal principle.

Chastising 'the current American system', Sunstein laments, 'it would not be an overstatement to say that much of the free speech "market" now consists of scandals, sensationalized anecdotes, and gossip, often about famous movie stars and athletes'.[98] Sunstein had earlier explained that, historically, this 'current system' emerges in contrast to the pre-1950s era of greater regulation.[99] His logic is clear enough, particularly in view of his aforementioned analogy to property rights.[100] If de-regulation does not improve the quality of the final product, then nor does greater regulation threaten to diminish it. Of course, many a historian would recall that 'low grade' speech is scarcely the invention of the twentieth century, even if mass and electronic media have more recently multiplied its outlets. Still, Sunstein warns that such chatter eclipses 'serious issues' and their 'in depth' discussion. It 'perpetuates a bland, watered-down version of conventional morality on most issues', such as 'to avoid real criticisms of existing [social and political] practice'.[101]

We can leave aside questions as to whether or how general public discourse might have differed in earlier times. The important point is that Sunstein rightly avoids suggesting any specific causation *from* American law's refusal to impose viewpoint-based punishments *to* those multiple and varied manifestations of media dross. Moreover, while noting the other 'flourishing democracies' that maintain bans,[102] Sunstein withholds comment on whether their regulations succeed in avoiding either 'scandals, sensationalized anecdotes, and gossip' or 'bland, watered-down version[s] of conventional morality on most issues', such that they would 'avoid real criticisms of existing practice'. One could scarcely hold such a view after a few minutes browsing Britain's *Daily Mail* or Germany's *Bild Zeitung*.

---

[97] Cf., e.g., Molnar & Post, 2012, p. 23.   [98] Sunstein, 1995, p. 23.
[99] Cf. Section 6.1, text accompanying notes 24 and 35.
[100] See Section 4.13, text accompanying note 195.   [101] Sunstein, 1995, pp. 22–3.
[102] Sunstein, 1995, pp. 15, 186; cf. p. 192 (referring to 'industrialized nations').

5.5 Consequentialist Oppositionism Revisited: Harms of Bans?

The argument thus far has been that no consequentialist claim can trump the higher-order citizen prerogative of non-viewpoint-punitive expression within the public discourse of an LSPD. For that same reason, no consequentialist–oppositionist claim can strengthen that prerogative as a matter of democratic legitimacy. As we have seen, however, the debates are concerned not only with political legitimacy, but also with practical effects. Consequentialist oppositionism cannot in any way decide the debates, then, and is subject to the same questions of empirical method as consequentialist prohibitionism. But it can dispel any suggestion that consequentialist claims stack up solely in the prohibitionist camp.

Some evidence suggests that bans, far from curbing, actively provoke and 'tutor' extremist groups. Wijnberg sketches the problem through a simple image:

Imagine that a group of schoolboys persistently mocks a classmate as 'fatso' (*dikzak*) … The teacher wants to call a stop to such conduct, and forbids the boys to use the word 'fatso'. So the boys just as doggedly decide to call the classmate 'beauty' (*schoonheid*). Does that improve the situation?[103]

Of course, only in a metaphorical sense, and not literally, is Wijnberg's scenario useful. Standard bullying remedies can protect individuals in educational, employment, and other such contexts. Such remedies accord with the aforementioned contexts of individually targeted harassment and 'fighting words' occurring outside public discourse. Within a situation of individually targeted aggression, speech can be scrutinized contextually. Even a word like 'beauty' can easily be identified as a form of harassment.

Rather, Wijnberg's scenario allegorizes a ubiquitous whitewashing process in Western Europe, which prohibitionists have largely ignored. A ban does not stop the speakers as long as they can dodge its terms by travestying their aggression in anodyne garb. Language and expression, as objects of legal regulation, inherently differ from conventional objects of regulation. Either one steals an apple or one doesn't. There is no sense in which one accomplishes such a theft by stealing the apple 'ironically'. There is no sense in which one succeeds in stealing the apple without specifically breaching the legal provision that sets forth the *actus reus* of the theft. Instead of crudely being called 'fatso' because he is overweight, the victim must instead endure the humiliation of cynically sanitized invective. Hate speech bans tutor extremists in the methods of Orwellian newspeak, as their propaganda has long illustrated.[104] Western European hate groups scornfully, even gleefully, adjust and re-adjust their speech to continually frustrate arrests and trials.

---

[103] Wijnberg, 2008, p. 35.
[104] See generally, e.g., British National Party, 2013; English Defence League, 2013; Freiheitliche Partei Österreichs, 2013; Front National, 2013; Nationaldemokratische Partei Deutschlands, 2013; Nederlandse Volks-Unie, 2013; Vlaams Belang, 2013. See also, e.g., Alduy & Wahnich, 2015 (examining the linguistic mainstreaming of extremist discourses).

Linguistic transformations spurred by bans often serve not to advance human dignity, but to sabotage it. In studies of German right-wing extremism, a number of authors show how bans systematically guide hate groups to become ever cleverer, to tread constantly at the edge of legality without overstepping it, regardless of how broadly the ban is defined. Problems of statistical evidence for those effects admittedly mirror-image the problems of the direct prohibitionist thesis. At the very least, however, they challenge prohibitionist consequentialism. 'After the wave of prohibitions against smaller neo-Nazi organisations in the years between 1992 and 1995', observe two experts on extremism, Andrea Röpke and Andreas Speit, 'some neo-Nazis began to construct a new organisational model'.[105] Similarly, examining the NPD, Toralf Staud observes,

After the Skinhead-network Blood & Honour was banned, [followers] started printing 'B&H' on their T-shirts or, according to the place of those two letters in the alphabet, the numerical code '28'. Once school teachers hear that '88' means 'Heil Hitler', pupils write '2 × 44' on their school packs or '87 + 1'.[106]

Drawing a consequentialist conclusion, albeit weighty in its deontological, dignitarian implications, Staud concludes, 'These cat-and-mouse games make a mockery of prohibitions',[107] and, by extension, of those whose dignity the bans purport to uphold. Another transparent substitution for 'Blood & Honour', notes one practising lawyer, Carsten Schrank, became, 'Glory and Honour' (*Ruhm und Ehre*).[108] The swastika has sometimes simply been replaced by a Nazi-era triangular figure (*das Gaudreieck*).[109] The Hitler greeting has at times just as simply been substituted by the 'Kühnen greeting', named after a post-war neo-Nazi leader, merely replacing the flat outstretched hand with three extended fingers.[110] The *quenelle*, similarly inverting the gesture, has been made famous by Dieudonné.[111] Like Wijnberg's

---

[105] Röpke & Speit, 2005, p. 8. Cf generally, Dornbusch & Raabe, 2005.
[106] Staud, 2006, p. 174.
[107] Staud, 2006, p. 174. Cf. Schrank, 2006, pp. 20–2, 26–8; Röpke, 2005, p. 44; Speit, 2005, pp. 15, 23–4, 37.
[108] Schrank, 2006, p. 28. Dornbusch, Raabe, Staud, Röpke, and Speit offer their investigations without legal analysis as such. They point to failures in existing approaches, but adopt no expressly prohibitionist or oppositionist stance. Some of these writers may, of course, maintain deontological reasons for favouring bans, despite their consequentialist showings of those bans' failures or defects. Schrank, by contrast, writes as a practising attorney. He professes overt scepticism towards existing German norms and methods. I include Schrank, aware that the monitoring group *Netz gegen Nazis* has sounded an alarm about his professional role as an experienced attorney for neo-Nazis. Schrank does publish an express disavowal of any links or sympathies with far-right organizations or ideologies (Schrank, 2006, p. 14), and goes some way towards alerting his readers about the inner workings of far-right groups. What remain are allegations, unfortunately unreferenced, of Schrank's support, in 2000, for neo-Nazi Horst Mahler's far-right Initiative *'Ja zu Deutschland, ja zur NPD'* ('Yes to Germany, yes to the NPD'). See *Schrank, Carsten*, 2008. See also, e.g., Kraudzun, 2011. What is important for present purposes is the parity of Schrank's observations with those of Dornbusch, Raabe, Staud, Röpke, and Speit, which compels us to examine the core observations that they all share in view of the consequentialist prohibitionism, irrespective of Schrank's individual politics.
[109] Schrank, 2006, p. 20.   [110] Schrank, 2006, p. 21; Zöchling, 2007.
[111] See, e.g., Geoghegan, 2013.

schoolboys, extremists systematically adjust their speech and symbols in response to each new regulatory advance.

A similar permutation has emerged under the name of the *Identitäre Bewegung*, following on from the French *Bloc identitaire* and *Génération identitaire*,[112] and incorporating neo-Nazi Russian hardbass music.[113] These movements propagate white supremacism, wherein racist language becomes systematically replaced by thinly veiled references to 'culture', including recourse to simulated social science discourses, such as 'ethnopluralism' (*Ethnopluralismus*). We find their message tailored to avoid the letter of bans, through such transparent slogans as 'Unconditionally defending what is OURS!' (*Das EIGENE bedingungslos verteidigen!*)[114]—not expressly naming any target group, and scarcely punishable, given that Ulpian's 'to each his own', *suum cuique, Jedem das Seine*, represents one of law's time-honoured maxims.[115] Similarly, as noted earlier, anti-Semitic expression broke out throughout most of the democratic world during the Gaza conflict of 2014. States with broad bans could scarcely boast their inhibiting effects, nor even any effect of limiting them to a traditional far right.[116] To the contrary, the platitude that one 'isn't allowed' to criticize Jews served more to fuel than to calm hateful expression.[117]

Staud notes that, having honed its law-dodging skills, the NPD grooms its mainstream image. Fragile individuals who might shun uncensored imagery, are easily comforted by messages manipulated to appear down-to-earth and commonsensical: 'If it hasn't been banned, it can't be so bad'.[118] Hence a result contrary to the bans' aims of deterring new recruits. Bans become 'How to' guides for hate groups to entrench themselves within culture, like disinfectants inadvertently spurring bacterial mutation into 'superbugs'. Staud argues that German bans on neo-Nazi political parties in the early 1990s led to increased NPD membership, by strengthening 'its (self-)image of martyrdom'.[119]

Some coded speech can, of course, through contextual readings, be punished in Germany, but far from challenging the results of these findings, that observation confirms Staud's vertiginous 'cat-and-mouse' image.[120] Prohibitionists voice concern for the effects of hate speech on the young or the poorly educated, but that danger cuts two ways. In the eyes of vulnerable onlookers, a hate group's opportunity to claim that it is denied equal standing allows it to confirm its alienation and martyrdom narrative, particularly once it has cosmetically altered its messages

---

[112] Clavel, 2012.

[113] Rechtsextreme wollen mit 'Hardbass' Jugendliche rekrutieren, 2012.

[114] Sieber, 2012. Cf., e.g., Majic, 2012.

[115] Cf. Heinze, 2013a, p. 81. Shakespeare observes the violence dormant in such facially equitable formulas as 'Stand for your own', *Henry V*, 1.2.101, *in* Shakespeare, 1982, p. 104; or, 'I come but for mine own', *Richard II*, 3.3.194, *in* Shakespeare, 2011, p. 227.

[116] See, e.g., Le Devin & Albertini, 2014.　　[117] See, e.g., Yücel, 2014.

[118] Staud, 2006, p. 58.

[119] Staud, 2006, pp. 58, 64. Cf. Molnar & Strossen, 2012, p. 382; Münch, 2002, p. 53; Preuß, 2002, p. 107.

[120] Cf., e.g., Kiyak, 2011.

to avoid the bans. The group can then cite the law as evidence of its view that democracy is a sham in pledging free speech to all while denying it to some.

One strand of consequentialist oppositionism sets forth 'bellwether' and 'steam valve' theories. Bellwether theorists claim that censoring speakers drives them underground, making it difficult for law enforcement to track their activities. When hate speech is admitted into public discourse, they claim, government can more easily monitor speakers whose activities might link to violent or other harmful conduct. Punishing hate speakers serves, on that view, only to tutor them in dissimulation, either pushing them underground or teaching them how to affect a deceptively mainstream veneer. Steam valve theorists share the same concern about the counter-productivity of censorship. They argue that bans make hate speakers feel unfairly excluded, perhaps provoking them to undertake more extreme action, including violence. The idea is that hate speakers may refrain from greater extremism when they have an equal chance to air their views, to 'let off steam'.

American writers have argued both for and against bans invoking the aforementioned bellwether or barometer arguments, but often in a purely speculative vein, given the lack of bans.[121] Manon Rescan and Nicolas Chapuis, by contrast, have adopted bellwether arguments based on the French experience: 'To dissolve an organisation is to run the risk of driving it into clandestinity.' An extremist group's decreased visibility demands, in turn, greater state resources 'required for surveillance', with police running 'the risk of losing track' of the members entirely.[122] Alexandre Lévy notes frustration on the part of police when surveillance of an extremist group is set back to zero after the group's forced dissolution.[123] In the German context, Morlock observes that refraining from bans renders 'a legal party much easier to monitor, and the political motives fuelling them can be examined.'[124] Morlock maintains, '[i]t is important that discontents be swiftly observed, precisely when those discontents manifest in constitutionally unacceptable demands.'[125] Open confrontation bars us, as Mill once counselled, from the 'deep slumber'[126] of complacency.[127] Schrank argues that German bans teach extremists to keep their activities underground, rendering law enforcement more difficult.[128]

One might wonder whether the consequentialist oppositionism with which I am now challenging prohibitionism strays towards an empiricism as flawed as that which I have ascribed to consequentialist prohibitionism. That is why I opened this section noting that consequentialist arguments are not decisive either

---

[121] See, e.g., Strossen, 1990, p. 560 (stating an oppositionist 'bellwether' or 'barometer' arguments); Delgado & Stefancic, 2004, pp. 205, 210–11 (prohibitionist challenge to 'bellwether' or 'barometer' arguments).

[122] Rescan & Chapuis, 2013.

[123] Lévy, 2013 (citing the example of the disbanding, in 2005, of the French neo-Nazi organization Elsass Korps).

[124] Morlock, 2002, p. 66.   [125] Morlock, 2002, p. 66.

[126] *On Liberty*, ch. 2, *in* Mill, [1869] 1991, p. 49.

[127] Cf., e.g., Smolla, 1993, pp. 6–8, 43–54, 151–69.

[128] Schrank, 2006, p. 19. Cf., e.g., Molnar & Strossen, 2012, pp. 382, 384, 386.

way for LSPDs. Given prohibitionists' failure to substantiate statistically reliable links between bans in public discourse and acts of violence or discrimination, it would be implausible for oppositionists to volley with equally tenuous claims. That said, nor are the risks posed respectively by prohibitionist and oppositionist consequentialisms shared equally between them, as mirror images. Those two sets of claims assume very different chains of causation. Both direct and indirect consequentialist prohibitionism assume far-reaching, socio-psychological effects of bans. The consequentialist oppositionism presented thus far assumes, by contrast, a narrower empirical field. It tracks only immediate and material responses of hate groups to bans.

But it is well worth assuming, for argument's sake, that both prohibitionist and consequentialist oppositionisms end up empirically indeterminate. Pointing to that substantive indeterminacy on both sides, prohibitionists might claim that it must then be left for legislatures and courts to balance the competing interests, again reverting to the default mode of value-pluralist proceduralism. However, prohibitionist indeterminacy cannot legitimately 'cancel out' oppositionist indeterminacy in that way. Prohibitionist indeterminacy is not a mirror-image counterpart of oppositionist indeterminacy. The two cannot, in an LSPD, be of equal weight. The citizen's prerogative loses any meaning as one of democracy's legitimating conditions, or even higher-order rights, if it can be abrogated for no reason other than the indeterminate prohibitionist one that its exercise may *possibly* cause harm.[129] Any assumption of equal indeterminacy on both sides does not weigh equally against the respective consequentialisms. To the contrary, given a background regime requiring a higher-order freedom of expression, any such indeterminacy must by definition weigh emphatically against the prohibitionist stance.

In other words, for an LSPD, non-viewpoint-punitive expression within public discourse offers nothing further to weigh or to balance. It is in this sense that we can best understand US Supreme Court Justice Hugo Black's long-debated suggestion that the 'unequivocal command' of the US First Amendment left no further government balancing to be done.[130] Black did not mean that view literally, given the many uncontroversial non-viewpoint punitive restrictions that we have already seen, and of which he was well aware. Once we set aside, as the LSPD concept does, non-viewpoint-selective regulations as in the aforementioned example of perjury, fraud, or 'time, manner, and place' along with doubts about the state's ability to protect the vulnerable, then balancing of interests becomes *categorically* illegitimate as to viewpoints expressed in public discourse. The burden of proof to trump expression within the public discourse of an LSPD remains with the prohibitionist, and not with the oppositionist to justify bans in view of some *prima facie* presumption of harm arising from the prohibitionist's speculative suppositions about material effects.

American oppositionists have lacked domestic empirical evidence of ineffectiveness, available on the continent, due to the post-1960s erosion and disappearance

---

[129] See, e.g., Greenawalt, 1989b, pp. 121–3.
[130] *Konigsberg v. State Bar of California*, 336 U.S. 36, 61 (1961) (Black, J., dissenting).

of American bans. They have nonetheless long warned against censorship's tendency to tutor speakers in re-packaging and re-coding hateful messages, transforming crude insults into what Nadine Strossen calls 'veiled innuendos'.[131] The Harvard African-American Studies scholar Henry Louis Gates, Jr. challenges those who 'spend more time worrying about speech codes than coded speech'. Historically, he notes, African Americans have not fared better in environments of polite speech. They have often still faced discrimination, yet without the blunt speech that would help them to make sense of it, and to plan their life strategies accordingly. '[T]he real power commanded by the racist', Gates recalls, 'is likely to vary inversely with the vulgarity with which it is expressed.'[132] Barack Obama makes a similar point in response to ongoing problems of US racism: 'it's not just a matter of it not being polite to say nigger in public. That's not the measure of whether racism still exists or not.'[133]

Those warnings echo Martin Luther King, Jr.'s earlier admonition, 'Lukewarm acceptance is much more bewildering than outright rejection.'[134] In his 2003 book *Nigger*, Gates's African-American Harvard colleague Randall Kennedy warns against a 'vocabulary of indirection' fostering a milieu in which 'the damaging but polite polemic is protected, while the rude but impotent epithet is not.'[135] That observation chimes with the veteran African-American civil rights attorney Theodore Shaw's confirmation that non-repression of hate speech facilitates the gathering of evidence for the enforcement of minorities' rights.[136]

Martin Imbleau, albeit defending French penalties for Holocaust denial, concedes that linguistic manipulations lead to mainstreamed hate speech.[137] But he fails to ask the crucial question—whether those manipulations emerge precisely from the need to avoid falling afoul of the French bans. Imbleau rightly counts 'taboos' around Nazism among the stimuli that spur Holocaust deniers.[138] Yet he fails to explain how so strongly exalting and entrenching that taboo—augmenting our response from moral outrage to a legal penalty—can diminish such an incentive. 'Scandal' following high-profile prosecutions, as Adriano Prosperi observes with respect to Holocaust denial in Italy, 'is the universal path to success'.[139] For Strossen, 'censored speech becomes more appealing and persuasive to many listeners merely by virtue of the censorship'.[140]

It is Imbleau's own chain of causation, then, which identifies bans as sources rather than remedies for intolerance. He condemns the right-wing extremist Jean-Marie LePen's self-styled image as a free speech martyr.[141] Yet he fails to notice that it is precisely the penalties for speech, which, over decades, placed LePen in that role. French bans spurred him to promote his narrative as the heroic outsider, the renegade

---

[131] Molnar & Strossen, 2012, p. 383.
[132] Gates, 1994, p. 47. Cf. Benz, 2005, pp. 9–11; Strossen, 1990, p. 560 (citing Lasson).
[133] Quoted in Yuhas, 2015. See also, e.g., Andrews, 2015.   [134] King, 1963.
[135] Kennedy, 2003, p. 124 (examining Obama's interview of 22 June 2015 with Marc Maron).
[136] Molnar & Shaw, 2012, pp. 399–400, 403–4.   [137] Imbleau, 2003, pp. 183–4.
[138] Imbleau, 2003, p. 177.   [139] Prosperi, 2013.   [140] Strossen, 1990, p. 554.
[141] Imbleau, 2003, pp. 185–6.

excluded by the state from equal access to public discourse. Imbleau warns against the dangers of Holocaust denial disseminated through the mediatization of 'star' anti-Semites like Robert Faurisson.[142] He fails to observe, however, that it is precisely the French ban, as with high-profile prosecutions of Holocaust deniers in Austria, Germany, and elsewhere, which have, in each case, triggered the media hype.[143]

A further qualification added by some prohibitionists is that bans should protect only the small subset of groups targeted for their 'immutable characteristics' such as race, over which one has little control, but not such as religion, which, involving 'ideas' (a more Western view of religion)[144] as well as free choices, must be open to criticism.[145] Muslims in the West, however, often form ethnic minorities. As a casual glance through the tabloids quickly reveals, stabs at Islam become ways of waging racism without reference to race,[146] even if grosser versions may end up being punishable in some LSPDs.

Once again, instead of diluting hatred, such a legal incentive tutors and invigorates it. Precisely opposite to any such view, many Muslims state that it is their faith, more than their ethnicity, that forms the more important part of their identity.[147] Far from calming the atmosphere, that 'narrow ban' position sets up a discriminatory, two-tier regime. It makes groups excluded from protection, because they are not defined racially, feel less respected than groups included under it. The excluded group feels *more* a victim of state discrimination than the protected group. State policy then pits one group against another in an unseemly rivalry of 'more victim than thou'.[148] Whatever anti-discrimination policies a state may prefer, one which itself discriminates between outsider groups can scarcely claim much moral high ground.

As a practical matter, some oppositionists claim that bans positively detract from non-punitive programmes against intolerance, even while appearing sympathetic to them. Bans have certainly proven easy to pass with little opposition. Mainstream political parties like to be seen as supporting gestures of tolerance, regardless of the substantive policies they otherwise pursue. Sustained and effective civic education, by contrast, requires harder work. For Strossen, 'regulating speech' is 'at best a distraction from, and sometimes an obstacle to, efforts to grapple with the real, concrete problems', such as discrimination in education or employment, or lack of investment in poor areas. Bans, Strossen argues, focus policy-makers on 'symbolism' instead of 'something real to promote actual equality.'[149] Throughout the late twentieth and early twenty-first centuries, while Germany scored questionable successes in punishing hate speech, it tended to be highly lax in punishing violent hate crimes, often failing to distinguish them from ordinary assaults and batteries.[150]

---

[142] Imbleau, 2003, p. 181.   [143] Cf. Strossen, 1990, p. 559.

[144] For Waldron, religious identity equates with holding an 'opinion'. Waldron, 2012a, p. 133. Cf., e.g., Snel, 2010, p. 46.

[145] Waldron, 2012a, p. 123; cf. p. 125.

[146] See, e.g., Cortese, 2006, pp. 53–76. See also, critically, Weinstein, 1999, pp. 166–7.

[147] Cf., e.g., Beatty, 2011.   [148] Cf., e.g., Heinze, 2009b.

[149] Molnar & Strossen, 2012, p. 381; cf. pp. 391–2.   [150] See, e.g., Popp, 2013.

Abstention from coercive censorship by no means debilitates a democracy's battle against intolerance. During the Danish cartoon crisis, some prominent continental media outlets reprinted the cartoons in a defensive posture of asserting their freedoms of expression, even after violent threats or responses had appeared.[151] Their American counterparts refrained from doing so, perhaps from their own fears of attack, yet also because they had no censorship battle to wage against the government. Several European news agencies reprinted the cartoons in the defensive posture of needing to capture still-unconquered, non-viewpoint-punitive territory within public discourse.[152]

For Tsesis, 'government also has many anti-criminal messages (e.g. campaigns against murder, rape, drug use, etc.), that don't preclude the use of criminal punishment against those who don't comply with the collective social ethos.'[153] It is again important to bear in mind, however, the aforementioned dual character of democratic law. In LSPDs, those punishments are legitimately directed only at non-compliance through the acts of committing those offences, and *not* at non-compliance solely through verbal disagreement with, i.e., verbal departure from the ethos of the laws.

'There is the greatest difference', writes Mill, 'between presuming an opinion to be true, because, with every opportunity for contesting it, it has not been refuted, and assuming its truth for the purpose of not permitting its refutation.'[154] That marketplace model admittedly instrumentalizes[155] the interests of the speakers, the audiences, and the targets of hatred. It subordinates those interests to the postulated greater good of procuring enlightened views throughout society as a whole. Even if we accept its premise, critical theorists counter that such arguments overlook the fact that the price hate speech exacts falls not evenly across the population, but on disempowered target groups.[156] When Mill was writing, the people or institutions targeted by provocative speech were often privileged and powerful, such as government, aristocracy, or the church. It is not obvious that Mill would agree, as his latter-day disciples have often had him do, that historically persecuted groups should bear a disproportionate burden, without our offering greater justification or compensatory balance for the targets.

The problem nevertheless seems more complex than some prohibitionists suggest. Both of those elements can, in some measure, be accomplished by the 'active state' element of the LSPD, whereby government intervenes as a constant and pervasive actor and speaker against intolerance, and an enabler

---

[151] See, e.g., Broder, 2010.   [152] See, e.g., Santi, 2011.
[153] Private communication of 7 January 2013 (on file with author).
[154] *On Liberty*, ch. 2, *in* Mill, [1869] 1991, p. 24. For critical examination, See, e.g., Barendt, 2007, pp. 7–11; Greenawalt, 1989b, pp. 130–4; Rosenfeld, 2012, pp. 251–2; Schauer, 2012; Sunstein, 1995, p. 19.
[155] Cf., e.g., Sunstein, 1995, p. 25.
[156] Cf. Fish, 1994, pp. 16–18; Fiss, 1996, pp. 17–18; Lawrence, 1993, p. 72; Matsuda, 1993, p. 18; Waldron, 2012a, pp. 30–3, 37, 155–7. Cf., critically, Molnar & Strossen, 2012, p. 378. For further critique of the marketplace and epistemology theories, see, e.g., Baker, 1989, pp. 12–17.

of disempowered targets of hate speech.[157] Once we move into the later twentieth century, and even while broader socio-economic and political imbalances persist, it becomes questionable whether the benefits and burdens of hateful expression within public discourse end up being distributed with the straightforward imbalances cited by Delgado. As Mchangama and others have noted, African Americans made their greatest gains in civil rights precisely during the post-Second World War era in which the US Supreme Court had begun striking down hate speech bans.[158] By contrast, as Western Europeans, during that same period, implemented and extended bans, racism over time certainly did not decrease, and has at times increased,[159] meaning that, if Delgado's reasoning be construed in terms of straightforward material causation, minorities are paying no lower price *with* the bans.

5.6 Prohibitionist Deontology (Dignitarianism)

In the immediate aftermath of the Second World War, a world lacking precedents for the LSPD model, consequentialist prohibitionism appeared not merely plausible, but manifest. As the LSPD has emerged over time, however, prohibitionists have relied increasingly on deontological claims[160] about human dignity. A new question then arises. Must oppositionist deontology be modified on deontological-prohibitionist, i.e., 'dignitarian' grounds?

Dignitarians reject the assumption that formal equality before the law can adequately redress discrimination. They echo the view that citizenship must surpass the purely administrative, 'birth certificates and passports' conception. If, as we have seen, democratic citizenship demands some stronger form of civic standing, that too, they argue, must be equal. Dignitarianism is a theory of egalitarian democratic citizenship. Dignitarians insist on bans as means of securing the citizenship status of groups that are disempowered, particularly through histories of discrimination.[161]

---

[157] See Section 4.11.

[158] See, e.g., Mchangama, 2012; Weinstein, 1999, pp. 106–18.

[159] Sources confirming incidents and attitudes of intolerance in Europe and elsewhere since the latter half of the twentieth century have included Opinions, Concluding Observations, and Comments of the UN Committee on the Elimination of Racial Discrimination and the UN Human Rights Committee; and regular reports of the European Commission against Racism and Intolerance, Minority Rights Group International, Amnesty International, and Human Rights Watch, as well as states' national and non-governmental monitoring bodies.

[160] Cf. Section 5.1, text accompanying note 11. See also, e.g., D'Souza, 1992, p. vii; Leggewie & Meier, 2002b, p. 11 (noting German prohibitionists' emphasis on arguments of principle over arguments of immediate or demonstrable danger posed by the far-right NPD party); Meier, 2002, pp. 14, 27.

[161] See, e.g., Abel, 1994; Barendt, 2007, pp. 31–4; Fiss, 1996, pp. 11–15; Heyman, 2008, p. 177 (applying Meiklejohn's dignitarian concept); Morange, 2009, p. 66; Pech, 2003, pp. 149–62. On Christian roots, see, e.g., Morange, 2009, p. 34. On Kantian elements of the claim, see, e.g., Nieuwenhuis, 2011, p. 144; Pech, 2003, pp. 156–8. Nieuwenhuis observes, however, that the Kantian conception of dignity also supports free expression. Nieuwenhuis, 2011, p. 24.

In Europe, the shift from consequentialist to dignitarian defences of bans parallels unfolding interpretations of colonial atrocities and the Holocaust, which have passed from immediate realities to phenomena raising concerns about indirect or symbolic effects. Deontological prohibitionism moderates, then, between two extremes. On the one hand, dignitarians generally insist that their claims are not too strong, posing no danger to public discourse overall. They seek only to promote balance by penalizing small quantities of speech carrying little social value. On the other hand, insofar as they forego claims about statistically grounded causal links between hatred and harm, they seek to avoid foundations that are too weak, for example, resting solely on notions of taste and decorum, which fail as trumps over higher-order legal interests.[162]

Deontological prohibitionism conceives of hate speech as being detrimental in itself. It is punishable not on grounds of harms that would demonstrably follow from it, but as a *malum in se*. Hate speech in public discourse must, on that view, be banned regardless of whether it triggers harms distinct from the expressive act itself. For dignitarians, hateful expression inherently degrades the very ingredient to which I am ascribing a peremptory status, namely democratic citizenship. They maintain that hatred in public discourse denies the equal integrity of all citizens, which is just as necessary to democratic legitimacy—just as much a legitimating element, therefore just as politically constitutive or pre-legal—as are citizens' prerogatives of speech within public discourse.

A *malum prohibitum*, often contrasted with the *malum in se*, is an act that entails wrongdoing only insofar as it is prohibited. It is not inherently harmful to drive on the right-hand or the left-hand side of the road. The one becomes harmful only once the law requires the other. By contrast, recalling the aforementioned discussion about the very possibility of ethical reason, we would call murder knowingly committed on the innocent, assuming agreed meanings for those terms, to be a *malum in se*, harmful in itself even if there were no law prohibiting it. The law which *does* prohibit it does not thereby create its ethical status, as it does in establishing driving rules, but merely ratifies that status. A *malum in se* is evil irrespective of the positive law governing it. It is evil not irrespective of the harm it causes, but rather insofar as that harm is intrinsic.

The suggestion that ideas contain intrinsic properties is not obvious. What is meant is the inherently dangerous philosophy or worldview that is conveyed. Deontological prohibitionism differs from consequentialist prohibitionism, then, not on the assumption that harm is irrelevant, but that it is inherent, irrespective of any empirical determination. Such a deontology does not so much detach from consequentialism, as it substitutes a contingent consequentialism for an absolute one. Hate speech is harmful not regardless of its impact, but because it can only ever have a harmful impact—essential and inherent, if not materially distinct. (Oppositionist deontology, by contrast, does not straightforwardly become its own

---

[162] See Section 5.7.

absolute consequentialism in any such way. Most oppositionist literature does not hold either that the actual messages of hate speech are, in themselves, generally good, nor even that they are *not* generally bad.)

Within LSPDs, then, dignitarianism entails a further kind of rhetorical consequentialism. Rhetorical consequentialism, again, evokes the dangerous results of hateful expression as essentially obvious. Detailed empirical support becomes superfluous. References to future harm operate metaphorically to underscore the importance of a claim presented as the product of the egregious histories of non-LSPDs. Here too, calling such arguments 'rhetorical' is not meant pejoratively. It reminds us that informal ethical reasoning often sidesteps analytic distinctions between consequentialist and deontological modes of argument.

One basic rhetorical consequentialism comes in the form of a cry, after the Holocaust but also in other contexts, 'Never Again!'[163] It implies that anything which might hypothetically lead to other such human catastrophes must be prevented. Nazi hate speech under the fragile Weimar Republic attracted popular support. Any hate speech, under any circumstances might therefore, on that view, and even in an LSPD, 'ultimately' lead either to crimes against humanity, or to less dramatic, yet nonetheless deleterious social effects. That categorical view renders the claims effectively deontological, albeit nominally consequentialist, illustrating how prohibitionist deontology may take the form of an absolutized consequentialism.

Buntenbach and Wagner invoke another common example, in the familiar formula that freedom of opinion 'is not absolute, and ought to be limited when it harms or limits the rights of others'.[164] Like many other such claims, it adopts the linguistic form of empirical causation, yet cites no empirical evidence for any such harm or limits. It certainly adopts the linguistic form of a balancing prescription. However, insofar as the authors seek in it justification for viewpoint-selective penalties within public discourse, hate speech within public discourse becomes a *malum in se*, as no insight is offered into the kinds of justiciable harms against which speech within public discourse ought *then* to be weighed.

Dignitarian, i.e., deontological-prohibitionist challenges to viewpoint absolutism within public discourse take two primary forms. One version would reject any notion that democracy presupposes conceptually pre-legal legitimating conditions. On that view, the procedurally Millian balancing of speech against government's determinations of harm would be no different than government weighing and balancing in other areas of law. Admittedly, few current regimes of positive law unequivocally bind themselves to the legitimating expressive conditions that have been described thus far. That approach, however, too readily collapses democratic legitimacy into proceduralism.

---

[163] See Section 1.1, text accompanying note 21.
[164] Buntenbach & Wagner, 2002, pp. 134–5. See generally Sections 1.1, 3.1, and 3.2.

Most dignitarians acknowledge the vital role of speech within democracy without abandoning distinctly normative notions of democratic legitimacy. They nonetheless maintain that hate speech must be banned *as part* of the formulation of law's pre-legal legitimating conditions.[165] Within LSPDs, that is arguably the strongest of the prohibitionist claims. Free expression admittedly counts, on that view, among democracy's necessary ingredients, but only alongside viewpoint-selective penalties in the form of hate speech bans, which, it is argued, supply a legitimating condition of equal normative stature.

An example of the foundational status of human dignity appears in the oft-cited German Basic Law of 1949. Its first article makes dignity paramount: 'Human dignity (*Die Würde des Menschen*) shall be inviolable. To respect and protect it shall be the duty of all state authority'[166] (GG article 1(1)). To be sure, the content and extent of human dignity as a legally protected interest have long remained unclear in German law.[167] The Federal Constitutional Court has nonetheless identified human dignity as 'the highest value' within the Basic Law,[168] along with other fundamental rights and liberties, as set forth in articles 1–19. Human dignity, in the view of many German jurists, is violated when someone, 'through contempt for the principle of equality, is depicted as "inferior", and [that individual's] right to live within the community (*Lebensrecht in der Gemeinschaft*) is contested or relativised.'[169]

Article 1(1) is often cited as a principle of peremptory authority, albeit, particularly outside Germany, with little attention to its case law. Its case-law interpretations scarcely distinguish it from similar principles in many democracies. Often in express contrast to that provision, prohibitionists chastise US law for what they see as its elevation of hate speakers' freedom above their targets' human dignity. Laurent Pech, for example, seeks to compare the differences between German and US approaches, claiming that the US Supreme Court has identified no such norm of human dignity for the specific purpose of limiting speech. 'American jurisprudence', he claims, refuses to recognize respect for human dignity as a legally binding norm (*une norme juridiquement contraignante*).'[170]

The US constitutional text, in its origins almost two centuries older than the German, indeed lacks a modern norm of human dignity as such. We must avoid, however, the age-old error of reducing law to black-letter texts. Pech overlooks one of the momentous developments in US Supreme Court history, namely, the vast case law on 'substantive due process', which emerged precisely to protect core elements of personal dignity[171] in ways altogether on par with Western European

---

[165] See, e.g., Heyman, 2008; Tillmanns, 2003.
[166] *Die Würde des Menschen* in art. 1 has been linked to Kant's categorical imperative, which depicts individuals as ends in themselves, and not as merely means for other individuals' or for the state's ends. Kant, [1785] 1968. See also, e.g., Bleckmann, 1997, pp. 541, 542–3, 552; Hochhuth, 2006, pp. 104–5.
[167] See generally, e.g., Bleckmann, 1997, pp. 539–90.
[168] See, e.g., BVerfGE 27, 1 (6). Cf., e.g., Bleckmann, 1997, pp. 539, 552.
[169] Geis, 1994, p. 226. Cf. Hochhuth, 2006, p. 100; Hoppe, 2008, p. 5; Schrank, 2006, p. 48.
[170] Pech, 2003, p. 150.   [171] See, e.g., Nowak & Rotunda, 2009, pp. 461–593.

jurisdictions as a general matter, irrespective of differences as to specific application, which vary as much among European states *inter se* as between Europe and the US.[172]

Dignitarians maintain that even if hate speech caused little detriment to *substantive* equality ('material equality' or 'equality of outcome'), it would still expressly deny the formal equality of citizens *qua* citizens.[173] For Parekh, hate speech ends up 'denying' its targets the equal 'capacity to live as responsible members of society'.[174] That critique aims at the purely formal or false universalism bestowed by the norm of equal citizenship, which would in reality foster the privileged status of citizens within the dominant classes. Such a view commits what can be called the *denial fallacy*. The fallacy proceeds by equivocating between two meanings of the word 'denial', whereby prohibitionists extrapolate from a metaphorical to a literal meaning of phrases like 'denial of citizenship'.

Hate speakers do 'deny' their targets' citizenship in an aspirational sense, wishing those targets to be deprived of all or some elements of citizen status. We err, however, in extrapolating from 'denial' in the sense of 'dislike' to 'denial' in the literal sense of a material negation of the targets' equal abilities to exercise all attributes of citizenship. In so doing, we again mistake a rhetorical consequentialism for a material one. A material *denial* of equal attributes of democratic citizenship takes place only if the hate speaker kills or injures the target citizen, or blocks the target citizen's access to the town hall, or to the polling station, or to the courthouse, or to the school, or to the political demonstration, and so forth—all of which have long had legal remedies within LSPDs, which can be strengthened without the state imposing viewpoint-selective bans within public discourse.

Hate speech certainly entails 'denial of citizenship' in the figurative sense of the hate speaker's *disdain* for democratic pluralism. But the fallacy of extrapolating from symbolic to material denial smuggles in another unsubstantiated consequentialism. Within LSPDs, it has not been shown in the statistically reliable way required by any claim of material 'denial' that, for example, ethnic, religious, national, linguistic, or sexual minorities have systemically found themselves barred from voting or speaking solely because racist, homophobic, or other such invective had at any given time been expressed within general public discourse. Within

---

[172] The US Supreme Court has developed over decades dignitarian applications of, e.g., the US Constitution's Fourth Amendment (guaranteeing '[t]he right of the people to be secure in their persons, houses, papers, and effects, against unreasonable searches and seizures'). Similarly, Robitaille-Froidure, accurately noting the US Supreme Court's apparent or tacit rejection of theories of group defamation, misleadingly interprets *New York Times v. Sullivan* as a protection of defamation generally. Robitaille-Froidure, 2011, p. 40. *Sullivan* in fact carves out the aforementioned, rather narrower, 'public official' exception, by no means annulling America's centuries-old common law torts of defamation. See, e.g., Section 2.9. Note indeed that any hate speech which, following traditional notions of libel or slander, attributes detrimentally false allegations of fact to non-public persons remains actionable under US law, in ways entirely consistent with the concept of non-*viewpoint*-punitive public discourse that I have thus far presented.

[173] Cf., e.g., Waldron, 2012a, pp. 39, 58, 60–1, 82–3, 86–7; see also Waldron, 2012a, pp. 105–43 (distinguishing between 'dignity' and 'offence').

[174] Parekh, 2012, p. 44.

LSPDs, such minority groups' citizenship has indeed been disdained by hate speakers. That disdain certainly expresses speakers' *attitude* of disrespect towards, or *disposition* to reject the targets as full citizens—which is as much as to say that it expresses the kind of intolerance that the active LSPD can combat through alternatives to viewpoint-selective bans in public discourse. But a poor attitude, an attitude of disrespect towards the target group, or a disposition to reject that group as full citizens represents, in itself, no step undertaken by the speaker that constitutes any demonstrable obstruction of the target's means of exercising full citizenship.

For Reiner Tillmanns, disdaining others' rights equates per se with 'disproportionately undermining'[175] them, hence his recurring imagery of quantification, and, in turn, of empirical causation. Tillmanns claims to identify the condition by which 'violations of human dignity' emerge as a countervailing interest of constitutional stature on par with the citizen prerogative of speech. He re-affirms the dominant, value-proceduralist norm that the two 'colliding' interests must be balanced against each other.[176] Having reified that 'collision' through recourse to the denial fallacy, Tillmanns then concludes: 'In such collision situations, the relevant constitutional interests (*Verfassungsgüter*) are to be mutually weighed up and limited according to the principle of *practical concordance*, such that all interests (*Güter*) achieve their optimal realisation (*Wirksamkeit*).'[177] One then enjoys 'a high degree' of 'freedom for developing one's personality'[178]—a formula which, albeit incorporating a constitutional value,[179] nevertheless fails to distinguish between the broadly liberal interest of 'freedom for developing one's personality' and the citizen's specifically democratic claim to participation in public discourse.

The fallacies linking these successive steps remain obscure, hence ubiquitous within prohibitionism, precisely because of the terseness, the assumption of obviousness, with which they are presented. After all, once the words 'human dignity' are pronounced, any challenge to any such explicit or tacit fallacies by which it is grounded can itself become construed as an affront to human dignity. The citizen's prerogative of expression within public discourse ends up effectively quantified through that dignitarian calculus by which the prerogative then comes to be parcelled out by the state in order to achieve a 'practical concordance' with the countervailing dignitarian interest.[180]

In the realm of public discourse, the traditional 'speech–conduct' distinction again backfires on those who challenge it. To extrapolate either from unequal *substantive*, for example, economic or social conditions, or from intolerant attitudes,

---

[175] Tillmanns, 2003, p. 28.   [176] Tillmanns, 2003, p. 28.
[177] Tillmanns, 2003, p. 28 (emphasis added).   [178] Tillmanns, 2003, p. 30.
[179] German Basic Law art. 2(1).
[180] Cf., e.g., Berlin, 1969, pp. 121–31 (warning against abuses arising from the view that some 'really' greater or higher form of freedom can be achieved through the curtailments of core elements of freedom—although 'citizenship' works even more powerfully than 'freedom' in that context).

to unequal *formal citizenship*, is to negate the possibility of even minimal legitimacy within any LSPD, since unequal material conditions and intolerant attitudes are legion, and far from limited to crude utterances. Even prohibitionist minimalism, so-called 'narrow' bans, cannot eschew that problem.

Recall Waldron's view, widespread among prohibitionists, that 'where there are fine lines to be drawn the law should generally stay on the liberal side of them'.[181] If that is the case, then it is not denial of the target's citizenship to which minimalist (or cautious or moderate) positions are really objecting. As Gates reminds us, the subtle denial is arguably more pernicious than the gross, particularly in circles of power. The real complaint then lies with the old problem of decorum, the sheer crudeness of the utterance. The term 'dignitarian' ends up merely re-clothing in new apparel the traditional civility arguments.[182]

Some might respond that what is wrongly overlooked by oppositionists is the viewpoint of vulnerable groups themselves. Yet that important identity-political point still runs into difficulties. Writers like Gates, Kennedy, or Mchangama remind us, from their own minority perspectives, as does Butler from the perspective of women's empowerment, that membership within a vulnerable group does not perforce entail unity of outlook towards bans.[183] That is the kind of essentialism which many seek to overcome, in view of histories of discrimination rooted in essentialisms.

The brilliant prohibitionist writer Steven Heyman has arguably been the subtlest exponent of the dignitarian position. Heyman praises John Locke, who 'condemns speech that denies the equal rights of others'.[184] Yet that conclusion, too, commits the denial fallacy. If Heyman believes that Locke identifies any kind of general speech within public discourse that, as such, *materially* voids anyone's citizenship beyond the expression of disdain, then he locates no such passage in Locke's writing. Heyman draws instead on Meiklejohn, Habermas, and Michael Walzer,

> Meiklejohn understands political debate on the model of the traditional town meeting. Everyone has a right to participate in this forum and to deliberate about the public good. At the same time, Meiklejohn observes that '[i]f a speaker … is abusive or in other ways threatens to defeat the purpose of the meeting, he may be and should be declared "out of order".'[185]

The risk of Meiklejohn's model is to overlook its limits as a metaphor. Heyman is certainly aware of the already-admitted restrictions on 'fighting words', stalking, and the like, as well as restrictions accepted by most oppositionists on agreed

---

[181] Waldron, 2012a, p. 126.   [182] See Section 5.7.

[183] I can, moreover, note that I openly belong to two particularly vilified minority groups of our time, whose representative organizations throughout Europe have overwhelmingly supported bans. See, e.g., Heinze, 2009b; Heinze, 2014a; Heinze, 2014b.

[184] Heyman, 2009, p. 167. Cf., e.g., Waldron, 2012a, pp. 204–33. Cf. also Section 4.12, text accompanying note 189.

[185] Heyman, 2008, p. 177.

procedures in political meetings, courtrooms, classrooms, workplaces, or 'time, manner, and place' when equally applicable to all speakers. Heyman is instead arguing that expression may turn out, solely on grounds of its viewpoint, to count as 'out of order'. When construed in that more metaphorical way—when expression is viewpoint-selectively turned into the equivalent of a 'time, manner, or place' restriction—the 'town hall' model collapses. There is no sense in which hate speech can 'defeat', or can even 'threaten to defeat' the 'purpose' of public discussion, except in the sense that lots of discussion in public discourse mis-carries through idiotic contributions, without that characteristic justifying a viewpoint-selective ban.

While clearly appreciating the difference between legitimating conditions and optimizing conditions, Heyman ends up conflating them. There was never any question that stupid and offensive discourse is generally inferior to enlight-ened and compassionate discourse. That insight obtains even when, on grounds of its worldview, speech 'disrupts' a discussion to the point of killing it. By analogy, a drunkard who cannot coherently string two sentences together, or a doomsday prophet who insists that we're all going to burn in hell, may frustrate a conversation to the point of destroying it. They may legitimately be removed for impeding the discussion through rules of disorderly conduct equally ap-plicable to all speakers, but not on viewpoint-punitive grounds.[186] We must distinguish between the 'purpose' of public discourse in the optimizing sense of deliberation about the best possible democracy and its 'purpose' in the democ-racy-legitimating sense of allowing citizens to air their views, be they about politics or about anything else. It could not plausibly fit the purpose of demo-cratic discourse in the optimizing sense for someone, for example, to advocate Stalinist gulags as a penalty for petty theft, yet such advocacy unquestionably forms part of a citizen's prerogative of speech within any LSPD.

For Habermas, Heyman continues, in the vein of standard rights discourse, 'relationships of mutual recognition are the foundation of rights: "[A]ll rights ul-timately stem from the system of rights that free and equal legal subjects would mutually accord to one another."'[187] If we replace 'rights' with 'democratic citi-zenship', that proposition's difficulties become more apparent. It is not as formally 'equal legal subjects', but as citizens whose formal equality manifests through non-viewpoint-punitive access to public discourse, that we ensure the legitimacy of our democracy. Only then can we legitimately be called 'legal subjects' who 'mu-tually accord' our 'system of rights ... to one another'. Yet let us assume *arguendo* that a dignitarian interest correlates to each of the 'rights that free and equal legal subjects would mutually accord to one another'. That dignitarian compo-nent soon becomes so vast as to be question-begging in its particular applications. Given that torture impairs not *only* a conceptually pre-legal citizenship interest as

---

[186] See Section 2.3, text accompanying note 34.
[187] Heyman, 2008, p. 178; cf. p. 178 n. 59 (discussing Walzer). See also Heyman, 2009, pp. 174–7. Cf. Gelber, 2010 (discussing Habermas and Nussbaum).

a necessarily legitimating element of democracy, we can admit that torture *also* impairs a dignitarian interest, or, for that matter, an altruistic interest, or a kindness interest, or many other interests of democracy-optimizing value. To include all of *those* among conceptually pre-legal, democracy-legitimating interests, however, would render impossible any serious determination of the legitimating elements of democratic norms and processes. All democracy-legitimating elements are also democracy-optimizing elements, but not all democracy-optimizing elements are also democracy-legitimating elements, unless we are to eliminate any serious enquiry into legitimacy altogether by collapsing the distinction , rendering any serious substantive defect within a democracy *ipso facto* a defect in democratic legitimacy. One scholar, however, notes a variant on Heyman's thesis, along the lines of Habermas's speech conditions:

One of the strongest deontological arguments for bans holds that, by its very nature, communication involves an interaction between two or more people who regard one another as persons (that is, as intelligent beings who are capable of understanding and expressing meaning); that this is true not only of interpersonal conversations but also of speech in the public realm; and that public discourse therefore should be understood as discussion between individuals who recognize one another as persons and members of the community. According to this argument, bans on hate speech (when understood as speech that denies recognition to others) does not violate Heinze's principle of democratic legitimacy because this speech does not fall within the legitimate bounds of public discourse in the first place (or at least is only a marginal, borderline instance of public discourse).[188]

As with Meiklejohn, we again risk confusing model with metaphor, reading too literally a template for private, interpersonal communication as the template for public discourse, and confusing an optimizing condition with a legitimating one. Even in a social situation, like a private house party, presenting no conventional forum of public discourse, someone may blurt out a remark, intelligent or stupid, but with no obvious interlocutor in mind *at all*, obviating any further determinations as to whether or in what way that speaker may be recognizing others present as sharing equal humanity. No more of an audience is strictly required for expression to count within public discourse. One is certainly more likely to engage in democracy-optimizing discussion by ensuring that one does recognize others' humanity, but such recognition cannot set a legitimate viewpoint-punitive limit on democratic public discourse.

Until recently in human history it was not uncommon for newborns with visible physical disabilities to be destroyed. That practice amounted to one basic type of eugenics, by definition failing to recognize the infant as co-equal. Democracies today reject that practice, but if someone wished to advocate such eugenics, nowhere would Mill's insistence on open refutation rather than coerced silence appear more appropriate. As a matter of democratic legitimacy,

---

[188] Comments of anonymous reviewer of this book (on file with author).

the citizen must *a fortiori* be entitled to state that view, however crudely or subtly its assumption of non-recognition of such children may be articulated. The prohibitionist might retort that such practices were performed out of compassion and not out of hateful non-recognition. At best, however, the ideal of compassionate eugenics tells only part of that story. It is by no means clear that some such children were not destroyed out of deepfelt horror. Even racists can embellish disdain in the veneer of compassion, through views such as 'They would be happier if they went back to where they came from.'

A variant on the democratic paradox is that some citizens may fully accept democracy, yet may recognize a value above it—most familiarly, the Sacred.[189] It is notable that the twentieth century, in which we witness the birth of the LSPD and of more secularized societies, also largely heralds the death of traditional blasphemy laws. Democracies today continue to include citizens who recognize the Sacred as a dignitarian value that stands even above the values of the democracy within which they otherwise willingly live in accordance with law. Either in lieu of or as a re-interpretation of blasphemy laws, some democracies include religious identities or sensibilities among the interests that must be weighed up within value-pluralist processes. Even as a legally protected interest, however, the Sacred can in no way justify viewpoint-selective penalties imposed within public discourse to protect it. Any legal protection for the Sacred must retain the duality, described in Section 3.5, which precludes viewpoint-selective penalties on such protections.

5.7 Civility, Decorum, and Symbolism

As noted in Section 4.8, expression within public discourse cannot legitimately be penalized on grounds of its ethical failings. *A fortiori* it cannot legitimately be banned on grounds of tastelessness, indecorousness, or incivility. In the West, regulation of public discourse on grounds of civility and decorum stem from an earlier era when democracies had not emerged under anything like an LSPD model. While the dominant value-pluralist proceduralism within most democracies today entails viewpoint-selective penalties to secure fundamental interests of safety, dignity, or equality, the interests balanced against speech were, in the past, far more casually construed. Curbs on speech were more readily accepted when deemed by some empowered authority to be 'reasonable'.[190]

It is certainly true that some laws can and should send moral or symbolic messages. Through seriously implemented anti-discrimination policies the state promotes material welfare, but also declares a value of civic pluralism. It becomes

---

[189] See, e.g., Hare 2009a; Marshall and Shea, 2011.
[190] See, e.g., Post, 2009, p. 129 (discussing the application of Charles Taylor's notion of dignity to hate speech). See also, e.g., Post, 1995, pp. 128–34, 268–89, 300–2; Weinstein, 1999, pp. 170–2; Weinstein, 2009a, pp. 55–8.

illegitimate, however, for an LSPD to abridge citizenship prerogatives for no other reason than that the state wishes to send a 'message',[191] indeed a 'symbolic'[192] message to citizens.[193] 'The favourable impression made upon foreigners', according to Grimm, 'plays no small role' in the implementation of German bans.[194] Klaus Günther praises viewpoint-punitive bans as means of countering Germany's historical 'dishonour'.[195] Such formulas trade citizenship itself against state-selected symbolism, inverting any notion of the citizenry as constitutive of democracy. Suddenly it is no longer the citizenry that legitimates the state, but the state that legitimates the citizenry.

For Julie Suk, French censorship 'enhances, rather than undermines, the state's legitimacy, because the state cannot govern legitimately unless it makes a strong, clear break with a past racist regime.'[196] She continues: 'In France, as in Germany and other European nations, criminal law has played a critical role in enabling the state and the society to face their collective responsibility for the Holocaust.'[197] The problem of a 'clear break with a past' is nothing new in law. Remedies include punishing individual perpetrators of atrocities, such as Wilhelm Boger or Maurice Papon, as well as compensating victims and their families. Those classical, retrospectively corrective remedies can never perform full justice. Nor do they fully 'break with a past'. Hence the panoply of prospective policies, including civic and educational campaigns and anti-discrimination policies, aimed at the nation as a whole. Lying at the heart of the *Rechtsstaat* in 'France, Germany, and other European nations', however, is the axiom that legal responsibility attaches to individual conduct.[198] Under the rule of law, higher-order legal interests cannot legitimately be instrumentalized for purposes of 'enabling the state and the society to face their collective responsibility' by silencing citizens as a way for the state to speak.

Elsewhere I have examined what I call a 'pseudo-realist fallacy' to criticize US-focussed prohibitionists writing both within the liberal tradition, such as Waldron,[199] and the critical tradition, such as Delgado and Matsuda.[200] Those writers vaunt their supposedly legal realist methods by confronting the black-letter of US First Amendment doctrine with reference to what they call 'real-world societies here on earth'[201] or the 'street wisdom' that 'Law is political'.[202] Fancying one's own views as 'in touch' while condemning rivals as 'ivory tower' is, of course, as old

---

[191] See, e.g., Bleich, 2011, p. 31; Buntenbach & Wagner, 2002, p. 135.

[192] See critically, Seils, 2002, p. 50.

[193] See, e.g., Meier, 2002, p. 27; Preuß, 2002, p. 104; Schrank, 2006, p. 18. Cf. Wijnberg, 2008, p. 110.

[194] Grimm, 2002, p. 143. That 'image abroad' concern remains shrouded in a sombre past. When Israel sought diplomatic relations with West Germany in 1963, Chancellor Konrad Adenauer indicated a willingness, on condition that Israel no longer insist on prosecutions of Holocaust perpetrators, which had become 'damaging (*unerträglich*) for Germany's image abroad'. Wiegrefe, 2014, p. 31.

[195] Günther, 2000, p. 66.

[196] Suk, 2012, p. 145. Cf., critically, Heinze, 2013, pp. 598–9.   [197] Suk, 2012, p. 149.

[198] See Section 5.3, text accompanying note 89.   [199] Heinze, 2013b, pp. 607–9.

[200] See Heinze, 2008a, pp. 121–33.   [201] Waldron, 2012a, p. 101.

[202] Matsuda, 1993, p. 19.

as academia itself.[203] However, in praising alternatives from other states, such as France, Germany, Scandinavian countries, or even the Soviet Union, they wholly sideline that selfsame realist approach. They instead simply cut and paste those states' policies off the page, with no such interest in how their real-world contexts bear upon them. Instead of comparing like with like—either purely formal US ideals with purely formal European ideals, or socially contextualized US realities with socially contextualized European realities—they rig their comparisons from the outset. The bleakest, most deeply contextualized accounts of US realities are merely held up to de-contextualized, black-letter European ideals. One is scarcely left in suspense about how the conclusions will work out. Leaving aside the gross abuses of bans within several non-LSPDs,[204] I have suggested in Section 5.5 that even the evidence from Germany or France is not nearly as salutary as their sheer black-letter texts, and the official rationales behind them, would make them seem.

Given France's modest efforts during the immediate post-war decades, questions arise about whether Suk, too, uncritically acquiesces in France's official 'break from the past' narrative, arguably designed more to manage today's troublemakers than to uphold any longstanding tradition of Holocaust remembrance, which, for many years, to state it kindly, blew hot and cold. Unlike a generation of German counterparts, even the government of the Socialist President Mitterand, as late as the 1990s, still declined to accept French responsibility for collaboration in the Holocaust, acknowledged only as late as 16 July 1995 in an address by President Chirac.[205] Suk never asks whether the immediate post-war concern had been to avoid offending constituencies with personal or family histories rooted in Nazi collaboration, while periodically punishing the token hate speaker, who represented no such constituency. And, as Grimm's observation reminds us, the PR was more than convenient for a state still aiming to be the leading EU power in the post-war decades, and to retain a leading role in the Francophone world and on the global stage. The problem is not that Suk is manifestly wrong or right, but that France's relationship to that past is steeped in many narratives. It is questionable whether we ought to take on face value only the official government account, particularly when it so tidily suits state interests—a bit of easy image boosting at the bargain-basement price of the citizen prerogatives of a few assorted neer-do-wells.

There is some irony to these instrumentalized views of citizenship, described by the former German Chancellor Gerhard Schröder as 'political hygiene',[206] given that 'past' from which these states purport to be making 'a strong, clear break', and in view of those past regimes' concepts of citizenship. To be sure, just as in Germany,[207] some French experts, too, challenge bans,[208] not the least of them

---

[203] Plato noticed it long ago. See *Gorgias* 484c–485c, *in* Plato, [4th century BCE] 1997, pp. 828–9.

[204] See Section 6.1, text accompanying notes 42–4.

[205] See, e.g., 'Vél' d'Hiv: Le long chemin vers la reconnaissance d'un crime d'État dans la déportation', 2012.

[206] Quoted in Seils, 2002, p. 44. On Waldron's similar justifications for curbing citizenship through recourse to pollution imagery, cf. Section 5.9, text accompanying notes 246–7.

[207] See this Section, text accompanying note 193.

[208] See Section 4.10, text accompanying note 144.

being the former President of the European Parliament, former member of the *Conseil constitutionnel*, and Auschwitz survivor Simone Veil.[209] One of Europe's pre-eminent historians of Nazism, Hans Mommsen, certainly recognizes the importance of state initiatives to confront the past. He warns, however, against doing so in crudely literal, ultimately self-contradictory ways. 'Just as unmediated applications cannot be drawn from history', he admonishes, nor should modern democracies be 'using Beelzebub to drive out the devil'.[210]

5.8 Narrow Bans and Advocacy of Violence

Some prohibitionists, emphatic in their commitment to democratic free speech, exhort us to adopt only narrow bans. They propose penalties only on the most overtly violent or extreme expressions of hatred, such as calls for the killing of some or all members of a group.[211] That stance is fundamentally dignitarian. After all, if one believes in some causation between hate and harm, drawing the line only around the hardest core seems patently inadequate, unless some other, distinct principle is at play. The narrow ban's deontological principle is that the hardest core of hatred offends any serious conception of democracy and ceases to play any plausible role in public discourse.

One oppositionist retort would be to dismiss such minimalism out of hand. If only a tiny subset of hateful utterances is to be banned, then, as was noted in Section 5.5, the only supposedly 'symbolic' message those utterances send to most hate speakers is how easily and mockingly the bans on them can be circumvented. Narrow bans end up *permitting* virtually all hate speech. That result pays little homage to the paramount status of humanity itself, which dignitarianism claims to vindicate.

Strong consensus has emerged against militant Islamists who call for violence against gays, Jews, or others. Muslims in Western Europe and elsewhere largely join that condemnation.[212] Moderates shun in particular the extremists' tendencies to reinforce stereotypes that the moderates crave to overcome. The moderates often note that extremists form peripheral minorities, and do not represent the 'real' Islam.[213] Despite the dignitarian justification for narrow bans, a consequentialist problem arises. Here too, no evidence has been cited that censorship dilutes extremism, and the analysis in Section 5.5 raises questions as to whether it pours fuel on the flames. A steam-valve question again arises as to whether censorship spurs the extremists' alienation and martyrdom narratives, similar to those of neo-Nazis, that our democracies are frauds, allowing political speech to some citizens but not to others. A further consequentialist reply might run along marketplace lines. If

---

[209] See *Robert Faurisson v. France*, Communication No. 550/1993, U.N. Doc. CCPR/C/58/D/550/1993(1996), para. 2.8.

[210] Mommsen, 2002, p. 148. Cf. Morlock's notion of 'self-paradox', Morlock, 2002, p. 64.

[211] See, e.g., Goodall, 2010, p. 92.   [212] See, e.g., Moussaoui, 2012.

[213] See, e.g., Litwin & Mansur, 2013.

the moderates are correct in deeming their numbers greater and their views better, then they enjoy a considerable advantage in countering hateful messages with better ones. Some moderates, however, reply that any such disproportion becomes skewed by the media's focus on extremism. But that worry is debatable. In addition to the opportunities for grassroots communication now afforded by social media, the mainstream media within LSPDs have made inroads into countering that view by seeking more socially diverse editorial and reporting staff, and opening their opinion pages to wider ranges of views.

Some minimalists suggest that their position avoids viewpoint censorship. Their position allows all 'viewpoints', they argue, but excludes only a small number of ways of expressing them. The most frequently cited example is injunctions against killing or violence: 'You can be intolerant, as long as you don't advocate violence.' Bans only on the most extreme utterances can, on that view, be rendered viewpoint-neutral, akin to a sheer 'time, manner, and place' regulation, for example, by prohibiting calls to kill *anyone*, irrespective of whether the targets belong to an identified social group. But separating a 'viewpoint' from a 'particular style of expressing a viewpoint', the age-old 'form' *versus* 'content' distinction, becomes an arbitrary enterprise. Viewpoint-selectivity does not vanish simply by finding a common, content-based denominator to be banned equally from all viewpoints. While viewpoint-selectivity takes centre stage in an analysis of hateful expression, recall that content-selective bans raise similar concerns about legitimacy.[214]

'Are you seriously arguing that people should be allowed to call for murder?' Yet advocacy of killing has informed politics for as long as political philosophy has existed. We might well oppose those who advocate reinstating the death penalty, particularly in view of its historically discriminatory applications, but it would be hard to justify censorship of such advocacy. Every non-utopian political philosophy is by definition a philosophy of legitimate killing, even if it is often only tacitly so. What differentiates political philosophies are the different grounds of legitimate killing that each adopts. John Rawls or Ronald Dworkin of course never expressly present their views *as* philosophies of legitimate killing, if only because the point is too obvious to be mentioned. But to conceive of their or anyone else's politics as precluding a theory of justified killings would be to collapse those theories utterly into utopias.

For Rawls or Dworkin, the scope of justified killing will include, at the very least, the actively engaged combatant who cannot reasonably be quelled without lethal force. The American Declaration of Independence of 1776 declares, in altogether generalized terms, an unequivocal justification for incitement to violence. It states, not in situation-specific or historically bound, but in universalist language along Lockean lines, the criteria by which violence is justified, along with the conditions under which those criteria can be deemed to have been met. For at least some revolutionary Marxists, it will include members of political or property-owning elites. For many radical clerics, it will include gays or adulterous women. My point is

---

[214] See Section 2.6, text accompanying note 51.

not the relativist one that all such philosophies are of equal worth. Rather, as was noted in Section 4.8, the democratic paradox means that, even assuming a premise of intellectual inequality, the LSPD nevertheless may not deduce from it a norm, imposed within public discourse, of viewpoint-punitive inequality. Implications for legitimate killing are germane to political theory. Those we dislike cannot be banned without censoring some canonic texts. Even just war theories, as the adjective suggests, are theories about when killing and violence are justified. As to their *ad bellum* element, they invariably justify violence in self-defence, yet (this is the part that often gets left out) what counts as legitimate 'defence' depends entirely on the background political assumptions, differing strongly for a liberal, a Marxist, a Maoist, an Islamist, an anarchist, a feminist, and so forth.

In order to justify the anomaly of banning discourses of militant Islamism while permitting those of revolutionary Marxism, some might argue, along the lines of a naïve secularism, that Marxism is distinctly 'political' in a way that ideas that we conventionally call 'religious' are not. One could, of course, write a book exploring the endless difficulties, both conceptual and historical, involved in any attempt to draw such conventional lines between the spheres of 'politics' and 'religion', particularly within the domain of popular worldviews as they arise within public discourse. Extremist Islamism is nothing if not political discourse, however intellectually unimpressive some may deem it to be.

There is no such thing as a political philosophy that is not a philosophy of who shall live and die. Every political philosophy, along with every visceral, un-theorized political preference, is a philosophy of death, whether or not its adherents choose to package it as such. Even pacifism or purportedly apolitical views, notwithstanding passionate protestations to the contrary, can only ever acquiesce to the strongest, hence most violent party, and thereby merely defaults to the inherent violence of a prevailing status quo consisting either of dominant or of clashing forces. Every political philosophy justifies, and through its sheer normativity incites, *some* form of violence, the target of which is cast as lethal to that philosophy's postulated social order.[215] The repulsive philosophy is repulsive not because the rest of us happen to lack a philosophy of who should die, but because it contradicts the one which we happen to prefer, and which seems natural, normal, obvious, or good to us—so much so that we may refuse to recognize our own as *being* a philosophy of violence.

The point is not ethically relativist since the fact that each of us proclaims or defaults to a politics of violence does not mean that all political philosophies are of equal value. Mandela has one just as Stalin does, even if Mandela's is better. Writers like Benjamin and Derrida make the point unmistakably[216]—albeit too circuitously, as if circumspect about relativist applications. Nor does the point entail any particular drift towards an intellectually linear or ethically abandoned *Realpolitik*. To the contrary, it is always intellectually impoverished, and ethically dangerous,

---

[215] As I have argued elsewhere, that result inevitability emerges as the product of a broader one, namely, that injustice is not the opposite, but the constant product of any programmatic regime of justice. See Heinze, 2013a.
[216] See Benjamin, [ca. 1920] 1965; Derrida, 2005.

to embrace one political philosophy merely by defining some contrary view as 'not' a philosophy, but 'simply' extremism.

Once again, what does or does not count as hateful expression, and the compromise solution of minimalism, amounts to imposing bans solely on grounds of decorum, of more or less blunt or polite formulations, with prohibitionists effectively privileging not those political positions which 'lack' a doctrine of legitimate death, but simply those that sufficiently dissimulate it. If prohibitionists' concern is with the violent effects of speech, we can scarcely overlook the tens of millions of people killed and brutalized in the name of Marxist–Leninist doctrines. That death toll exponentially surpasses the numbers sacrificed to Islam. It rather compares—leaving aside the weary old debates about likening Stalin or Mao to Hitler on other grounds—in sheer numbers, to the victims of the same Nazi ideologies whose expression is banned in many LSPDs.

Prohibitionists may retort that Marxist killings did not envisage vulnerable groups. Leaving aside questions about that assertion as a factual matter, including the enormous violence that Soviet or Maoist forces did indeed visit on such groups, once violence reaches numbers on such a scale it would be astonishing to claim that status as an outsider group would be the only criterion, if one is concerned about the long-term effects of speech promoting violence. Prohibitionists may also claim that such actions were not 'true' Marxism. On both the textual and the historical record, that reply is in fact far more problematical than such an objection might lead us to believe. But leaving aside that complex enquiry, the central point is that moderate Muslims wish to ban extremist speech because it, too, betrays the 'true' Islam.

Even assuming those kinds of Marxist, or Muslim, purity theses to be true, it remains implausible for the advocacy of violence to be banned in the name of betraying some 'purer' Islam, but not in the name of betraying some 'purer' Marxism, or indeed some 'purer' liberalism. Speech cannot legitimately be banned for its deviation from an orthodoxy which some believers, or even non-believers, feel it betrays. The analogy to Marxism also raises questions about post-9/11 bans on 'support for' or indeed 'glorification of' terrorism, particularly given the Islamist context, which cannot be separated from related concerns about hate speech. Classical Marxism, like liberalism, and notwithstanding any number of revisions, is nothing if not glorification of the 'right' kind of violence.

Some might argue that, in LSPDs, threats from Marxism have seemed too weak in the early twenty-first century, as compared to threats from radical Islam. Yet *that* view is altogether consequentialist, and simply leads us back to square one, i.e., to the problem of showing plausible causation between speech and harms. At any rate, the Soviet Union may have collapsed, but verbal, and not only verbal, assaults on capitalism are, understandably, permanent features of newer anti-globalization movements, and are the immediate heirs of Marxism in a post-industrial and electronic age. By analogy, the platforms of various militant leftist groups in the 1960s and 1970s were dominated by Marxist ideas and influences. Those groups were rightly banned as demonstrably engaged in organized violent *conduct*. Yet the idea of equally banning Marxist–Leninist texts as 'incitements' to terrorism would have appeared McCarthyist.

Recall also the consequentialist oppositionist theses examined in Section 5.5. Within LSPDs it is by no means clear that banning even advocacy of murder aids vulnerable groups. Contrary to a dominant consensus, for example, gays as targets of extreme Islamism benefit little from bans on consequentialist grounds. It can be difficult to convince the wider society of the constant dangers faced by gays. Pushing the bigotry further from public view only turns it from a visible to an invisible risk, rendering gays' fears that much less obvious to the ordinary observer, and thereby, as bellwether theories warn, inviting not action but complacency.[217]

5.9 Incitement

In July 2007, the Islamist activist Mizanur Rahman, was sentenced to a six-year prison term (reduced to four years) for his 2006 protest in London against the Danish Muhammad cartoons. Rahman had held a placard demanding the deaths of British soldiers in Iraq, and the 'beheading of those who insult Islam'.[218] Rahman's case illustrates the arbitrariness of a legal catch-all like 'incitement', in this case 'incitement to racial hatred'—particularly curious, as Rahman's message neither refers to race, nor targets any traditionally excluded racial, ethnic, or religious minority group. The only other racial hatred that can be inferred is that Rahman belongs to one racial group, despite the fact that Islam as referred to in his statement cuts across races; and that 'those who insult Islam' somehow belong to some other racial group, despite the fact that many ex-Muslims, like Ayaan Hirsi Ali, 'incite' against Islam in far more strident language, and indeed with a far greater public and media presence.

What is most striking about the case is neither the conviction nor the sentence. The remarkable element is the overwhelming consensus—among the political class, legal professionals, and the media—that rallied around it, on the right, on the left, and from minority communities. No leading public figure in Britain even tentatively questioned it.[219] Few if any voices in Britain's legal, professional, or academic community objected, nor did mainstream Muslims or their organizations, again happy to distance themselves from extremists. At no point was it shown how any member of Rahman's 'audience' might have taken any step towards committing any harmful act in a way that might have been 'incited' by his message. Nor did the British government attempt to show (and nor do other Western European states in such cases generally attempt to show[220]) that any link had ever been established between that kind of general utterance and any specific act of violence—no

---

[217] See Section 5.5, text accompanying note 125.

[218] 'Even odious ideas must be allowed expression', 2006 (despite its title, the *Observer* leader endorses Rahman's conviction). On the sentencing order, see 'Six Years for Muslims who called for killings over newspaper cartoon', 2007.

[219] A rare exception was the writer and free speech advocate Kenan Malik. See Malik, 2007. See also Bleich, 2011, p. 41.

[220] Cf. Section 5.1, text accompanying notes 9–11.

more than a link has been found between violent films, or readers of revolutionary Marxist texts, and violent social acts.

In order to understand what Rahman did, we must consider what he did not do. Imagine Rahman exhorting some random passers-by to find weapons and to join him in 'beheading' some perceived enemy of Islam, or saying to them 'Westerners are killing us! There are some just across the road! C'mon everyone, let's get 'em!' Those scenarios underscore how different Rahman's message was. Rahman's conviction was based on the state's ability to imagine a sequence of 'incited' events that never occurred, and lacking any judicial requirement that any likelihood of their occurrence be demonstrated. His 'crime' can make sense only on the assumption that there *might* have been an onlooker, who *might* have seen Rahman's placard or heard his words, and who *might* then have *either* agreed with those views *or* taken offence at them, and then *might*, prompted by such passion, have responded by finding some victim, and therefore *might* then have caused some physical or material harm to that person.[221]

Alternatively, the charge makes sense if the state drops all pretence of material causation even lower that already rock-bottom threshold, insisting not even on any such speculatively material result, but merely on incitement to 'hatred' in the literal sense (itself a crime in some democracies), i.e., punishing the act of *possibly* causing *someone* to embrace or to experience a *bad emotion*, or, in the words of the European Court of Human Rights, 'an emotion of rejection of and hostility' (*un sentiment de rejet et d'antagonisme*) towards a targeted population.[222] Either assumption relies either on the consequentialist theory—but, again, with no showing of material causation either attempted or judicially required—that such hateful speech leads first to hateful emotions, which then, in turn, lead to hateful acts; or on the deontological view that speech 'aiming to deny' the rights of others in fact does so *ipso facto*, irrespective of any evidence of others' rights being in fact 'denied'.

Even on a classically liberal reading, any attempt to square either of those interpretations of Rahman's act with any plausible interpretation of Mill's harm principle would offer an intellectual spectacle indeed. If all of us were prosecuted for harms that *might* somehow flow from our conduct through such a protracted chain of hypothetical causation (in Rahman's case, even a civil tort standard of causation could scarcely have been shown, let alone a criminal standard), few of us could go free. That is the very model of the kind of dragnet device—creating crimes in order to punish people for things that *could within some imaginable scenario* result from their actions—that, we might have hoped the rule of law, the *Rechtsstaat*, was long ago created to avoid.[223] When you sit behind the wheel of a car, that is statistically far more likely to unleash a chain of harmful effects. Every year, thousands of

[221] Cf. on such speculative reasoning, Section 5.1, text accompanying notes 10–11.
[222] *Soulas v. France*, ECtHR, No 15948/03 (2008), para. 43. As with Rahman, no requirement was made that the petitioners' open-ended calls for 'ethnic war' (and no more than Marxists who have open-endedly advocated class warfare) be causally linked to any violent action.
[223] See Section 5.3, text accompanying note 89.

people in Western Europe are killed or injured in road traffic incidents. As we have seen, no such statistics have been linked to such speech acts within LSPDs.

Liability may legitimately arise when such statements are uttered as part of an effort to engage other, identifiable individuals to undertake some immediate unlawful act. Such speech, known as criminal *solicitation*, has long been subject to punishment. But Rahman did no such thing. No evidence has suggested that such vague and general statements uttered within an altogether conventional forum of public discourse actually result in violent or other illegal conduct, or formed part of any demonstrable plot to do so. Hate speech may moreover be punished if it becomes part of a distinct act of criminal *conspiracy*. Conspiracy involves agreement by two or more persons to engage in unlawful conduct (often also properly requiring evidence of material steps already undertaken). One speaker may say to one or more identified others, with their assent and subsequent cooperation, 'Westerners are killing us! One of you get the petrol, someone else get the matches, I'll get the timer, and we'll meet back here at midnight!' In addition, we have precedent for speech not merely speculating about, or abstractly favouring, but rather expressed in furtherance of some overt act to overthrow a democratic government, punished as treason, as in the famous prosecution of William Joyce, aka Lord Haw-Haw.

Under the famous US *Brandenburg* rule, government may punish 'incitement to imminent lawless action that is *likely* to produce such conduct'.[224] That standard does not slightly modify, but rather categorically differs from allowing government to punish expression solely on grounds of far-flung speculation about social harms. By extension from the concept of conspiracy, organizations, including political parties, can be banned on principles of criminal *syndicalism* or *terrorism* if their central operations[225] comprise criminal activity, which can certainly include hate-motivated activity *other* than expression of viewpoints within public discourse.[226] Factually or normatively borderline controversies obviously arise between, on the one hand, 'pure speech', and, on the other hand, what has been called 'speech plus', conduct sufficient to count as criminal solicitation, conspiracy, or syndicalism, beyond the purely general expression of viewpoints.[227] Those hard cases, too, legitimately remain under the purview of judicial scrutiny. As elsewhere, however, the existence of hard cases cannot justify penalties on conduct for which no evidence suggests any such 'speech plus'.[228]

The German Basic Law provides that political parties which 'by reason of their aims or the behaviour of their adherents,[229] seek to undermine or abolish the liberal democratic order[230] or to endanger the existence of the [state] shall

---

[224] *Brandenburg v. Ohio*, 395 U.S. 444, 447 (1969) (emphasis added). Weinstein, 1999, p. 169. See also Weinstein, 1999, pp. 16–26, 34–5. See also, e.g., Nowak & Rotunda, 2009, pp. 1291–7.

[225] See, e.g., Meier, 2002, pp. 22–3; Morlock, 2002, p. 75; Preuß, 2002, p. 110.

[226] See *Dennis v. United States*, 341 U.S. 494, 579–81 (1951) (Black, J., dissenting), and at 581–91 (Douglas, J., dissenting).

[227] *Brandenburg*, 395 U.S. at 455 (Douglas, J., concurring).

[228] Cf. Busch, 2002; Leggewie & Meier, 2002b, pp. 11–12 (citing Kelsen); Meier, 2002, pp. 20–2; Preuß, 2002, p. 110.

[229] Cf. this Section, text accompanying note 225.   [230] Cf. Section 3.2, note 22.

be unconstitutional'.[231] Such a provision raises no difficulties, and is upheld by every modern democracy, insofar as the terms 'aim' and 'seek' are applied to actual or attempted acts of material harm (including preparatory acts, *Vorbereitungshandlungen*,[232] beyond sheer expression of aspiration), such as actual or attempted acts of full-blown criminal syndicalism, terrorism, sabotage, murder, rape, or individual physical assaults. But illegitimacy arises from extensions beyond that criterion, to constructions of 'aim' or 'seek' which reach to general expressions of viewpoint within public discourse.

For the German Constitutional Court, a political party can be banned when it 'desires deliberately to undermine the functioning' of the liberal democratic order, 'and ultimately to abolish it'.[233] Grimm distinguishes 'between opinion (*Meinen*) and desire to effectuate (*Verwirklichenwollen*)'.[234] However, a 'desire to effectuate' itself arises solely as a purely subjective or a purely communicated act. The sheer feeling or expression of a desire to undermine the liberal democratic order implies nothing about material steps undertaken to effectuate that desire. Similarly, Thiel concedes that the preparatory acts cannot encompass what he calls 'differences of opinion of various political leanings, carried out in a traditional way'.[235] On his view, however, they may well include conduct which shows what he calls a 'persistently aggressive *tendency*'.[236] That element would pose no problem, and would correspond to universal democratic practice, if 'aggressive' were, again, limited to such material acts as terrorism or individual assault, but Thiel withholds any such qualification.

Thiel again concedes that 'the Basic Law's guaranty of free expression protects even opinions that challenge the liberal-democratic order', but only to pursue his view that penalties may be imposed when the actor's conduct shows that the liberal–democratic order '*ought* to be undermined or eliminated in an abusive manner'.[237] Grimm's and Thiel's own formulations make clear that acts from which we infer the actor's ideal of what *ought* to be remain distinct from those material acts undertaken to bring it about. Absent actual or attempted acts of specific material harm—and despite Grimm's or Thiel's, like Parekh's or Waldron's, assurances of prudently drawn limits—any of these other notions about conduct merely expressing an individual or even a collective desire to 'undermine or abolish the liberal democratic order' remain in Morlock's words, 'wholly unbounded and all-encompassing',[238] which US First Amendment jurisprudence refers to as 'overbreadth'.

In much of Europe, it has been legitimate for governments to combat right-wing, left-wing, or religious extremism when groups can be found undertaking material steps to inflict harm on persons or on public or private property, or dealing in contraband—crimes in which elements of solicitation, conspiracy, or aiding and

---

[231] German Basic Law art. 21(2).   [232] Morlock, 2002, p. 75.
[233] Cited in Grimm, 2002, p. 142.   [234] Grimm, 2002, p. 142
[235] Thiel, 2003d, p. 182.   [236] Thiel, 2003d, p. 182 (emphasis added).
[237] Thiel, 2003d, p. 182 (original emphasis).
[238] Morlock, 2002, p. 75. Cf. Groh, 2002, pp. 95–6.

abetting can be demonstrated. By contrast, insofar as such activity lacks any evidence of actual or attempted material harm, any residual pseudo-crime of 'incitement' merely masks the state's failure to identify such harm. Concepts like 'solicitation', 'conspiracy', 'treason', or 'aiding and abetting' certainly contain their own potential for peripheral vagueness. However, definitions of illegal acts always present definitional or evidentiary problems in law. The concept of 'incitement' is not merely vague at the 'periphery', however, as in so-called 'hard' cases. It is unsustainable at the core, even in 'easy' (in the sense of wholly undisputed) cases, like Rahman's,[239] suggesting its outright illegitimacy as a crime under the rule of law. Throughout Europe, the concept of hate-based 'incitement' has turned into the new, i.e., secular, blasphemy: The state punishes supposed perpetrators despite their having failed to cause what any democratic *Rechtsstaat* could legitimately designate as cognizable harm.

Imagine the worst nightmare of many a white, middle-class European. A local bearded imam, eyes fiery, fist raised, preaches to a crowd of young, agitated followers, with a heavy foreign accent: 'Being unarmed makes you despised!' and 'It is much safer to be feared than loved!' and 'Weigh all the harmful things you must do, and do them all at once, so as not to have to repeat them every day!' Several Western European states today might well bring a prosecution for 'incitement', as they would if such words were spoken by far-right extremists against a racial minority.

Those words were in fact written by one of the West's flagship thinkers, Machiavelli,[240] and that scenario certainly cannot assume a sheer misinterpretation or misappropriation of the original ideas. As with Rahman, we are happy to imprison the easy targets, the ineffectual nobodies, while remaining indifferent to violent messages that have long proved able to shake the world. (Certainly by the 1970s, it would have been unthinkable for British authorities to round up masses of Northern Irish Catholics collectively chanting for death to the British in every corner pub, despite such sentiments being far more conspicuously linked to active, violent conflict.) Anyone responding that *The Prince* is simply a harmless 'classic', of purely historical and scholarly interest, has read it poorly indeed.[241] A central thesis of *The Prince* is that, from the point of view of acquiring and preserving power, killing and cruelty are justified. Does that message differ from the messages increasingly falling under anti-fascist or anti-terror laws? As Mary Riddell has noted, 'Crimes of "glorifying and condoning terrorism" hark back to the 18th-century offence of seditious libel, under which pamphleteers disagreeing with the state were clapped in jail.'[242]

---

[239] Cf. Post, 1995, pp. 154–6 (discussing 'rhetorical hyperbole').

[240] Machiavelli, [1532] 1979, pp. 33, 49, 56. On prohibitionists' own terms, Machiavelli's nuance in his *Discourses* can in no way be said to alter the literal content of *The Prince*'s theses, no more than the state can legitimately adjudicate orthodoxies about 'the real' Marx or 'the real' Islam.

[241] Of course, after power is secured, Machiavelli favours a republican government rather different from that sought by militant Islamists. But the Islamists' ultimate political vision, like that of any run-of-the-mill demagogue, also purports to be a peaceful and harmonious one.

[242] Riddell, 2005.

The free speech advocacy organization Article 19 has supported hate speech bans, albeit narrow ones. In a 2012 report, the organization recognizes the risks of overbreadth and abuse surrounding crimes of incitement, proposing stringent guidelines for legal liability.[243] The authors understandably propose guidelines aimed at avoiding the arrant randomness commonly associated with prosecutions. They clear away old ambiguities, however, only by introducing new ones. A brief glance is worthwhile since Article 19, too, uncritically assumes the dominant posture of liberal rights embedded within value-pluralist proceduralism.

Article 19's guidelines can certainly be read to justify penalizing much politically revolutionary agitation. The question as to whether the report's unacknowledged anti-revolutionary commitment is good or bad per se would lead us into deep philosophical water. As with Grimm's or Thiel's views, the report nevertheless indicates that the organization's proposal by no means maintains the kind of ideological neutrality that its rule of law apparel might suggest. To cite only one of several examples of the report's lack of clarity, the guidelines admonish: 'Courts should carefully distinguish between publications which exhort the use of violence and those which offer a genuine critique on a matter of public interest.'[244]

For great volumes of politically provocative speech, classical and contemporary, that distinction certainly ends up more obfuscatory than illuminating. Do the authors mean that, as long as intellectually upmarket statements 'offer a genuine critique on a matter of public interest', then such speech must enjoy unqualified freedom to 'exhort the use of violence'? If so, then incitement to violence can scarcely constitute the danger which the recommendation seeks to avoid. Or does the report mean the opposite, namely, that as long as utterances 'exhort the use of violence', then they may be penalized, even if they do 'offer a genuine critique on a matter of public interest'? (Can statements 'which exhort the use of violence' simultaneously 'offer a genuine critique' and can such a critique be tacit, or must it be explicit?)

Within the context of the report as a whole, either of those two interpretations could be said to follow from that passage, despite their mutual incompatibility. If the authors prefer the former interpretation, then they write a *carte blanche* to any speaker minimally clever enough to toss some intellectual jargon onto the incitement, which most extremist or hate groups easily do, particularly since the report refrains from defining what counts as 'genuine critique'. If, by contrast, the authors prefer the latter interpretation, then the proposed distinction becomes vacuous. The incitement will then trump *any* of the intellectual content which the distinction had been introduced to protect. The report's frequent references to 'context'—whereby it introduces full-blown, legislative or judicial weighing and balancing—might suggest that, depending on the circumstances, either interpretation might be warranted. Yet if neither construction is satisfactory on its face, then the additional reference to context or relegation of the problem to purely proceduralist mechanisms add nothing.

---

[243] See Article 19, 2012.   [244] Article 19, 2012, p. 35.

One might, with Waldron, argue that the offence of such a statement lies not in its literal likelihood of causing violence, but merely in its 'ugly',[245] 'disfiguring' effect on 'our social environment'.[246] Waldron presents that kind of 'harm' as a violation of what he calls 'political aesthetics'. As I argue elsewhere, such an appeal merely revives under a new name the age-old civility and decorum arguments that were discussed in Section 5.7.[247] The value of Waldron's insights lies not on his own premises, but on precisely the opposite premises, in what he inadvertently teaches us. Given the implausibility of justifying such crimes of 'incitement' on any empirically credible harm-based rationale, we suddenly find strong grounds for suspecting that individuals like Rahman *really are* being thrown into prison for no reason other than the 'ugliness' of their views. Of course, no LSPD could ever openly declare that it imprisons people for public expression on grounds of expressive 'ugliness'. How far would such an offence reach: 'strict liability ugliness'? 'aiding and abetting ugliness'? 'attempted ugliness'? Understandably, as Waldron inadvertently suggests, that sense of ugliness must surely be what many a lawmaker and judge feels, while being clever enough not to declare it. Only from that perspective does it make sense that the largely pre-modern and indeterminate crime of 'incitement' serves to dress the *real*, but officially unacknowledged crime of sheer expressive 'ugliness'. Once again we witness the effects of democracy collapsed into the conventional paradigm of liberal rights embedded within the value-pluralist proceduralism of routine legislative and judicial balancing.

5.10 Free Expression in the Public University

From the outset of the hate speech debates, universities have taken centre stage. The current concept of 'hate speech' traces its origins largely back to racist incidents within US university campuses in the 1980s.[248] Such controversies have emerged also within state-funded universities in other countries.[249] Censorship of far-right or radical Islamist speakers has become routine on Western European campuses.[250] Higher education raises problems different from those posed by compulsory, primary schooling. Primary schooling in LSPDs, particularly at younger ages, is where the active state, as speaker, expressly and rightly inculcates pluralist values to the individuals it is still educating as citizens. The public university, by contrast, faces the active society's democratic dilemma. On the one hand, as a state-affiliated institution, it, too, must promote tolerance. On the other hand, 'enforced tolerance'—which, again, we value for the compulsory civic education of legal minors—takes on a different meaning for higher education. The university is

---

[245] Waldron, 2012a, p. 65.   [246] Waldron, 2012a, p. 33.
[247] See Heinze, 2013b, pp. 610–15.   [248] See Matsuda et al. (eds), 1993.
[249] Sunstein recalls that private universities in the US can constitutionally ban as much public discourse as they like. Many of them nonetheless 'like to follow the Constitution even if they are not required to do so'. Sunstein, 1995, p. 197.
[250] See, e.g., Batty, 2013.

a community designed for adult, full-fledged citizens[251] who are enrolled by choice (although references to them as impressionable 'kids' are revealing). It is precisely the state's affiliation which seems to render illegitimate any limits on those citizens' speech prerogatives within those spheres of university life that can be dentified as forums of democratic public discourse.[252]

A marketplace theory, while inadequate to challenge bans within LSPDs at large, more persuasively supplements the democratic legitimacy argument within institutions that exist for no other reason than training their members in the scrutiny of thoughts. Western public universities pride themselves on exploring complex ideas, yet display little talent for defeating stupid ones. Universities must obviously maintain the regulated contexts of formal instruction, or of other events, such as conferences, requiring procedurally structured frameworks, just as parliaments must enforce procedural rules. Within those confines, controlled speech indeed becomes 'a defining characteristic'.[253] It requires discretion and judgement on the part of professional staff in steering discussion. A student spouting hate speech during a chemistry lecture, even if not targeting other individuals through 'fighting words' can be silenced or removed for interrupting the lesson plan.[254]

Not all campus speech takes place, however, under formal or staff-supervised conditions. In Western Europe, viewpoint-punitive bans on public discourse have become routine for universities, following whatever bans prevail for society generally. A dilemma arises when commitment to tolerance clashes with the duty to forge students adept at defending pluralist values—adept not merely because they can recite drilled pluralist dogmas, but through tested ability. Anyone who thinks that ability need not be actively honed and improved, rather than being laid to rest by silencing hateful expression, is pursuing tolerance not for the sake of democracy, but instead of democracy.

My view in this book might at first seem to authorize bans for universities. I have argued that democracy's legitimating expressive conditions in no way entail affirmative duties on the state to facilitate hate speakers. Within society at large, citizens can publicly support the legalization of heroin, or the abolition of capitalism, without the state having any duty to provide a dedicated forum for them to do so. Conversely, as we have seen, the state can choose certain forums for promoting its view without having to open up those forums to conflicting views, for example, a state-operated billboard dedicated solely to public awareness campaigns expressing the state's preferred view, encouraging people to avoid drunk driving, or to advertise battered women's shelters.

From the correct premise that the public university offers countless and diverse state-furnished forums, the conclusion does not, however, follow that the

---

[251] Legal minors do occasionally enrol in universities. Their apparent precocity, however, must therefore be deemed suitable for the academic community across the board.

[252] Cf. Post, 1996–97, pp. 1528–9 (discussing Fiss) (contrasting 'parliamentary' and 'pedagogical' modes of speech).

[253] Sunstein, 1995, p. 199.   [254] See, e.g., Posner, 2015.

university is itself *nothing but* a state-sponsored speech forum in the way that such a billboard can be. If the university were such an entity, then the state's preference, say, for capitalism over socialism, or for closed versus open borders, would equally entitle universities to bar the advocacy of socialism or of open borders. The public university offers countless and diverse state-directed forums, including classrooms. But it cannot in its entirety reduce to one, without sacrificing its aforementioned purpose as a forum consecrated to nothing other than the testing of *all* ideas. Some irreducible portion of university life must be understood as consisting of citizen communications conducted outside state-directed speech forums, even if they are conducted on state-operated university premises. Those communications include contacts with citizens unaffiliated with the university.[255] The state's monopoly on facilities cannot equate with a monopoly on ideas.

An overriding aim of higher education must, then, be the cultivation of practices of difficult and vigorous public exchange. Such skill, Mill reminds us, never emerges from truth enforced by law.[256] Mill might certainly despair to visit our public universities today, where pretty much anyone can recite pluralist norms by rote, yet no one can rigorously defend them against even rather ludicrous challenges. When norms become dogma, their truth or cogency becomes not manifest, but simply irrelevant. Some staff or students may refuse to answer extremists to avoid dignifying or mainstreaming extremism, to avoid flattering irrationality with a rational reply. That personal or strategic preference to withdraw from the sphere of others' distasteful utterances scarcely amounts, however, to a justification for banning provocative speakers.

It might be argued that universities must serve not merely as replicas, but as improved models of society. As a micro-social laboratory for implementing and experiencing better human interactions, the university must, on that view, become a community for testing more humane conditions in life, prompting its members to carry those better values into society. As with state-directed management of decorum or symbolism, however, that democracy-optimizing ideal cannot override democracy-legitimating conditions. It cannot legitimately be implemented to the extent of diminishing university members' necessary attributes of citizenship. In lieu of censorship, universities, like LSPDs generally, can legitimately implement pluralist and minority-empowering, but not viewpoint-punitive policies. Moreover, as with LSPDs generally, the imperatives of democratic public discourse in no way deter universities from punishing acts of inter-personal harassment, stalking, or 'fighting words'.

In March 2013, University College London (UCL) hosted a debate entitled 'Islam or Atheism: Which Makes More Sense?', organized by a group calling itself the Islamic Education and Research Academy (IERA). Stewards attempted, according to their interpretations of Muslim precepts, to segregate the men from the women. In subsequently banning the group,[257] the university's response

---

[255] But on the status of foreign nationals, see Section 4.11, text accompanying note 169.
[256] See Section 5.5, text accompanying note 154. See also Heinze, 2016a.
[257] Batty, 2013.

exemplifies our public officials' ongoing failures to recognize distinctions between viewpoint-punitive and non-viewpoint-punitive regulation of speech. If, by comparison, a campus prayer group enforces sex segregation, that practice, which is not offered as part of the open debate of university life, can be presumed voluntary on the part of all participants. (Anyone rejecting religious sex segregation would remain free either to protest against the practice or to organize alternative prayer.)

The advertised IERA debate, by contrast, was neither devotional nor had it grounds for assuming that members of the general public would consent to segregation. The university therefore rightly demands adherence to viewpoint-neutral, conduct-based rules, which include non-discriminatory admission and seating for all events, yet which must allow speakers to *advocate* sex segregation, or outright male supremacy, or pushing gays from rooftops, or any other such ideas, if they so please.

From that correct premise as to background forum rules, however, UCL nonetheless draws a faulty conclusion. It states its policy as follows: 'We do not allow enforced segregation on any grounds at meetings held on campus.' From that legitimate premise it certainly follows that the event 'be cancelled if there were any attempt to enforce such segregation'. But we must distinguish between, on the one hand, cancelling a single event for breach of a universally applicable rule governing conduct (which could be as ordinary as, e.g., failure to comply with fire safety standards), and, on the other hand, imposing an outright ban on the group even if it is willing to abandon its sex segregation practices. The university had notified the IERA in advance that the segregation would be disallowed. When one of the invited speakers refused to consent to the segregation, however, an event organizer did agree to abandon the sex separation.[258]

One might retort that segregated seating forms part of IERA's viewpoint, being itself a form of expressive conduct.[259] But, once again, *democratic* public discourse becomes a nonsense without some necessary speech–conduct distinction (however unsatisfying that distinction may be from a phenomenological or deconstructionist standpoint), since any viewpoint-neutral, 'time, manner, or place' regulation could otherwise turn out to be viewpoint-punitive, such as disregarding noise limits through a desire to performatively dramatize the stresses of urban life. Accordingly, the university can prohibit people from 'expressively' or 'performatively' smoking cannabis at an assembly without banning the speech of cannabis advocates, just as the state can allow speakers to advocate lower taxes while punishing those who express such a message by 'expressively' or 'performatively' dodging their tax bill. Once again we see that, however defective the distinction between ideas and things may be as an ontological or social matter, it remains a legal imperative for the very possibility of democracy.

For its total ban of IERA, the university offered only the all-purpose explanation that IERA's 'interests' run 'contrary' to UCL's 'ethos'. But a state-funded university is not a tea house. Similarly, Muslim staff and students have often favoured

---

[258] 'IERA event at UCL on 9 March', 2013.   [259] See, e.g., Strossen, 1990, pp. 491–3.

banning radical Islamists. Moderate Muslims often resent what they see as the extremists' appropriation of their religion. However justified that hostility may be as a matter of personal or community preference, it cannot be the role of the public, democratic university—no more than of the state generally—either to enforce a particular position on a theological or philosophical dispute, or to promote one faction by censoring another.

Hate preachers have been blamed for inspiring young people to become radicalized (again, acknowledgement of their status as legal adults goes curiously astray). Universities, understandably, do not wish to feed those trends. Leaving aside, however, the fact that such material is easily available elsewhere, questions still arise about the university's disposition to bad ideas in principle. It would be more legitimate to limit regulations to time, manner, and place rules governing university facilities. Any university members requesting university venues can be accommodated on condition of compliance with regulations more appropriate to an educational community. The university can legitimately require that all details of all organizers' and speakers' names and institutional affiliations along with details of the event, be formally announced (as is indeed customarily done with more conventionally academic speakers) and open to the entire academic community, and that they abide by ordinary conduct-based rules of participation. Those non-viewpoint-punitive rules can apply irrespective of whether the events are about militant Islamism, revolutionary Marxism, or English-countryside butterfly collecting.

A more difficult question arises outside those spheres of public discourse. Again, within formal instruction, the university can, as an employer, legitimately regulate hate speech on the part of its professional teaching staff.[260] Lecturers ordinarily dominate within a disproportionate power dynamic, in view of their composite roles as authorities, moderators, and assessors. The lecture hall or seminar room cannot always be a forum of open public discourse in view of such power imbalances. The public university, in that respect, mirrors society more broadly. Those of its activities which more resemble regimented employment and educational contexts may legitimately impose bans as part of the active democracy's rightful pursuit of civic pluralism. By contrast, activities, such as those run by students, some of which become forums for public discourse, furnish less justification for bans.

---

[260] See Section 2.8.

6
Democratic Historicism

In the early twenty-first century, debates about hateful expression within comparative law and politics were structured by a schism between, on the one hand, the US, where the Constitution has been interpreted to preclude viewpoint-punitive bans within public discourse; and, on the other hand, Western Europe, a centre of gravity for democracies that have adopted bans, and in that sense representing such states as Australia, Canada, and New Zealand.[1] Those pro-ban LSPDs encompass a range of approaches, nonetheless united by a minimal consensus.[2] Non-US prohibitionists often explain the schism with reference to a cultural divide between an imperially brash, excessively individualist US, and at least minimally egalitarian assumptions elsewhere. US oppositionists often explain it with reference to everyone else's 'less democratic cast'.[3]

Those explanations become implausibly essentialist. They lead to an historically determinist scepticism about the appropriateness of oppositionism outside the US. Having thus far considered the LSPD model in descriptive terms, it is now worth placing it in historical perspective in order to explore those differences. The trans-Atlantic schism certainly begs an explanation, but culturally reductionist accounts turn out to be mostly folklore. The basic tenet of a constitutive, as opposed to purely administrative conception of citizenship is certainly not a US invention. It has equally strong roots in European thought.

6.1 Historical Determinism

States throughout the world have known centuries of regulating one or another kind of provocative speech,[4] blasphemy being a prominent example.[5] Debates around banning far-right political parties arise in Europe immediately after the end of the Second World War.[6] Meanwhile, a US First Amendment notion of hate speech emerge against a backdrop of post-war critiques of racial, ethnic, national,

---

[1] e.g., Bleich, 2011; Colliver (ed.), 1992, Nieuwenhuis, 2011; Pech, 2003; Robitaille-Froidure, 2011; Waldron, 2012a.
[2] See Section 4.2, text accompanying note 37.
[3] See Section 2.1, text accompanying notes 12–13.
[4] See, e.g., Lewis, 2008; Rohrßen, 2009 (on *Volksverhetzung*).
[5] See, e.g., Hare, 2009b.   [6] See, e.g., Leggewie & Meier, 2002a.

post-colonial, patriarchal, normative–heterosexual, and other such traditionally repressive politics.[7] Throughout the later twentieth century, European jurists and scholars, increasingly aware of crystallizing trans-Atlantic differences,[8] could write off US debates as irrelevant to a continent that had achieved consensus about the need to balance speakers' freedoms with others' human dignity, particularly within the framework of the European Convention on Human Rights (ECHR) and other international instruments. To the post-war generation, that restraint seemed necessary to starve attitudes that had culminated in the Holocaust, colonial atrocities, and internal repression of minorities. By the end of the twentieth century, what was striking about dominant European attitudes was not, in itself, the acceptance of bans on hate speech in public discourse. It was the sense of those bans as obvious, requiring no real discussion, except as to details of content and scope.[9] The European political and legal consensus had deemed extreme speech appropriate for routine legislative or judicial restrictions, with no theorized critique required. That assumption left 'a serious gap'[10] in public discussion and in scholarly enquiry.

The new century shook any such confidence to the core. The attacks in the US of 11 September 2001 were followed by the murder of Dutch filmmaker Theo van Gogh, the Danish cartoon controversy, Belgian and French bans on burqas, Swiss bans on minarets, ethnic minority riots outside Paris or Stockholm, terrorist attacks in London, Madrid, and Oslo, increased far-right and anti-Semitic activity in France and Germany, and the growth of ever more mainstreamed far-right political parties. Discussions about free expression suddenly exploded. Some in Europe pursued the earlier, post-war logic, calling for continued and indeed ever broader hate speech bans.[11] Others have increasingly challenged that consensus.[12] Once the re-evaluation of arguments for and against bans had begun, trans-Atlantic comparisons became inevitable. Studies and conferences increasingly became structured as 'Europe *versus* the US' enquiries.[13]

---

[7] See, e.g., Delgado, 1989; Delgado, 1996; Delgado & Stefancic, 2004; Heinze, 2008a; Heinze, 2009b; Langton, 1993; Maitra, 2012, Maitra & McGowan, 2012a; Maitra & McGowan, 2012b; McGowan, 2012; Matsuda et al., 1993.

[8] See, e.g., Mchangama, 2011.

[9] See, e.g., Akkermans et al., 1999, pp. 61–71; Berka, 1999, pp. 313–41; Bleckmann, 1997, pp. 787–878; Lebreton, 1999, pp. 111–22; Robert & Duffar, 1996, pp. 653–6; Wachsmann, 1998, pp. 389–452; See also, e.g., European Commission against Racism and Intolerance (ECRI) General Policy Recommendation No. 1: 'Combating racism, xenophobia, anti-semitism and intolerance', adopted on 4 October 1996.

[10] Nieuwenhuis, 2011, p. 14. See also, e.g., Greene, 2012, pp. 94–6; Noorloos, 2012, pp. 1, 229. At the same time, as Frederick Schauer has noted, a widespread First Amendment consensus had formed in the US. Schauer, 1992.

[11] See, e.g., ECRI, General Policy Recommendation No. 7 on national legislation to combat racism and racial discrimination, adopted on 13 December 2002; ECRI General Policy Recommendation No. 8, adopted on 17 March 2004; ECRI General Policy Recommendation No. 9 on the fight against anti-Semitism, adopted on 25 June 2004.

[12] See, e.g., Hare, 2009a; Hare, 2009b; Malik K., 2007; Molnar & Malik, 2012; Mchangama, 2011; Mchangama, 2012; Vaneigem, 2003; Wijnberg, 2008.

[13] See, e.g., Belavusau, 2013; Bleich, 2011; Hare & Weinstein, 2009; Herz & Molnar, 2012; Nieuwenhuis, 2011; Pech, 2003; Robitaille-Froidure, 2011. For pre-2001 comparative projects, see, e.g., Colliver et al., 1992; Loveland, 1999.

That Euro-American exchange first came into prominence, then, not at a random moment, but at an historically laden one. Far from mannerly, Wilsonian internationalism, the US was, in the immediate post-9/11 years, pursuing a dramatically mediatized political exceptionalism. Already rooted in nationalist and neo-conservative moods spawned after the Nixon and Carter years, America's go-it-alone positions on areas of global concern, particularly during the presidency of George W. Bush, could readily be viewed as reactionary per se, in contrast to Western European preferences for balance. The trans-Atlantic hate speech debate often collapsed into caricatures of 'the' historically European acceptance of view-point-punitive bans on public discourse, pitted against 'the' historically American rejection of them. That Euro-American schema straightforwardly equates prohibitionism with Europe, and oppositionism with the US. The discussion often falls prey to, in Karl Popper's sense, a cultural or historical determinism,[14] a teleological or essentialist view of the two continents' parallel histories.[15]

That error can be called the *fallacy of historical and cultural determinism*. It recapitulates the age-old misstep of construing history as destiny. It begins with the correct observation (the 'is') that Europe and the US currently take opposite approaches to viewpoint-punitive bans within public discourse. It then draws the normative conclusion (the 'should') that such bans are *ipso facto* appropriate for European or otherwise non-American social conditions. The seeming American exceptionalism on an issue critical to the foundations of democracy has motivated heady explorations, tracing some mystically American concept of liberty back to colonial times, from George Washington's plucky Minutemen through to the Wild West's frontier spunk and America's laissez-faire economic fetishes. That panorama supposedly captures an American 'spirit' at odds with their distant, equally caricatured cousins—a continent of anguished Europeans, brooding their way through a history that has left them sheepishly balancing away their rights.[16]

The familiar folklore of Americans having 'a greater distrust of government'[17] often pays little attention to the histories of popular movements within non-US democracies. In the immediate post-Second World War period, ideals of strong social welfare states, as exemplified in what were, at the time, still demographically

---

[14] The term 'historicist' introduces problems of its own, as it has been used in divergent ways. In the twentieth century, Karl Popper used the term derisively, to condemn social theorists who assume fixed laws to be underpinning human history. Popper, [1945] 2002a; Popper, [1957] 2002b. In the early nineteenth century, by contrast, Savigny (whom Popper never mentions) had used the term approvingly, and in a rather different sense, to characterize the reaction against law construed as abstract, universalist formulations of norms 'on paper', associated with Napoleonic, pan-European codification movements. Savigny insisted on concepts of law as products of culture. See, e.g., Goyard-Fabre, 1992, pp. 194–206; Goyard-Fabre, 1997, pp. 296–312; Heinze & Marcou, 2016. More recently, Robert Gordon, closer to Savigny's notion, has identified 'historicism' within specific practices of law to signal an anti-universalist assumption that 'a social practice or a document is a product of the preoccupations of its own time and place.' Gordon, 2012, p. 200.

[15] See generally, e.g., Popper, 2002b.

[16] See Section 2.1, text accompanying notes 6–12, and this Section, text accompanying notes 47–8. Cf. Heinze, 2009a.

[17] Weinstein, 2009b, p. 91.

homogeneous Northern European states, admittedly reflected a trust in government that would later clash with a strand of US neo-conservatism prominent since the presidency of Ronald Reagan. Of course, even that contrast fails to account for bans in states like Australia, Canada, or New Zealand. But trust in a certain ideal of good government does not always translate as trust in the particular government of the day, as suggested by comparative surveys casting doubt on the view that Western Europeans take less critical stances towards government.[18] For example, German popular opinion has reacted with far greater outrage than American against electronic surveillance, not least through a belief in its chilling effects on speech.[19]

In questioning the significance of that seemingly gaping divide, I do not deny social and philosophical differences across the ocean. Commenting on paradigm shifts identifiable in the 1930s, Post writes,

[A]bout the time the [US] Supreme Court was fashioning its special concept of public discourse, American sociologists were developing a strikingly analogous notion of the public, which they viewed as a form of social organization transcending particular communities and existing only in the presence of diverse and conflicting forms of communal life.[20]

That emergence of parallel legal and sociological pluralism comes as no surprise for an immigrant society, very different from most Western European national demographics of that pre-war era. By the early twenty-first century, however, European patterns had dramatically shifted. If Western Europe still contains demographically homogenous pockets, as does the US, vast population centres now host far greater ethnic and cultural diversity than before the Second World War, lending them to a similar sociological model.[21]

The Euro-American dichotomy in the hate speech debate reflects the perennial error of viewing history as a mere projection backwards from, therefore as a preparation for, current circumstances. Throughout several centuries of a parallel European and US history, no clean divide existed between their respective approaches to provocative speech. Overall differences were as evident between any two European states as between them and the US.[22] Holmes penned his 'fire in a theatre' dictum[23] to confirm the same general regulatory power over speech that could be found in Europe. He did change his view, but solely to usher in a preference for stronger protections, which, for several decades, was embraced only by a minority on the Supreme Court.

In the immediate aftermath of the Second World War, when human rights began to emerge as strongly proclaimed values within Western legal regimes, the core principles governing free speech had, for centuries, still remained comparable on both continents. Values of free speech, certainly acknowledged throughout Western democracies, were still generally deemed to compete on an even field with

---

[18] See, e.g., Greene, 2012, p. 107.
[19] See, e.g., Hausmitteilung, 2013, p. 5 (*Der Spiegel* editors advocating German political asylum for Edward Snowden), and that edition, pp. 22–39. Cf. Section 2.6, note 60.
[20] Post, 1995, p. 140.   [21] See, e.g., Tillmanns, 2003, pp. 25, 31.
[22] The qualifier 'overall' remains crucial. Historical differences can certainly be identified as to more particular matters, such as blasphemy. Cf. works cited in this Section, notes 4–5.
[23] See Section 2.8, text accompanying note 83.

routine government claims of state interest in their regulation on such open-ended grounds as morality or public order.[24] In the early twentieth century, American judges like Holmes or Louis Brandeis might well have begun nurturing a vanguard, urging stronger protections, thereby heralding the later Euro-American divide. At the start, however, they were doing so solely in dissenting opinions,[25] far from a political, judicial, or popular consensus.

An embryonic paradigm shift, away from routine restrictions on speech towards greater protections, may well have surfaced as early as the 1930s.[26] By the 1950s, however, the US Supreme Court would still, like European courts, find that the state may impose viewpoint-selective penalties on public discourse under the heading of group defamation.[27] As a matter of sheer black-letter law, Post may rightly observe that, '[s]ince the 1930s the [US] Supreme Court has regularly expressed a specifically constitutional vision of a "world of debate about public affairs" *that transcends the bounds and perspectives of any particular community.*'[28] In those dawning years of America's paradigm shift, however, any such 'vision' stayed largely confined to an intellectual elite. It reflected no unequivocal shift in overall American norms or institutions. Beyond the Supreme Court's placid corridors, the legal systems of southern US states had, over decades, still been implementing or acquiescing in pervasive and systemic racial segregation and subordination. 'Free' speech witnessed de-segregationists and their families lynched, brutalized, and terrorized, with the acquiescence of state officials, hence, from any legal-realist perspective, of state law.[29]

That deeply anti-democratic regime begins to decay only with the help of coercive federal intervention in the 1950s and 1960s.[30] From 1776 through to the 1960s, then, the best that can be said is that the US was more or less democratic and rights-based, depending on the locality, even if its liberal rhetoric and political mythology postured as universal within or beyond its borders. It would be fantasy[31] to suggest that the US *generally*, before the 1960s, maintained any vision of 'unmolested and unobstructed' speech,[32] or of '"a cleared and safe space" within which can occur that "uninhibited, robust, and wide-open" debate on public issues'.[33] Despite long histories of progressively emerging democratic norms and practices, and despite varying degrees of democratic character, the society in which

---

[24] See this Section, notes 9 and 27. See also, e.g., Sunstein, 1995, pp. 2–5.

[25] See, e.g., Lewis, 2008, pp. 28–9, 34–8. On respective differences between the two Justices' views, see, e.g., Sunstein, 1995, pp. 24–8.

[26] See, e.g., Post, 1995, pp. 137–8.

[27] *Beauharnais v. Illinois*, 343 U.S. 250 (1952). Waldron correctly observes that story, but his attempt to revive *Beauharnais* by challenging interpretations of the 1964 case of *New York Times v. Sullivan* (Waldron, 2012a, pp. 61–4), omits discussion about the US Supreme Court's views on viewpoint discrimination, insofar as it relates, e.g., to such cases as *R.A.V. v. St Paul*, 505 U.S. 377 (1992) or *Virginia v. Black*, 538 U.S. 343 (2003). Cf., e.g., Weinstein, 2009b, pp. 84–8. On exaggerated interpretations of US defamation law, see Section 5.6, text accompanying notes 170–2.

[28] Post, 1995, p. 137 (emphasis added). Cf. Post, 1995, pp. 179, 187, 188.

[29] See generally, e.g., Hoffer, 2012.   [30] See, e.g., Fiss, 1996, pp. 6–10.

[31] See, e.g., Greene, 2012, pp. 96–7.

[32] Post, 1995, p. 138 (citing *Cantwell v. Connecticut*, 310 U.S. 296 (1940)); See also Post, 1995, p. 141.

[33] Post, 1995, p. 138 (citing *West Va. State Bd. Of Educ. v. Barnette*, 319 U.S. 624 (1943))

a pluralist worldview becomes the norm for popular consciousness remains a distinctive, but only recent political form on either side of the Atlantic.

Post later concedes that the 'public forum' doctrine, protecting a public space 'that the citizen can commandeer',[34] finds limited support in US Supreme Court jurisprudence through the 1940s.[35] Nor is it surprising that such a doctrine had not yet emerged when segregationist legal regimes were not even punishing, but were instead deeply complicit in, racist lynchings and other forms of persecution, let alone creating public forums for all citizens, equally, including minorities, to 'commandeer'. Any analysis that stresses US myths of public discourse, without taking concurrent socio-legal realities into account, perpetuates the fallacy of historical determinism, that sister myth about a Euro-American socio-political, i.e., more-than-black-letter schism as being more momentous than it has in fact been.[36]

The US as a whole fails to present, except on paper, any distinct ethos of free speech for all citizens until well into the 1960s. Only then do Holmes's and Brandeis's legacy conquer a durable Supreme Court majority, within the socio-legal context of civil rights movements enjoying progressively greater support among federal lawmakers. An economically and culturally confident America would, in part to face down the Soviet Union,[37] start celebrating its faith in democracy's ability to triumph over undemocratic ideas through public dialogue, without resorting to viewpoint-punitive bans.[38] Such free speech pioneers as William O. Douglas or Hugo Black, New Deal supporters, and judicial defenders of civil rights, dwelled far from the later, insular chauvinism of the George W. Bush era, within which the post-2001 trans-Atlantic hate speech debates were born.

Only by the late 1960s do the Court's 1930s *obiter dicta* witness comprehensive legislative, and aggressive judicial intervention to dismantle racial segregation, anticipating later gains for women, gays, and other minorities—events again belying Waldron's and others' suggestions of a value-neutral ethos underlying the Court's rejection of viewpoint-punitive bans. Only then does the myth of speakers' and dissidents' prerogatives for all citizens begin to emerge as legal reality on the American horizon, even while racism, sexism, homophobia, and other discriminatory attitudes persist. That historical canvas bars superficial links drawn between US protections of speech and an early twenty-first century, insular, and reactionary politics. US protections of speech were the creation of legal visionaries, first vigorously opposed by a conservative as well as a racist and patriarchal establishment.[39] Figures later associating themselves with critical and progressive thought, like Vaneigem or Butler, oppose speech bans in a spirit akin to that of Holmes, Brandeis, Douglas, and Black.

---

[34] Post, 1995, p. 201 (citing Kalven).
[35] Post, 1995, pp. 202–5. Cf. Sunstein, 1995, p. 7 (noting that outright weighing and balancing approaches within US law were still rivalling positions more protective of speech in the 1950s and 1960s), and Sunstein, 1995, pp. 2–5.
[36] See, e.g., Heinze, 2008a; Heinze, 2009a.
[37] See Section 4.8, note 101. Cf., e.g., Greene, 2012, p. 93.
[38] See, e.g., Post, 1995, p. 193 (examining Warren Court jurisprudence as a reaction to McCarthyism).
[39] See, e.g., Weinstein, 1999, pp. 16–26.

After the Second World War, along with the spirit of militant democracy, Western European hate speech bans came to be seen as a weapon against the enemies of pluralism. The rest of the world joined Western Europe in approving internationally agreed bans,[40] yet often through cynical motives. Soviet and other dictatorial regimes eagerly seized the humanist patina of hate speech bans[41] to justify internal repression, as several post-Soviet successor states have continued to do with little interruption.[42] Members of disempowered ethnic minorities throughout the East bloc could be punished, under the banner of high-minded human rights ideals, for 'stirring up hatred' by criticizing the political domination of ethnic or national majority governments of socialist states.[43] Similarly, Turkey used hate speech bans to prosecute advocates of Kurdish independence.[44]

Prohibitionists often betray an eerie myopia, heralding the 'universal acceptance' of hate speech bans as a global triumph,[45] thereby deploying the rhetoric of fashioning such universality as evidence of an ethical obviousness—and rejection of bans therefore as manifestly unethical—without even parenthetically acknowledging their manipulative and repressive deployment in one-party states, which endorsed them in order to stamp their conduct with the imprimatur of an international legal and ethical code. Only through dozens of such unsavoury reinforcements did our planet end up with what Kevin Boyle, an exemplar of that strand of ahistorical, de-contextualized prohibitionism, could brand 'The United States *versus* the Rest of the World'.[46]

Legal culture and popular culture interact, of course, in complex ways. By the late twentieth century, American protections of speech since the 1960s had arguably come to appear just as self-evident, in the eyes of an American mainstream establishment, as regulations appeared in the eyes of many Europeans, not to mention the views of citizens within societies saddled with altogether long traditions of repressing speech, and whose governments had never seen a restriction on speech they didn't like. The debate becomes impoverished indeed when it slips into an automatic reflex, uncritically defaulting to an historically

---

[40] See Section 1.1, text accompanying note 22.

[41] See, e.g., Heinze, 2008a, pp. 122–33; Mchangama, 2011.

[42] See, e.g., Richter, 2012. Although the Soviets took a forceful lead (Mchangama, 2011), Western European national laws generally came to accept various degrees of regulation.

[43] See, e.g., Molnar, 2009, p. 243; Richards, 1999, pp. 178–9. On post-communist Central and Eastern Europe, see, e.g., Belavusau, 2013, pp. 20–32, 116–65; Molnar, 2009, pp. 239–40; Richter, 2012, pp. 290–305; Speit, 2005, p. 17.

[44] See, e.g., Belavusau, 2013, pp. 52–3. On repressive use of hate speech bans in Pakistan, see, e.g., Abrams, 2012, pp. 120–1; on their abuse in Ethiopia, see Mengistu, 2012, pp. 353–4, 370–2. On the use of bans against minorities critical of majorities, including abuses of blasphemy laws, often cast as 'inciting hatred against religion' in Greece, Poland, or several Muslim majority countries, see, e.g., Marshall & Shea, 2011. In the West, too, abuse of hate speech bans has prompted suspicion about them among advocates of minority rights. See, e.g., Greene, 2012, pp. 97–8; Molnar & Strossen, 2012, pp. 390–1.

[45] See, e.g., Boyle, 2001; Delgado & Stefancic, 2004, p. 197; Delgado & Stefancic, 1999, pp. 56–7, 123; Lee, 1990, pp. 39–40; Matsuda, 1993, pp. 26–30; Tsesis, 2002, pp. 180–2.

[46] Boyle, 2001. See also, e.g., Matsuda, 1993, pp. 26–31; Colliver, 1992. But see critically, Heinze, 2008a, pp. 117–39. Cf., e.g., Greene, 2012, pp. 108–11; Weinstein, 2009b, pp. 81–2, 84. Molnar has further challenged assumptions about the absoluteness of the Euro-American schism. See Molnar, 2009; Molnar, 2012, pp. 186–7.

determinist dichotomy between semi-civilized Americans revering aggressive individualism above all other values *versus* lethargically timorous Europeans yoked to government-dictated notions of the collective good. The fallacy of historical determinism becomes augmented when one ideological basis is ascribed to US law and another, contrasting one to European laws. The black-letter differences certainly make it tempting to draw broader cultural comparisons; and yet the aforementioned similarities in actual public discourse across Western democracies—or, at any rate, differences which do not obviously cut across a trans-Atlantic divide—raise questions as to whether those black-letter differences really do reflect deeper schisms.

To illustrate the fallacies of historical and cultural determinism, let's start with a random hypothetical. Assume that a given Irish commercial law in the 1990s was more 'libertarian' than a corresponding English one, while English law was more 'libertarian' on abortion. If a comparative scholar, Smith, had deduced a broader *cultural* libertarianism in Ireland based solely on that commercial rule, a glaring doubt would have arisen if a second scholar, Jones, were then to introduce an area, like abortion, where it is English law that seemed, at least by comparison, more libertarian. Smith's attribution of a general 'libertarianism' to Irish culture would prove circular,

Jones: I understand that the particular Irish commercial rule is relatively less restrictive than the English one. But does that make it 'libertarian'?
Smith: Yes, because Ireland is more generally libertarian.
Jones: What is your evidence that Ireland is more generally libertarian?
Smith: Well, just look at the differences between these two respective commercial rules.

Smith's only way out of that circle is to provide more general evidence of Irish legal or cultural libertarianism exceeding England's, independently of the particular rule being examined—which, for anyone familiar with England and Ireland in the 1990s, would seem unlikely. I stress this analogy because such circular reasoning undergirds the fallacies of historical or cultural determinism. Euro-American differences are offered as confirmation of broader cultural differences—with reference to high-blown ideological categories like 'libertarianism', 'egalitarianism', and the like—but then the evidence adduced for those broader cultural differences in the first instance turns out mostly to consist of those divergent approaches to hate speech regulation. That circularity feeds, in turn, the fallacies of historical or cultural determinism.

Grimm, for example, calls the hate speech debate a 'problem [of] identifying the exact boundary between legitimate public discourse and objectionable speech'.[47] He 'identifies' that 'boundary' through a familiar comparison,

---

[47] Grimm, 2009a, p. 19. By 'objectionable', Grimm apparently means 'legitimately subject to prohibition', in contrast to what he calls 'legitimate', and therefore presumably protected 'public discourse'. After all, if 'objectionable' simply meant, as it means for oppositionists, 'objectionable but nevertheless protected', then there would be no need for 'identifying the exact boundary' between the two types of speech.

In the United States there *seems* to be a *tendency* to assume that a multicultural and mul-tireligious society needs more speech than a homogeneous society. ... In Europe there is a *tendency* to assume that multicultural and multireligious societies are in need of more consideration among the various groups. Consequently, greater restrictions of speech in the interest of peaceful coexistence *seem* justifiable.[48]

Grimm does not state whether he intends that observation to be legal-realist and sociological, or whether he intends it solely as an impressionistic com-ment on the putative values underlying the differences in black-letter law. Surely, however, the former option is excluded. Grimm cannot be envisaging a broad-based, legal-realist or sociological analysis in the space of a brief para-graph that lacks any social science references. Any serious cross-cultural analysis pitched at such a vast level of generality would require a volume of its own. Grimm instead seems to assume only the norms already reflected in the extant, black-letter formalisms, extrapolating from those to the broader 'tendencies' they are supposed to embody. Grimm's dignitarian principle rests, then, on a vi-cious circle. Is 'Europe' justified in retaining its hate speech bans? Yes, because it 'seems' to maintain different social 'tendencies'. Why do those tendencies 'seem' different? Since no serious sociological analysis is suggested, any evidence for that difference simply lies in an abstraction from the fact that Europe, unlike the US, has bans. Those tendencies do indeed 'seem' different because Europe *has* hate speech bans.

Like 'absolutism', such vast concepts as 'libertarianism', 'egalitarianism', 'utilitar-ianism', or 'pragmatism' maintain a seductive appeal. They are grand ideas—vintage concepts throughout the history of legal and political theory. Their deployment in law and politics nevertheless requires that we ask whether they are uncritically re-capitulating casual mythologies (in our case, mythologies which construct cultural difference), or are performing some substantive, heuristic function—whether, as lawyers like to say, such concepts are more probative than prejudicial. The grand 'isms' work powerfully when they genuinely account for cultural differences be-yond the narrow, logically circular confines of this or that particular norm or prac-tice; but they work misleadingly when they are merely extrapolated onto whole cultures from rules otherwise examined in isolation *from* the whole of the re-spective legal systems.

In *Freedom of Speech: Importing European and US Constitutional Models in Transitional Democracies*, Uladzislau Belavusau ushers the Euro-American com-parisons into a new historical phase. Most comparisons with the US have focussed at national levels, with European or international norms mentioned mostly in-sofar as they are incorporated and applied domestically. Belavusau joins a growing scholarship that moves beyond national frameworks. He pinpoints a distinctly *Euro*-American divide, contrasting US law with what he calls the 'ever-harmonising "European freedom of expression"',[49] spawned within the European Union (EU)

---

[48] Grimm, 2009a, p. 19 (emphasis added).
[49] See Section 4.2, text accompanying note 37.

and the Council of Europe (CoE). Belavusau's study is more than academic. It seeks a path for the 'transitional democracies of Central and Eastern Europe (CEE)'.[50] The author examines CEE nations as places with distinct cultures, including grievous local histories of intolerance, which, he argues, must not hastily be assigned pre-fabricated legal models. He contrasts the US and pan-European models with an eye towards the immediate problem of choosing the best model for CEE states.

Belavusau proposes a distinction between the 'pragmatic American and preventive European approaches'.[51] The adjective 'pragmatic' is indeed commonly applied to the US, whose intellectuals, notably since William James and John Dewey, have often associated themselves, and their nation, with a 'pragmatic' politics. It also emerges in Huckleberry Finn-type popular culture, recalling an American mythology and folklore. To depict European approaches as 'preventive' seems equally appealing, in view of European responses to the Second World War and colonialism.

But that again is the type of contrast that runs into difficulties. First, we ordinarily view 'prevention' not as negating or rejecting, but at the heart of 'pragmatism'. Thiel, for example, expressly praises Germany's preventive approach for its pragmatic advantages.[52] Two such terms form no clear dichotomy, much less the kind of binarism that would distinguish European from US approaches. Second, if 'pragmatism' offers a conceptual construct, is it not the European approaches to hate speech that embrace it more strongly? The essence of pragmatism is avoidance of categorical rules, in favour of flexibility.[53] The US doctrine covering viewpoint-punitive bans within public discourse is, if nothing else, certainly categorical, often condemned as overly rigid and ideological.[54] Belavusau himself later depicts the US approach as nothing less than 'absolute',[55] but that is the polar opposite of 'pragmatic'. If either side of the ocean is aiming at pragmatism, it would be the prevailing European preference for compromise solutions and for malleable weighing and balancing, proportionality, and totality of the circumstances formulas within the dominant value-pluralist proceduralism. That preference contrasts to a US viewpoint absolutism which would render difficult or impossible most hate speech bans, even if, in certain situations, some Americans could find pragmatic grounds for favouring them. That might have been the case, for example, in the Skokie, Illinois controversy concerning neo-Nazis who marched in a town inhabited by Jewish Holocaust survivors.[56] A problem with the notion of pragmatism is that, despite having been particularly embraced in American thought and folklore, its sense of fluidity or flexibility is far from being the distinct preserve of Americans. Many political and legal

---

[50] Belavusau, 2013, p. 1. Cf. pp. 4, 5, 116–65.
[51] Belavusau, 2013, p. 3.
[52] Thiel, 2003d, p. 187. See also, e.g., Meier, 2002, p. 21; Thiel, 2003c, pp. 129–30.
[53] See, e.g., James, [1907] 1981. Cf., e.g., Amin & Thrift, 2013, pp. 32–3 (discussing Dewey and Rorty).
[54] See, e.g., Matsuda, 1993, pp. 31–5; Delgado & Stefancic, 1999, pp. 41–5.
[55] See this Section, text accompanying note 70.   [56] See, e.g., Strum, 1999.

traditions boast, in one or another sense, their pragmatism, even if each displays it in ways different from the others.[57]

For now, let's leave to one side the empirical doubts raised in Section 5.5 as to whether European polices have proven to be 'preventive'. Within the context of hate speech, the European balancing approaches posit ethical principles *on both sides* of the equation: *free speech* precepts furnish reasons of high principle to maintain whichever hate speech national, European, and international norms aim to protect; and *dignitarian*, *anti-discrimination*, or *harm-based* precepts furnish reasons of high principle to justify punishing whichever hate speech those norms aim to ban. Belavusau notes the views of observers objecting to European solutions which, in their view, too readily allow political expedience to assume the guise of ethical principle.[58] That malleability, he suggests, as reflected in the familiar 'proportionality' or 'margin of appreciation' tests, means that legislators or courts can bend to the political winds, while always being able to justify the outcomes in the principled language of human rights requirements.

European flexibility, then, offers the recipe for a greater nuts-and-bolts tinkering, for a 'pragmatism', denied to American lawmakers or judges, even under circumstances that might prompt pro-ban sentiments in some areas of the US to run strong, along with any attendant political or judicial opportunism. Far from being deemed 'pragmatic', the categorical US First Amendment viewpoint absolutism is constantly derided for pushing one narrow and socially abstracted view of civil liberties, for being out of touch with 'real-world societies here on earth',[59] and, as Belavusau himself often notes, for safeguarding individual speakers' rights regardless of viewpoint. American culture frequently reveals quasi-absolutist ideological polarization on matters such as abortion or religious education, for which Europeans have long been satisfied with, at least by comparison, seemingly pragmatic accommodations. There is no denying a spirit of pragmatism in US history, but it is by no means obvious that Europe has lacked similar approaches, indeed throughout a very long history.

Another popular characterization of the Euro-American comparison arises from a supposedly American 'libertarianism'.[60] While marketplace metaphors remain mostly the preserve of free speech specialists, 'libertarian' has become a mediatized, catch-all adjective. The label's meanings seem variable, but it is frequently employed in contrasts between the US and some—or rather, virtually *any*—other culture, far beyond the confines of the hate speech debate. The US Tea Party movement of the early twenty-first century, or conservative American 'shock jock' culture dating back a few decades earlier, shroud the US with a libertarian folklore. Even among scholars, we might well find a stronger libertarian strain within the US than outside.[61] But does libertarianism explain the distinctness of the US approach to free speech?

---

[57] Cf. Section 3.2, text accompanying note 27.
[58] See Section 3.2, text accompanying note 28.
[59] See Section 5.7, text accompanying note 201. Cf. critically, Heinze, 2013b, pp. 607–9.
[60] See, e.g., Belavusau, 2013, pp. 5, 34, 49.   [61] See, e.g., Caine, 2004–05.

A 'strong', minimal state libertarianism would admit no regulation except insofar as it demonstrably preserves the formally equal and maximum autonomy of all individuals. Creation of such a regime, which is unknown in recorded history, would represent not a minor variation, but a revolutionary overthrow of countless existing government structures. A 'weak' or ad hoc libertarianism, by contrast, stands loosely for countless positions, taken on any particular issue of the day. They are not necessarily supported by a Nozick-type overarching theory of the state. That weaker, colloquial libertarianism merely denotes a preference that, given a range of feasible alternatives, opts for some relatively less regulatory one.

As an historical matter, one problem with attributing the current US First Amendment position to libertarianism is that it emerges from a post-1960s Supreme Court that was far from libertarian on strongly related social issues. It had, again, imposed intrusive racial integration measures during the same years in which it was clawing back restrictions on speech.[62] During those same years, the Court had also accepted a *de facto* power of general federal regulation under the Constitution's Commerce Clause—a power still largely intact, except where more recently limited on expressly federalist, and not libertarian grounds.[63]

Even if the Court was far from libertarian in its original motives, one might argue that its First Amendment jurisprudence gradually came to incorporate libertarian rationales after the more politically conservative Reagan years. The avowedly jurisprudential conservative US Supreme Court Justice Antonin Scalia, appointed to the Court by Reagan in 1986, has taken the lead in crucial free speech cases. If any judicial opponent of bans in the late twentieth and early twenty-first centuries were to meet the test of a post-Reagan American libertarianism, either Scalia would have to run as a leading candidate, or it would become hard to guess how the Court's approach could be called libertarian at all. Scalia also offers a valuable test case, since he has virulently rejected European and other foreign legal doctrines in the area of human rights,[64] thus associating him with an impetus to preserve distinctive principles of US law, in express contrast to European or international ones. Yet, however Scalia's free speech principles may be characterized, they have not turned out to be libertarian, at least, no more libertarian than are the principles of most other Western democracies. There 'is no basis for thinking', this Justice proclaims in a 1991 case, 'that American public opinion has ever embraced that "'you may do what you like so long as it does not injure someone else" beau ideal—much less for thinking that it was written into the Constitution.'[65]

---

[62] See Section 5.5, text accompanying note 158.

[63] See, e.g., Nowak & Rotunda, 2009, pp. 182–225.

[64] See, e.g., *Thompson v. Oklahoma*, 487 U.S. 815, 868 n. 4 (1988) (Scalia, J., dissenting); *Lawrence v. Texas*, 539 U.S. 558, 598 (2003) (dissenting).

[65] *Barnes v. Glen Theatre, Inc.* (Scalia, J.), 501 U.S. 560, 574–75 (1991). Similarly, Scalia's anti-gay opinion in *Lawrence* is conspicuously anti-libertarian, *Lawrence*, 539 U.S. at 586 (dissenting). Nor is the majority opinion in that case, striking down a sodomy law, although certainly compatible with familiar libertarian views, written in terms conspicuously more libertarian than those of comparable rulings in Europe or elsewhere.

Only a year later, we again find Scalia authoring a Court opinion in the high-profile *R.A.V. v. St. Paul* case, striking down a criminal conviction for a racist cross-burning on the private property of a black family.[66] The opinion recognizes the cross-burning's performative or illocutionary character, even if Scalia avoids that terminology. Scalia emphasizes that such an act is *not* 'pure speech', but, to the contrary, includes an inseparable, conduct-based element which *can* be punished without violating the First Amendment. Given all nine Justices' unanimous agreement that a criminal penalty was entirely admissible, their disagreement remains confined to questions about a law based on viewpoint-selective penalties. The view that such a ruling 'omits the victim's story'[67] is not as obvious as some have suggested.

The Court majority never characterizes the cross-burning as expression meriting constitutional protection for no reason other than that it *is* expression.[68] Such a rationale remains as alien to First Amendment law as it does to the great numbers of cases in which European states would protect expression. The US Supreme Court certainly finds itself obliged to focus on the vandalism's expressive content in *R.A.V.* That focus does not, however, flow from any discernibly libertarian principle. The error of reading libertarianism into the US First Amendment position parallels the error of reading absolutism into it. Nothing in the *R.A.V.* ruling contradicts an illocutionary interpretation of the defendant's malice. The Euro-American comparison wanders astray through any premise that principles of US free speech law differ from European law in specifically disregarding linguistic performativity.

For the *R.A.V.* Court, lawmakers *may* constitutionally penalize the vandalism, but must do so in ways that punish comparable expressive offenses in comparable ways, so as not to implicate state action in viewpoint-selective penalties. We must admittedly read that notion of 'comparable' with a critical eye; but, even if we reject the Court's application of it, to label as 'libertarian' the opinion's insistence on consistent standards for policing expression is to fall into a sheer category error. A judicial standard requiring the even-handed policing of expression—regardless of any controversies about its application—differs from a judicial standard requiring state abdication from policing expression.

Belavusau deems it 'clear that both the public policy derogation of Article 10(2) ECHR and an anti-discrimination defence of Article 14 ECHR outweigh the value of pure *l'expression pour l'expression*' which he and others associate with the US.[69] Yet that kind of rigorously libertarian approach would have rendered many cases decidable in a line or two, obviating any need for the hundreds of pages of painstaking casuistry which, for decades, have earmarked US law on free speech, and rendered it altogether difficult to subsume under any all-encompassing principle. Belavusau periodically returns to his basic

---

[66] See, e.g., *R.A.V. v. St. Paul*, 505 U.S. 377, 380 n. 1 (1992).
[67] Cf., e.g., Belavusau, 2013, p. 97 (discussing Matsuda).
[68] Cf., e.g., Belavusau, 2013, p. 92.   [69] Belavusau, 2013, p. 92 (original italics).

comparison, claiming that 'the European human rights agenda has been essentially driven by the ethos of the European Court of Human Rights, whose stance on racism, sexism, and homophobia has been based on non-discrimination rather than on *absolute* free speech'.[70] But, once again, numerous cases have, over decades, confirmed that US law on speech is far from absolute in any libertarian sense.

A similar misconstruction of the concept of neutrality rears its head in a passage in which Belavusau certainly does convey the strengths, but also the limits of recourse to linguistic theory for purposes of the trans-Atlantic comparison. Belavusau rightly observes that 'the perception of language by critical scholars is essentially *post*-structuralist.'[71] He also insightfully adds, echoing Fish, that there 'is no ideal speaker suitable for legal neutrality'.[72] Language indeed transmits, recapitulates, and thereby perpetuates socio-political imbalances. But a label like 'libertarian' accepts the myth of a state neutrality which fails to withstand analysis of how US law governing both speech and discrimination has developed since the modern doctrine emerged in the 1960s. Belavusau may be right, then, to suggest that '[t]he label *viewpoint neutralists* references the opponents of *performative* insights'.[73] However, as we have seen, both the doctrine and the history of US free speech law demonstrate that it is mistaken to extrapolate from the Supreme Court's very narrow refusal to allow viewpoint-selective punishments to the broader suggestion of an overall US viewpoint neutrality within the law relevant to speech or to discrimination.

6.2 Universals and Their Limits

Democracy's legitimating expressive conditions can, as we have seen, be articulated independently of rights jurisprudence. But that has not been the trend in practice. Protagonists on both sides continue to assume the prevailing, rights-based contexts. Mill supplies a typical starting point for liberal oppositionism. Recall that he proposes 'one very simple' harm principle[74] to resolve once and for all a vast array of social problems, as different as free speech, gambling, and alcohol consumption. Other examples of that liberal, formulaic impulse include Kant's 'categorical imperative', Rawls's 'veil of ignorance',[75] or Dworkin's 'rights as trumps'.

Two objections are frequently raised against those classical liberal algorithms. First, the formulas proposed, instead of solving perennial problems, often just turn them into new ones. As was noted in Section 3.6, for example, Mill's proposal that

---

[70] Belavusau, 2013, p.113 (emphasis added).
[71] Belavusau, 2013, p. 109 (original italics).   [72] Belavusau, 2013, p. 109.
[73] Belavusau, 2013, p. 109 (original italics).
[74] See Section 3.6, text accompanying note 88.
[75] My references to Rawls in this Section focus on *A Theory of Justice* (Rawls, 1999) rather than *Political Liberalism* (Rawls, 1993) insofar as (a) Rawls deems those two works to be generally reconcilable, and (b) the former from the outset elicits classical liberal characteristics of Rawls's method.

freedom be protected when it causes no 'harm' merely displaces the vast question 'What freedoms ought we to have?' onto equally vast questions as to what constitutes 'harm'. Those questions plague both deontological and consequentialist approaches to hate speech.

One option, as we have seen, is for value-pluralism to move from a substantive to a procedural Millianism, which accepts determinations of harm insofar as they proceed from some duly constituted state authority, such as a legislature, court, or administrative agency. Yet that approach, too, merely displaces the vast question 'What constitutes harm?' onto equally vast questions as to the appropriate scope of 'duly constituted state authority'. Is such authority self-legitimating, or must it follow independent legitimating criteria? Centuries of public law teach us that sheer investiture of state power scarcely removes all questions as to its legitimate exercise and limits. It was that problem to which Mill had sought to respond in the first place, by seeking a formula that government ought to apply. In that respect, however, he falls into his own vicious circle. He displaces the question 'What is the appropriate scope of duly constituted state authority?' onto the equally vast question with which *On Liberty* begins, which runs, in essence: 'What freedoms ought we to have?'. Mill's slippery step in *On Liberty* is to assume that 'harm' is the more concrete, objective, or ideologically neutral notion, which can then fill in the notion of 'liberty' with apolitical or politically transcendent content.[76]

The point is not that the harm principle is vacuous. It does succinctly formulate an heuristics, a template of the kind of discussion that will commonly inform questions as to the content of individual liberties. As controversies have arisen around legalizing inter-racial marriage or recognizing gay rights, 'Who is harmed?' has provided a useful start. Still, the harm principle's inherent indeterminacy is not a problem specific to Mill. It haunts other ahistoristist, liberal-universalist formulaics. Whether we would, for example, choose hate speech bans within what Rawls deems to be the ideally deliberative situation decked by a 'veil of ignorance',[77] even accepting for ourselves the anonymized identities he would have us imagine behind that veil, remains debatable.[78] For argument's sake, one might well maintain, by contrast, that, behind the veil of ignorance, all would necessarily choose that system which would leave them, in their post-deliberative ('post-veil') social position, socially or materially best off. That kind of calculus involves factors very different from those relevant to the role and character of public discourse. Far from unequivocally answering the question, Rawls, too, merely re-formulates it (not unlike Habermas), as to those social elements which are not as straightforwardly amenable to such a calculus.

Similarly, Kant's categorical imperative leaves a host of indeterminacies. Questions as to whether or when it commands democracy, let alone a particular form of democracy, remain speculative. By extension, any purely liberal Dworkinian

---

[76] See Section 3.6, text accompanying note 89.
[77] Or, as Waldron proposes, within Rawls's model of the 'well ordered society'. Waldron, 2012a, pp. 77–81. Cf. critically, Heinze, 2013b, p. 606.
[78] Cf., e.g., Waldron, 2012a, p. 70.

formula which would straightforwardly have rights of speech override hate speech bans remains indeterminate for as long as so many LSPDs, in their positive law, following the dominant, value-pluralist balancing approach, formally or function-ally elevate dignitarian aims to the status of trumps over non-viewpoint-punitive expression within public discourse.

There is a second, but related objection to classical, liberal formulaics. Aiming to apply indifferently across local histories or cultural contexts, they in fact overlook those contexts' vital roles.[79] Liberal formulaics rarely confess to 'ignoring' history. Their theorists suggest the contrary, namely, their ability to overcome historically intractable problems by surmounting the vicissitudes of time and culture, relegating those to the status of discrete 'factors' which their formulas purportedly take into account. Mill certainly never suggests that the concept of 'harm', nor does Kant suggest that the categorical imperative, must be assessed with decisive reference to traditional or popular attitudes. Those are the kinds of factors they want to overcome. Historical and cultural contexts become nominally acknowledged, but functionally subordinated. That is why Dworkin commits a deductive fallacy when he applies uniform criteria of pol-itical legitimacy to all democracies, irrespective of various states' histories and political circumstances.

A democratic–historicist[80] theory must seek an alternative to naïve universal-isms. Aporias between formulaic, liberal universalisms and historically grounded relativisms are certainly not new. In the early nineteenth century, universalist legal rationalism, following the French revolution, included both Kantian idealism and Napoleonic codification movements. Those movements frowned on 'back-wards' regimes of customary law, grounded in local traditions. In a guise still characteristic of much liberalism today, Enlightenment intellectuals often viewed pre-existing arrangements as frozen in centuries of 'medieval' law—history and custom viewed as shackles of irrationalism, which had to be shaken off, as liberal reform arrived to replace cluttered histories and traditions with ordered reason and system.

Historicist thinkers like Savigny condemned those abstract universalisms. They argued that local and customary norms had emerged organically and piecemeal, in response to immediate but intricately changing needs. Those holistic systems would be undermined by overarching statutory systems imposed by Europe's emer-ging, statist regimes, which made law a tool of centralized control and therefore of popular alienation.[81] Prohibitionist proceduralists condemn a categorical rejection of bans in the same vein. Non-viewpoint-punitive expression within public dis-course may, in their view, suit the historical and cultural contexts of some societies, such as the US, while remaining inappropriate for others.

Historicism in that sense must be distinguished from Popper's meaning, which is both narrower and broader. Popper's notion of historicism is narrower than

---

[79] Cf. Section 4.6, text accompanying note 78.   [80] See Section 6.1, note 14.
[81] See, e.g., Goyard-Fabre, 1992, pp. 194–206; Goyard-Fabre, 1997, pp. 296–312.

Savigny's. Popper's concern is not with overall cultural contexts, but only with views which identify particular historical 'laws' (like orthodox Hegelian or Marxist dialectics) as inexorable. And Popper's concept is simultaneously broader, insofar as those historical 'laws' in fact turn out to be universalist abstractions of their own, extracted from particular cultural contexts, and in some instances, like Hegel's or Marx's, universalized to apply to all of world civilization.[82] We can distinguish, then, between the closed historicism, which Popper rejects, and a post-Savigny open historicism.

Open historicist criticisms remain relevant to today's hate speech debates, in view of histories of oppression based on race, ethnicity, nationality, sex, sexuality, and other identities, often taking distinct forms in particular societies. Dworkin's generally formulaic, liberal insistence on free speech rings hollow in the ears of prohibitionists who point to bleak local histories. Leaving aside the *lex lata* that viewpoint-punitive bans have been embraced within universalist human rights norms and institutions, prohibitionists view bans as offsetting a de-contextualized, rights-based ethos of free speech. Using again Mill's example, the concept of 'harm' comes to be seen not as bearing a fixed, ahistorically empirical meaning, but as arising from experiences and perceptions grounded in history and culture (once again, that same observation applies, substituting Mill's criterion of 'harm', to Kant's rules which could be 'universally valid' or to or Rawls's 'decisions agreed behind the veil of ignorance'). Even if few observers today call themselves, without qualification, 'historicist', philosophies stressing social and cultural elements of law continue to cast doubt on traditionally universalist liberal formulaics, and to influence critical, republican, or communitarian theories.

No sooner had those nineteenth-century historicist objections to liberalism emerged than were some intellectuals attempting to overcome them. They sought a liberalism that does not descend into simplistic, ahistorical formulas, and an historicism that does not descend into outright relativism. For the young Hegel, that synthesis means not straightforwardly 'refuting' liberalism, particularly in its Kantian formulaics, but instead incorporating it[83] within some historically and culturally grounded context. If the later Hegel's political model is shunned for its insufficiently democratic execution of that synthesis, Hegel's broader grasp of the necessity of *some* democratic–historicist synthesis remains compelling. In the twenty-first century, something like an LSPD model may be taking its place within that tradition of synthesizing liberal and historicist demands.

Liberal pluralism was once deemed to be diametrically opposed to notions of history as hidebound traditionalism. Throughout much of the post-Second World War West, however, it has come to form a part of culture, largely through the cardinal role of the state as educator and speaker. Liberal pluralism need no longer stand as, in Savigny's sense, a diametric opposite to Western history and culture. It actively shapes history and culture. That is not to say, recalling Vaneigem, that

---

[82] Popper 2002a; Popper 2002b.   [83] See, e.g., Hegel, [1807] 1970b, pp. 310–15.

culture must irrevocably collapse into unbridled, Wild West, consumerist individualism, nor that the challenges of critical, civic republican, or communitarian
schools have lost force. Conflict persists between dominant universalisms and the
alienated groups whom they disfavour. Resolutions of that conflict cannot legitimately be framed, however, in the mutually exclusive terms of strictly dignitarian or strictly anti-dignitarian responses to the alienation or disempowerment of
disadvantaged groups.

Hegel grasps that both liberalism and historicism become in themselves
dead-ends, each forever mechanically negating the other. When Hegel's demand
for a synthesis goes ignored, that vicious circle continues, as reflected in today's
hate speech debates, in which citizenship interests and dignitarian interests fall into
a hollow deadlock. By the early nineteenth century, Hegel had already theorized
Recht (as 'right') in broader as well as subtler terms, structurally incorporating
non-coercive means of promoting ethical values. If that insight seems of unclear
utility, given Hegel's unfortunate (if understandably anti-Jacobin) diminution of
democratic structures, the point, for us, is not to adopt the Hegelian model literally or in its entirety, but rather to seek a democratic–historicist synthesis through
a shift from the archaic, punitive model of law towards the model of the state as,
itself, an active and powerful, yet a non-viewpoint-punitive participant in public
discourse, beyond the red herring of a 'night watchman' state that is morally neutral, indifferent, or impotent.

Post does glimpse the problem of navigating between abstract universalism and
historical context. He questions the 'highly internationalist doctrine of human
rights that extend universally throughout the globe',[84] advising that 'history, customs, traditions, and political circumstances'[85] must be taken into account. But
without more, as was noted at the outset, that view swings to the opposite extreme
of Dworkin's abstract liberalism, becoming so 'highly contextualist'[86] as to leave
no critical standard for citizens *generally* to assess the regulation of public discourse
within various societies throughout the world.[87]

Weinstein and Hare are almost right in their warning that 'democracies tend
to overreact to what at the time seemed to be imminent threats to core societal
values.'[88] Although formulated only in general terms, that view fails to account for
the anomaly that those fearing, for example, the dissemination of Nazi propaganda
under the Weimar democracy, or hate speech in Rwanda or the former Yugoslavia,
did not overreact. The democratic–historicist model assists in re-phrasing their
claim, adding the qualification that in LSPDs—outside of those legitimately
declared and independently reviewable states of emergency which precisely suspend their LSPD character—such threats do indeed run the risk of being countered by speech restrictions that prove to be overreactions.

---

[84] Molnar & Post, 2012, pp. 23, 30–1.
[85] Molnar & Post, 2012, p. 24, cf. p. 25.   [86] Molnar & Post, 2012, p. 24.
[87] For further discussion of this problem in Post, see Heinze, 2013b, pp. 593–4.
[88] Weinstein & Hare, 2009, p. 5 (discussing Justice William O. Douglas's rejection of a ban on a
Ku Klux Klan march).

A grasp of the synthesis between liberalism and historicism can invoke the young Hegel's critique of *Positivität*, 'positivity', in the sense of punitive authority deployed to impose moral doctrine.[89] Georg Lukács traces that analysis of authority to Hegel's confrontation with coercively institutionalized Christianity. Hegel rejects 'positivity' in the sense of an ethical positivism that includes the punitive disciplining of public or individual opinion.[90] Essential to Hegel's concept of mind (*Geist*) is his view that ethical opinion formation, the education of the citizen as an actively ethical and civic agent (Aristotle's influence is apparent), is achieved only through critical reflection, as both an individual and socially interactive process. Crucial ethical principles such as altruism or forgiveness lose all meaning when they become coerced by institutional authority, as does a principle like tolerance.

An individual can be constrained to act in a desired way, as can an animal or robot, but it is the human's appreciation of that choice, that person's interactive understanding of the social world, which makes it ethical. External authority still retains legitimacy in controlling countless actions—killings, thefts, frauds, etc. Yet even those norms reflect ethics, and not merely coerced rules, insofar as they assume individuals' abilities to deliberate.[91] To erase the decisive line between, on the one hand, action, and, on the other hand, the expression of a worldview within public discourse, an erasure that reduces ethics to the enforceable prescription of desirable actions irrespective of individual thought, is to erase ethics itself as to those speakers who are coerced in that way.

The removal of that viewpoint-punitive power, not from law altogether, but only from the expressive manifestation of individual deliberative capacity, was already an Enlightenment project, still pursued in the nineteenth century. Mill does state a similar position in *On Liberty*, focussed less on Hegel's example of church authority, and more on state authority: 'the peculiar evil of silencing the expression of an opinion'—in our case, a hateful opinion—'is, that it is robbing the human race; posterity as well as the existing generation; those who dissent from the opinion, still more than those who hold it.' Even 'if the opinion is … wrong, they lose … the clearer perception and livelier impression of truth, produced by its collision with error.'[92] That view coincides with Mill's insistence on the airing of contradictory views for purposes of avoiding complacency and promoting critical understanding of our views.[93]

The young Hegel's assumptions are subtler than those of Mill's overarching empiricism. In our world, Hegel's critique of ethical positivity (*Positivitäts-Kritik*), of coerced morality, means that racism, sexism, or other forms of intolerance become immoral not because any institutional authority deems it so, but only insofar as

---

[89] See, e.g., Hegel, 1970a, pp. 216 ff.   [90] Lukács, 1967, pp. 52–67.
[91] Cf. Aristotle, *Nicomachean Ethics*, 3.1–3, *in* Aristotle, [4th century BCE] 1984, vol. 2, pp. 1752–7.
[92] Mill, 1991a, p. 21.
[93] See Section 4.7. See also Scanlon, 1977, pp. 162–8 (finding support in Mill and, to some degree, Kant).

we retain the socially interactive capacity to reach that insight.[94] To the hater's incentives to speak, government diktat indeed adds a second incentive, namely, to spurn government diktat *as such*. Recalling the discussion in Section 5.5, hate speakers gain an incentive to deny the Holocaust precisely *because* the state's censorship of public denials confirms their conspiracy theory of state complicity in the Holocaust 'myth'. They gain an incentive to voice racist remarks precisely *because* the state's punishment of them confirms its complicity in policies, which, by silencing dissenters, can be pursued with fewer challenges.

The young Hegel's critique of positivity foreshadows certain values of free speech identified in the twentieth century by Meiklejohn. Meiklejohn's overly narrow concept of 'political speech' has won little support,[95] but the overall aim of speech in a democracy, on his view, does rightly hold 'that all the citizens shall, so far as possible, understand the issues which bear upon our common life. That is why no idea, no opinion, no doubt, no belief, no counterbelief ... may be kept from them.'[96] In Scanlon's words, '[t]he harm of coming to have false beliefs is not one that an autonomous man could allow the state to protect him against through restrictions on expression.... In order to be protected by such a law a person would thus have to concede to the state the right to decide that certain views were false and, once it had so decided, to prevent him from hearing them advocated.'[97]

Again, as with other classic figures, from Plato and Aristotle through to Locke, Rousseau, or Kant, contrary interpretations of Hegel have been ventured, and my task is not to seek meticulous historical reconstructions, but to seek probative readings of those thinkers within the enquiry into the legitimating requirements of post-Second World War democracies. Central to Hegel's critique of Kant is a rejection of the categorical imperative's ahistorical, abstract absolutism, which reduces citizens to automatons, for whom, strictly speaking, no stronger link need exist than sheer obedience to positive law (*Legalität*).[98] For Hegel, intermediary social networks between the individual and the state, not only the family but also broader collective entities, are not merely incidental nor indeed altogether voluntarist. They are as fundamental to the ethical, or just, society as is Kant's prescription of individual citizenship.[99]

Citizenship requires not merely obedience to positive law, but a foundation of equal and mutual respect among citizens. Dignitarians argue that hate speech mars any such respect. On that view, hate speech bans merit fundamental, even constitutional stature. Heyman argues that 'hate speech clearly conflicts with what Hegel regards as the basic principle underlying the system of rights: the duty to *"respect others as persons"*.'[100] If, however, as Heyman rightly observes, Hegel 'does

---

[94] See, e.g., Vaneigem, 2003, pp. 14–15, 18–19, 22, 34–8. See also objections raised in France to the Gayssot law, which punishes Holocaust denial. Robitaille-Froidure, 2011, pp. 67–70; Vaneigem, 2003, pp. 25–6.

[95] See, e.g., Post, 1995, pp. 268–89.   [96] Meiklejohn, 1960, p. 75.

[97] Scanlon, 1977, p. 164.   [98] Hegel, [1807] 1970b, pp. 310–15.

[99] Hegel, [1820] 1970c, pp. 338–98.   [100] Heyman, 2009, p. 168 (quoting Hegel).

not explicitly address the problem of speech that denies recognition to others',[101] then Hegel *a fortiori* prescribes no penalties for the sheer expression of evil views, even in an evil way, and that duty of respect remains precisely in the realm of more general ethical concern, within broadly democracy-optimizing as opposed to democracy-legitimating conditions.

The problem with Heyman's appeal to Hegel is that it contradicts Hegel's always-peremptory concept of *Geist*, mind, as immersed within cultural and historical processes, which includes Hegel's critique of positivity, his critique of authoritatively decreed ethical truth, from which Hegel's own political models, on their own premises, draw their necessary justification. The whole point of Hegel's philosophy of mind is that no view or utterance can lie 'beyond' that which might be legitimately pondered by the mind as a product of interaction with the world. Even if we deem the crudest hate speech to be that which expresses not an idea but merely an 'inarticulate grunt', we must not forget that Hegel, unlike some of his Enlightenment predecessors, does not define one's human nature as a mutually exclusive opposite or negation of one's animal nature, but, to the contrary, locates visceral or animal responses at the outset, or 'first stage', in the mind's long trajectory to realize itself.

Some blame for Heyman's not uncommon view lies with Hegel himself for any real or apparent contradiction, as the hierarchical, not to mention undemocratic, structure of his later political philosophy indeed raises questions about its grounding in his philosophy of mind. I can therefore readily concede a role for bans to those who, reading the later Hegel literally, pre-suppose a constitutionally undemocratic state. It nevertheless remains that it is, on the terms of Hegel's own broader system, the legal model which must serve consciousness in and for itself (*das Bewußtsein an und für sich*), i.e., critical ethical consciousness, and not consciousness which must serve law.

Precisely insofar as we might resolve the contradiction in favour of bans within constitutionally undemocratic states, we must resolve it against them for any state that would retain Hegel's expressly foundational value of ethics acquired through critical reflection and not through positive law diktat, coercion, and compulsory liability. Hegel's view of a society and a culture that are not superseded by, but form integral parts of, law and politics is, moreover, nothing new. It had already been a cornerstone of Aristotle's ethical and political thought. Aristotle may indeed provide a less complex account. Crucial for Aristotle is that individual character and social interaction, far from being separate from politics, form its paramount foundation. His *Nicomachean Ethics* states essential traits of the active, participatory citizen, for whom the civic 'polity' of his *Politics* is designed.

Surely inspiring Hegel is the *Nicomachean Ethics*'s emphasis on friendship (φιλία, *philia*), not merely as a private relationship, but as the cornerstone of civic relationships.[102] As with Hegel, one might *prima facie* draw the conclusion

---

[101] Heyman, 2009, p. 168.   [102] See Section 4.12, text accompanying note 177.

that respect is not merely a teleological but a constitutionally foundational element of citizenship, easily legitimating the limits on expression represented by bans (unsurprisingly, Aristotle and Hegel have counted among the leading classical inspirations for contemporary communitarian thought). Aristotle's approach nevertheless casts doubt on that interpretation. As with Hegel, a cornerstone of Aristotle's thought is the character of truth itself. Truth, for Aristotle, is not of any one nature, but depends on its object. 'Theoretical' (abstract, logical, speculative, metaphysical), 'practical' (ethical, political), and 'productive' (industrial, artistic) modes of truth are all examined with respect to their properties and roles.

For Aristotle truth does include our experience of ethical rightness. His approach to the acquisition or expression of ethical ideas, however, is not in itself viewpoint-punitive. As with such everyday activities as eating or drinking, earning or spending—none of which, for Aristotle, have the highly individualist character we might attribute to them today, but are rather seen as deeply affecting our relationships to others and our capacities to help or to harm them—Aristotle constantly avoids bans as means of avoiding excesses. He instead insists that the citizen cultivate individual experience in order to appreciate ethics not by rote or through higher authority, let alone by coercion. Aristotle recognizes that regulations—criminal law, contract law, etc.—are necessary, but avoids punitive censorship as a means of engendering ethical truth or rightness.

If post-Second World War LSPDs have emerged through historically unprecedented practices, their gestational years find a mirror in Eastern and Central Europe. As we have seen, bans were implemented as part of broader controls, within a system strictly policing what would otherwise be recognized as broad-based, participatorily self-critical government. Soviet-dominated regimes 'taught' non-discrimination not with respect to their own histories or cultures, but with respect to intolerance in the West, instrumentalizing anti-discrimination values as sheer means of furthering a strictly monolithic party line. A figure like Angela Davis zealously promoted those regimes' condemnations of Western imperial or ethnic supremacist histories—histories always overlooking their own oppression of countless peoples and identities within the Soviet empire.[103] Unsurprisingly, within weeks or months of those regimes' collapse, the most hideous racisms and nationalisms were not so much born anew, but rather rose to the surface, having never had a chance to die.[104] One of Aristotle's famous observations is that all of us 'by nature desire to know.'[105] Albeit without reference to Aristotle, Vaneigem inadvertently radicalizes and more overtly politicizes that view. He ironically deems 'our natural propensity towards curiosity' to be a 'natural indiscretion'. He calls it an 'immoderate taste for investigation', which

---

[103] See Heinze, 2013c. Cf. Heinze, 2008a, pp. 121–33.
[104] See, e.g., Richter, 2012.
[105] *Metaphysics* 1.1.980ª22, in Aristotle, [4th century BCE] 1984, p. 1552.

'our civilisation's predatory mores have merchandised and appropriated within the odious cohort of inquisitorial and police practices.'[106] To protect human dignity through selective punishment of incorrect worldviews or viewpoints is to sacralize—the very sacralization that does not honour but rather 'kills' its adored object: 'Execration is born of adoration.'[107]

More accessible than Hegel in generating a serviceable model of the pluralist, post-Enlightenment democracy, are the insights of Benjamin Constant. Constant comes of age amidst the French Revolution. He holds office under Napoleon, witnessing Europe as a battleground between rationalist revolution and local, anti-universalist tradition.[108] Sharing Hegel's horror at the excesses of Jacobinism, Constant develops a strong liberal philosophy, while wary about the pitfalls of de-contextualized universalisms. Constant perhaps most clearly anticipates what I am calling democratic–historicism. He develops his positions not as a project for finding solutions not in the form of universalist algorithms transcending cultural contexts, but rather as emerging out of those contexts.[109] Methodologically, he therefore resembles Hegel more than Locke, Kant, Mill, Rawls, or Dworkin. Constant's liberalism seeks not to dissolve history into liberalism, but to situate liberalism within history. If the older Hegel tilts the synthesis of liberalism and historicism towards the latter's subordination of individual to state interests, Constant steers that synthesis in the opposite direction, underscoring necessary limits to that subordination.

No more than Aristotle, Rousseau, Kant, Hegel, Mill, or other classical figures can Constant yield tailored replies to our contemporary questions about hate speech bans. His culturally conscious liberalism nevertheless paves the way for a model of democratic public discourse more persuasive than formulaically liberal or stridently anti-liberal approaches.[110] A double synthesis is now at work—on the one hand, between democracy and historicism, to locate nodes at which they converge; and, on the other hand, between European and American approaches, whose divide is more of a surface, black-letter type, while the philosophical fundamentals for a concept of speech are shared through common Western roots. Those two syntheses are linked. The principles of speech that have emerged through the US First Amendment can be shown to be grounded within a synthesis of liberal and historicist traditions, in particular within the historical emergence of the LSPD.

Albeit not commenting on those early nineteenth-century synthetic projects of Constant or Hegel, Post describes a 'complex dialectic between two distinct and antagonistic but reciprocally interdependent forms of social organization', which he calls 'responsive democracy' and 'community'. Leaving aside Post's

---

[106] Vaneigem, 2003, p. 17.   [107] Vaneigem, 2003, p. 18.

[108] See, e.g., Todorov, 2004, pp. 31–65.   [109] Constant, [1815] 1997, pp. 483–91.

[110] Cf. Post's view of the 'complementary but hostile relationship' between democracy and community at Post, 1995, pp. 14–15, 17.

occasional penchant for theories of American exceptionalism, which exaggerate the Euro-American divide, we see how his book's salient theory of free speech turns out to have deep roots in a shared Western history. Post explains, '[w]hen the law attempts to organize social life based on the principle that persons are socially embedded and dependent'—and that, although Post does not specifically note it, is the open historicist concern running from Savigny and Hegel through to recent communitarian and critical writers—'it instantiates the social form of community.'[111]

Post continues with the contrasting point that when, on the other hand, the law 'attempts to organize social life based on the contrary principle that persons are autonomous and independent'—a hallmark of classical liberalism from Locke through to Kant, Mill, Rawls, and Dworkin—'it instantiates the social form of responsive democracy.'[112] Although Post does not expressly inscribe his project within those longer traditions, he re-discovers the synthesis that Constant had sought. Post invokes that 'dialectic' precisely in view of his, like Constant's, presumable scepticism towards traditional liberalism's ahistorical, formulaic approaches, rejecting 'any general "free speech principle"'.[113] Post's synthesis of those two strands in his concept of 'democratic community'[114] strongly echoes what I have ventured to call Constant's democratic–historicist synthesis.

Revisiting debates, alive since the Renaissance, about differences between ancient and modern politics, Constant recognizes that, in an industrializing, post-Enlightenment modernity, states are growing too large, both geographically and demographically, to warrant any return to an ideal of ongoing dialectic between individual and collective interests. By the nineteenth century, the increasing and centralizing power of modern states means that some sphere of individual liberty, active in the state yet beyond the reach of the state, must be safeguarded.[115] (Such views are sometimes voiced to justify not merely speech, but all civil and political rights, as fundamental within post-industrial states, even if such human rights cannot be called absolute in any trans-historical sense.)

Such a view bars the state from banning the expression of disapproved and offensive opinions from public discourse.[116] While acknowledging the loss, in any foreseeable future, of Athenian democratic and Roman republican citizenship ideals, Constant envisages the modern individual's protected sphere as a basis for preserving and exercising the role of the active citizen within the modern, ever more powerful state. Through an ideal of liberty anchored in inviolable citizenship, as

---

[111] Post, 1995, p. 179. Cf. Post, 1995, pp. 180–91.

[112] Post, 1995, p. 179. Cf. Post, 1995, pp. 180–91.

[113] Post, 1995, p. 16 (criticizing F. Schauer and G. Stone). See also Post's scepticism about algorithms taking the form of 'opaque phrases and tests'. Post, 1995, p. 177. Post, in turn, parallels his distinction between responsive democracy and community to that between, respectively, liberalism and communitarianism. Post, 1995, p. 193.

[114] Post, 1995, p. 179. Cf. Post, 1995, p. 191–6.

[115] Cf. Barendt, 2007, pp. 21–3; Nieuwenhuis, 2011, p. 35; Post, 1995, pp. 7, 137, 188–9.

[116] Cf. Post, 1995, p. 188.

a necessary guarantee for civic participation, the citizen-dissident secures some home, if far from an ideal one, within the modern bureaucratic, administrative, and regulatory state. The pluralist LSPD turns out to have been both strongly anticipated, yet also an important development within the history of democracies. Only by appreciating the historical specificity of the character and legitimating conditions of today's democracies can we find a politically legitimate solution to hateful expression as a broader social problem.

7

Conclusion

Hate speech has unquestionably led to violence and discrimination in democracies such as Germany's Weimar Republic, the immediate post-Cold War Yugoslavia, or Rwanda, and in less devastating but still grievous ways elsewhere. Since the 1960s, however, the model of the longstanding, stable, and prosperous democracy (LSPD) has been notable for its categorically different social dynamics, in which no such sweeps of devastating public mobilization have occurred. LSPDs have conspicuously lacked statistically demonstrable causation traceable from hate speech to cognizable patterns of discrimination or violence, despite ample quantities of hateful expression, over decades in LSPDs, irrespective of whether they maintain or lack bans.

The LSPD has proved historically distinctive in its capacity to undertake universal, pluralist primary education, to combat violence and discrimination against vulnerable groups, and to facilitate those groups' civic empowerment, even if improvements can certainly be made on those fronts, as a process that must always remain ongoing and vigilant. LSPDs are never viewpoint-neutral. They dispose of resources sufficient to protect vulnerable groups through pluralist and anti-discrimination policies, however, without having to impose viewpoint-selective penalties within public discourse.

Prohibitionists as well as oppositionists hit impasses when they assume static notions of democracy. Prohibitionists commit an inductive fallacy when they deem concrete dysfunctions of some societies designated as democratic to inhere within democracies generally. Oppositionists, on the other hand, commit a deductive fallacy when they apply identical criteria of political legitimacy to all democracies, irrespective of various states' histories and political circumstances. That assumption has posed problems for applications of Mill's famous harm principle, or for a writer like Dworkin, as formulaic approaches to free speech fail to take historically distinct forms of democracy into account. It is mistaken to assume any given society to be established as a democracy fully accountable for its legitimating conditions, merely through its adoption of constitutional texts or acts. That mistaken oppositionist deduction results from its universalist abstraction, neglecting an account of political history that must fundamentally distinguish between different kinds or phases of democracy, in particular, between LSPDs and non-LSPDs.

All LSPDs maintain liberal and rights-based elements. One reason their respectively liberal and democratic strands become difficult to distinguish is because, both conceptually and in practice, each element ends up entailing the other to a greater or lesser degree; but also because, historically, Western democracies emerged largely within cultures of pre-existing liberal values that had gained force within what were still constitutionally monarchical and aristocratic power structures. In view of that history, we still spontaneously formulate questions like, 'How much freedom of expression should "we"—i.e., the state—"give" to racists?', since that question does not conceptually conflict with conventional *liberal* values, which inherently entail legislative, judicial, or other government balancing of 'rights' against substantively or procedurally identified 'harms'. With respect to non-viewpoint-punitive expression in public discourse, however, such a question in its sheer formulation entails the erosion of democratic legitimacy.

Democracy ensues not from one-size-fits-all constitutional instruments but from textured cultural histories. We must recognize that not all democracies can always fully observe their legitimating conditions. Empirical considerations determine, at least in part, achievement and maintenance of LSPD status. But that role for a necessarily consequentialist calculus by no means precludes the distinct status of a deontological criterion governing the regulation of public discourse once LSPD status is plausibly achieved. In moral reasoning, it is coherent to assert that consequentialist reason must govern unless and until certain (i.e., LSPD) conditions are fulfilled; *and* that, once those conditions are met, and for as long as they prevail, deontological principles must then prevail.

Those latter principles justify this book's primary thesis, namely: *A longstanding, stable, and prosperous democracy (LSPD) can be fully held to its legitimating expressive condition, which requires the citizen's prerogative of non-viewpoint-punitive expression within public discourse.* Those general observations, and their ramifications, can be formulated through a series of general points, surveying some of this book's main arguments. Each point first states in italic typeface a familiar prohibitionist claim, then offers a response based on the ideas that have been set forth in the preceding chapters.

1. *The 'anti-absolutist' claim: No rights are absolute. Rights must be limited by respect for others and by the needs of society as a whole. There are many regulations of speech to which no one objects, punishing for example, commercial fraud or courtroom perjury. Hate speech bans are no different.*

Reply: It is the opponents of bans themselves, misleadingly branding themselves 'free speech absolutists', who are often at fault for provoking that straw-man thesis. None of the serious opponents of hate speech bans advocates free speech 'absolutism'. Nor can that concept have any serious meaning. If free speech were 'absolute', you could even lawfully kill someone, as long as you were doing it to make some statement.

The phrase 'free speech absolutism' has been replaced in this book with 'viewpoint absolutism'. Under that doctrine, a democracy cannot legitimately restrict expression within public discourse solely on grounds of its undesirable or even dangerous worldview. Viewpoint-selective bans on expression differ, then, from acts like fraud or perjury. Governments may certainly impose viewpoint-neutral and least-restrictive 'time, manner, and place' regulations on noise levels or on avoiding obstructions to free circulation, as long as the rules apply equally to all speakers.

2. *The 'not speech' claim: The crudest hate speech is not speech at all. It is the kind of 'inarticulate grunt' that can legitimately be banned because it forms 'no essential part of any exposition of ideas'.*

Reply: That thesis undoes itself. It is the bans themselves which elevate mindless growls into expression of an identifiable worldview, through their customary formulations, and through the motives invoked for combating hate speech. Both of those elements identify some content in the speech that is intelligible as hateful. An inarticulate content is a lack of meaningful content. It conveys, by definition, neither a hateful, nor a loving, nor any other message. If it were devoid of meaning, there would be no basis for comprehending it at all, let alone banning it as hateful.

3. *The 'Weimar' (or 'snowball') claim: Democracy under the Weimar Republic and other democracies show that unbridled speech can lead to atrocities. Some offensive remarks may, on the surface, appear harmless. But seemingly innocuous offences snowball into more pernicious forms. Once speech reaches a Nazi-like extreme, it becomes too late to avert the dangerous consequences.*

Reply: Not all democracies are alike. I have proposed the concept of the long-standing, stable, and prosperous democracy, as its three adjectives elicit a political model of historically recent vintage, dating no further back than the 1960s. Formal and informal structures of LSPDs have developed many buffers to intolerance, absent in weaker democracies. Social scientists diagnose multiple causes of discrimination within LSPDs. But none have traced hatred expressed within public discourse to anything like the levels of mobilization that hate speech has prompted in weaker democracies. Our freely and massively available media portrayals of violence show no proportionate correlation to incidents of violence in LSPDs, and have even correlated to periods of decreased violence.

4. *The 'direct harm' claim: Hate speech can cause psychological harm, just as hate-motivated violence causes physical harm. Children who are called 'nigger', 'Paki', 'dirty Jew', or 'queer' suffer just as much as when they are physically bullied. For adults, verbal abuse can render workplace, educational, or other environments unbearable.*

Reply: A more literally libertarian, 'sticks and stones' argument would indeed allow people to insult each other face-to-face. A position based chiefly on democratic principles, by contrast, entails no such view. Democracy requires only non-viewpoint-punitive expression within the sphere of open, public discourse. Rules governing stalking, harassment, interpersonal aggression, or codes of employment can continue to regulate expression outside democratic public discourse within democracies' established frameworks of individual rights. Here too, within LSPDs, no statistically reliable causation from patterns of hate speech within public discourse to patterns of violence or discrimination has been demonstrated, despite the proliferation of hateful and violent speech within our public (e.g., electronic) forums. There is even weighty evidence that, within Western democracies, hate speech bans, far from reducing, are prompting incidents of hate speech, as hate groups routinely refine their responses to existing bans and penalties.

5. *The 'indirect harm' claim: The harms of hate speech do not manifest in a conventionally empirical sense. From some phenomenological and socio-linguistic perspectives, hateful expression is 'illocutionary', i.e., not merely denoting hatred but enacting discrimination, and 'perlocutionary', disseminating adverse psychological effects regardless of any materially evident impact. Anthony Cortese describes a 'cultural transmission theory', whereby cultures 'pass hate on to each succeeding generation', making intolerance 'normal or conventional'. Hate speech germinates intolerance, not through discrete, causally traceable chains of events, but through cumulative effects. We must overcome conventional speech–conduct distinctions in order to achieve a more nuanced view of the harms of hate speech.*

Reply: An obstacle for those theories of indirect causation is not that they are wrong, but that they are too right by half. They prove more than any normative model of democracy can support. To designate the culturally transmissive, illocutionary, or perlocutionary force of utterances as a legally cognizable harm draws no obvious line around hateful expression as such. It reaches so far into expression, including violence or offence in countless works of film, music, art, literature, or colloquial speech, that recognizing such effects as harms would oblige the state to turn public expression into the wholly subordinated object of a government-operated licence.

One might reply, 'Perhaps we cannot curb all harmful speech, but surely we can curb the most extreme.' Yet that view merely presupposes what these theories of direct or indirect harm need to prove, namely that, in addition to generally harmful speech, there is a particularly egregious type which must be banned from public discourse. To be sure, we can and should challenge conventional speech–conduct distinctions on compelling phenomenological and socio-linguistic grounds. But it remains the case that precisely that distinction underlies both the rule of law and democratic citizenship, both of which shun the imposition of penalties on grounds of dangers which citizens *may* hypothetically pose through their unacceptable ideas.

6. *The 'dignitarian' claim: Everyone in a democracy ought to be able to exercise essential attributes of citizenship, but not so far as to impair either other individuals' equal citizenship prerogatives or their inherent human dignity.*

Reply: That claim merely transposes an argument about overall human freedom into an argument about citizenship. Individual freedoms can indeed be abused, and any democracy has endless norms to avoid or penalize such abuse. The fact that freedom can be abused does not, however, mean that citizenship can be abused. One citizen may certainly exercise certain citizen prerogatives to express disdain, hence symbolic denial, of other citizens, even in very crude ways. Within an LSPD, however, there is no sense in which the expression of a viewpoint within public discourse materially 'denies', i.e., abrogates, the citizenship prerogatives of any other individual.

7. *The 'hate crime' claim: The bans are necessary because hate speech is commonly connected to hate-based acts of murder, battery, rape, assault, and property theft or damage.*

Reply: Given the necessity both for democracy and for the rule of law of maintaining a speech–conduct distinction, the state can legitimately punish hate-motivated acts of murder, battery, and otherwise criminal acts without taking the additional step of viewpoint-selective bans on speech generally uttered in public discourse. That premise does not entail the conclusion that viewpoints expressed within public discourse can qualify as 'conduct' for purposes of prohibiting hate crimes.

8. *The 'disproportionate impact' claim: It's easy for those in privileged positions to oppose hate speech bans. They do not bear the brunt of hatred. But 'individual freedom' looks different from the viewpoint of subordinated groups.*

Reply: Contrary to the suggestions of some supporters of bans, members of minority groups do not all support bans, particularly after rigorous discussion has taken place. To suppose they do would essentialize those groups in ways that anti-discrimination efforts largely wish to challenge. Strong support for bans has been voiced, for example, by some African-American scholars; but others, including Harvard University Professors Henry Louis Gates, Jr. and Randall Kennedy, express doubts about bans as tools against discrimination.

A further component of the LSPD model, and a further reason why that model eschews a libertarian or 'value neutral' myth of the state, is that Western democracies have witnessed comprehensive deployments of state resources to combat discrimination in material ways that have proved both more politically legitimate, and more pragmatically effective, than viewpoint-selective penalties within public discourse. Those methods include such techniques as workplace non-discrimination laws, pluralist education in primary schools, and public awareness initiatives, particularly through the media.

9. *The 'morals and symbols' claim: Perhaps hate speech bans cannot be proven to reduce violence or discrimination. But governments still ought to take a clear stand in principle against hatred and intolerance. Even if democracies fight discrimination in other ways, they should ban hate speech to set an example both for their citizens and on the world stage. That is why Jeremy Waldron reproaches oppositionists for insisting that vulnerable groups must 'just learn to live with' hate speech.*

Reply: The notion that oppositionists assume a 'value-neutral state' remains one of the recurring myths in the free speech debates. There could never be any such thing as a 'value-neutral' state, nor have leading oppositionists advocated any such thing. LSPDs can overwhelmingly be shown to have taken such moral and symbolic stands—not always perfectly or without contradiction, but certainly in more than peripheral, lip-service ways. Measures like non-discrimination laws, pluralist primary education, and bans on individually targeted stalking, harassment, or 'fighting words', do indeed convey the state's moral and symbolic messages against intolerance or violence. In the arena of ideas, government still remains, by far, the loudest speaker. LSPDs have many legitimate ways of taking a moral stand, without having to censor views that depart from it. They have sound reasons for 'sending a message' or indeed 'sending a symbolic message' of pluralism either to their own societies or to the rest of the world; but they sacrifice legitimacy when they make such symbolic gestures by abridging the citizen's prerogative of non-viewpoint-punitive expression within public discourse.

10. *The 'civility' or 'decorum' claim: Perhaps in a democracy we must put up with intolerant speech, even at the risk of disproportionate impact on minorities. There is nevertheless a difference between 'message' and 'manner'. People may express hateful ideas, if they wish, but at some point it is legitimate for the state to punish the crudest forms. Society is right to care about common courtesy and basic decency. No society ever perished just because some sheer callousness was eliminated.*

   Reply: Gates recalls that, historically, African-Americans have not fared better in environments of polite speech. They have often still faced discrimination, yet without the blunt speech that would help them to make sense of it, and to plan their life strategies accordingly.

11. *The 'climate' claim: Waldron also proposes what he calls a theory of 'political aesthetics'. He observes that hate speech creates overall 'ugliness' or 'slow-acting poison', all of which 'become a disfiguring part of the social environment'.*

   Reply: Defenders of bans who invoke distinctly aesthetic considerations would, on their own logic, legalize, for example, T.S. Eliot's upmarket anti-Semitism, and even Brigitte Bardot's mid-market Islamophobia, but not Omar Bakri Mohammad's downmarket homophobia. As I have argued elsewhere,[1] Waldron's appeal to 'political aesthetics' merely re-phrases the age-old civility and decorum arguments, without acknowledging those rebuttals furnished by writers such as Gates, Kennedy, Shaw, and many others. If public discourse indeed is not merely important, but constitutive of democracy—even on a traditional, rights-based rationale—then governments cannot legitimately eliminate undesirable views on grounds of their sheer 'ugliness'.

12. *The 'Western tolerance' claim: Waldron further cites writers such as Locke, Diderot, Bayle, or Voltaire to elicit a firm tradition of liberalism which nevertheless remains compatible with hate speech bans.*

   Reply: Leaving aside some disheartening views of those writers, such as Voltaire's anti-Semitism or Locke's denigration of 'savage' peoples, most early modern writers had little or no experience of democracy, and in some cases—famously in Voltaire's case—did not support democratizing movements. In proposing the LSPD model, I seek to distinguish modern democracy's 'minimal' from its 'optimal' conditions. Comprehensive campaigns for pluralism and tolerance must certainly form part of government's democracy-optimizing initiatives, but not at the price of abrogating democracy's minimal, constitutively legitimating conditions, which include all citizens' prerogatives of non-viewpoint-punitive expression in public discourse.

---

[1] See Heinze, 2013b, pp. 610–15.

13. *The 'positive law' claim: Whether we like it or not, hate speech bans are a fait accompli. International, regional, and national legal systems have overwhelmingly approved at least minimal, and often capacious, hate speech bans. It's too late now to turn back the clock. The law has spoken.*

Reply: Societies like Israel, India, or Northern Ireland, at least at certain points in their histories, illustrate democratic areas in which stronger arguments can be made for hate speech bans, precisely because of their lack of a sufficiently stable character (although, as we have seen, in weaker democracies or non-democracies, hate speech bans are often used *against* vulnerable groups). It cannot be ruled out that, if applied in good faith, hate speech bans may assist law enforcement in stabilizing volatile situations. That does not, however, render bans legitimate within LSPDs.

14. *The 'majoritarian' claim: Western European democracies have hate speech bans because majorities of their citizens and politicians support bans in some form.*

Reply: It is a perennial mistake to confuse democracy with majoritarianism. Majority rule does constitute one rule of decision, but by no means exhausts forms of democratic lawmaking. The principle of majority rule only legitimately applies within a polity already constituted through certain inviolable principles of citizenship, which include citizens' essential democratic prerogatives of expression within public discourse.

15. *The 'balance of interests' claim: Freedom of speech is important, but must be balanced against other individuals' or groups' interests in fundamental dignity, respect, or non-discrimination. The imperative of individual freedom must be balanced against the imperative of equality.*

Reply: Here again, the distinct and recent LSPD model sets a necessary limit to our customary expectations of wholesale legislative or judicial balancing of rights or interests. There are countless ways in which governments can and rightly do balance competing interests in order to promote pluralism, but the limit of such legal powers lies at the point of a citizenry that constitutionally confers those powers. Within an LSPD, lawmakers retain no legitimacy in abridging constitutive citizen prerogatives in order, instrumentally, to pursue social goods, notably when those democracies have demonstrated more legitimate (and more effective) ways of achieving those social goods.

16. *The 'globalization' claim: The 2005 Danish Mohammad cartoons demonstrated how free speech in the West, even if harmless at home, can have violent repercussions around the world. In an era of electronic communications, overly broad freedoms of speech can have dangerous consequences.*

Reply: It is illegitimate to suggest that one society's norms of democratic citizenship must be abridged because members of another society respond adversely to its exercise. By analogy, in many societies, electronic communications revealing scantily clad Western women also provoke hostility, which, however, would scarcely justify calls for Western women to start covering themselves up.

17. *The 'incitement' claim: Hateful utterances are not merely expressive when they incite people to hatred, discrimination, or violence.*

Reply: The concept of criminal 'incitement' remains one of our vestiges of pre-modern law. The state retains power to punish people for harms that might, on a wholly speculative chain of causation, result from expressing ideas. To be sure, the criminal law rightly punishes acts of criminal solicitation or conspiracy, where material acts towards the commission of a crime can be identified. Crimes of 'incitement' do the opposite. They furnish the state with a dragnet device for sweeping up undesirables without having to show even a highly remote probability of harm actually resulting from the public expression of ideas.

18. *The 'regulated media' claim: If citizens retain a democratic prerogative to utter hate speech, then surely that means the state must give them air time.*

Reply: The only democratic imperative is that citizens not face legal penalties for their general viewpoints aired in public discourse. That condition does not impose, either in logic or in practice, any further requirement that the state actively facilitate the expression of hateful ideas. The state may not impose fines or prison sentences on speakers solely on grounds of their viewpoints aired in public discourse, but nor is the state obliged to offer them platforms.

19. *The 'cultural relativist' claim: Abolition of hate speech bans would represent yet another unwelcome Americanization. Unbridled speech may well suit US culture, but Europe has different histories and traditions.*

Reply: Attempts to explain the divergent trans-Atlantic approaches to hate speech on grounds of broader cultural differences between the US and Europe have failed. If prohibitionists were right about the dangers of hate speech, Western Europe would have progressed towards ever greater tolerance, and the US towards ever greater intolerance. The facts suggest no such straightforward causation. Intolerance breeds from many social factors. LSPDs share historically unprecedented levels of open, public debate, and cross-cultural comparison offers no evidence to suggest that the overall quality of European public discourse would be particularly degraded by abolishing bans on viewpoints expressed in the public sphere.

20. *The 'communitarian' claim: Western societies have become too individualist. Individual liberties are valued to the exclusion of the needs of others, and of society as a whole. Rights carry responsibilities, and freedom of speech should be exercised with due regard for the sensitivities of others.*

Reply: Here too, the distinct and recent LSPD model has, in the late twentieth and early twenty-first centuries, shown itself able to adopt rafts of measures to bolster such values, without having to punish individuals for publicly voicing general viewpoints delinquent in those values. Even ardent communitarians in the West recognize limits to the abridgment of individual freedom where core elements of democracy are at stake.

Many of the states best situated today to fulfil a democracy's legitimating expressive conditions are those that continue to impose extensive viewpoint-selective penalties within public discourse. That irony finds its explanation largely in a history of persecution at home or colonialism abroad. Explanation, however, cannot persist as justification. Under conditions of good-faith implementation, themselves often debatable, viewpoint-selective penalties within public discourse may offer justifiable means of preventing violence or discrimination, within societies which have not attained LSPD status, or when that status has become impaired. But such a concession means only that democracies must sometimes sacrifice legitimacy for purposes of assuring immediate safety or security.

Suppose for argument's sake that, as a normative matter, any one of our contemporary democracies draws its political legitimacy not only from the integrity of its duly empowered officials, institutions, and procedures, but also from certain substantive democratic norms. The irony remains that such substantive norms become effective, they enter positive law, only through those procedural channels. Non-viewpoint-punitive expression within public discourse may well constitute a democracy's legitimating expressive condition; but that condition remains purely hortatory, *de lege ferenda*, until it be incorporated into law.

As a practical matter, outside of revolutionary or otherwise foundational constitutional moments, officials spend little time pondering the minutiae of their regime's legitimating conditions. It seems unlikely, moreover, that many votes will ever be gained by *repealing* hate speech bans. Even people who strongly oppose them are unlikely to go so far as to make their repeal a central voting criterion. Once bans, which stand as symbolic gestures of inclusion for minorities, have become part of law, proposals for their repeal would set off alarm bells of distrust, irrespective of well-intentioned references to democratic legitimacy. Officials can certainly take steps to rein in bans, although such steps inevitably raise questions about their even-handed application. However, most politicians are unlikely to propose repealing them outright. Given such political realities, nothing argued in this book can offer any prediction on the likelihood that a more critical approach to bans will emerge within government or the judiciary. However, to lack certainty as to the constitutive role of public discourse is to lack a necessary feature of democratic citizenship.

Works Cited*

Abel, R. (1994). *Speech and Respect*. London: Stevens & Sweet & Maxwell.

Abrams, F. (2012). 'On American Hate Speech Law'. In M. Herz, & P. Molnar (eds.), *The Content and Context of Hate Speech: Rethinking Regulation and Responses* (pp. 116–26). Cambridge: Cambridge University Press.

Accattoli, L. (21 February 2006). 'Intolleranza e violenza non sono mai giustificate'. *Corriere della Sera (UK edition)*, p. 5.

Adorno, T. W. (1971). *Erziehung zur Mündigkeit* (1st edn). Frankfurt a.M.: Suhrkamp.

Akkermans, P., Bax, C., & Verhey, L. (1999). *Grondrechten: Grondrechten en grondrechtsbescherming in Nederland*. Deventer: Tjeenk Willink.

Alduy, C., & Wahnich, S. (2015). *Marine Le Pen prise aux mots: Décryptage du nouveau discours frontiste*. Paris: Seuil.

Alexander, L. (2005). *Is There a Right of Freedom of Expression?* Cambridge: Cambridge University Press.

Altman, A. (2012). 'Freedom of Expression and Human Rights Law: The Case of Holocaust Denial'. In I. Maitra, & M. K. McGowan (eds.), *Speech & Harm: Controversies over Free Speech* (pp. 24–49). Oxford: Oxford University Press.

Amin, A., & Thrift, N. (2013). *Arts of the Political: New Openings for the Left*. Durham, NC: Duke University Press.

Anderson, B. (4 February 2006). 'Stop Cringing and Stand Up for Our Own Values'. *The Times*, p. 29.

Andrews, K. (24 June 2015). *Obama's N-word Interview Shows America Needs Action, Not Talk, on Race*. Retrieved 1 October 2015, from *the Guardian*: http://www.theguardian.com/commentisfree/2015/jun/24/obama-n-word-interview-america-race-black-poor

Aristotle. ([4th century BCE] 1984). *The Complete Works of Aristotle: The Revised Oxford Translations* (Vols. 1 & 2). (J. Barnes, ed.) Princeton, New Jersey: Princeton University Press.

Aristotle. ([4th century BCE] 1999). *Nicomachean Ethics* (2nd rev'd ed.). (T. H. Irwin, trans.) Indianapolis: Hackett.

Article 19. (21 December 2012). *Prohibiting Incitement to Discrimination, Hostility or Violence*. Retrieved 1 October 2015, from Article 19: http://www.article19.org/resources.php/resource/3572/en/prohibiting-incitement-to-discrimination,-hostility-or-violence

Ash, T. G. (8 January 2015). *Against the Assassin's Veto*. Retrieved 1 October 2015, from Free Speech Debate: http://freespeechdebate.com/en/2015/01/against-the-assassins-veto/

Aslan, R. (8 February 2006). *Depicting Mohammed: Why I'm Offended by the Danish Cartoons of the Prophet*. Retrieved 1 October 2013 from Slate: http://www.slate.com/id/2135661/

Attacks Reported on Ugandans Newspaper 'Outed' as Gay. (22 October 2010). Retrieved 1 October 2015 from BBC News: http://www.bbc.co.uk/news/world-africa-11608241

---

* For citations to passages of classic texts originally published with chapter or section divisions predating modern editions, the full name of the work and original location of the cited passage appears in the corresponding footnote.

Austin, J. (1962). *How to Do Things with Words*. (J. Urmson, & M. Sbisà, eds.) Oxford: Oxford University Press.

Backes, U. (2011). 'Extremismus in Frankreich'. In E. Jesse, & T. Thieme (eds.), *Extremismus in den EU-Staaten* (pp. 131–48). Wiesbaden: Springer.

Baker, C. E. (1989). *Human Liberty and Freedom of Speech*. New York: Oxford University Press.

Baker, C. E. (2009). 'Autonomy and Hate Speech'. In I. Hare, & J. Weinstein (eds.), *Extreme Speech and Democracy* (pp. 139–57). Oxford: Oxford University Press.

Baker, C. E. (2011). 'Is Democracy a Sound Basis for a Free Speech Principle?' *Virginia Law Review*, 97(3), 515–29.

Baker, C. E. (2012). 'Hate Speech'. In M. Herz, & P. Molnar (eds.), *The Content and Context of Hate Speech: Rethinking Regulation and Responses* (pp. 37–80). Cambridge: Cambridge University Press.

Barendt, E. (2007). *Freedom of Speech* (2nd edn). Oxford: Oxford University Press.

Barghoorn, F. C., & Remington, T. F. (1986). *Politics in the USSR* (3rd edn). New York: Little, Brown & Co.

Basic Law for the Federal Republic of Germany. (2012). Retrieved 1 October 2015, from Juris: http://www.gesetze-im-internet.de/englisch_gg/englisch_gg.html

Batty, D. (15 March 2013). *UCL Bans Islamic Group from Campus in Row Over Segregated Seating*. Retrieved 1 October 2015 from *the Guardian*: http://www.guardian.co.uk/world/2013/mar/15/ucl-bans-islamic-group-over-segregation

BBC News. (19 February 2006). *Muslim Cartoon Row Timeline*. Retrieved 1 October 2015, from http://news.bbc.co.uk/1/hi/world/middle_east/4688602.stm

BBC World Service. (7 June 2015). *Newshour*. Retrieved 1 October 2015, from http://www.bbc.co.uk/programmes/p02slhqk

Beatty, M. (11 October 2011). *The 2010 Census: Race and Ethnicity*. Retrieved 1 October 2015, from Islamic Insights: http://islamicinsights.com/news/opinion/the-2010-census-race-and-ethnicity.html

Belavusau, U. (2013). *Freedom of Speech: Importing European and US Constitutional Models in Transitional Democracies*. London: Routledge.

Benedict-XVI. (13 May 2007). *Inaugural Session of the Fifth General Conference of the Bishops of Latin America and the Caribbean: Address of His Holiness Benedict XVI*. Retrieved 1 October 2013, from The Holy See: http://www.vatican.va/holy_father/benedict_xvi/speeches/2007/may/documents/hf_ben-xvi_spe_20070513_conference-aparecida_en.html

Benjamin, W. ([*ca.* 1920] 1965). 'Zur Kritik der Gewalt'. In W. Benjamin, *Zur Kritik der Gewalt und andere Aufsätze* (pp. 29–65). Frankfurt a.M.: Suhrkamp.

Bentham, J. ([1789] 2001). 'An Introduction to the Principles of Morals and Legislation'. In J. Bentham, *On Utilitarianism and Government* (pp. 75–309). London: Wordsworth.

Bentham, J. ([1843] 2001). 'Anarchical Fallacies'. In J. Bentham, *On Utilitarianism and Government* (pp. 383–459). London: Wordsworth.

Benz, W. (2005). *Was ist Antisemitismus?* (2nd edn). Munich: Beck.

Berka, W. (1999). *Die Grundrechte: Grundfreiheiten und Menschenrechte in Österreich*. Vienna: Springer.

Berlin, I. (1969). *Four Essays on Liberty*. Oxford: Oxford University Press.

Bleckmann, A. (1997). *Staatsrecht II—Die Grundrechte* (4th edn). Cologne: Carl Heymanns.

Bleich, E. (2011). *The Freedom to Be Racist?: How the United States and Europe Struggle to Preserve Freedom and Combat Racism*. New York: Oxford University Press.

Bodelier, R. (13 January 2006). *Extreme porno is een misdaad.* Retrieved 1 October 2015, from Liberales: http://www.liberales.be/essays/bodelierporno

Boyle, K. (2001). 'Hate Speech: The United States versus the Rest of the World?' *Maine Law Review,* 53, 487.

Brettschneider, C. (2010). 'When the State Speaks, What Should It Say? The Dilemmas of Freedom of Expression and Democratic Persuasion'. *Perspectives on Politics,* 8(4), 1005–16.

Brettschneider, C. (2012). *When the State Speaks, What Should It Say?: How Democracies Can Protect Expression and Promote Equality.* Princeton, NJ: Princeton University Press.

British National Party. (n.d.). Retrieved 1 October 2015, from https://www.bnp.org.uk/

Broder, H. M. (2 January 2010). *Der Westen und die Mohammed-Karikaturen: Im Mauseloch der Angst.* Retrieved 1 October 2015, from Spiegel Online: http://www.spiegel.de/politik/ausland/der-westen-und-die-mohammed-karikaturen-im-mauseloch-der-angst-a-669793.html

Brown, A. (2015). *Hate Speech Law: A Philosophical Examination.* Abingdon: Routledge.

Brudholm, T. (2015). 'Hate Crimes and Human Rights Violations'. *Journal of Applied Philosophy,* 32(1), 82–97.

Buntenbach, A., & Wagner, B. (2002). 'Warum wir trotzdem für ein Verbot der NPD sind'. In C. Leggewie, & H. Meier, *Verbot der NPD oder mit Rechtsradikalen leben?* (pp. 132–7). Frankfurt a.M.: Suhrkamp.

Burke, J. (7 November 2004). *The Murder that Shattered Holland's Liberal Dream.* Retrieved 1 October 2015, from *the Guardian*: http://www.theguardian.com/world/2004/nov/07/terrorism.religion

Busch, H. (2002). 'Der Beitrag des Verfassungsschutzes zum NPD-Verbotsantrag'. In C. Leggewie, & H. Meier, *Verbot der NPD oder mit Rechtsradikalen leben?* (pp. 56–63). Frankfurt a.M.: Suhrkamp.

Butler, J. (1997). *Excitable Speech: A Politics of the Performative.* New York: Routledge.

Caine, B. (2004–05). 'Trouble with Fighting Words: Chaplinsky v. New Hampshire Is a Threat to First Amendment Values and Should Be Overruled'. *Marquette Law Review,* 88(3), 441–562.

Cavalli, G. (21 February 2006). 'Mimun, nuove accuse Petruccioli lo difende'. *Corriere della Sera (UK edition),* p. 7.

Centre for Social Cohesion. (2010). *Radical Islam on UK campuses.* London: The Centre for Social Cohesion.

Christian Wins Case Against Employers Over Gay Marriage Comments. (16 November 2012). Retrieved 1 October 2105, from *the Guardian*: http://www.guardian.co.uk/law/2012/nov/16/christian-wins-case-gay-marriage-comments

Clavel, G. (3 November 2012). *Convention du Bloc Identitaire: dix ans de provocations de l'extrême droite radicale à l'ombre du FN.* Retrieved 1 October 2015, from the *Huffington Post*: http://www.huffingtonpost.fr/2012/11/01/convention-du-bloc-identitaire-provocations-extreme-droite-radicale_n_2057513.html

Cohen-Almagor, R. (2005). *Speech, Media and Ethics: The Limits of Free Expression.* Basingstoke, UK: Palgrave.

Colliver, S. (ed.) (1992). *Striking a Balance: Hate Speech, Freedom of Expression and Non-Discrimination.* Colchester, UK: Human Rights Centre, University of Essex.

Constant, B. ([1815] 1997). 'Principes de politique'. In B. Constant, & M. Gauchet (eds.), *Écrits politiques* (pp. 303–588). Paris: Gallimard.

Corcoran, M. G. (1989). 'Last Judgment of Plato's Gorgias: Mythos to You, Logos to Me'. *Iowa Law Review,* 74, 827.

Cornell, D., Rosenfeld, M., & Carlson, D. G. (eds.). (1992). *Deconstruction and the Possibility of Justice*. London: Routledge.

Cortese, A. (2006). *Opposing Hate Speech*. Westport, CT: Praeger.

Cram, I. (2006). *Contested Words: Legal Restrictions on Freedom of Speech in Liberal Democracies*. Aldershot, UK: Ashgate.

Cram, I. (2009). 'The Danish Cartoons, Offensive Expression, and Democratic Legitimacy'. In I. Hare, & J. Weinstein (eds.), *Extreme Speech and Democracy* (pp. 311–30). Oxford: Oxford University Press.

Cram, I. (2012). 'Coercing Communities or Promoting Civilised Discourse? Funeral Protests and Comparative Hate Speech Jurisprudence'. *Human Rights Law Review*, 12(3), 455–78.

Cranston, M. (1967). *Freedom*. New York: Basic Books.

Crouch, C. (2004). *Post-Democracy*. London: Polity.

Danish Cartoons Depicting the Prophet Muhammad Abuse Our Freedoms. (30 November 2005). Retrieved 1 October 2015, from Muslim Council of Britain: http://www.mcb. org.uk/danish-cartoons-depicting-the-prophet-muhammad-abuse-our-freedoms/

de Tocqueville, A. ([1835] 1999). *De la démocratie en Amérique* (Vol. 1). Paris: Garnier Flammarion.

Dearden, L. (28 February 2015). *George Galloway Demands £5,000 from Twitter Users Over 'Anti-Semitism' Libel and Threatens Legal Action*. Retrieved 1 October 2015 from *the Independent*: http://www.independent.co.uk/news/people/george-galloway-demanding-5000-from-twitter-users-over-antisemitism-libel-10077205.html

Delgado, R. (1989). 'Storytelling for Oppositionists and Others: A Plea for Narrative'. *Michigan Law Review*, 87, 2411.

Delgado, R. (1993). 'Words that Wound: A Tort Action for Racial Insults, Epithets, and Name Calling'. In M. Matsuda, C. Lawrence III, R. Delgado, & K. Crenshaw (eds.), *Words that Wound: Critical Race Theory, Assaultive Speech, and the First Amendment* (pp. 89–110). Boulder, CO: Westview Press.

Delgado, R. (1996). *The Rodrigo Chronicles: Conversations About America and Race*. New York: New York University Press.

Delgado, R. (2006). 'Foreword'. In A. Cortese, *Opposing Hate Speech* (pp. ix–xiii). Westport, CT: Praeger.

Delgado, R., & Stefancic, J. (1999). *Must We Defend Nazis?: Hate Speech, Pornography, and the New First Amendment*. New York: New York University Press.

Delgado, R., & Stefancic, J. (2004). *Understanding Words That Wound*. Boulder, CO: Westview.

Derrida, J. (2005). *Force de loi*. Paris: Galilée.

Dodd, V. (24 May 2013). *'I Still Have Influence', Says Preacher Who Claims He Schooled Woolwich Suspect*. Retrieved 1 October 2015, from *the Guardian*: http://www.theguardian. com/uk/2013/may/24/woolwich-murder-influence-preacher-suspect-adebolajo

Dollimore, J. (2004). *Radical Tragedy* (3rd edn). Basingstoke: Palgrave.

Dollimore, J., & Sinfield, A. (eds.). (1994). *Political Shakespeare: Essays on Cultural Materialism* (2nd edn). Manchester: Manchester University Press.

Dornbusch, C., & Raabe, J. (2005). 'Rechtsrock fürs Vaterland'. In A. Röpke, & A. Speit (eds.), *Braune Kameradschaften. Die militanten Neonazis im Schatten der NPD* (Vol. 2, pp. 67–86). Berlin: Links Verlag.

Dreier, R. (2002). 'Verfassung und "streitbare" Ideologie'. In C. Leggewie, & H. Meier, *Verbot der NPD oder mit Rechtsradikalen leben?* (pp. 81–8). Frankfurt a.M.: Suhrkamp.

D'Souza, F. (1992). 'Introduction'. In S. Colliver (ed.), *Striking a Balance: Hate Speech, Freedom of Expression* (pp. v–ix). London: Article 19.

Dworkin, R. (1977). *Taking Rights Seriously*. Cambridge, Massachusetts: Harvard University Press.

Dworkin, R. (11 June 1992). 'The Coming Battles over Free Speech'. *The New York Review of Books*, pp. 55–58, 61–64.

Dworkin, R. (1996). *Freedom's Law*. Oxford: Oxford University Press.

Dworkin, R. (2009). 'Foreword'. In I. Hare, & J. Weinstein, *Extreme Speech and Democracy* (pp. v–ix). Oxford: Oxford University Press.

Dworkin, R. (2012). 'Reply to Jeremy Waldron'. In M. Herz, & P. Molnar (eds.), *The Content and Context of Hate Speech: Rethinking Regulation and Responses* (pp. 341–4). Cambridge: Cambridge University Press.

Economist Intelligence Unit. (2014). *Democracy Index 2013*. London: *The Economist*.

Emerson, T.I. (1963). 'Toward a General Theory of the First Amendment'. *Yale Law Journal*, 72, 877–956.

Evans, C. (2009). 'Religious Speech that Undermines Gender Equality'. In I. Hare, & J. Weinstein (eds.), *Extreme Speech and Democracy* (pp. 357–74). Oxford: Oxford University Press.

Even Odious Ideas Must Be Allowed Expression. (12 November 2006). Retrieved 1 October 2015, from *Guardian/Observer*: http://www.theguardian.com/commentisfree/2006/nov/12/leaders.comment

Farrell, I. P. (17 September 2006). *Is There a Right of Freedom of Expression?* Retrieved 1 October 2015, from Notre Dame Philosophical Reviews: http://ndpr.nd.edu/news/25119-is-there-a-right-of-freedom-of-expression/

Faux, E. (6 January 2014). *Alain Vidalies: 'l'antisémitisme ce n'est pas une opinion, c'est un délit'*. Retrieved 1 October 2015, from Europe 1: http://www.europe1.fr/mediacenter/emissions/europe-nuit/videos/alain-vidalies-l-antisemitisme-ce-n-est-pas-une-opinion-c-est-un-delit-1763805

Feldman, S. M. (2000). *American Legal Thought from Premodernism to Postmodernism*. New York: Oxford University Press.

Fennema, M. (2009). *Geldt de vrijheid van meningsuiting ook voor racisten?* Amsterdam: Elsevier.

Fetscher, I. (1975). *Rousseaus politische Philosophie: Zur Geschichte des demokratischen Freiheitsbegriffs*. Frankfurt a.M.: Suhrkamp.

Fish, S. (1994). *There's No Such Thing as Free Speech: And It's a Good Thing, Too*. New York: Oxford Paperbacks.

Fisk, R. (6 February 2006). 'The Fury: Violent Protests Sweep Europe and Middle East as Cartoon Crisis Escalates'. *The Independent*, p. 1.

Fiss, O. (1996). *The Irony of Free Speech*. Cambridge, MA: Harvard University Press.

Foucault, M. (2009). *Le gouvernement de soi et des autres: Tome 2, Le courage de la vérité—Cours au Collège de France (1983–1984)*. Paris: Seuil.

Fredet, J.-G. (9–15 February 2006). 'Régis Debray: résistance, oui, inconscience, non!' *Le Nouvel Observateur* (No. 2153), pp. 56–7.

Freedman, R. (2013). *The United Nations Human Rights Council: A Critique and Early Assessment*. Oxford: Routledge.

Freiheitliche Partei Österreichs. (n.d.). Retrieved 1 October 2015, from http://www.fpoe.at/

Freitag, J., & Thieme, T. (2011). 'Extremismus in Schweden'. In E. Jesse, & T. Thieme (eds.), *Extremismus in den EU-Staaten* (pp. 329–43). Wiesbaden: Springer.

Front National. (n.d.). Retrieved 1 October 2015, from http://www.frontnational.com/

Gates, H. L. (1994). 'War of Words: Critical Race Theory and the First Amendment'. In H. L. Gates, A. Griffin, D. Lively, & N. Strossen (eds.), *Speaking of Race, Speaking of Sex: Hate Speech, Civil Rights, and Civil Liberties* (pp. 17–47). New York: NYU Press.

Gaus, G. (2010). *Liberalism*. Retrieved 1 October 2015, from Stanford Encyclopedia of Philosophy: http://plato.stanford.edu/entries/liberalism/

Geis, M.-E. (1994). 'Meinungsfreiheit und das Verbot rechtsradikaler Äußerungen'. *Recht der Jugend und des Bildungswesens*, 218–28.

Gelber, K. (2010). 'Freedom of Political Speech, Hate Speech and the Argument from Democracy: The Transformative Contribution of Capabilities Theory'. *Contemporary Political Theory*, 9(3), 304–24.

Gelber, K. (2012a). 'Reconceptualizing Counterspeech in Hate Speech Policy (with a Focus on Australia)'. In M. Herz, & P. Molnar (eds.), *The Content and Context of Hate Speech: Rethinking Regulation and Responses* (pp. 198–216). Cambridge: Cambridge University Press.

Gelber, K. (2012b). '"Speaking Back": The Likely Fate of Hate Speech Policy in the United States and Australia'. In I. Maitra, & M. K. McGowan (eds.), *Speech & Harm: Controversies over Free Speech* (pp. 50–71). Oxford: Oxford University Press.

Geoghegan, T. (30 December 2013). *Who, What, Why: What is the Quenelle Gesture?* Retrieved 1 October 2015, from BBC: http://www.bbc.co.uk/news/blogs-magazine-monitor-25550581

Gilens, M., & Page, B. I. (2014). 'Testing Theories of American Politics: Elites, Interest Groups, and Average Citizens'. *Perspectives on Politics*, 12(3), 564–81.

Gonzalvez, S. (11 December 2014). *Christiane Taubira: "Le racisme n'est pas une opinion. C'est un délit."*. Retrieved 1 October 2015, from Lyon Bondy Blog: http://lyonbondy-blog.fr/nouveau/christiane-taubira-le-racisme-nest-pas-une-opinion-cest-un-delit/

Goodall, K. (2010). 'Challenging Hate Speech: Incitement to Hatred on Grounds of Sexual Orientation in England, Wales and Northern Ireland'. In P. C. Chan (ed.), *Protection of Sexual Minorities since Stonewall* (pp. 79–100). London: Routledge.

Gordon, R. W. (2012). 'Critical Legal Histories Revisited: A Response'. *Law & Social Inquiry*, 37(1), 200–15.

Goyard-Fabre, S. (1992). *Les fondements de l'ordre juridique*. Paris: Presses Universitaires de France.

Goyard-Fabre, S. (1997). *Les Principes philosophiques du droit politique moderne*. Paris: Presses Universitaires de France.

Greenawalt, K. (1989a). *Speech, Crime and the Uses of Language*. Oxford: Oxford University Press.

Greenawalt, K. (1989b). 'Free Speech Justifications'. *Columbia Law Review*, 89, 119–55.

Greene, J. (2012). 'Hate Speech and the Demos'. In M. Herz, & P. Molnar (eds.), *The Content and Context of Hate Speech: Rethinking Regulation and Responses* (pp. 92–115). Cambridge: Cambridge University Press.

Grimm, D. (2002). 'Über den Umgang mit Parteiverboten'. In C. Leggewie, & H. Meier (eds.), *Verbot der NPD oder mit Rechtsradikalen leben?* (pp. 138–44). Frankfurt a.M.: Suhrkamp.

Grimm, D. (2009a). 'Freedom of Speech in a Globalized World'. In I. Hare, & J. Weinstein (eds.), *Extreme Speech and Democracy* (pp. 11–22). Oxford: Oxford University Press.

Grimm, D. (2009b). 'The Holocaust Denial Decision of the Federal Constitutional Court of Germany'. In I. Hare, & J. Weinstein (eds.), *Extreme Speech and Democracy* (pp. 557–61). Oxford: Oxford University Press.

Groh, K. (2002). 'Reanimation der "wehrhaften" Demokratie?' In C. Leggewie, & H. Meier (eds.), *Verbot der NPD oder mit Rechtsradikalen leben?* (pp. 89–97). Frankfurt a.M.: Suhrkamp.

Günther, K. (2000). 'The Denial of the Holocaust: Employing Criminal Law to Combat Anti-Semitism in Germany'. *Tel Aviv University Studies in Law*, 15, 51–66.

Habermas, J. (1973). 'Wahrheitstheorien'. In H. Fahrenbach (ed.), *Wirklichkeit und Reflexion* (pp. 211–65). Pfüllingen: Neske.

Hadfield, A. (2005). *Shakespeare and Republicanism*. Cambridge: Cambridge University Press.

Hare, I. (2009a). 'Extreme Speech under International and Regional Human Rights Standards'. In I. Hare, & J. Weinstein (eds.), *Extreme Speech and Democracy* (pp. 62–80). Oxford: Oxford University Press.

Hare, I. (2009b). 'Blasphemy and Incitement to Religious Hatred: Free Speech Dogma and Doctrine'. In I. Hare, & J. Weinstein (eds.), *Extreme Speech and Democracy* (pp. 289–310). Oxford: Oxford University Press.

Hare, I., & Weinstein, J. (eds.). (2009). *Extreme Speech and Democracy*. Oxford: Oxford University Press.

Hart, H. (1994). *The Concept of Law* (2nd edn). (P. A. Bulloch, & J. Raz (eds.) Oxford: Oxford University Press.

'Hausmitteilung'. (4 November 2013). *Der Spiegel*, p. 5.

Haworth, A. (1998). *Free Speech*. London: Routledge.

Healy, T. (2013). *The Great Dissent: How Oliver Wendell Holmes Changed His Mind—and Changed the History of Free Speech in America*. New York: Metropolitan Books.

Hegel, G. W. (1970a). 'Frühe Schriften'. In G. W. Hegel, *G.W.F. Hegel: Werke* (Vol. 1). Frankfurt: Suhrkamp.

Hegel, G. W. ([1807] 1970b). 'Phänomenologie des Geistes'. In G. W. Hegel, *Georg Wilhelm Friedrich Hegel: Werke* (Vol. 14). Frankfurt: Suhrkamp.

Hegel, G. W. ([1820] 1970c). 'Grundlinien der Philosophie des Rechts'. In G. W. Hegel, *G.W.F. Hegel: Werke* (Vol. 7). Frankfurt: Suhrkamp.

Heinze, E. (2003). *The Logic of Liberal Rights*. London: Routlege.

Heinze, E. (2005). *The Logic of Constitutional Rights*. Aldershot: Ashgate.

Heinze, E. (2006). 'Viewpoint Absolutism and Hate Speech'. *Modern Law Review*, 69, 543–82.

Heinze, E. (2007). 'Towards the Abolition of Hate Speech Bans'. In T. Loenen, & J. Goldschmidt (eds.), *Religious Pluralism and Human Rights* (pp. 295–309). Antwerp: Interstentia.

Heinze, E. (2008a). 'Truth and Myth in Critical Race Theory and LatCrit: Human Rights and the Ethnocentrism of Anti-Ethnocentrism'. *National Black Law Journal*, 20, 107–62.

Heinze, E. (2008b). 'Even-handedness and the Politics of Human Rights'. *Harvard Human Rights Journal*, 21, 7–46.

Heinze, E. (2009a). 'Wild-West Cowboys versus Cheese-Eating Surrender Monkeys: Some Problems in Comparative Approaches to Extreme Speech'. In I. Hare, & J. Weinstein (eds.), *Extreme Speech and Democracy* (pp. 182–203). Oxford: Oxford University Press.

Heinze, E. (2009b). 'Cumulative Jurisprudence and Hate Speech: Sexual Orientation and Analogies to Disability, Age and Obesity'. In I. Hare, & J. Weinstein (eds.), *Extreme Speech and Democracy*. Oxford: Oxford University Press.

Heinze, E. (2009c). 'Heir, Celebrity, Martyr, Monster: Legal and Political Legitimacy in Shakespeare and Beyond'. *Law & Critique*, 20(1), 79–103.

Heinze, E. (2009d). 'Imperialism and Nationalism in Early Modernity: The "Cosmopolitan" and the "Provincial" in Shakespeare's Cymbeline'. *Journal of Social & Legal Studies*, 18(3), 139–68.

Heinze, E. (2009e). 'Power Politics and the Rule of Law: Shakespeare's First Historical Tetralogy and Law's "Foundations"'. *Oxford Journal of Legal Studies*, 29, 230–63.

Heinze, E. (2009f). 'The Metaethics of Law: Book One of Aristotle's Nicomachean Ethics'. *International Journal of Law in Context*, 6(1), 23–44.

Heinze, E. (2010). '"This Power Isn't Power if It's Shared": Law and Violence in Jean Racine's La Thébaïde'. *Law & Literature*, 22(1), 76–109.

Heinze, E. (2012a). '"Where Be His Quiddities Now?": Law and Language in Hamlet'. In M. Freeman, & F. Smith (eds.), *Law and Language: Current Legal Issues* (Vol. 15) (201–20). Oxford: Oxford University Press.

Heinze, E. (2012b). 'Victimless Crimes'. In R. Chadwick (ed.), *Encyclopedia of Applied Ethics* (2nd edn, Vol. 4, pp. 471–82). London: Elsevier/Academic Press.

Heinze, E. (2013a). *The Concept of Injustice*. London: Routledge.

Heinze, E. (2013b). 'Hate Speech and the Foundations of Democracy'. *International Journal of Law in Context*, 9(4), 590–617.

Heinze, E. (25 November 2013c). *Angela Davis's Racism: A Glance at Morality and History*. Retrieved 1 October 2015, from Critical Legal Thinking: http://criticallegalthinking.com/2013/11/25/angela-daviss-racism-glance-morality-history/

Heinze, E. (5 June 2014a). *Are All Forms of Prejudice Really Equal?* Retrieved 1 October 2015, from Left Foot Forward: http://leftfootforward.org/2014/06/are-all-forms-of-prejudice-really-equal/

Heinze, E. (15 August 2014b). *Anti-Semitism is Not Held to Account in the Same Way as Other Forms of Bigotry*. Retrieved 1 October 2015, from *the Conversation*: https://theconversation.com/anti-semitism-is-not-held-to-account-in-the-same-way-as-other-forms-of-bigotry-30482

Heinze, E. (11 February 2015a). *British MP Exploits Vague Defamation Law to Sue Guardian Journalist*. Retrieved 1 October 2015 from *the Conversation*: https://theconversation.com/british-mp-exploits-vague-defamation-law-to-sue-guardian-journalist-37486

Heinze, E. (1 January 2015b). 'Torture Allegations, Racial Conflicts … and Leadership on Human Rights?' *People's Daily (China)*, p. 1 [English translation at: http://www.qmul.ac.uk/media/news/items/hss/146305.html].

Heinze, E. ((forthcoming 2016a)). 'Ten arguments for—and against—"no-platforming"'. In *Free Speech Debate*: http://freespeechdebate.com/en/

Heinze, E. (forthcoming 2016b). 'Towards a Legal Concept of Hatred: Democracy, Ontology, and the Limits of Deconstruction'. In T. Brudholm, & B. S. Johansen (eds.), *Hate, Politics and Law*. Oxford: Oxford University Press.

Heinze, E., & Marcou, A. (forthcoming 2016). 'Review of *The Struggle for European Private Law: A Critique of Codification* by Leone Niglia'. *Journal of Comparative Law*, 10(1).

Herz, M., & Molnar, P. (eds.). (2012). *The Content and Context of Hate Speech: Rethinking Regulation and Responses*. Cambridge: Cambridge University Press.

Heyman, S. (2008). *Free Speech and Human Dignity*. New Haven, CT: Yale University Press.

Heyman, S. J. (2009). 'Hate Speech, Public Discourse, and the First Amendment'. In I. Hare, & J. Weinstein (eds.), *Extreme Speech and Democracy* (pp. 158–81). Oxford: Oxford University Press.

Hobbes, T. ([1651] 1998). *Leviathan*. (J. C. Gaskin (ed.)) Oxford: Oxford University Press.

Hochhuth, M. (2006). *Die Meinungsfreiheit im System des Grundgesetzes*. Tübingen: Mohr Siebeck.

Hoffer, W. H. (2012). *Plessy v. Ferguson: Race and Inequality in Jim Crow America*. Lawrence, KS: University Press of Kansas.

Holmes, S. (2012). 'Waldron, Machiavelli, and Hate Speech'. In M. Herz, & P. Molnar (eds.), *The Content and Context of Hate Speech: Rethinking Regulation and Responses* (pp. 345–51). Cambridge: Cambridge University Press.

Hoppe, C. (2008). *Ist es gerecht, das Grundrecht auf Meinungsfreiheit zugunsten des Rechts der Menschenwürde in bestimmten Fällen einzuschränken?* Norderstedt: Grin Verlag.

Howe, A. (1998). 'Review of Judith Butler, Excitable Speech'. *International Journal for the Semiotics of Law*, 11(31), 95–104.

IERA event at UCL on 9 March. (11 March 2013). Retrieved 1 October 2015, from UCL: http://www.ucl.ac.uk/news/news-articles/0313/11032013-meeting

Imbleau, M. (2003). *La négation du génocide nazi, liberté d'expression ou crime raciste?: Le négationnisme de la Shoah en droit international et comparé*. Paris: L'Harmattan.

International Convention on the Elimination of All Forms of Racial Discrimination. (regularly updated). Retrieved 1 October 2015 from United Nations Treaty Collection: https://treaties.un.org/Pages/ViewDetails.aspx?src=treaty&mtdsg_no=iv-2&chapter=4&lang=en

International Covenant on Civil and Political Rights. (regularly updated). Retrieved 1 October 2015 from United Nations Treaty Collection: https://treaties.un.org/pages/viewdetails.aspx?chapter=4&src=treaty&mtdsg_no=iv-4&lang=en

Jacobson, A., & Schlink, B. (2012). 'Hate Speech and Self-Restraint'. In M. Herz, & P. Molnar (eds.), *The Content and Context of Hate Speech: Rethinking Regulation and Responses* (pp. 217–41). Cambridge: Cambridge University Press.

James, W. ([1907] 1981). *Pragmatism*. Indianapolis, IN: Hackett.

Jaschke, H.-G. (2006). *Politischer Extremismus*. Wiesbaden: VS Verlag für Sozialwissenschaften.

Jesse, E. (2011). 'Extremismus in Deutschland'. In E. Jesse, & T. Thieme (eds.), *Extremismus in den EU-Staaten* (pp. 83–98). Wiesbaden: Springer.

Josende, L. (2010). *Liberté d'expression et démocratie: Réflexion sur un paradoxe*. Brussels: Bruylant.

Jourde, P. (9–15 February 2006). 'La pédagogie par le blasphème'. *Le Nouvel Observateur* (No. 2153), p. 55.

Kailitz, S. (2004). *Politischer Extremismus in der Bundesrepublik Deutschland*. Wiesbaden: VS Verlag für Sozialwissenschaften.

Kant, I. ([1785] 1968). 'Grundlegung zur Metaphysik der Sitten'. In W. Weischedel (ed.), *Werkausgabe* (Vol. 7, pp. 5–104). Frankfurt: Suhrkamp.

Kelly, P. (2003). 'J.S. Mill on Liberty'. In D. Boucher, & P. Kelly (eds.), *Political Thinkers: From Socrates to the Present* (pp. 324–42). Oxford: Oxford University Press.

Kelsen, H. ([1949] 2005). *General Theory of Law & State*. New Brunswick, NJ: Transaction.

Kelsen, H. (1920). *Vom Wesen und Wert der Demokratie*. Tübingen: J.C.B. Mohr.

Kennedy, R. (2003). *Nigger: The Strange Career of a Troublesome Word*. New York: Vintage.

King, M. L. (16 April 1963). *Letter from Birmingham Jail*. Retrieved 1 October 2013, from Martin Luther King, Jr., Research & Education Institute (Stanford University): http://mlk-kpp01.stanford.edu/index.php/resources/article/annotated_letter_from_birmingham/

Kiyak, M. (13 December 2011). *Lieber deutscher Nazi!* Retrieved 1 October 2015, from Frankfurter Rundschau: http://www.fr-online.de/meinung/kolumne-lieber-deutscher-nazi-,1472602,11445174.html

Kraudzun, H. (3 March 2011). *Fußball-Profi Owomoyela verliert gegen die NPD*. Retrieved 1 October 2015, from Märkische Oderzeitung: http://www.moz.de/artikel-ansicht/dg/0/1/285599/

Kühn, A., & Rosenbach, M. (8 July 2013). *Das Grauen am Abend*. Retrieved 1 October 2015, from *Der Spiegel*: http://www.spiegel.de/spiegel/print/d-102241790.html

Langton, R. (1993). 'Speech Acts and Unspeakable Acts'. *Philosophy and Public Affairs*, 22, 305–30.

Langton, R. (2012). 'Beyond Belief: Pragmatics in Hate Speech and Pornography'. In I. Maitra, & M. K. McGowan (eds.), *Speech & Harm: Controversies over Free Speech* (72–93). Oxford: Oxford University Press.

Lawrence, C. (1993). 'If He Hollers Let Him Go: Regulating Racist Speech on Campus'. In M. Matsuda, C. Lawrence III, R. Delgado, & K. Crenshaw (eds.), *Words that Wound: Critical Race Theory, Assaultive Speech, and the First Amendment* (53–88). Boulder, CO: Westview Press.

Le Devin, W., & Albertini, D. (22 July 2014). *Antisémitisme, les réseaux de la haine*. Retrieved 1 October 2015, from Libération: http://www.liberation.fr/societe/2014/07/22/antisemitisme-les-reseaux-de-la-haine_1068556

Le Monde. (1 January 2014). *Dieudonné: une décision exceptionnelle*. Retrieved 1 October 2015, from *Le Monde*: http://www.lemonde.fr/idees/article/2014/01/11/dieudonne-une-decision-exceptionnelle_4346435_3232.html

Le Nouvel Observateur. (13 November 2013). 'Le racisme n'est pas une opinion, c'est un gnon aux valeurs de la République'. Retrieved 1 October 2015, from http://tempsreel.nouvelobs.com/politique/20131113.OBS5169/le-racisme-n-est-pas-une-opinion-c-est-un-gnon-aux-valeurs-de-la-republique.html

Lebreton, G. (1999). *Libertés publiques et droits de l'homme* (4th edn). Paris: Armand Colin.

Lee, S. (1990). *The Costs of Free Speech*. London: Faber & Faber.

Leggewie, C., & Meier, H. (2002a). *Verbot der NPD oder mit Rechtsradikalen leben?* Frankfurt a.M.: Suhrkamp.

Leggewie, C., & Meier, H. (2002b). 'Das NDP-Verbot in der Diskussion'. In C. Leggewie, & H. Meier (eds.), *Verbot der NPD oder mit Rechtsradikalen leben?* (pp. 9–13). Frankfurt a.M.: Suhrkamp.

Leigh, I. (2009). 'Homophobic Speech, Equality Denial, and Religious Expression'. In I. Hare, & J. Weinstein (eds.), *Extreme Speech and Democracy* (pp. 375–99). Oxford: Oxford University Press.

Lévy, A. (11 June 2013). *Les groupes violents, plus faciles à fustiger qu'à interdire*. Retrieved 1 October 2015, from *L'Opinion*: http://www.lopinion.fr/9-juin-2013/groupes-violents-plus-faciles-a-fustiger-qu-a-interdire-868

Lewis, A. (2008). *Freedom for the Thought We Hate: A Biography of the First Amendment*. New York: Basic Books.

Litwin, F., & Mansur, S. (29 January 2013). *Mistaking Islamism for Islam*. Retrieved 1 October 2015, from *Ottawa Citizen*: http://www2.canada.com/ottawacitizen/news/archives/story.html?id=eb717a8e-e8a0-4040-a4c7-72001d184655&p=2

Lobban, M. (1991). *The Common Law and English Jurisprudence 1760–1850*. Oxford: Oxford University Press.

Locke, J. ([1689] 1983). *A Letter Concerning Toleration*. (J. Tully (ed.)) Indianapolis, IN: Hackett.

Locke, J. ([1689] 1988). 'Second Treatise of Civil Government'. In P. Laslett (ed.), *Two Treatises of Government* (pp. 284–445). Cambridge: Cambridge University Press.

Loveland, I. (ed.). (1999). *Importing the First Amendment: Freedom of Speech and Expression in American, English and European Law*. Chicago: Northwestern University Press.

Lucardie, P., Voerman, G., & Wielenga, F. (2011). 'Extremismus in den Niederlanden'. In E. Jesse, & T. Thieme (eds.), *Extremismus in den EU-Staaten* (pp. 247–63). Wiesbaden: Springer.

Lukács, G. (1967). 'Der junge Hegel: Über die Beziehungen von Dialektik und Ökonomie'. In G. Lukács, *Georg Lukács Werke* (3rd edn, Vol. 8). Zurich: Luchterhand.

Macchiavelli, N. (1995). *Il Principe*. (G. Inglese (ed.)) Turin: Einaudi.

Machiavelli, N. ([1532] 1979). *The Prince*. (P. Bondanella, & M. Musa, Trans.) Oxford: Oxford University Press.

MacIntyre, A. (2007). *After Virtue* (3rd edn). Notre Dame, Indiana: University of Notre Dame Press.

MacKinnon, C. A. (1996). *Only Words*. Cambridge, MA: Harvard University Press.

Maitra, I. (2012). 'Subordinating Speech'. In I. Maitra, & M. K. McGowan (eds.), *Speech & Harm: Controversies over Free Speech* (pp. 94–120). Oxford: Oxford University Press.

Maitra, I., & McGowan, M. K. (2012a). *Speech & Harm: Controversies over Free Speech*. Oxford: Oxford University Press.

Maitra, I., & McGowan, M. K. (2012b). 'Introduction and Overview'. In I. Maitra, & M. K. McGowan (eds.), *Speech & Harm: Controversies over Free Speech* (pp. 1–23). Oxford: Oxford University Press.

Majed, R. (11 January 2013). *Tunisian Activists Call for "National Kissing Day" Saturday*. Retrieved 1 October 2015, from NOW News: https://now.mmedia.me/lb/en/international/tunisian_activists_call_for_national_kissing_day_satur day

Majic, D. (11 November 2012). *Neueste Rechte*. Retrieved 1 October 2015, from *Frankfurter Rundschau*: http://www.fr-online.de/die-neue-rechte/rechtsextremismus-neueste-rechte,10834438,20843510.html

Malanczuk, P. (1997). *Akehurst's Modern Introduction to International Law*. London: Routledge.

Malik, K. (July 2007). *Don't Incite Censorship*. Retrieved 1 October 2015, from Index on Censorship: http://www.indexoncensorship.org/2007/07/don%E2%80%99t-incite-censorship/

Malik, M. (2009). 'Extreme Speech and Liberalism'. In I. Hare, & J. Weinstein (eds.), *Extreme Speech and Democracy* (pp. 96–120). Oxford: Oxford University Press.

Mann, H. (2010). *Der Untertan* (16th edn). Frankfurt am Main: Fischer.

Marshall, P., & Shea, N. (2011). *Silenced: How Apostasy and Blasphemy Codes are Choking Freedom Worldwide*. New York: Oxford University Press.

Martinet, A. (2008). *Eléments de linguistique générale* (5th edn). Paris: Armand Colin.

Marx, K. ([1843] 1976). 'Bemerkungen über die neueste preußische Zensurinstruktion'. In K. Marx, & F. Engels, *Werke* (Vol. 1, pp. 3–25). Berlin: Dietz Verlag.

Marx, K. ([1844] 1956). 'Zur Judenfrage'. In IML/ZK-SED (ed.), *Karl Marx—Friedrich Engels: Werke* (Vol. 1, pp. 347–77). Berlin: Dietz.

Matsuda, M. et al. (eds.). (1993). *Words that Wound: Critical Race Theory, Assaultive Speech, and the First Amendment*. Boulder, CO: Westview Press.

Matsuda, M. (1993). 'Public Response to Racist Speech: Considering the Victim's Story'. In M. Matsuda, C. Lawrence III, R. Delgado, & K. Crenshaw (eds.), *Words that Wound: Critical Race Theory, Assaultive Speech, and the First Amendment* (pp. 17–51). Boulder, CO: Westview Press.

Matussek, M. (12 February 2014). *Ich bin wohl homophob. Und das ist auch gut so*. Retrieved 1 October 2015, from *Die Welt*: http://www.welt.de/debatte/kommentare/article124792188/Ich-bin-wohl-homophob-Und-das-ist-auch-gut-so.html#disqus_thread

McCormack, N. (2009). 'Peer Review and Legal Publishing: What Law Librarians Need to Know about Open, Single-Blind, and Double-Blind Reviewing'. *Law Library Journal*, 10(1), 59–70.

McGoldrick, D. (2009). 'Extreme Religious Dress: Perspectives on Veiling Controversies'. In I. Hare, & J. Weinstein (eds.), *Extreme Speech and Democracy* (pp. 400–29). Oxford: Oxford University Press.

McGowan, M. K. (2012). 'On "Whites Only" Signs and Racist Hate Speech: Verbal Acts of Racial Discrimination'. In I. Maitra, & M. K. McGowan (eds.), *Speech & Harm: Controversies over Free Speech* (pp. 121–47). Oxford: Oxford University Press.

Mchangama, J. (1 December 2011). *The Sordid Origin of Hate-Speech Laws.* Retrieved 1 October 2015, from *Policy Review*, No. 170: http://www.hoover.org/publications/policy-review/article/100866

Mchangama, J. (1 December 2012). *The Harm in Hate Speech Laws (review of J Waldron, 'The Harm in Hate Speech')*. Retrieved 1 October 2015, from *Policy Review*, No. 176: http://www.hoover.org/publications/policy-review/article/135466

Meier, H. (2002). '"Ob eine konkrete Gefahr besteht, ist belanglos": Kritik der Verbotsanträge gegen die NPD'. In C. Leggewie, & H. Meier (eds.), *Verbot der NPD oder mit Rechtsradikalen leben?* (pp. 14–29). Frankfurt a.M.: Suhrkamp.

Meiklejohn, A. (1948). *Free Speech and Its Relation to Self-Government.* New York: Harper & Bros.

Meiklejohn, A. (1960). *Political Freedom: The Constitutional Powers of the People.* Westport, CT: Greenwood.

Mengistu, Y. L. (2012). 'Shielding Marginalized Groups from Verbal Assaults without Abusing Hate Speech Laws'. In M. Herz, & P. Molnar (eds.), *The Content and Context of Hate Speech: Rethinking Regulation and Responses* (pp. 352–77). Cambridge: Cambridge University Press.

Merleau-Ponty, M. (1945). *La phénoménologie de la perception.* Paris: Gallimard.

Michaelman, F. (1988). 'Law's Republic'. *Yale Law Journal*, 97, 1539.

Mill, J. S. ([1861] 1991b). 'Utilitarianism'. In J. S. Mill, & J. Gray (eds.), *On Liberty and Other Essays* (pp. 129–201). Oxford, Oxford University Press.

Mill, J. S. ([1869] 1991a). 'On Liberty'. In J. S. Mill, & J. Gray (eds.), *On Liberty and Other Essays* (pp. 11–28). Oxford: Oxford University Press.

Milton, J. ([1644] 1991). 'Aereopagitica'. In S. Orgel, & J. Goldberg (eds.), *John Milton* (pp. 236–73). Oxford: Oxford University Press.

Miranda A. H. Horvath et al. (2013). '"Basically … Porn is Everywhere": A Rapid Evidence Assessment on the Effect that Access and Exposure to Pornography has on Children and Young People'. London: Office of the Children's Commissioner (UK)/Middlesex University.

Molnar, P. (2009). 'Towards Improved Law and Policy on "Hate Speech"—The "Clear and Present Danger" Test in Hungary'. In I. Hare, & J. Weinstein (eds.), *Extreme Speech and Democracy* (pp. 237–64). Oxford: Oxford University Press.

Molnar, P. (2012). 'Responding to "Hate Speech" with Art, Education, and the Imminent Danger Test'. In M. Herz, & P. Molnar (eds.), *The Content and Context of Hate Speech: Rethinking Regulation and Responses* (pp. 183–97). Cambridge: Cambridge University Press.

Molnar, P. (ed.). (2015). *Free Speech and Censorship Around the Globe.* Budapest: Central European University Press.

Molnar, P., & Malik, K. (2012). 'Interview with Kenan Malik'. In M. Herz, & P. Molnar (eds.), *The Content and Context of Hate Speech: Rethinking Regulation and Responses* (pp. 81–91). Cambridge: Cambridge University Press.

Molnar, P., & Post, R. (2012). 'Interview with Robert Post'. In M. Herz, & P. Molnar (eds.), *The Content and Context of Hate Speech: Rethinking Regulation and Responses* (pp. 11–36). Cambridge: Cambridge University Press.

Molnar, P., & Shaw, T. (2012). 'Interview with Theodore Shaw'. In M. Herz, & P. Molnar (eds.), *The Content and Context of Hate Speech: Rethinking Regulation and Responses* (pp. 399–413). Cambridge: Cambridge University Press.

Molnar, P., & Strossen, N. (2012). 'Interview with Nadine Strossen'. In M. Herz, & P. Molnar (eds.), *The Content and Context of Hate Speech: Rethinking Regulation and Responses* (pp. 378–98). Cambridge: Cambridge University Press.

Mommsen, H. (2002). 'Die stumpfe Waffe: Parteiverbote in der Weimarer Republik'. In C. Leggewie, & H. Meier (eds.), *Verbot der NPD oder mit Rechtsradikalen leben?* (pp. 145–48). Frankfurt a.M.: Suhrkamp.

Montesquieu, C.-L. ([1748–49] 1993). *De l'esprit des lois* (Vols. 1 & 2). (V. Goldschmidt, (ed.)) Paris: Garnier Flammarion.

Morange, J. (2009). *La liberté d'expression*. Brussels: Émile Bruylant.

Morlock, M. (2002). 'Schutz der Verfassung durch Parteiverbot?' In C. Leggewie, & H. Meier (eds.), *Verbot der NPD oder mit Rechtsradikalen leben?* (pp. 64–80). Frankfurt a.M.: Suhrkamp.

Moussaoui, M. (13 September 2012). *Le CFCM appelle à un front uni contre les prêcheurs de haine*. Retrieved 1 October 2015, from Le Conseil Français du Culte Musulman: http://www.lecfcm.fr/?p=3002

Mowbray, A. (2004). *Cases and Materials on the European Convention on Human Rights*. Oxford: Oxford University Press.

Münch, I. v. (2002). 'Ist das Bundesverfassungsgericht für "Signale" zuständig?' In C. Leggewie, & H. Meier (eds.), *Verbot der NPD oder mit Rechtsradikalen leben?* (pp. 51–55). Frankfurt a.M.: Suhrkamp.

Muslim Head Says Gays 'Harmful'. (3 January 2006). Retrieved 1 October 2015, from BBC News: http://news.bbc.co.uk/1/hi/uk/4579146.stm

Nancy, J.-L. (1990). *La communauté désoeuvrée*. Paris: Christian Bourgois.

Nancy, J.-L. (2013). *La haine, le sens coagulé*. Retrieved 1 October 2015, from Council of Europe: http://www.coe.int/fr/web/portal/search?p_p_id=coesearch_WAR_coesearchportlet&p_p_lifecycle=0&p_p_state=maximized&p_p_mode=view&p_p_col_id=column-1&p_p_col_count=1&_coesearch_WAR_coesearchportlet_mvcPath=%2Fhtml%2Fsearch%2Fview_content.jsp&_coesearch_WAR_

Narr, W.-D. (2002). 'Weshalb ich als radikaler NPD-Gegner fast ebenso radikal gegen ein Verbot derselben votiere'. In C. Leggewie, & H. Meier (eds.), *Verbot der NPD oder mit Rechtsradikalen leben?* (pp. 126–32). Frankfurt a.M.: Suhrkamp.

Nathanson, S. (n.d.). *Act and Rule Utilitarianism*. Retrieved 1 October 2015, from Internet Encyclopedia of Philosophy: www.iep.utm.edu/util-a-r/#H2

Nationaldemokratische Partei Deutschlands. (n.d.). Retrieved 1 October 2015, from http://www.npd.de/ Nederlandse Volks-Unie. (n.d.). Retrieved 1 September 2013, from http://www.nvu.info/

Neumann, V. (2002). 'Feinderklärung gegen Rechts?: Versammlungsrecht zwischen Rechtsgüterschutz und Gesinnungssanktion'. In C. Leggewie, & H. Meier (eds.), *Verbot der NPD oder mit Rechtsradikalen leben?* (pp. 155–68). Frankfurt a.M.: Suhrkamp.

New Statesman. (28 May 2015). *What Can't You Say? Stephen Fry, Slavoj Žižek, Elif Shafak and More Say the Unsayable*. Retrieved 1 October 2015, from *New Statesman*: http://www.newstatesman.com/politics/2015/05/what-can-t-you-say-stephen-fry-slavoj-i-ek-elif-shafak-and-more-say-unsayable

Nieuwenhuis, A. (2011). *Over de grens van de vrijheid van meningsuiting: Theorie, rechtsvergelijking, discriminatie, pornografie* (3rd edn). Nijmegen: Ars Aequi Libri.

Noorloos, M. (2012). *Hate Speech Revisited: A Comparative and Historical Perspective on Hate Speech Law in the Netherlands and England & Wales*. Mortsel, BE: Intersentia.

Norrie, A. (ed.). (1993). *Closure or Critique: New Directions in Legal Theory*. Edinburgh: Edinburgh University Press.

Nowak, J. E., & Rotunda, R. D. (2009). *Constitutional Law* (8th edn). St. Paul, Minnesota: West.

Nozick, R. (1977). *Anarchy, State, and Utopia*. New York: Basic Books.

Owen, R., & Erdem, S. (16 September 2006). 'Muslims Vent Fury at Pope's Speech'. *The Times*, pp. 1–2.

Paolucci, E. O., Genuis, M. L., & Violato, C. (2001). 'A Meta-Analysis of the Published Research on the Effects of Child Sexual Abuse'. *The Journal of Psychology: Interdisciplinary and Applied*, 135(1), 17–36.

Parekh, B. (2012). 'Is There a Case for Banning Hate Speech?' In M. Herz, & P. Molnar (eds.), *The Content and Context of Hate Speech: Rethinking Regulation and Responses* (37–56). Cambridge: Cambridge University Press.

Pech, L. (2003). *La liberté d'expression et sa limitation: Les enseignements de l'expérience américaine au regard d'expériences européennes*. Clermont-Ferrand: Les Presses Universitaires de la Faculté de Droit de Clermont-Ferrand.

Perry, B. (2005). 'A Crime By Any Other Name: The Semantics of Hate'. *Journal of Hate Studies*, 4(1), 121–37.

Pettit, P. (2012). *On the People's Terms: A Republican Theory and Model of Democracy*. Cambridge: Cambridge University Press.

Pitkin, H. F. (November 1988). 'Are Freedom and Liberty Twins?' *Political Theory*, 16(4), 534–52.

Plato. ([4th century BCE] 1997). *Plato: Complete Works*. (J. M. Cooper (ed.)) Indianapolis, Indiana: Hackett.

Popp, M. (25 November 2013). *Rechts liegen gelassen*. Retrieved 1 October 2015, from *Der Spiegel*: http://www.spiegel.de/spiegel/print/d-122579478.html

Popper, K. ([1945] 2002a). *The Open Society and Its Enemies* (Vols. 1 & 2). London: Routledge.

Popper, K. (2002b). *The Poverty of Historicism*. London: Routledge.

Posner, E. (15 February 2015). *Universities Are Right—and Within Their Rights—to Crack Down on Speech and Behavior*. Retrieved 1 October 2015 from Slate: http://www.slate.com/articles/news_and_politics/view_from_chicago/2015/02/university_speech_codes_students_are_children_who_must_be_protected.single.html

Posner, R. (2005). 'The Supreme Court, 2004 Term—Foreword: A Political Court'. *Harvard Law Review*, 119, 31–102.

Posner, R. (5 September 2002). *The Best Offense*. Retrieved 1 October 2015, from The New Republic Online: http://www.powells.com/review/2002_09_05.html

Post, R. (1994–95). 'Recuperating First Amendment Doctrine'. *Stanford Law Review*, 47, 1249–81.

Post, R. (1995). *Constitutional Domains: Democracy, Community, Management*. Cambridge, MA: Harvard University Press.

Post, R. (1996–97). 'Equality and Autonomy in First Amendment Jurisprudence'. *Michigan Law Review*, 95, 1517–41.

Post, R. (2006). 'Democracy and Equality'. *Annals of the American Academy of Political and Social Science*, 603, 24–36.

Post, R. (2009). 'Hate Speech'. In I. Hare, & J. Weinstein (eds.), *Extreme Speech and Democracy* (pp. 123–38). Oxford: Oxford University Press.

Post, R. (2011a). 'Participatory Democracy and Free Speech'. *Virginia Law Review*, 97(3), 477–90.

Post, R. (2011b). 'Participatory Democracy as a Theory of Free Speech: A Reply'. *Virginia Law Review*, 97(3), 617–32.

Preuß, U. K. (2002). 'Die empfindsame Demokratie'. In C. Leggewie, & H. Meier (eds.), *Verbot der NPD oder mit Rechtsradikalen leben?* (pp. 104–19). Frankfurt a.M.: Suhrkamp.

Prosperi, A. (24 October 2013). 'Negazionismo: Se una legge vuole punire chi cancella la Shoah'. *La Repubblica*, p. 52.

Qvortrup, M. (2004). *The Political Philosophy of Jean-Jacques Rousseau*. Manchester, UK: Manchester University Press.

Rachedi, M. (16 July 2014). *Le racisme est une opinion et un délit*. Retrieved 1 October 2015, from Libération: http://www.liberation.fr/debats/2014/07/16/le-racisme-est-une-opinion-et-un-delit_1064868

Rancière, J. (2004). *Aux bords du politique*. Paris: Gallimard.

Rancière, J. (2005). *La haine de la démocratie*. Paris: La Fabrique.

Rawls, J. (1993). *Political Liberalism*. New York: Columbia University Press.

Rawls, J. (1999). *A Theory of Justice* (2nd edn). Oxford: Oxford University Press.

Raz, J. (1994). *Ethics in the Public Domain*. Oxford: Clarendon Press.

Rechtsextreme wollen mit 'Hardbass' Jugendliche rekrutieren. (11 October 2012). Retrieved 1 October 2015, from *Der Standard*: http://derstandard.at/1348285647348/Rechtsextreme-wollen-mit-Hardbass-Jugendliche-rekrutieren

Reichman, A. (2009). 'Criminalizing Religiously Offensive Satire: Free Speech, Human Dignity, and Comparative Law'. In I. Hare, & J. Weinstein (eds.), *Extreme Speech and Democracy* (pp. 331–54). Oxford: Oxford University Press.

Reporters Without Borders. (n.d.). Retrieved 1 October 2015 from http://en.rsf.org/

Reporters Without Borders. (2014). *World Press Freedom Index 2014*. Retrieved 1 October 2015, from Reporters Without Borders: http://rsf.org/index2014/en-index2014.php#

Rescan, M., & Chapuis, N. (6 June 2013). *Au nom de quoi le gouvernement peut-il dissoudre des groupes ultra?* Retrieved 1 October 2015, from *Le Monde*: http://www.lemonde.fr/politique/article/2013/06/06/au-nom-de-quoi-le-gouvernement-peut-il-dissoudre-des-groupes-ultra_3425520_823448.html

Richards, D. A. (1999). *Free Speech and the Politics of Identity*. Oxford: Oxford University Press.

Richter, A. (2012). 'One Step Beyond Hate Speech: Post-Soviet Regulation of "Extremist" and "Terrorist" Speech in the Media'. In M. Herz, & P. Molnar (eds.), *The Content and Context of Hate Speech: Rethinking Regulation and Responses* (pp. 290–305). Cambridge: Cambridge University Press.

Riddell, M. (7 August 2005). *Fight Fear with Freedom*. Retrieved 1 October 2015, from *the Guardian*: http://www.guardian.co.uk/politics/2005/aug/07/media.pressandpublishing

Robert, J., & Duffar, J. (1996). *Droits de l'homme et libertés fondamentales* (6th edn). Paris: Montchrestian.

Robitaille-Froidure, A. (2011). *La liberté d'expression face au racisme: Étude de droit comparé franco-américain*. Paris: L'Harmattan.

Rohrßen, B. (2009). *Von der 'Anreizung zum Klassenkampf' zur 'Volksverhetzung' (§ 130 StGB): Reformdiskussion und Gesetzgebung seit dem 19. Jahrhundert*. Berlin: De Gruyter.

Röpke, A. (2005). 'Bomben, Waffen, Terror in der Kameradschaftsszene'. In A. Röpke, & A. Speit (eds.), *Braune Kameradschaften. Die militanten Neonazis im Schatten der NPD* (2nd edn, pp. 40–66). Berlin: Links Verlag.

Röpke, A., & Speit, A. (2005). 'Einleitung'. In A. Röpke, & A. Speit (eds.), *Braune Kameradschaften. Die militanten Neonazis im Schatten der NPD* (2nd edn, pp. 8–12). Berlin: Links Verlag.

Rorty, R. (1 April 2004). 'Post-Democracy'. *London Review of Books*, 26(7), 10–11. Retrieved from London Review of Books.

Rosenfeld, M. (2012). 'Hate Speech in Constitutional Jurisprudence: A Comparative Analysis'. In M. Herz, & P. Molnar (eds.), *The Content and Context of Hate Speech: Rethinking Regulation and Responses* (pp. 242–89). Cambridge: Cambridge University Press.

Rousseau, J.-J. ([1762] 1964). 'Du Contrat social'. In B. Gagnebin, & M. Raymond (eds.), *Oeuvres Complètes* (Vol. 3) (347–470). Paris: Gallimard [Pléiade].

Russell, B. (2000). *History of Western Philosophy* (2nd edn). London: Routledge.

Sandel, M. J. (1998). *Liberalism and the Limits of Justice* (2nd edn). Cambridge: Cambridge University Press.

Santi, P. (3 November 2011). *2006: 'Charlie Hebdo' publie les caricatures de Mahomet.* Retrieved 1 October 2015, from *Le Monde*: http://www.lemonde.fr/a-la-une/article/2011/11/03/2006-charlie-hebdo-publie-les-caricatures-de-mahomet_1597782_3208.html

Saussure, F. d. (1981). *Cours de linguistique générale.* (T. d. Mauro (ed.)) Paris: Payot.

Scanlon, T. (1977). 'A Theory of Freedom of Expression'. In R. Dworkin (ed.), *The Philosophy of Law* (pp. 153–71). Oxford: Oxford University Press.

Scanlon, T. (2011). 'Why Not Base Free Speech on Autonomy or Democracy?' *Virginia Law Review*, 97(3), 541–48.

Schabas, W. A. (2000–01). 'Hate Speech in Rwanda: The Road to Genocide'. *McGill Law Journal*, 46, 141–71.

Schauer, F. (1992). 'The First Amendment as Ideology'. *William & Mary Law Review*, 33, 853.

Schauer, F. (2012). 'Social Epistemology, Holocaust Denial, and the Post-Millian Calculus'. In M. Herz, & P. Molnar (eds.), *The Content and Context of Hate Speech: Rethinking Regulation and Responses* (pp. 129–43). Cambridge: Cambridge University Press.

Schauer, F. F. (1982). *Free Speech: A Philosophical Enquiry.* Cambridge: Cambridge University Press.

Schmitt, C. ([1922] 2009). *Politische Theologie: Vier Kapitel zur Lehre von der Souveränität* (9th edn). Berlin: Duncker & Humblot.

Schmitt, C. ([1928] 1993). *Verfassungslehre* (8th edn). Berlin: Duncker & Humblot.

Schmitt, C. (1996). *Der Begriff des Politischen* (6th edn). Berlin: Duncker & Humblot.

Schopenhauer, A. ([1819] 1996). *Die Welt als Wille und Vorstellung.* (W. Freiherr von Löhneysen (ed.)) Frankfurt am Main/Leipzig: Insel.

Schrank, C. (2006). *Rechts-Staat Deutschland?: Zum Kampf der Justiz gegen Rechtsextremisten.* Norderstedt: Books on Demand.

Schrank, Carsten. (1 May 2008). Retrieved 1 October 2015, from Netz gegen Nazis: http://www.netz-gegen-nazis.de/lexikontext/schrank-carsten

Schubert, T. (2011). 'Extremismus in Dänemark'. In E. Jesse, & T. Thieme (eds.), *Extremismus in den EU-Staaten* (pp. 54–82). Wiesbaden: Springer.

Seils, C. (2002). 'Selbstläufer symbolischer Politik: Wie ein Verbot der NPD auf die politische Agenda kam'. In C. Leggewie, & H. Meier (eds.), *Verbot der NPD oder mit Rechtsradikalen leben?* (pp. 44–50). Frankfurt a.M.: Suhrkamp.

Sekyiamah, N. D. (17 November 2013). *I Thought the US was the Land of Gold. Now I See It as Rude and Disrespectful.* Retrieved 1 October 2015, from *the Guardian*: http://www.theguardian.com/commentisfree/2013/nov/17/ghana-america-exchange-expats-immigration-war

Shakespeare, W. (1982). *Henry V.* (G. Taylor (ed.)) Oxford: Oxford University Press.

Shakespeare, W. (1994). *Coriolanus.* (R. B. Parker (ed.)) Oxford: Oxford University Press.

Shakespeare, W. (2011). *Richard II.* (A. B. Dawson, & P. Yachnin (eds.)) Oxford: Oxford University Press.

Shiffrin, S. (2011). 'Dissent, Democratic Participation, and First Amendment Methodology'. *Virginia Law Review*, 97, 559–65.

Shiffrin, S. V. (2011). 'Methodology in Free Speech Theory'. *Virginia Law Review*, 97, 549–58.

Sieber, R. (16 December 2012). *Neonazis übernehmen die 'Identitäre Bewegung'*. Retrieved 1 October 2015, from Zeit Online: http://blog.zeit.de/stoerungsmelder/2012/12/16/neonazis-ubernehmen-die-identitare-bewegung_10828

Sim, C. (2011). 'The Singapore Chill: Political Defamation and the Normalization of a Statist Rule of Law'. *Pacific Rim Law & Policy Journal*, 20(2), 319–53.

Six Years for Muslims Who Called for Killings Over Newspaper Cartoon. (19 July 2007). *The Daily Telegraph*, p. 18.

Smolla, R. A. (1993). *Free Speech in an Open Society*. Vintage: New York.

Snel, J. (2010). *Recht van Spreken*. Zoetermeer: Uitgeverij Boekencentrum.

Social Progress Imperative. (2015). *Social Progress Index 2015*. Retrieved 1 October 2015, from The Social Progress Imperative: http://www.socialprogressimperative.org/data/spi

Soubrouillard, R. (27 May 2015). *Kamel Daoud: 'La France a une collection de tabous extraordinaires'*. Retrieved 1 October 2015 from Marianne: http://www.marianne.net/kamel-daoud-france-collection-tabous-extraordinaires-100233854.html

Speit, A. (2005). 'Wir marschieren bis zum Zieg'. In A. Röpke, & A. Speit (eds.), *Braune Kameradschaften. Die militanten Neonazis im Schatten der NPD* (2nd edn, pp. 13–39). Berlin: Links Verlag.

Staud, T. (2006). *Moderne Nazis: Die neuen Rechten und der Aufstieg der NPD* (3rd edn). Cologne: Kiepenheuer & Witsch.

Stefancic, J., & Delgado, R. (1992–93). 'A Shifting Balance: Freedom of Expression and Hate Speech Regulation'. *Iowa Law Review*, 78, 737.

Strossen, N. (1990). 'Regulating Racist Speech on Campus: A Modest Proposal'. *Duke Law Journal*, 484–549.

Strum, P. (1999). *When the Nazis Came to Skokie*. Lawrence, KA: University Press of Kansas.

Suk, J. C. (2012). 'Holocaust Denial and the Free-Speech Theory of the State'. In M. Herz, & P. Molnar (eds.), *The Content and Context of Hate Speech: Rethinking Regulation and Responses* (pp. 144–63). Cambridge: Cambridge University Press.

Sumner, L. (2009). 'Incitement and the Regulation of Hate Speech in Canada: A Philosophical Analysis'. In I. Hare, & J. Weinstein (eds.), *Extreme Speech and Democracy* (pp. 204–20). Oxford: Oxford University Press.

Sunstein, C. (1988). 'Beyond the Republican Revival'. *Yale Law Journal*, 97, 1539.

Sunstein, C. (1995). *Democracy and the Problem of Free Speech*. New York: Free Press.

Taguieff, P.-A. (2002). *La Nouvelle judéophobie*. Paris: Mille et Une Nuits.

Taguieff, P.-A. (2004). *Prêcheurs de haine: Traversée de la judéophobie planétaire*. Paris: Mille et Une Nuits.

Taylor, C. (1992). 'Atomism'. In S. Avineri, & A. de-Shalit (eds.), *Communitarianism and Individualism* (pp. 29–50). Oxford: Oxford University Press.

Thiel, M. (ed.). (2003a). *Wehrhafte Demokratie: Beiträge über die Regelungen zum Schutze der freiheitlichen demokratischen Grundordnung*. Tübingen: Mohr Siebeck.

Thiel, M. (2003b). 'Zur Einführung: Die "wehrhafte Demokratie" als verfassungsrechtliche Grundentscheidung'. In M. Thiel (ed.), *Wehrhafte Demokratie: Beiträge über die*

Regelungen zum Schutze der freiheitlichen demokratischen Grundordnung (pp. 1–24). Tübingen: Mohr Siebeck.

Thiel, M. (2003c). 'Die Verwirkung von Grundrechten gemäß Art. 18GG'. In M. Thiel (ed.), *Wehrhafte Demokratie: Beiträge über die Regelungen zum Schutze der freiheitlichen demokratischen Grundordnung*. Tübingen: Mohr Siebeck.

Thiel, M. (2003d). 'Das Verbot verfassungswiedriger Parteien (Art. 21 Abs. 2GG)'. In M. Thiel (ed.), *Wehrhafte Demokratie: Beiträge über die Regelungen zum Schutze der freiheitlichen demokratischen Grundordnung* (pp. 173–207). Tübingen: Mohr Siebeck.

Tillmanns, R. (2003). 'Wehrhaftigkeit durch Werthaftigkeit—der ethische Grundkonsens als Existenzvoraussetzung des freiheitlichen Staates'. In M. Thiel (ed.), *Wehrhafte Demokratie: Beiträge über die Regelungen zum Schutze der freiheitlichen demokratischen Grundordnung* (pp. 25–55). Tübingen: Mohr Siebeck.

Todorov, T. (2004). *Benjamin Constant: La Passion démocratique*. Paris: Livre de Poche.

Transparency International. (n.d.). *Corruption perceptions index (annual)*. Retrieved 1 October 2015, from http://www.transparency.org/research/cpi/overview

Traufetter, G. (6 February 2006). 'Die Schere im Kopf: Ayaan Hirsi Ali über Gründe und Folgen des islamischen Protests'. *Der Spiegel*, pp. 96–7.

Tsesis, A. (2002). *Destructive Messages: How Hate Speech Paves the Way for Harmful Social Movements*. New York: New York University Press.

Unger, R. M. (1998). *Democracy Realized: the Progressive Alternative*. New York: Verso.

US Bureau of Public Affairs (Office of the Historian). (1971–72). *Foreign Relations of the United States, 1969–1976* (Vol. 14). Washington, DC: US Department of State.

US Bureau of Public Affairs (Office of the Historian). (2007). *Soviet–American Relations: The Detente Years, 1969–1972*. Washington, DC: US Department of State.

van Walsum, S. (10 February 2006). 'De muur tussen vrij en onvrij zal vallen'. *De Volkskrant*, p. 1.

Vaneigem, R. (2003). *Rien n'est sacré, tout peut se dire: Réflexions sur la liberté d'expression*. Paris: La Découverte.

Vél' d'Hiv: Le long chemin vers la reconnaissance d'un crime d'État dans la déportation. (16 July 2012). Retrieved 1 October 2015, from *L'Humanité*: http://www.humanite.fr/politique/le-long-chemin-vers-la-reconnaissance-d%E2%80%99un-crime-d%E2%80%99etat-dans-la-deportation-500825

Vlaams Belang. (2013). Retrieved 1 October 2015, from http://www.vlaamsbelang.org/

Volokh, E. (2011a). 'The Trouble With "Public Discourse" as a Limitation on Free Speech Rights'. *Virginia Law Review*, 97(3), 567–94.

Volokh, E. (2011b). 'In Defense of the Marketplace of Ideas/Search for Truth as a Theory of Free Speech Protection'. *Virginia Law Review*, 97(3), 595–601.

Voltaire. ([1751] 1957). 'Le Siècle de Louis XIV'. In Voltaire, & R. Pomeau (ed.), *Oeuvres historiques* (pp. 601–1274). Paris: Gallimard: Bibliothèque de la Pléiade.

Voltaire. ([1763] 1961). 'Traité sur la tolérance'. In Voltaire, & J. Van Den Heuvel (ed.), *Mélanges* (pp. 563–650). Paris: Gallimard: Bibliothèque de la Pléiade.

Wachsmann, P. (1998). *Libertés publiques* (2nd edn). Paris: Dalloz.

Waldron, J. (2012a). *The Harm in Hate Speech*. Boston, MA: Harvard University Press.

Waldron, J. (2012b). 'Hate Speech and Political Legitimacy'. In M. Herz, & P. Molnar (eds.), *The Content and Context of Hate Speech: Rethinking Regulation and Responses* (pp. 329–40). Cambridge: Cambridge University Press.

Waldron, J., & Weinstein, J. (26 October 2012). *The Legal Response to Hate Speech: Should the U.S. Be More Like Europe?* Retrieved 1 October 2015, from Sandra Day O'Connor College of Law, Arizona State University: http://online.law.asu.edu/Events/2012/HateSpeech/

Wassermann, R. (2002). 'Revitalisierung eines totgesagten Verfassungsprinzips'. In C. Leggewie, & H. Meier (eds.), *Verbot der NPD oder mit Rechtsradikalen leben?* (pp. 98–103). Frankfurt a.M.: Suhrkamp.

Weinrib, E. J. (1989). 'Law as Myth: Reflections on Plato's Gorgias'. *Iowa Law Review*, 74, 787.

Weinstein, J. (1999). *Hate Speech, Pornography, and the Radical Attack on Free Speech Doctrine*. Boulder, CO: Westview Press.

Weinstein, J. (2001). 'Hate Speech, Viewpoint Neutrality, and the American Concept of Democracy'. In T. Hensley (ed.), *The Boundaries of Freedom of Expression & Order in American Democracy* (pp. 161–6). Kent, OH: Kent University Press.

Weinstein, J. (2009a). 'Extreme Speech, Public Order, and Democracy'. In I. Hare, & J. Weinstein (eds.), *Extreme Speech and Democracy* (pp. 23–61). Oxford: Oxford University Press.

Weinstein, J. (2009b). 'An Overview of American Free Speech Doctrine and its Application to Extreme Speech'. In I. Hare, & J. Weinstein (eds.), *Extreme Speech and Democracy* (pp. 81–95). Oxford: Oxford University Press.

Weinstein, J. (2011a). 'Participatory Democracy as the Central Value of American Free Speech Doctrine'. *Virginia Law Review*, 97(3), 491–514.

Weinstein, J. (2011b). 'Participatory Democracy as the Basis of American Free Speech Doctrine: A Reply'. *Virginia Law Review*, 97(3), 633–79.

Weinstein, J., & Hare, I. (2009). 'General Introduction'. In I. Hare, & J. Weinstein (eds.), *Extreme Speech and Democracy* (pp. 1–7). Oxford: Oxford University Press.

Weiss, V. (7 August 2014). *Ein fatales Bündnis: Welche Wurzeln hat der aktuelle Antisemitismus?* Retrieved 1 October 2015, from *Die Zeit*: http://www.zeit.de/2014/33/antisemitismus-europa/komplettansicht

Wieder, T. (13 January 2014). *Jack Lang sur l'affaire Dieudonné: "La décision du Conseil d'Etat est une profonde regression"*. Retrieved 1 October 2015, from *Le Monde*: http://www.lemonde.fr/politique/article/2014/01/13/jack-lang-la-decision-du-conseil-d-etat-est-une-profonde-regression_4346841_823448.html

Wiegrefe, K. (25 August 2014). 'Die Schande nach Auschwitz'. *Der Spiegel*, pp. 28–35.

Wijnberg, R. (2008). *In Dubio: Vrijheid van meningsuiting als het recht om te twijfelen*. Amsterdam: Prometheus.

Williams, S. H. (2011). 'Democracy, Freedom of Speech, and Feminist Theory: A Response to Post and Weinstein'. *Virginia Law Review*, 97(3), 603–15.

Withnall, A. (16 September 2014). *Sports Direct security Guard Allegedly Banned Jewish Schoolboys and Told Them: 'No Jews, No Jews'*. Retrieved 1 October 2015, from *the Independent*: http://www.independent.co.uk/news/uk/home-news/sports-direct-security-guard-banned-jewish-schoolboys-and-told-them-no-jews-no-jews-9735919.html

Wynne-Jones, R. (2 June 1996). *Poets Clash Over 'Anti-Semitic' Eliot*. Retrieved 1 October 2015, from *the Independent*: http://www.independent.co.uk/news/uk/home-news/poets-clash-over-antisemitic-eliot-1335055.html

Yücel, D. (30 July 2014). *Nein, du darfst nicht*. Retrieved 1 October 2015, from Taz.de: http://www.taz.de/Debatte-Israelkritik/!143349/

Yuhas, A. (22 June 2015). *Barack Obama invokes N-word during interview on racism in America*. Retrieved October 1, 2015, from *Guardian*: http://www.theguardian.com/us-news/2015/jun/22/barack-obama-n-word-racism-marc-maron-interview

Zöchling, C. (28 January 2007). *FPÖ: Drei rechte Finger*. Retrieved 1 October 2015, from Profil-Online: http://www.profil.at/articles/0704/560/162845/fpoe-drei-finger

Zwagerman, J. (2009). *Hitler in de polder & Vrij van God*. Amsterdam: Arbeiderspers.

Index

Printed and bound by CPI Group (UK) Ltd, Croydon, CR0 4YY